**Federal and State
Court Systems
— A Guide**

Federal and State Court Systems —A Guide

Fannie J. Klein, LL.B., LL.M.,
Associate Professor, Emerita,
New York University School
of Law

With contributions by Associate
Professor Edward J. Bander,
Associate Librarian, New York
University School of Law
and Associate Professor
John P. Richert, Stockton State
College, Pomona, New Jersey

Published for
The Institute of Judicial Administration

Ballinger Publishing Company • Cambridge, Massachusetts
A Subsidiary of J.B. Lippincott Company

This book is printed on recycled paper.

Copyright © 1977 by Ballinger Publishing Company. All rights reserved. No part of this publication may be reproduced, stored in a retrievel system, or transmitted in any form or by any means, electronic mechanical photocopy, recording or otherwise, without the prior written consent of the publisher.

International Standard Book Number: 0−88410−219−X

Library of Congress Catalog Card Number: 76−47480

Printed in the United States of America

Library of Congress Cataloging in Publication Data

Klein, Fannie J
  Federal and State court systems.

  Includes bibliographies and index.
  1. Courts—United States. 2. Court congestion and delay—
United States. 3. Justice, Administration of—United States.
I. Bander, Edward J., joint author. II. Richert, John, joint author.
III. Institute of Judicial Administration. IV. Title.
KF8700.K6   347'73'1   76−47480
ISBN 0−88410−219−X

Dedication

TO THE MEMORY OF

ARTHUR T. VANDERBILT

Late Chief Justice of the
State of New Jersey

Dean of New York
University School of Law

"The great work of Chief Justice Arthur T. Vanderbilt was in judicial administration, organization of courts, and remaking American legal procedure to the needs of the crowded and hypermechanized world and complex social order of today. His work for law reform, organization of courts, organization of administrative work of the courts and for legal education make a consistent whole and mark him as entitled to a high place among those who had raised our institutions of justice to their highest possibilities."

—Dean Roscoe Pound
Harvard Law School

Contents

List of Figures   xi

List of Tables   xiii

Foreword   xv

Preface   xix

Acknowledgments   xxi

Chapter 1
The Dual Court System   1

Introduction   1
Court Structure of the American Colonies Under the Articles
  of Confederation   2
Creation of the Judicial Power of the United States: The Judiciary
  Act of 1789   5
Bibliography   5

Chapter 2
State Courts Generally   7

Structure and Jurisdiction   7
Judicial Conduct   27

Continuing Judicial Education   45
Court Administration   46
Bibliography   58

Chapter 3
The Grand Jury   61

Development and Functions   61
Analyses and Critique   63
Bibliography   65

Chapter 4
The Petit Jury   67

History, Development, and Use of the Civil and Criminal Jury   67
Selection of Jurors for the Venire   69
Trends   71
Bibliography   73

Chapter 5
Selected State Court Systems   75

Alaska   75
California   80
Colorado   87
The District of Columbia   95
Hawaii   99
Illinois   103
Massachusetts   108
New Jersey   115
New York State   121
Puerto Rico   156
Bibliographies by State   163

Chapter 6
The United States Court System:
Court Structure, Jurisdiction,
Judicial Personnel, Administration   167

Historical Background   167
Cases the United States Court Can Decide   168
The Supreme Court of the United States   168
United States Courts of Appeals   172

The Workload of the Appellate Courts in the Federal Court System   175
United States District Courts   179
Three-Judge District Courts   186
Special Courts of the United States   187
Tax Court of the United States   189
United States Emergency Court of Appeals   190
United States Court of Military Appeals   191
United States Magistrates   191
Administration of the United States Courts   192
Bibliography   194

Appendixes   199

Appendix A
Legal Research—*Edward J. Bander*   201

Legal Research Books   202
Authority   204
Reports   205
Digests   209
Annotations   211
Loose-Leaf Services   212
Encyclopedias   213
Treatises   213
Restatements   214
Law Reviews   214
Case Citations   216
Transition   217
Constitutions   217
Statutes and Regulations   218
Legislative History   220
Bowling v. Sperry   222
Shepard's Citations, Specimen Pages   228
American Law Reports Chart   232
Alphabetical Appendix (Index and Bibliography)   233

Appendix B
Courts: A Comparative Perspective
—*John P. Richert*   255

The Organization of Courts   256
Rules Applied by Courts   260
Staffing the Courts   266

Glossary 275

Index 293

About the Author 301

About the Contributors 303

List of Figures

5−1	Alaska Judicial System	76
5−2	California Judicial System	81
5−3	Colorado Judicial System	89
5−4	District of Columbia Local Court System	96
5−5	Hawaii Court System	100
5−6	Illinois Judicial System	104
5−7	Massachusetts Judicial System	109
5−8	New Jersey Judicial System	116
5−9	Outline of New York State Court Structure	123
5−10	New York State General Court Structure	124
5−11	Courts of Limited Jurisdiction *Within* New York City	132
5−12	Courts of Limited Jurisdiction *Outside* New York City	138
5−13	Puerto Rico Judicial System	158
6−1	The United States Court System	169

List of Tables

2–1	Names of Courts in the States and Numbers of Judges of Appellate Courts and Trial Courts of General Jurisdiction	14
2–2	Final Selection of Judges	22
2–3	Methods of Removal of Judges and Filling of Vacancies	29
2–4	Selected Data on Court Administrative Offices	49
2–5	Selected Data on Court Administrative Offices	53
2–6	Judicial Administration Education and Training Programs (1975)	57
6–1	United States Courts of Appeals	174
6–2	United States District Courts	183
6–3	Special Courts	189

Foreword

Bernard G. Segal

By any standard, Arthur Vanderbilt was one of the giants of the legal profession. Whether as practicing lawyer, as Law School Dean, as leader of the organized Bar of the Country, or as State Supreme Court Chief Justice, his career is a lodestar for all who follow in any of these capacities.

The last time I had the privilege of talking with this remarkable man was when, as Chairman of the American Bar Association Standing Committee on Federal Judiciary, I called to secure his views concerning the qualifications of William J. Brennan for nomination as Associate Justice of the Supreme Court of the United States. He responded in the most glowing terms, and as in so much that Chief Justice Vanderbilt said and did, his responses concerning Justice Brennan's potential for distinguished and exemplary service on the Supreme Court have proved to be prophetic.

It was in that same conversation that Chief Justice Vanderbilt talked of the Institute of Judicial Administration, which he founded, and of Fannie Klein who has been connected with the Institute since its inception. The Chief Justice spoke of her fondly and favorably. In the years since then, she has made a very large contribution to the improvement of judicial administration in America by her teachings, her writings, and her work for the Institute and other organizations.

Virtually all of Fannie Klein's writings have been concerned with our justice system. Her two-volume bibliography published this year, *The Administration of Justice in the Courts*, a greatly expanded and broad ranging revision of her *Judicial Administration and the Legal Profession* which first appeared in 1963, is the most useful tool I know for anyone working on any aspect of our justice system and particularly our courts. It reflects an enormous amount of talented effort and provides an incredibly complete guide to the prolific writings in these fields.

Fannie Klein, however, has not written for the profession alone. Over a period of more than two decades, her unexcelled zeal and considerable talents have produced articles, papers, pamphlets, and other publications, providing valuable materials for use in educating high school and college students on the administration of justice at federal and state levels.

In my own work in the fields of judicial selection, tenure, compensation, and administration Fannie Klein has been a source of information and guidance to me over the years. Accordingly, when she requested that I write this Foreword for her most recent publication, *Federal and State Court Systems—A Guide*, I accepted with enthusiasm. I also had another reason for doing so.

Of all our historic American traditions, none is more basic than citizens' respect for law. Further, the citizens' esteem for their courts and for the judges who preside in them is of the very essence of our kind of society.

We cannot hope to maintain this essential regard for our judicial system unless our courts are efficient and afford prompt justice to our citizens. Yet, the sobering fact is that despite the very substantial measures which have been taken during the last quarter of a century and particularly in the past decade, under present conditions our courts cannot be as efficient as we would like and certainly cannot render prompt justice. Judges and lawyers through the organized Bar have been doing a great deal to remedy these conditions, but in more recent years, they, and government officials as well, have come to the realization that if the degree and quality of change that are needed are to be attained, it will only be if our entire citizenry is drawn into the process and becomes an integral part of it.

Where real progress has been made in improving our judicial system, experience has demonstrated that the reforms are attained only through an aroused public. In New Jersey, where it took seventeen years to secure a new judicial article for that state's Constitution, Chief Justice Vanderbilt said that when success was finally achieved, it was by virtue of a grass roots uprising. Since then, this has been proved many times as major reforms have been adopted in state after state—a unified judicial system, merit selection of judges, a program for the removal, discipline, or compulsory retirement of the badly behaving or the mentally or physically disabled judge, and numerous others.

Before we can secure an aroused citizenry, we must have an informed citizenry. In a free, democratic society, it is urgent that citizens understand their basic institutions. It is imperative that children in grade schools and high schools begin to be indoctrinated with the essentials of our justice system. Chief Justice Warren E. Burger of the Supreme Court of the United States has given eloquent emphasis to the need to have our people understand how justice operates in our country, and to start the process of learning early in a child's education. However, there has been no authoritative, educational treatise which tells the whole story in one place. In enlarging her prior rather modest effort in the form of a booklet, which went through five editions, into the present impressive volume, Fannie Klein achieves this objective. In direct and understandable style, she traces our dual court system from its structure under the Articles of Confederation to the present day, giving both historical perspective and current understanding. Certainly for high school and college students, and the citizenry at large, there is no available work which meets the coverage and the quality of this one.

The book fills another important need, due to a major development in the practice of law at all levels—in private law offices, in corporate law departments, in public interest law offices, and in bureaus and departments of government. This has been the appearance, and phenomenal growth in the number and use, of paralegals, or legal assistants as they have more recently been called by the American Bar Association. The phenomenon of the legal assistant is of very recent vintage. In the late 1960's, leaders of the organized Bar suddenly realized that as costs of legal services were inevitably mounting, it was no longer enough to be concerned only about providing legal services for the poor. A very large number of persons in the lower and the middle income ranges were beginning to find that they could not afford the rising costs of legal services. At the same time, lawyers were performing a multitude of routine tasks, necessarily at lawyers' hourly rates, which non-lawyers could do equally well, probably better when fully trained. Faced with this challenge to provide quality legal services at lower cost, and realizing that our profession was rapidly approaching the place where only the more affluent citizens would be able to afford legal services, the need for developing a system of career legal assistants became obvious.

The organized Bar reacted magnificently. In August, 1968, the ABA House of Delegates adopted a resolution which recognized that many tasks in servicing a client's needs could be performed by a trained, non-lawyer assistant working under the direction and supervision of a lawyer, and this of course at much lower cost than if the lawyer were performing these functions. At that time, very few law firms had ever heard of legal assistants, to say nothing about employing them, and not one college in the United States offered a training program for legal assistants.

During much of 1969 and 1970, the ABA put on a crash program. The then President of the American Bar Association scarcely gave an address to any state or local bar association in the country in which he did not urge that it undertake actively promoting the use of legal assistants and motivating qualified people to prepare and apply for such positions. In 1970, a three-week pilot project, co-sponsored by the American Bar Association and the San Francisco Bar Association, was conducted in San Francisco in an attempt to develop a model on-the-job training program participated in by both lawyers and legal assistants, working as a team to endeavor to apply scientific principles to develop techniques and procedures for the use of legal assistants in dealing with specific legal problems. The ensuing five years witnessed phenomenal progress in the movement. Today, legal assistants are employed in virtually every area of legal services, and more than 180 educational institutions now offer formal training programs for legal assistants. Now there is talk of developing courses offering a formal certificate or degree to those completing prescribed courses of training and qualifying as legal assistants. Much more needs to be done, but there is scarcely a precedent for the progress made in a very few years.

It is to this new group operating within the legal profession that Fannie Klein's new book will in my judgment prove to be invaluable. It must be understood that this volume is not a "how to do it" manual. Rather it tells in simple, readable style what every legal assistant should know of the general background, structure, problems, and functioning of our courts and the judges who preside over them.

The author has had the wisdom to enlist Edward J. Bander, Associate Librarian and Associate Professor at the New York University Law School, to prepare, with the advice and counsel of the author, a chapter on legal research. Like the author's chapters, this is superbly done and will be of great assistance not only to legal assistants but also to college and high school students in their research in any field of the law.

I believe that the book should become required reading in the educational institutions offering formal training for legal assistants. My hope, indeed my expectation, is that many of my fellow lawyers will also recognize the value and need of this publication as part of core curriculum in in-house training programs for legal assistants who may come directly to law offices without attending university courses or schools for paralegals. In my opinion, every legal assistant should read this book for the general background and understanding it will provide: Certainly, it is indispensable for the legal assistant assigned to any phase of litigation.

In short, Fannie Klein's treatise fills a critical need for citizens interested in the workings of our justice system, for students concerned in their research or other work with the structure and functioning of our dual court system, and for legal assistants desirous of acquiring an enriching background on our courts and the judges who preside in them and on the basic tools of legal research.

I cannot close this Foreword without expressing my continuing admiration for Fannie Klein's contributions to the administration of justice in America. This volume is just one more of the rich benefits we derive from her ceaseless efforts in this respect. I am proud to be a very small part of this latest result by having written this Foreword to this splendid addition to the literature in the critical field with which the volume is concerned.

Preface

In 1957 the Institute of Judicial Administration published a pamphlet of seventy-eight pages entitled a *Guide to Court Systems.* As stated in its introduction, the objective was to present to the beginning law student, to the interested layman, and to foreign students of our courts an uncomplicated narrative regarding court structure and the interrelationship of state and federal courts. In addition, because of the activities of the Institute of Judicial Administration in the field of court reform, additional information was given on court personnel and court administration. Under the editorship of this author, former associate director of the Institute, the first pamphlet was prepared mainly by Leon Schneider, then a research associate, now a practicing lawyer in New York City.

Thereafter periodically through the years, the statistical and other information in the original pamphlet were updated.

Recently, there were considerably increasing requests for the pamphlet from students in the colleges, from high school students competing in competitions, from various court reform organizations, and particularly from faculty members who had organized courses for paralegals or legal assistants in law offices.

It was then decided that an entirely new book was needed; one which would not only update the information in the pamphlet, but which would considerably expand the information into areas of current importance to all interested in the structure, personnel, internal operation, and administration of state and federal courts.

The format was entirely changed; and details of developments across the nation in the administration of civil and criminal justice in both state and federal courts, not covered in the pamphlet, have been added. Civil and criminal delays in trial courts are described and the problems in juvenile justice receive comment.

There are new chapters on the grand jury and the petit jury. Whereas previously only the New York courts were discussed in detail, presently nine states, selected because they vary in size and represent various geographic sections, receive similar treatment.

The federal court system also is extensively described, including a narrative on delay in the federal appellate courts and what is being recommended to remedy this increasing problem.

A generous number of tables and diagrams illustrate the narrative, and each chapter is supplemented by a list of additional readings. A full glossary of terms has been added.

One extremely important addition is Appendix A by Associate Professor Edward Bander, associate law librarian at New York University Law School, entitled "Legal Research." He not only describes methods of finding precedent, but presents a full panoply of law books and research materials that a basic law library should have.

Another dividend for the reader is the Appendix by Associate Professor Richert in which he gives an insight into foreign civil law country court systems.

Acknowledgments

In the course of researching and writing this book it became necessary for me to consult numerous materials and to speak to many authorities. I present my list of acknowledgments with expressions of deep gratitude. Any misstatements or errors of omission or commission are entirely my own; for the data found accurate and valuable, I thank my sources of information.

First and foremost, I acknowledge with thanks the substantial research assistance of Norman Reimer, a third year law student at New York University School of Law, research assistant at the Institute of Judicial Administration. Mr. Reimer has also written Chapter 5, "Selected State Court Systems," except the sections on New York and the District of Columbia. He has assisted me for many months researching, checking, and writing.

Ms. Cynthia Philip, senior research associate at the Institute of Judicial Administration, read the preliminary draft. She offered numerous helpful suggestions which I used, and I thank her.

Mr. Kent Huie, secretarial assistant at the Institute of Judicial Administration, patiently typed and retyped the various drafts. The final draft was typed by Mrs. Anna Schwartzberg, long a valued secretary at the Institute. Mrs. Geraldine Hansen, office manager, with her usual competence, facilitated the typing of the manuscript. Mr. Calvin Hudson, library technical assistant, unfailingly and promptly responded to my call for materials. For all of this help I am exceedingly grateful. For suggesting that the original pamphlet be expanded into a book and obtaining a publisher, I ower thanks to Mr. Paul Nejelski, former director of the Institute of Judicial Administration.

I list the organizations and individuals who have permitted me to quote from their publications and to Xerox charts and other items. After compiling the data for Chapter 5, the first draft was sent to each state court administrator and in one case, to the chief justice in order to establish the current accuracy of the data. To these friends, very busy people, who, yet, responded promptly and constructively, I express my deep gratitude.

Council of State Governments—Bevard Crihfield, Executive Director; Paul Albright, Director of Publications.

American Bar Association—Bert Early, Executive Director.

Arizona Law Review—Law Review Editors.

Conference of State Court Administrators—Jag Uppal, Executive Secretary.

State of New York, Office of Court Administration—Peter R. Gray, Deputy State Administrator; Harold Wolf, Public Information Officer; Michael F. McEneny, Director, Education and Training Office.

New York State Temporary Commission on Judicial Conduct—Gerald Stern, Administrator.

Administrative Office of the United States Courts—Joseph F. Spaniol, Jr., Executive Assistant to the Director.

Administrative Assistant to the Chief Justice of the United States—Mark W. Cannon, for statistics on the numbers of cases filed and docketed in the Supreme Court.

Many thanks go to the following individuals who read the report on their state:

The Hon. J.A. Rabinowitz, Chief Justice, Supreme Court of Alaska.

Ralph N. Kleps, Director, Administrative Office of California.

Harry O. Lawson, State Court Administrator, Colorado.

Roy O. Gulley, Director, Administrative Office of the Illinois Courts.

Lester E. Cingcade, Administrative Director, Office of the Courts, Hawaii.

The Hon. J. Simpson, Jr., Judge, Superior Court, Appellate Division, Administrative Director of the Courts, New Jersey.

Arnold W. Malech, Executive Officer, District of Columbia Courts, Washington, D.C.

Antonio S. Negron Garcia, Estado Libre, Associado de Puerto Rico, Tribunal Supremo.

**Federal and State
Court Systems
— A Guide**

does not purport to define these problems. Its objective is to outline the judicial framework within which cases are tried in state and federal courts in the United States.

COURT STRUCTURE OF THE AMERICAN COLONIES UNDER THE ARTICLES OF CONFEDERATION

The preponderance of early American settlers emigrated from England and most of the colonial charters provided that laws should conform to the policy and forms of law in England. The Privy Council in England served as a court of last resort and provided some guarantee that there would be no significant departure from English custom and law. A brief description of the colonial courts will illustrate their similarity to the courts then existing in England.

Highest Court of Review in the Colonies

Colonial government was marked by a lack of distinction between legislative, executive, and judicial functions. While the seventeenth century witnessed a gradual contraction of the judicial powers exercised by colonial legislatures, the governor and council (fashioned after the House of Lords in England) had general appellate jurisdiction. The names of these supreme appellate tribunals varied in the colonies—e.g., supreme court, governor and council, general court. In the seventeenth century they were often known as Courts of Assistants and were composed of the governor and his assistants. In Massachusetts, in 1699, a superior court with appellate and original jurisdiction was created. A direct appeal from the superior court lay to the King in Council in England. A similar court was established in Pennsylvania in 1722. In Rhode Island, Connecticut, Virginia, and New Hampshire, superior courts with appellate and original jurisdiction were created, but the General Assembly of each colony functioned as the highest appellate court, final appeal being to the Privy Council in England.

At the time of the American Revolution, therefore, the colonies' highest appellate courts were of two types. One was similar to the House of Lords in England, i.e., the upper branch of the legislature. The other was similar to the King's Bench in England, and acted as an appellate court and a court of first instance.

Courts of First Instance

Colonial courts of original jurisdiction adhered to the distinction between law and equity as it had developed in England. The common law of England consists of the principles and usages and rules of action based on custom as enforced by the courts. Procedures developed for the bringing of specific categories of suits became technical and inflexible. This, together with the high cost of bringing suit, led to efforts for improvement. The king, who retained supreme judicial power, granted, through his Curia Regis, or council, the petitions of those who claimed they could not obtain justice in the common law courts. The chief officer of the Curia Regis was the chancellor, "the keeper of the King's conscience," and later keeper of the Great Seal. Eventually, the work of the chancellor increased so much in volume and importance that a permanent court of chancery was established. A system of rules, procedures, and remedies applicable to the chancery courts became known as equity, and functioned to supplement the common law.

Courts of Law

Colonial courts of first instance at law were variously known as the provincial court, superior court, supreme court, general court, or court of common pleas. Their jurisdiction was often a combination of that exercised by different law courts in England, e.g., the King's Bench, common pleas, and the exchequer court. In some colonies a minimum amount of money had to be involved before one could invoke the judicial power of these courts. The judges of such courts were appointed by the governor. Generally there was one chief justice and three or five associate justices in each colony. In some colonies the judges of the court of general jurisdiction rode circuit in each county, while in others there were jurisdictional districts or circuits with specially assigned judges for each district or circuit.

Courts of Equity

Separate courts of equity were also established in some colonies; Maryland, for example, in 1694 created as its equity court the court of chancery. Judicial powers were generally vested in the governor and council or in the governor alone, but legislatures also exercised some equity jurisdiction. Many of the colonies gave equity powers of some degree to the courts of first instance at law, and in some colonies to the lower courts.

Criminal Courts

As in England, the colonial legislatures exercised some criminal jurisdiction, e.g., by bills of attainder whereby a person was punished for a felony or treason without a trial. Criminal jurisdiction was exercised by courts variously named: courts of oyer and terminer and jail delivery, magistrates, general sessions of the peace and general sessions.

Courts of Limited or Special Jurisdiction

The courts of limited civil jurisdiction were called court of common pleas or county courts. In several of the colonies the minor courts were known as justices of the peace of the courts of sessions, or quarter sessions. Courts of limited jurisdiction were often established by county or precinct.

Many colonial judges of the lower courts exercised administrative as well as judicial functions. They could assess and levy taxes, license certain trades, authorize the building and repairing of jails and courthouses, and appoint certain public officials.

Separate probate courts were established in some colonies to deal with the administration of decedents' estates. In others, the legislature or the governor, through his commissioners or surrogates, supervised the administration of decedents' estates. Probate jurisdiction was granted to the court of general jurisdiction of first instance in some cases or, if small estates were involved, to the inferior courts. By 1973, Pennsylvania, Delaware, and Maryland had separate probate courts. Developing along similar lines were the orphans' courts, established to handle child custody and other domestic cases.

For very minor civil matters arising in cities or boroughs, the court of the mayor, recorder and alderman or corporation court had been established. Other commercial problems were dealt with by an extraordinary court of common pleas. A separate admiralty court also existed to handle matters involving shipping.

The King in Council

Final review from the colonial courts was reserved to the King-in-Council. However, since appeals to England were slow and costly, attempts were made by the colonies to limit this right of final appeal.

Immediately after the Revolution, the still autonomous states had the opportunity to reexamine their judicial structures. The prevailing idea of a system of checks and balances led to a separation of the higher judiciary from the legislative and, eventually, from the executive branches. Supreme courts and courts of error and appeals replaced the legislatures as the ultimate courts of review (except in political matters, e.g., impeachment trials). In some states, distrust of legislative power led to the constitutional establishment of inferior courts. In others, the authority to establish inferior courts was delegated to the legislatures.

A constitutional court is one provided for in the constitution while a legislative court is one created by statute. It is far simpler to change, modify or eliminate a legislative court than a constitutional court, as any changes in state constitutions usually require passage by two successive legislatures followed by approval at a duly constituted election by the voters.

Many of the features of the colonial judiciary have survived. Some of the old courts were reestablished and retained their jurisdiction. Those states admitted later to the Union modeled their judicial systems after the original thirteen colonies. It is therefore not surprising that the state judicial systems are even today similar in many respects, although there is little uniformity in the names of courts of like jurisdiction.

CREATION OF THE JUDICIAL POWER OF THE UNITED STATES: THE JUDICIARY ACT OF 1789

The federal judicial power was first created under the Articles of Confederation submitted to the states in 1777, ratified in 1781. This power was extremely limited. It gave authority to Congress to appoint courts for the trial and appeal of piracies and felonies on the high seas; it also enabled Congress itself to act as a last appellate court in disputes between two or more states.

The great change in the relationship of states to the national government came about in 1789 with the final adoption of the United States Constitution which, under article III, section 1, provided for the judicial power of the United States. It called for the establishment of one Supreme Court, with appellate and limited original jurisdiction and inferior courts to be created by the Congress. Within the first six months of its existence, the first Congress followed through by enacting the Judiciary Act of 1789. Under this Act there were created the one Supreme Court of the United States consisting of a chief justice and five associate justices and a system of inferior federal courts.

BIBLIOGRAPHY

AMERICAN Law Institute. Study of the division of jurisdiction between state and federal courts. Philadelphia, 1969. 587 p.

BALDWIN. The American judiciary. Chapter X, relations of state to federal courts. New York, 1905.

BEATTY. State court evasion of United States supreme court mandates during the last decade of the Warren court. Valparaiso University Law Review 6:260 (1972).

BELL. State courts and the federal system. Vanderbilt Law Review 21:949 (1968).

FARNSWORTH. An introduction to the legal system of the United States. Dobbs Ferry, New York, 1963. 184 p. Revised 1975.

FIELD. Jurisdiction of federal courts, a summary of American Law Institute proposals. Federal Rules Decisions 46:141 (1969).

FRANK. Maintaining diversity jurisdiction. Yale Law Journal 73:7 (1963).

FRANKFURTER. Distribution of judicial power between United States and state courts. Cornell Law Review 13:499 (1928).

HART and WECHSLER. The federal courts and the federal system (2d ed.) Mineola, New York, 1973. 1657 p.

JACKSON. The machinery of justice in England. Cambridge, 1972. 589 p.

KURLAND. The distribution of judicial power between national and state courts. Judicature 42:159 (1959).

McGOWAN. Organization of judicial power in the United States Evanston, Illinois, 1969. 133 p.

MAYERS. The American legal system; the administration of justice in the United

States by judicial, administrative, military and arbitral tribunals. New York, 1964. 594 p.

MOORE and WECKSTEIN. Diversity jurisdiction: past, present, and future. Texas Law Review 43:1 (1964).

SCHWARTZ. The law in America: a history. New York, 1974. 382 p.

SWINDLER, Seedtime of an American judiciary: From independence to the Constitution, William and Mary Law Review 17:503 (1976).

U.S. ADVISORY Commission on Intergovernmental Relations. State-local relations in the criminal justice system. Washington, 1971. 308 p.

 *Chapter 2*

State Courts Generally

STRUCTURE AND JURISDICTION

Courts of Ultimate Review

All state constitutions provide for one court of ultimate review, with the exception of New Hampshire, where the highest court was established by the legislature in conformity with its constitutional authority. Colonial history reveals the basis for the one supreme judicial authority in each of the states. It was recognized that the uniformity of result attained by the right of ultimate appeal to the Privy Council in England from the colonial courts was advantageous. However, while the states fashioned their courts of ultimate appeal after the English model, they sought to separate the judicial entity from the political body—the legislature.

In most of the states the highest appellate court is called the supreme court. The name court of appeals is employed in Kentucky, Maryland, and New York. In Maine and Massachusetts, it is the supreme judicial court. In West Virginia, the highest court is designated as the supreme court of appeals.

The courts of last resort hear appeals from designated state courts, either the lower state trial courts or courts of intermediate appeal, usually without regard to the amount of money involved. A variety of criminal cases are appealable to the court of last resort. Being at the apex of a state's court system, the highest court has ultimate jurisdiction over controversies involving the interpretation of the state constitution and state statutes.

The number of justices in the highest state courts varies from three to nine. This number includes a chief or presiding justice and associate justices. The justices serve for terms of from six to ten years in most states, but among the states the terms vary from two years to life. The justices in twenty-four states are elected by the people in either partisan or nonpartisan elections. In Delaware, Hawaii, and New Jersey, justices are appointed by the governor with the approval of the state senate. In Massachusetts, Maine, and New Hampshire, the governor's appointment must be ratified by the executive council. Vermont, Rhode Island, South Carolina, and Virginia provide for legislative appointment without subsequent ratification. Supreme court justices in Connecticut are nominated by the governor and appointed by the general assembly.

The method of judicial selection in Missouri was changed in 1940, by constitutional amendment, from a political party primary and election system to a nonpartisan system known as the Missouri or the American Bar Association Plan. In Missouri this method of selection applies only to the judges of the Missouri Supreme Court, the three courts of appeal, circuit and probate courts of St. Louis, Clay, Platte, and Jackson Counties and the city of St. Louis, and municipal courts of Kansas City. The plan employs the following steps:

1. Judges are nominated by a nonpartisan, nonsalaried commission of an equal number of lawyers, selected by the bar of the state, and laymen, appointed by the governor.

2. The judge is appointed by the governor from a list of three nominees presented by the commission.

3. After a brief trial period of at least twelve months, the judge must be voted on and approved by the people in order to remain in office. At the next general election following a year of service by an appointed judge, the judge's name is placed on a separate judicial ballot without party designation and on the ballot appears the question, "Shall Judge ＿＿＿＿＿ of the ＿＿＿＿＿ Court be retained in office? Yes ＿＿＿ No ＿＿＿ ." The voters X in one answer, leaving the other blank.

The nucleus of the Missouri Plan is the appointment of judges to office from a list of qualified candidates nominated by a nonpolitical commission. Subsequently, after a period of probationary service, those judges stand for election on their records, rather than in contest against other candidates; in some cases other candidates, who conform to requirements of the statute, may run against them, but on a nonpartisan basis. There is a continuing movement in the United States in favor of such a plan to deemphasize politics in the selection of judges and to keep the ones who have proven themselves on the bench. Forms of both merit selection and merit retention have been adopted for the appellate courts in Alaska, Arizona, Colorado, Indiana, Iowa, Kansas, Missouri, Nebraska, Oklahoma, Utah, and Vermont. In some states only the merit retention feature is used for certain courts, as in California (all appellate courts). In other states the mayor or the governor has from time to time set up a merit selection plan by executive order or on a voluntary basis, as in New Mexico, New York City, recently in New York State, Puerto Rico, California, Maryland, and Florida.

Salaries of the justices of the highest state courts range from $26,000 in Maine to $60,575 for judges of the Court of Appeals of New York. In many of the states, chief justices receive a larger salary than do their associate justices; for example the chief justice of Arkansas receives $32,250 per year and an associate justice of that court receives $29,563. The average salary received by associate justices of the various courts of last resort was reported in 1976 at $38,152 and $32,527 for general trial court judges. These figures are up from $30,316.46 for supreme court justices and $27,518.82 for trial court judges, formerly reported in a 1972 judicial salary survey.

In addition, states have provided improved retirement pensions and benefits for a surviving spouse as well as funds for judges' expenses. Several legislatures have provided for automatic salary increases based on a consumer price index while Maryland provides automatic salary increases for the judiciary based on general salary increases awarded to all state employees. Rhode Island entitles judges and all court personnel to longevity increments, depending upon years of service, i.e., "longevity after seven years 5%; after eleven years 10%; after fifteen years 15% and after twenty-five years 20%."

The majority of the courts of last resort hold their sessions and terms at the state capitol. In several states the court meets in different cities, as in California, Idaho, Oregon, Pennsylvania, and Tennessee. The commencement and completion of the court terms vary and are generally controlled by the courts. Some courts have only one term annually, others have as many as five or more terms during the year.

Intermediate Appellate Courts

Economic development and proliferating criminal appeals have resulted in heavily increasing the caseloads of some of the highest state courts. For example, in January 1959, there were 483 cases pending before the seven-member Colorado supreme court. Ten years later, 972 appeals were on that court's docket — an increment of 489 cases or a 49 percent increase in the court's workload, exclusive of more than 3,000 motions also on the calendar. To lighten this increasing burden, Colorado and twenty-two other states have established by constitution or statute intermediate appellate courts. Ordinarily, these courts are denominated courts of appeal. The name appellate court is employed in Illinois and Indiana, and in Pennsylvania the intermediate appellate court is the state superior court. Intermediate appellate jurisdiction is given to the appellate divisions of the New Jersey superior court and the New York supreme court. Arkansas has authorized the creation of intermediate appellate courts in the event its supreme court becomes too heavily burdened.

There is little uniformity in the jurisdiction exercised by intermediate appellate courts. Some of them are given original jurisdiction in special cases. Generally, however, they exercise appellate jurisdiction. Their appellate jurisdiction may be limited to cases involving a certain maximum monetary amount. For example, the court of appeals in Missouri has appellate jurisdiction in all cases where the amount in dispute does not exceed $30,000. It also takes appeals in criminal cases from the circuit courts of Missouri. In other states, the appellate jurisdiction is usually confined, subject to a few exceptions, to appeals from final orders of specified courts. Some states define the jurisdiction of their intermediate appellate courts in terms of the types of cases they may hear, e.g., only civil cases may be appealed to the Texas Court of Civil Appeals. All of the states having intermediate appellate courts provide for some permissive means of review by the highest state court. And, in some cases, a litigant is given the right of direct appeal to the highest state court without permission of the intermediate appellate court. Pennsylvania, for example, is one state where an appeal is taken directly to the state supreme court in cases of felonious homicide.

The number of judges sitting in the intermediate appellate courts varies from three in Alabama to forty-two in the civil court of appeals in Texas. In most of the states having intermediate appellate courts, the judges are selected in the same manner provided for the selection of the justices of the highest state court. However, in New York, where the judges of the Court of Appeals are elected, the justices of the appellate division are appointed by the governor from elected justices serving in the supreme court. The terms of office vary from six years in Oklahoma to fifteen years in Maryland, and in some states the term is eventually for life. Salaries range from $26,000 in Oklahoma to $51,627 for justices of the appellate divisions in New York. Generally, presiding judges of intermediate appellate courts receive the same salary as associate judges.

Trial Courts of Original and General Jurisdiction

Trial courts of general jurisdiction may be called upon to handle civil, criminal, equity, and probate cases. The extent of jurisdiction exercised over these classes of litigation varies in each state depending upon whether separate courts exist to handle any of these types of litigation. In states such as Arkansas, Mississippi, Delaware, and Tennessee, separate chancery or equity courts still exist. However, most states have abolished the procedural distinctions between law and equity and the same court can dispose of both equity and law matters. The most populous states, with the exception of California, maintain separate probate or surrogate's courts to dispose of decedent estate matters; for example, New York, Massachusetts, and Michigan. Some states maintain separate criminal and civil divisions. In South Carolina, for instance, the circuit courts are divided into courts of common pleas, which handle civil cases, and courts of general sessions, which handle criminal cases.

When a state court exercises both civil and criminal jurisdiction, it may do so concurrently with courts of limited jurisdiction. Reference must be made to the constitution, statutes, and the cases judicially decided to determine exactly the jurisdiction of a particular trial court of general jurisdiction.

Special courts to hear domestic relations or family matters have often been established in heavily populated jurisdictions. Arizona provides for a court of conciliation to be created by the superior court rather than the legislature. New

Jersey has courts of juvenile and domestic relations and the New York Family Court hears all family matters with the exception of divorce, separation, and annulment proceedings.

The *National Survey of Court Organization* conducted in 1973 by the U.S. Department of Justice, Law Enforcement Assistance Administration, estimates that as of July 1, 1971, there were 4,929 judges of the courts of general jurisdiction in the United States. This estimate excludes the many trial courts which hear only special civil cases or only criminal cases. The major trial courts are usually authorized to hear appeals from minor courts. In many cases, in appealing from a decision of a minor court, the litigant can get a completely new trial, that is, a trial de novo, or retrial, in the trial court of general jurisdiction. There is a movement to abolish such a system of double trials. Automation, in providing for the keeping of a record of the trial in the lower court, is leading to appeal on the record rather than going through the process of an entirely new trial in many states where trial de novo has existed.

The number of judges in the trial courts of general jurisdiction varies in different states. In a few states, the number of judges per judicial area is limited in the constitution. However, in the majority of the states the legislature is authorized to increase the number of judges as population and caseload increase. (In California there are 171 authorized superior court judges for the county of Los Angeles serving a population of approximately seven million.) Florida has an unusual constitutional provision which automatically increases the number of judgeships as population increases.

Usually judges of the trial courts of general jurisdiction are selected by the same process as judges of the highest state court. In Rhode Island, however, justices of the supreme court are elected by the legislature and trial judges of the superior court are appointed by the governor with the consent of the state senate. In Massachusetts and Rhode Island, a trial judge has tenure for life, during good behavior. And in New Jersey, judges of both the supreme and the superior courts are appointed by the governor with the consent of the State Senate to serve initially for seven years, and then on reappointment, for life, during good behavior. Except for judges in these states, the terms served by trial judges range from two to fifteen years; the average is six years. At the present time, at least nine states require trial judges to submit to merit retention or nonpartisan elections at the expiration of their terms.

The geographic location of trial courts of general jurisdiction is usually set by statute. In most states sessions are held in the county seats. However, some states require that at least one of the major trial courts be held in each judicial area during the year. The length of trial court sessions may be set by statute or left to the trial judges. Some trial courts are in continuous session. Others determine the length of their sessions by the amount of litigation in the judicial area in which they sit. It has not been the practice to hold trials during the summer months in most jurisdictions, although some states have enacted statutes requiring trial courts to do so. Many courts are finding it necessary to conduct trials during the summer in order to maintain current calendars. For instance, the New York Supreme Courts in New York City have been trying criminal cases, and some civil cases, during the past several summers in order to help reduce the growing backlog of cases. Trial courts in Delaware and California regularly try cases on a year-round basis.

Courts of Limited or Special Jurisdiction

These courts dispose of "petty" litigation, or "small causes," and petty criminal cases. Traditionally, such courts were justice of the peace courts. In many states, justices of the peace were elected officials, did not have to be attorneys, and were compensated by the amount of fees collected. By the nineteenth century, there was an increasing tendency to replace the justices of the peace with magistrates or local inferior courts with somewhat increased jurisdiction. For some cases, county courts were given jurisdiction concurrent with the justices of the peace. For others, especially in the larger cities, municipal courts were established to handle the most minor civil matters. In cases involving more limited sums of money a relatively simple procedure has been established. Designated as small claims courts, these civil courts of lesser jurisdiction are currently found in some twenty-eight states.

Where the justices of the peace have not been supplanted by district or county courts in rural areas, or by municipal courts in larger cities, they continue to exercise petty criminal jurisdiction and petty civil jurisdiction. A common feature of justice of the peace courts is that a trial de novo may be had in a court of original general jurisdiction. Appellate review of the trial court's judgment is then available in a court of intermediate appeal or court of ultimate review. Violation of traffic ordinances or other local ordinances usually result in payment of a fine to the justice of the peace, or the police justice as he is known in some towns and villages. Larger cities have created special traffic courts or special parts of the magistrates courts to deal with the increasing volume of traffic violations. New York established a process for the administrative adjudication of traffic violations in 1970.

While in many jurisdictions domestic relations problems are handled by the trial courts of general jurisdiction, special courts have been created to dispose of these matters in Delaware, Louisiana, Mississippi (Harrison County), New Jersey, New York (except divorce, separation, and annulment), South Carolina, and West Virginia. Separate juvenile courts exist in several states. Elswhere, authority to act as a juvenile court, or through a juvenile division of the trial court, is vested in the trial court of general jurisdiction, or in the probate or domestic relations court. When a court acts as a juvenile court, the procedures employed have been informal, rather than in accord with standard criminal procedure for adults, on the theory that the state stands in the relation of a parent to the child. The U.S. Supreme Court, in the case of *In re Gault*, 387 U.S. 1 (1967), has held that the concept of due process embodied in the fourteenth amendment to the U.S. Constitution must be applied to juvenile proceedings. Among the constitutional guarantees cited by the Supreme Court were the rights to adequate notice of a delinquency hearing, to representation by counsel, to confront and cross-examine witnesses, and the privilege against self-incrimination. Increasingly, juvenile courts are making extensive use of auxiliary services—legal guardians, social workers, psychological testing—in an attempt to rehabilitate the delinquent youth offender.

The difficulties these courts have in dealing with increasing juvenile crime has caused a reexamination and reevaluation of their philosophies and procedures. There is a movement on the part of courts and legislatures to reshape the laws relating to the problems of youth. The American Bar Association jointly with the Institute of Judicial Administration has for the last five years been preparing basic standards for the administration of juvenile justice. As explained by the Honorable Irving R. Kaufman, chief judge of the U.S. Second Circuit Court of Appeals and chairman of the Joint IJA—ABA Project, the standards to be submitted for approval cover constructive, concrete, and comprehensive reform.

Summarizing comments on court systems, in some states it is not unusual for jurisdiction to be so fragmented among different courts that a litigant may have to go to more than one court to obtain a final decision on all aspects of what he or she considers is his or her case.

Table 2–1. Names of Courts in the States and Number of Judges of Appellate Courts and Trial Courts of General Jurisdiction*

State or Other Jurisdiction	Appellate Courts	Number of Judges	Trial Courts of General Jurisdiction	Number of Judges	Courts of Limited Jurisdiction
Alabama	Supreme Court Court of Criminal Appeals Court of Civil Appeals	9 5 3	Circuit courts	108	Courts of probate County courts (a) Justice courts (a) Recorder's courts (b)
Alaska	Supreme Court	5	Superior courts	17	Magistrates courts District courts
Arizona	Supreme Court Court of Appeals	5 12	Superior courts	67	Justice courts City & town magistrate courts
Arkansas	Supreme Court	7	Chancery & probate courts Circuit courts	26 29	County courts Municipal courts Courts of common pleas Justice courts Police courts City courts
California	Supreme Court Courts of Appeal	7 56	Superior courts	522	Municipal courts Justice courts
Colorado	Supreme Court Court of Appeals	7 10	District Court	94	Superior Court Juvenile Court] Denver Probate Court] County courts Municipal courts
Connecticut	Supreme Court	6(c)	Superior Court	45(c)	Court of Common Pleas Juvenile Court Probate courts

State	Court of last resort / appellate courts	No.	Trial courts	No.	Inferior courts
Delaware	Supreme Court	3	Court of chancery; Superior court	3; 11	Family Court; Municipal Court (Wilmington); Justice courts
Florida	Supreme Court; District Courts of Appeal	7; 20	Circuit courts	263	County courts; Municipal courts
Georgia	Supreme Court; Court of Appeals	7; 9	Superior courts	86	Probate courts; Civil & criminal courts; Justice courts; Small claims courts
Hawaii	Supreme Court	5	Circuit courts	13	District courts
Idaho	Supreme Court	5	District courts	24	Magistrate's Division of District Court
Illinois	Supreme Court; Appellate Court	7; 34	Circuit court (approx.) and Associate Judges	360; 250	....
Indiana	Supreme Court; Court of Appeals	5; 9	Circuit courts; Superior courts; Criminal courts	88; 78; 4	County courts; Municipal courts; Magistrate courts; Probate courts; Juvenile courts; City & town courts(d); Justice of peace courts(d)
Iowa	Supreme Court	9	District court(e)	292(e)	....
Kansas	Supreme Court	7	District courts	64	Probate courts; City courts (Magistrate); County courts; Juvenile courts; Municipal courts

(Table 2–1 cont'd overleaf . . .)

Table 2–1. continued

State or Other Jurisdiction	Appellate Courts	Number of Judges	Trial Courts of General Jurisdiction	Number of Judges	Courts of Limited Jurisdiction
Kentucky (i)	Supreme Court	7	Circuit courts	83	County courts Justice courts Police courts
Louisiana	Supreme Court Courts of Appeals	7 29	District courts	125	City courts Juvenile courts Mayors' courts Justice courts Traffic courts Family courts Municipal courts Parish courts
Maine	Supreme Judicial Court	6	Superior Court	14	Probate courts District courts
Maryland	Court of Appeals Court of Special Appeals	7 12	Circuit courts of counties Courts of Supreme Bench of Baltimore City	63 22	Orphans' courts District Court
Massachusetts	Supreme Judicial Court Appeals Court	7 6	Superior Court	46	Land Court Probate courts Municipal Court (Boston) District courts Juvenile courts Housing courts
Michigan	Supreme Court Court of Appeals	7 18	Circuit courts Recorder's Court (Detroit)	138 23	Common Pleas Court (Detroit) Municipal courts District courts Probate courts

State	Highest Court		Trial Court		Lower Courts
Minnesota	Supreme Court	9	District courts	72	County courts Probate courts Municipal courts
Mississippi	Supreme Court	9	Chancery courts Circuit courts	25 24	Family Court (Harrison County) County courts City police courts Justice courts
Missouri	Supreme Court Court of Appeals	7 22	Circuit courts	112	Probate courts Court of Criminal Correction (St. Louis) Magistrate courts Municipal courts
Montana	Supreme Court	5	District courts	28	Municipal courts Justice courts City courts Workmen's Compensation Judge
Nebraska	Supreme Court	7	District courts	45	County courts Municipal courts Juvenile courts Workmen's Compensation Court
Nevada	Supreme Court	5	District courts	25	Municipal courts Justice courts
New Hampshire	Supreme Court	5	Superior court	13	Probate courts District courts Municipal courts
New Jersey	Supreme Court Appellate Division of Superior Court	7 22	Superior Court County courts	120 103	County district courts Juvenile & Domestic Relations Court Municipal courts

(Table 2–1 cont'd overleaf . . .)

Table 2–1. continued

State or Other Jurisdiction	Appellate Courts	Number of Judges	Trial Courts of General Jurisdiction	Number of Judges	Courts of Limited Jurisdiction
New Mexico	Supreme Court Court of Appeals	5 5	District courts	32	Probate courts Municipal courts Small Claims Court Magistrate Court
New York	Court of Appeals Appellate Divisions of Supreme Court(f)	7 24(g)	Supreme Court	257	Court of Claims Surrogate's Court Family Court County courts Civil Court (N.Y. City) Criminal Court (N.Y. City) District courts City courts Town & village courts
North Carolina	Supreme Court Court of Appeals	7 9	Supreme Court	55	District Court
North Dakota	Supreme Court	5	District courts	19	County courts with increased jurisdiction County courts County justice courts Municipal courts
Ohio	Supreme Court Courts of Appeals	7 38	Courts of common pleas	296	Municipal courts County courts Court of Claims

State	Appellate courts		Trial courts (general)		Trial courts (limited)
Oklahoma	Supreme Court	9	District Court	185	Municipal courts
	Court of Criminal Appeals	3			
	Court of Appeals	6			
Oregon	Supreme Court	7	Circuit courts	70	County courts
	Court of Appeals	6			District courts
					Justice courts
					Municipal courts
Pennsylvania	Supreme Court	7	Courts of common pleas	285	Municipal Court of Philadelphia
	Superior Court	7			Traffic Court of Philadelphia
	Commonwealth Court	7			Justices of the peace
Rhode Island	Supreme Court	5	Superior Court	15	District courts
					Probate courts
					Family Court
					Police Court (Providence, Pawtucket, Johnston)
South Carolina	Supreme Court	5	Circuit Court	16	County courts
					Probate courts
					Magistrate courts
					City recorders courts
					Family courts
South Dakota	Supreme Court	5	Circuit courts	36	Five law-trained magistrates and others
Tennessee	Supreme Court	5	Chancery courts	26	County courts
	Court of Appeals	9	Circuit courts	54	General sessions courts
	Court of Criminal Appeals	7	Criminal courts	22	Municipal courts
			Law-equity courts	5	Juvenile courts
					Domestic relations courts

(Table 2–1 cont'd overleaf . . .)

Table 2–1. continued

State or Other Jurisdiction	Appellate Courts	Number of Judges	Trial Courts of General Jurisdiction	Number of Judges	Courts of Limited Jurisdiction
Texas	Supreme Court Court of Criminal Appeals Court of Civil Appeals	9 5 42	District courts	220	Criminal district courts Courts of domestic relations Juvenile courts County courts at law County civil courts at law Probate courts County criminal courts County criminal courts at law County criminal courts of appeal County courts Justice courts Municipal courts
Utah	Supreme Court	5	District courts	21	Juvenile courts City courts Justice courts
Vermont	Supreme Court	5	Superior courts	7	District courts Probate courts
Virginia	Supreme Court	7	Circuit courts	103	General district courts Juvenile & domestic relations courts
Washington	Supreme Court Court of Appeals	9 12	Superior courts	100	District courts Municipal courts
West Virginia	Supreme Court of Appeals	5	Circuit courts	50	Police courts

Wisconsin	Supreme Court	7	Circuit courts County courts	53 128	Municipal courts
Wyoming	Supreme Court	5	District courts	13	Justice courts Municipal courts
Dist. of Col.(h)	Court of Appeals	9	Superior Court	44	County courts
Guam	Supreme Court	3	Superior Court	5	Traffic Court Small Claims Court
Puerto Rico	Supreme Court	8	Superior Court	89	District Court Municipal Court Justice courts

*When the same judges preside over two or more classes of courts, only one of the classes is shown. Also, certain types of specialized courts, such as tax courts or industrial relations courts, have been omitted from this compilation.

(a) Effective January 1977, the county courts and justice courts will be abolished and replaced by a state trial court of limited jurisdiction named the district court.

(b) Effective December 1977, recorder's courts will more correctly be referred to as municipal courts.

(c) Does not include senior judges (i.e., judges between the ages of 65 and 70 who are eligible for assignment to judicial duties but who have retired from full-time service as a judge).

(d) Scheduled to be replaced by the county courts except that justice of the peace courts will continue in Marion County.

(e) A unified system with 85 district court judges who possess the full jurisdiction of the court. An additional 19 district associate judges, 19 full-time judicial magistrates, and 169 part-time judicial magistrates have limited jurisdiction.

(f) The appellate divisions may establish appellate terms to hear appeals from local courts; 2 of the 4 appellate divisions have done so. In addition, the county courts, although basically trial courts, may hear appeals from certain local courts.

(g) Twenty-four justices permanently authorized; in addition, as of November 1, 1975, 18 justices and certificated retired justices had been temporarily designated.

(h) Reflects 1974 survey. Later information not available.

(i) Kentucky adopted a new judicial article at the November 1975 general election. Some implementing legislation will be before the General Assembly for its consideration. This table reflects information prior to implementation of new judicial article.

Reproduced by permission of the Council of State Governments from its publication *State Court Systems Revised 1976*.

Table 2–2. Final Selection of Judges

State	
Alabama	Appellate, circuit, district, and probate judges elected on partisan ballots. Judges of municipal courts are appointed by the governing body of the municipality as of 1977.
Alaska	Supreme Court Justices, superior, and district court judges appointed by Governor from nominations by Judicial Council. Approved or rejected at first general election held more than 3 years after appointment. Reconfirmed every 10, 6, and 4 years, respectively. Magistrates appointed by and serve at pleasure of the presiding judges of each judicial district.
Arizona	Supreme Court Justices and court of appeals judges appointed by Governor from a list of not less than 3 for each vacancy submitted by a 9-member Commission on Appellate Court Appointments. Maricopa and Pima County superior court judges appointed by Governor from a list of not less than 3 for each vacancy submitted by a 9-member Commission on Trial Court Appointments for each county. Superior court judges of other 12 counties elected on nonpartisan ballot (partisan primary); justices of the peace elected on partisan ballot; city and town magistrates selected as provided by charter or ordinance, usually appointed by mayor and council.
Arkansas	All elected on partisan ballot.
California	Supreme Court and courts of appeal judges appointed by Governor with approval of Commission on Judicial Appointments. Run for reelection on record. All judges elected on nonpartisan ballot.
Colorado	Judges of all courts, except Denver County and municipal, appointed initially by Governor from lists submitted by nonpartisan nominating commissions; run on record for retention. Municipal judges appointed by city councils or town boards. Denver County judges appointed by mayor from list submitted by nominating commission; judges run on record for retention.
Connecticut	All appointed by Legislature from nominations submitted by Governor, except that probate judges are elected on partisan ballot.
Delaware	All appointed by Governor with consent of Senate.
Florida	All elected on nonpartisan ballot.
Georgia	All elected on partisan ballot except that county and some city court judges are appointed by the Governor with consent of the Senate.
Hawaii	Supreme Court Justices and circuit court judges appointed by the Governor with consent of the Senate. District magistrates appointed by Chief Justice of the State.

State	
Idaho	Supreme Court and district court judges are elected on nonpartisan ballot. Magistrates appointed by District Magistrate's Commission for initial 2-year term; thereafter, run on record for retention for 4-year term on nonpartisan ballot.
Illinois	All elected on partisan ballot and run on record for retention. Associate judges are appointed by circuit judges and serve 4-year terms.
Indiana	Judges of appellate courts appointed by Governor from a list of 3 for each vacancy submitted by a 7-member Judicial Nomination Commission. Governor appoints members of municipal courts and several counties have judicial nominating commissions which submit a list of nominees to the Governor for appointment. All other judges are elected.
Iowa	Judges of Supreme and district courts appointed initially by Governor from lists submitted by nonpartisan nominating commissions. Appointee serves initial 1-year term and then runs on record for retention. District associate judges run on record for retention; if not retained or office becomes vacant, replaced by a full-time judicial magistrate. Full-time judicial magistrates appointed by district judges in the judicial election district from nominees submitted by county judicial magistrate appointing commission. Part-time judicial magistrates appointed by county judicial magistrate appointing commissions.
Kansas	Supreme Court Judges appointed by Governor from list submitted by nominating commission. Run on record for retention. Nonpartisan selection method adopted for judges of courts of general jurisdiction in 23 of 29 districts.
Kentucky (a)	Judges of Supreme Court and circuit court judges elected on nonpartisan ballot. All others elected on partisan ballot.
Louisiana	All elected on open (bipartisan) ballot.
Maine	All appointed by Governor with consent of Executive Council except that probate judges are elected on partisan ballot.
Maryland	Judges of Court of Appeals, Court of Special Appeals, Circuit Courts and Supreme Bench of Baltimore City appointed by Governor, elected on nonpartisan ballot after at least one year's service. District court judges appointed by Governor subject to confirmation by Senate.
Massachusetts	All appointed by Governor with consent of Executive Council. Judicial Nominating Commission, established by executive order, advises Governor on appointment of judges.
Michigan	All elected on nonpartisan ballot, except municipal judges in accordance with local charters by local city councils.
Minnesota	All elected on nonpartisan ballot. Vacancy filled by gubernatorial appointment.
Mississippi	All elected on partisan ballot, except that city police court justices are appointed by governing authority of each municipality.

(Table 2–2 cont'd overleaf . . .)

Table 2-2. continued

Missouri	Judges of Supreme Court, Court of Appeals, circuit and probate courts in St. Louis City and County, Jackson County, Platte County, Clay County and St. Louis Court of Criminal Correction appointed initially by Governor from nominations submitted by special commissions. Run on record for reelection. All other judges elected on partisan ballot.
Montana	All elected on nonpartisan ballot. Vacancies on Supreme or district courts and Workmen's Compensation Judge filled by Governor according to established appointment procedure.
Nebraska	Judges of all courts appointed initially by Governor from lists submitted by bipartisan nominating commissions. Run on record for retention in office in general election following initial term of 3 years; subsequent terms are 6 years.
Nevada	All elected on nonpartisan ballot.
New Hampshire	All appointed by Governor with confirmation of Executive Council.
New Jersey	All appointed by Governor with consent of Senate except that magistrates of municipal courts serving one municipality only are appointed by governing bodies.
New Mexico	All elected on partisan ballot.
New York	All elected on partisan ballot except that Governor appoints judges of court of claims and designates members of appellate division of Supreme Court, and Mayor of the City of New York appoints judges of the criminal and family courts in the City of New York.
North Carolina	All elected on partisan ballot.
North Dakota	All elected on nonpartisan ballot.
Ohio	All elected on nonpartisan ballot except court of claims judges who may be appointed by Chief Justice of Supreme Court from ranks of Supreme Court, court of appeals, court of common pleas, or retired judges.
Oklahoma	Supreme Court Justices and Court of Criminal Appeals Judges appointed by Governor from lists of three submitted by Judicial Nominating Commission. If Governor fails to make appointment within 60 days after occurrence of vacancy, appointment is made by Chief Justice from the same list. Run for election on their records at first general election following completion of 12 months' service for unexpired term. Judges of Court of Appeals, district and associate district judges elected on nonpartisan ballot in adversary popular election. Special district judges appointed by district judges. Municipal judges appointed by governing body of municipality.
Oregon	All elected on nonpartisan ballot for a 6-year term, except that most municipal judges are appointed by city councils (elected in three cities).

Pennsylvania	All originally elected on partisan ballot; thereafter, on nonpartisan retention ballot.
Rhode Island	Supreme Court Justices elected by Legislature. Superior, family and district court justices and justices of the peace appointed by Governor, with consent of Senate (except for justices of the peace); probate and municipal court judges appointed by city or town councils.
South Carolina	Supreme Court and circuit court judges elected by Legislature. City judges, magistrates, and some county judges and family court judges appointed by Governor—the latter on recommendation of the legislative delegation in the area served by the court. Probate judges and some county judges elected on partisan ballot.
South Dakota	All elected on nonpartisan ballot, except magistrates (law trained and others), who are appointed by the presiding judge of the judicial circuit in which the county is located.
Tennessee	Judges of intermediate appellate courts appointed initially by Governor from nominations submitted by special commission. Run on record for reelection. The Supreme Court judges and all other judges elected on partisan ballot.
Texas	All elected on partisan ballot except municipal judges, most of whom are appointed by municipal governing body.
Utah	Supreme and district court judges appointed by Governor from lists of three nominees submitted by nominating commissions. If Governor fails to make appointment within 30 days, the Chief Justice appoints. Judges run for retention in office at next succeeding election; they may be opposed by others on nonpartisan judicial ballots. Juvenile court judges are initially appointed by the Governor from a list of not less than 2 nominated by the Juvenile Court Commission, and retained in office by gubernatorial appointment. Town justices of the peace are appointed by town trustees. City judges and county justices of the peace are elected.
Vermont	Supreme Court Justices, superior court judges (presiding judges of county courts) and district court judges appointed by Governor with consent of Senate from list of persons designated as qualified by the Judicial Selection Board. Supreme, superior, and district court judges retained in office by vote of Legislature. Assistant judges of county courts and probate judges elected on partisan ballot in the territorial area of their jurisdiction.
Virginia	Supreme Court and all major trial court judges elected by Legislature. All judges of General District Juvenile and Domestic Relations Courts elected by Legislature. Committee on District Courts, in the case of part-time judges, certifies that a vacancy exists. Thereupon all part-time judges of General District Courts and General District Juvenile and Domestic Relations Courts are appointed by circuit judges.
Washington	All elected on nonpartisan ballot except that municipal judges in second, third and fourth class cities are appointed by mayor.
West Virginia	Judges of all courts of record elected on partisan ballot.

(Table 2–2 cont'd overleaf . . .)

Table 2–2. continued

Wisconsin	All elected on nonpartisan ballot.
Wyoming	Supreme Court Justices and district court judges appointed by Governor from a list of 3 submitted by nominating committee and stand for retention at next election after 1 year in office. Justices of the peace elected on nonpartisan ballot.
District of Columbia	Appointed by President of the United States upon the advice and consent of the United States Senate.
Guam	All appointed by Governor with consent of Legislature from list of 3 nominees submitted by Judicial Council for term of 5 years; thereafter run on record for retention every 5 years.
Puerto Rico	All appointed by Governor with consent of Senate.

(a) Kentucky adopted a new judicial article at the November 1975 general election. Some implementing legislation will be before the General Assembly for its consideration. This table reflects information prior to implementation of new judicial article.

Reproduced by permission of the Council of State Governments from its publication *State Court Systems Revised 1976*.

JUDICIAL CONDUCT

Judges in all courts must maintain constant vigilance lest their personal conduct reflect bias or misconduct in the exercise of judicial authority. The American Bar Association's Canons of Judicial Ethics, first drafted in 1924, were carefully restudied for almost three years (1970–1972) by a Special Committee on Standards of Judicial Conduct, chaired by the Hon. Roger J. Traynor, then chief justice of California. The extensive restudy of the original canons may be related to the incidents surrounding the resignation of one of the United States Supreme Court justices and the nomination by President Nixon of a number of federal court judicial candidates. A Code of Judicial Conduct, replacing the Canons of Judicial Ethics, was developed and was adopted by the House of Delegates in August 1972. It embraces off-the-bench activities as well as courtroom conduct and obligations. Indicative of the advisory nature of the Code are those sections which caution a judge against becoming influenced or giving the impression of being influenced by partisan demands, self-interest, or conflicting obligations — either pecuniary or charitable. Canon Six calls upon a judge to regularly file reports of compensation received for quasi-judicial and extra-judicial activities, giving standards for compensation, expense reimbursement, such reports to be made annually and filed as a public document in the office of the clerk of the court.

Discipline and Removal of State Court Judges

The U.S. Constitution provides that federal judges may be removed from office only for cause, and then only by process of impeachment. Almost all the states have adopted this method. *Address*, which is also used, is a method of removal by which the legislature, after a two-thirds vote based upon a showing of cause, may require a judge to resign, or direct the governor to remove him. Another means by which state judges are removed is the device known as *Recall*. Currently authorized by the constitution of eight states, recall requires that a judge submit to a popular election if a petition is filed charging him with misconduct. If the judge fails to receive a majority of the votes cast, he will forfeit his office. The above methods are cumbersome and political and are rarely used. For these reasons simpler methods of dealing with "bad" or incompetent judges have evolved.

Courts on the Judiciary exist in a number of states. They are composed either of high court judges or judges of different levels of state courts. Courts on the judiciary may consider a wide range of causes for removal, including willful misconduct in office, and physical or mental inability to perform judicial functions. A judge tried before a court on the judiciary is guaranteed procedural due process. An adverse ruling may result in the judge's retirement, censure, or removal. In 1975, thirty-eight states and the District of Columbia had created various types of commissions to deal with undesirable judicial conduct. They are usually composed of state court judges from different courts, bar members, and sometimes laymen. These commissions are empowered to recommend censure, suspension, retirement, or removal upon their determination that a judge has been delinquent in his judicial activities. Like proceedings before a court on the judiciary, action by a commission is conducted with a view toward guaranteeing a judge procedural due process and fairness, and freedom from publicity until found guilty. Hearing by the state court of last resort is generally available. This procedure is usually in addition to, and not in place of, the other removal procedures provided in constitutions discussed above. Other states have moved in the direction of providing some means, other than impeachment, for removing undesirable judges. Rarely does the plan affect the lower court judges. There are more informal methods of dealing with lower court judges.

Although the names of these bodies differ and their procedures may also be different, their objectives are the same: to keep a vigilant watch on the conduct and performance of judges and to supply a method more simple than impeachment to deal with such problems.

Table 2-3. Methods for Removal of Judges and Filling of Vacancies

State or Other Jurisdiction	How Removed	Vacancies: How Filled
Alabama	All judges subject to impeachment. All except justices of Supreme Court may be removed by Supreme Court. A Judicial Inquiry Commission and Court of the Judiciary were created in new constitution for purpose of investigating and acting upon complaints. Court of the Judiciary is empowered to remove, suspend, censure, or otherwise discipline a judge.	By Governor, until the next general election, when judge is elected to fill unexpired term. Ad interim appointees customarily elected for a full term.
Alaska	All justices and judges subject to impeachment for malfeasance or misfeasance. Impeachment by 2/3 vote of Senate; trial in House, with a Supreme Court justice, designated by the court, presiding. Concurrence of 2/3 vote of House required for removal.	Filled by Governor from nominations by Judicial Council.
	On recommendation of Judicial Qualifications Commission or on own motion, Supreme Court may suspend judge from office without salary when in U.S. he pleads guilty or no contest or is found guilty of a crime punishable as a felony under Alaska or federal law or of any other crime involving moral turpitude under that law. If conviction is reversed, suspension terminates, and he shall be paid salary for period of suspension. If conviction becomes final, removal from office by Supreme Court.	
	On recommendation of Judicial Qualifications Commission, Supreme Court may (1) retire judge for disability that seriously interferes with performance of duties and is or is likely to become permanent, and (2) censure or remove judge for action occurring not more than 6 years before commencement of current term which constitutes willful misconduct in office, willful and persistent failure to perform duties, habitual intemperance, or conduct prejudicial to the administration of justice that brings the judicial office into disrepute.	

(Table 2-3 cont'd overleaf . . .)

Table 2–3. continued

State or Other Jurisdiction	How Removed	Vacancies: How Filled
Arizona	Every public officer subject to recall. Electors, equal to 25% of votes cast at last preceding general election, may petition for recall. All judges, except justices of courts not of record, subject to impeachment by 2/3 of vote of Senate. Upon recommendation of Commission on Judicial Qualifications, Supreme Court may remove judges from all courts (except city magistrate) for willful misconduct in office, willful and persistent failure to perform duties, habitual intemperance, or conduct prejudicial to the administration of justice that brings the judicial office into disrepute, or may retire them for disability that seriously interferes with performance of duties and is, or is likely to become, permanent.	Supreme Court justices, Court of Appeals judges, and Pima County Superior Court judges selected in manner provided for in original appointment. Superior Court judges of the other 12 counties by Governor, until the next general election when judge is elected to fill unexpired term. Justices of the peace by county board of supervisors for balance of term. City magistrates by the mayor and council.
Arkansas	Judges of the Supreme and circuit courts and chancellors are subject to removal by impeachment or by the Governor upon the joint address of 2/3 of the members elected to each house of the General Assembly.	By Governor until next general election. Ad interim appointees ineligible for election.
California	Judges of all state courts subject to impeachment. All judges subject to recall by voters. Suspension without salary by Supreme Court when they plead guilty or no contest or are found guilty of a crime punishable as a felony under California or federal law or of any other crime that involves moral turpitude, and removal by the Supreme Court upon final conviction of such crimes. Upon recommendation of Commission on Judicial Qualifications, Supreme Court may remove judges from all courts for willful misconduct in office, willful and persistent failure to perform duties, habitual intemperance, or conduct prejudicial to the administration of justice that brings the judicial office into disrepute, or may retire them for disability that seriously interferes with performance of duties and is, or is likely to become, permanent.	Supreme Court and Courts of Appeal judges, by Governor with approval of Commission on Judicial Appointments, until next gubernatorial election. If elected, fills unexpired term of predecessor. Superior court judges, by Governor, until next election. Judge then elected serves full term. Municipal court judges, by Governor, for unexpired term of predecessor. Justice court judges, by

		board of supervisors of county or by special election, until next election, when judge is elected to serve unexpired term.
Colorado	Judges of Supreme, Appeals, District, and county courts, by impeachment or (except judges of the Denver County Court) on recommendation of the Commission on Judicial Qualifications, by the Supreme Court, for willful misconduct in office, willful or persistent failure to perform duties, or habitual intemperance, as well as for disability seriously interfering with performance of duties and likely to become of a permanent character. Denver County Court and municipal judges may be removed according to charter and ordinance provisions.	By the Governor, from lists submitted by Judicial Nominating Commissions.
Connecticut	Judges of the Supreme and Superior Courts may be removed by impeachment. Governor shall also remove them on the address of 2/3 of each house of the General Assembly. All judicial officers may be removed by impeachment; tried by the Senate, 2/3 vote. Judges of Supreme, Superior, Common Pleas, Circuit and Juvenile Courts may retire or be retired for disability. The Judicial Review Council may, after hearing, recommend that a judge not be reappointed, that he be retired for disability, or that impeachment proceedings be instituted against him.	By Governor until the next General Assembly or until a successor shall be elected or appointed.
Delaware	Court on the Judiciary has power to retire judge for permanent mental or physical disability, or to censure or remove judge from office for misconduct. All civil officers may be impeached.	As in case of original appointment.
Florida	Justices of the Supreme Court, and judges of the District Courts of Appeal and circuit courts may be impeached for misdemeanor in office. Any such justice or judge may be disciplined or removed by the Supreme Court on recommendation of a Judicial Qualifications Commission for willful or persistent failure to perform his duties or for conduct unbecoming a member of the judiciary, or may be retired for disability seriously interfering with the performance of his duties, which is, or is likely to become, of a permanent nature.	By the Governor, until the next general election, from recommendations provided by an appropriate Judicial Nominating Commission.

(Table 2–3 cont'd overleaf . . .)

Table 2–3. continued

State or Other Jurisdiction	How Removed	Vacancies: How Filled
Georgia	Judges are subject to impeachment for cause, and removed from office. Trial by Senate, 2/3 vote. A Judicial Qualification Commission investigates charges of alleged misconduct or incapacity and certifies its findings to the Supreme Court. Any justice or judge may then be retired, removed, or censured by the Supreme Court upon recommendation of the Judicial Qualification Commission.	By the Governor, until the next general election.
Hawaii	A Commission for Judicial Qualification investigates charges of alleged misconduct or incapacity and certifies its findings to the Governor. Any justice or judge then may be retired or removed by the Governor upon recommendation by an especially appointed board of judicial removal.	Supreme and Circuit Court vacancies by Governor, by and with advice and consent of Senate. Pending official appointment, chief justice may assign circuit judge to serve temporarily on Supreme Court or on any vacant circuit court bench. District court vacancies filled by chief justice.
Idaho	Judges are subject to impeachment for cause, and removed from office. Impeachment trial by Senate, 2/3 vote. Supreme and district court judges subject to removal by Supreme Court after investigation and recommendation by Judicial Council. Magistrates may be removed by district court judges of judicial district sitting en banc, upon majority vote, in accordance with Supreme Court rules.	Supreme and District Court vacancies filled by Governor, from names recommended by Judicial Council, for unexpired term; magistrates by district magistrate's commissions for unexpired term.
Illinois	After notice and hearing, any judge may be removed for cause by a commission composed of one judge of the Supreme Court selected by that court, two judges of the Appellate Court selected by that court, and two circuit judges selected by the Supreme Court. Such commission is permanently convened by the Supreme Court rule for disciplinary action against judges to consider complaints of physical or mental disability. All civil officers may be impeached by the Legislature.	By election at the next general election.

State		
Indiana	Appellate judges may be removed by vote of the Supreme Court on own motion or that of Judicial Qualifications Commission. Nonappellate judges are also subject to disciplinary power of Supreme Court, which includes the power to suspend a judge without pay.	Appellate vacancies are filled in the same manner as initial selection. If a trial judge is suspended, Supreme Court appoints a pro tem to serve. If a trial judge is removed, Governor appoints a person to serve until next general election.
Iowa	Supreme and District Court judges subject to impeachment. Upon recommendation of Commission on Judicial Qualifications, such judges and district associate judges also may be retired for permanent disability or removed for failure to perform duties, habitual intemperance, willful misconduct, or substantial violations of the canons of judicial ethics, by order of the Supreme Court. Judicial magistrates may be removed by a tribunal consisting of 3 district court judges in the judicial election district of the magistrate's residence.	All vacancies created by removal are filled in the same manner as original final selection.
Kansas	All officers under constitution subject to impeachment. In addition to impeachment, all judges below Supreme Court level are subject to retirement for incapacity, and to discipline, suspension, and removal, for cause, by the Supreme Court after appropriate hearing.	For Supreme Court, by Governor from list submitted by Nominating Commission, until next general election, when appointee runs on his record. For district court in 23 districts by Governor from list submitted by district judicial nominating commission until next general election when appointee runs on record; in 6 districts the Governor appoints until next general election.
Kentucky(a)	Removal by Governor on the address of 2/3 of each house of the General Assembly. All civil officers subject to impeachment.	By the Governor, until the next regular election.

(Table 2–3 cont'd overleaf . . . .)

Table 2–3. continued

State or Other Jurisdiction	How Removed	Vacancies: How Filled
Louisiana	Upon investigation and recommendation by Judiciary Commission, Supreme Court can censure, suspend with or without salary, remove from office, or retire involuntarily a judge for misconduct relating to his official duties or willful and persistent failure to perform his duties, persistent and public conduct prejudicial to the administration of justice that brings the judicial office into disrepute, conduct while in office which would constitute a felony, or conviction of a felony, as well as retire a judge for disability which is, or is likely to become, of a permanent character. All state and district officers may be impeached.	By special election called by the Governor and held within 6 months after the vacancy occurs. Until the vacancy is filled, the Supreme Court appoints a qualified person, who is ineligible as a candidate at the election.
Maine	Judges may be impeached by the House; removal upon 2/3 vote at trial by Senate. Judges also may be removed by the Governor with the advice of the Council on the address of both branches of the Legislature. Judges of Supreme Judicial, Superior and district courts may be retired for disability.	Vacancies filled as in case of original appointment, except that vacancies in office of judges of probate are filled by the Governor, with the advice and consent of the Council, until January 1 after the next November election.
Maryland	Judges of Court of Appeals, Court of Special Appeals, trial courts of general jurisdiction, and District Court by the Governor, on conviction in a court of law or on impeachment; or on the address of the General Assembly, 2/3 of each house concurring in such address. Impeachment trial by Senate, conviction on 2/3 vote. Removal or retirement by Court of Appeals after hearing and recommendation by Commission on Judicial Disabilities, for misconduct in office, persistent failure to perform duties, conduct prejudicial to the proper administration of justice, or disability seriously interfering with the performance of duties, which is, or is likely to become, of a permanent character. Elected judge convicted of felony or misdemeanor relating to his public duties and involving moral turpitude is removed from office by operation of law when conviction becomes final.	By the Governor, from Nominating Commission list, until first biennial election for congressional representative after the expiration of the term or the first general election 1 year after the occurrence of the vacancy. Appointees customarily elected to full term. District Court judges appointed and confirmed by Senate (no election).

Massachusetts	The Governor, with the consent of the Executive Council, may remove judges upon the address of both houses of the Legislature. Also, after hearing, he may, with the consent of the Council, retire a judge because of advanced age or mental or physical disability. All officers may be removed by impeachment.	As in the case of an original appointment.
Michigan	House of Representatives directs impeachment by a majority vote. Impeachment trial by Senate, 2/3 vote for conviction. Governor may remove judge for reasonable cause insufficient for impeachment with concurrence of 2/3 of the members of each house of the Legislature. On recommendation of Judicial Tenure Commission, Supreme Court may censure, suspend with or without salary, retire, or remove a judge for conviction of a felony, physical or mental disability, or persistent failure to perform duties, misconduct in office, or habitual intemperance or conduct clearly prejudicial to the administration of justice.	For all courts of record, by Governor, until January 1, next succeeding first general election held after vacancy occurs, at which successor is elected for unexpired term of predecessor. Vacancies on municipal courts filled by local city councils. Supreme Court may authorize persons who have been elected and served as judges to perform judicial duties for limited periods or specific assignments.
Minnesota	Supreme and district court judges may be impeached. On recommendation of Judicial Tenure Commission, Supreme Court may censure, suspend with or without salary, retire, or remove a judge for conviction of a felony, physical or mental disability, or persistent failure to perform duties, misconduct in office, or habitual intemperance or conduct prejudicial to the administration of justice.	Filled by Governor until next general election occurring more than 1 year after appointment.
Mississippi	Presentment, indictment by a grand jury, and conviction of a high crime or misdemeanor in office. All civil officers may be impeached by 2/3 of members present of the House, and removed after trial by Senate. Also, for reasonable cause which shall not be sufficient ground for impeachment, the Governor shall, on the joint address of 2/3 of each branch of the Legislature, remove from office the judges of the Supreme and inferior courts.	By Governor during recess of Senate. Filled at next congressional election if there is one prior to the expiration of the term.

(Table 2–3 cont'd overleaf . . .)

Table 2-3. continued

State or Other Jurisdiction	How Removed	Vacancies: How Filled
Missouri	All judges are subject to retirement, removal, or discipline on recommendation of a majority of members of a committee composed of two citizens (not members of the Bar) appointed by the Governor, two lawyers appointed by the governing body of the Missouri Bar, one judge of the Court of Appeals elected by a majority of that court, and one circuit judge selected by a majority of circuit judges in the State.	By Governor until next general election, except that vacancies in the Supreme Court, Court of Appeals, circuit and probate courts of City of St. Louis, St. Louis, Clay, Platte, and Jackson Counties, and the St. Louis Court of Criminal Correction are filled by Governor from nominations by a nonpartisan commission until the next general election after the judge has been in office at least a year.
Montana	All judicial officers subject to impeachment. Impeachment by 2/3 vote of House. Upon recommendation of Judicial Standards Commission, Supreme Court may suspend a judicial officer and remove same upon conviction where a felony or other crime involves moral turpitude; also, can order censure, suspension, removal, or retirement for cause.	Justices of Supreme Court, district court judges, and Workmen's Compensation judge by Governor; justices of peace by boards of county-commissioners. Judge so appointed holds until next general election.
Nebraska	Impeachment by majority of Legislature; in case of impeachment of Supreme Court justice, all judges of district courts sit as court of impeachment—2/3 concurrence required; in case of other judicial impeachments, heard by Supreme Court as court of impeachment. Also, provisions similar to those in California for removal of judges by Supreme Court on recommendation of a Judicial Qualifications Commission.	By Governor, from lists submitted by nonpartisan judicial nominating commissions.
Nevada	All judicial officers except justices of peace subject to impeachment. Impeachment by 2/3 vote of each branch of Legislature, provided that no member of either branch shall be eligible to fill the vacancy so created. Trial by Senate, 2/3 vote. Also subject to removal by legislative resolution and by recall.	By Governor.

New Hampshire	Governor with consent of Council may remove judges upon the address of both houses of the Legislature. Any officer of the State may be impeached.	Vacancies filled by Governor with consent of Council.
New Jersey	Proceedings can be initiated by either house of the Legislature, the Governor, or the Supreme Court on its own motion for removal of judges of all but Supreme Court, for misconduct in office, willful neglect of duty or other conduct evidencing unfitness for judicial office, or for incompetence. Hearing, not to be held until conclusion of any independent criminal or administrative proceeding involving the grounds for removal, by Supreme Court en banc or by a panel of 3 justices or judges designated by chief justice. Pending determination of removal proceeding, court may suspend a judge with or without pay for a maximum of 90 days. Justices of Supreme Court, and judges of Superior Court and county courts subject to impeachment. Because of prerequisite of bar membership, they also may lose qualifications for judicial office by disciplinary proceedings resulting in disbarment. Effective July 1974, the Supreme Court created an Advisory Committee on Judicial Conduct. The Committee is authorized to receive complaints against judges alleging facts indicating the following: (1) misconduct in office; (2) willful failure to perform their duties; (3) incompetence; (4) habitual intemperance; (5) engagement in partisan politics; (6) conduct prejudicial to the administration of justice that brings the judicial office into disrepute; or, (7) may be suffering from a mental or physical disability which is disabling him and may continue to disable him indefinitely or permanently from the performance of his duties. Whenever the committee concludes from a preliminary investigation that circumstances, if established at a plenary hearing, may call for censure, suspension, or removal of the judge, the committee makes such a recommendation to the Supreme Court, together with the documentation supporting its position. On certification of Supreme Court, Governor may appoint 3-man commission to inquire into incapacity of Supreme, Superior or county court judge. On its recommendation, Governor may retire judge from office.	By Governor, with advice and consent of Senate.
New Mexico	All state officers and judges of the district courts may be impeached. Through the judicial standards commission, any justice, judge, or magistrate may be disciplined or removed for willful misconduct in office or willful and persistent failure to perform his duties or habitual intemperance, or may be retired for disability seriously interfering with the performance of his duties, which is, or is likely to become, of a permanent character. *(Table 2–3 cont'd overleaf . . .)*	Governor appoints to fill vacancy until next general election.

Table 2–3. continued

State or Other Jurisdiction	*How Removed*	*Vacancies: How Filled*
New York	Any judge may be removed by impeachment. Judges of the Court of Appeals and justices of the Supreme Court may be removed by 2/3 concurrence of both houses of the Legislature. Judges of the Court of Claims, county courts, Surrogate's Court, Family Court, the Civil and Criminal Courts of the city of New York, and district courts may be removed by 2/3 vote of the Senate, on recommendation of the Governor. All judges of superior courts may be removed for cause or retired for disability by a Court on the Judiciary. Judges of the Civil and Criminal Courts of the city of New York, district courts, city courts, town courts, and village courts may be removed for cause or retired for disability by the appropriate Appellate Division of the Supreme Court.	Vacancies in elective judgeships filled at the next general election for full term; until the election, Governor makes the appointment (with the concurrence of the Senate if it is in session), except in the following cases: Civil Court of the city of New York appointed by the Mayor; district courts appointed by the appropriate district governing body; city courts (outside the city of New York), town courts, and village courts appointed by appropriate governing body as prescribed by the Legislature.
North Carolina	Upon recommendation of the Judicial Standards Commission, the Supreme Court may censure or remove any justice or judge for willful misconduct in office, willful and persistent failure to perform his duties, habitual intemperance, conviction of a crime involving moral turpitude, or conduct prejudicial to the administration of justice that brings the judicial office into disrepute. Any justice or judge may be removed by the same process, for mental or physical incapacity interfering with the performance of his duties which is or is likely to become permanent.	By Governor until next general election. Ad interim appointees customarily elected for remainder of unexpired term.
North Dakota	Supreme and district court judges by impeachment for habitual drunkenness, crimes, corrupt conduct, malfeasance, or misdemeanor in office. County judges by Governor after hearing. Impeachment trial by Senate, conviction 2/3 vote. All judges may be recalled. Upon recommendation of Commission on Judicial Qualifications, Supreme Court may remove judges from all courts for willful misconduct in office, willful and persistent failure to perform duties, habitual intemperance, or conduct prejudicial to the	Supreme Court judges by Governor until next general election. District court judges appointed by Governor to fill unexpired term.

administration of justice that brings the judicial office into disrepute, or may retire them for disability that seriously interferes with performance of duties and is, or is likely to become, permanent.

Ohio	By concurrent resolution of 2/3 of members of both houses of the General Assembly.	By Governor until next election, when judge is elected to fill unexpired term.
	All judges may be removed by impeachment. Trial by Senate, conviction on 2/3 vote.	
	By disqualification as a result of disciplinary action as provided in Rule V, Supreme Court.	
	Removal for cause upon filing of a petition signed by at least 15% of the electors in the preceding gubernatorial election; trial by court or jury.	
	Removal, retirement, or suspension without pay for cause following complaint filed in the Supreme Court; hearing before a commission of judges named by the Supreme Court. Appeal from commission to Supreme Court.	
Oklahoma	By impeachment for willful neglect of duty, corruption in office, habitual drunkenness, incompetency, or any offense involving moral turpitude.	Vacancies on Supreme Court and Court of Criminal Appeals by Governor, as in case of original appointment. Appointee to vacancy occurring during unexpired term serves for remainder of that term if retained by election after completing 12 months' service.
	Removal by order of Court on the Judiciary for gross neglect of duty, corruption in office, habitual drunkenness, commission while in office of any offense involving moral turpitude, gross partiality in office, oppression in office, or any other grounds hereinafter specified by the Legislature. Compulsory retirement, with or without compensation, for mental or physical disability preventing proper performance of office duties, or incompetence to perform duties of the office.	Vacancies on Court of Appeals and District Court filled by Governor for unexpired term; in making appointment, he may but need not use aid of Judicial Nominating Committee.

(Table 2–3 cont'd overleaf . . . .)

Table 2–3.   continued

State or Other Jurisdiction	How Removed	Vacancies: How Filled
Oregon	Any judge may be involuntarily retired for mental or physical disability after certification by a special commission; he may appeal to Supreme Court. On recommendation of Commission on Judicial Fitness, Supreme Court may remove a judge of any court for conviction of a felony or a crime involving moral turpitude, willful misconduct in a judicial office involving moral turpitude, willful or persistent failure to perform judicial duties, habitual drunkenness, or illegal use of narcotic drugs.	By Governor until next general election, at which time a judge is elected to fill the unexpired term.
Pennsylvania	All judges, as all civil officers, may be impeached by House for any misdemeanor in office. Trial by Senate, 2/3 vote for conviction. Upon recommendation of the Judicial Inquiry and Review Board, any justice or judge may be suspended, removed, or otherwise disciplined by the Supreme Court for specified forms of misconduct, neglect of duty, or disability.	By Governor, until the first Monday of January following next judicial election which shall occur more than 10 months after vacancy occurs. If Senate is in session, advice and consent of 2/3 of its members, except majority for justices of the peace.
Rhode Island	Supreme Court judges, by a resolution of the General Assembly voted by a majority in each house at the annual session for the election of public officers. All judicial officers may be impeached. Trial by Senate, 2/3 vote of all members elected thereto for conviction.	In case of vacancy on Supreme Court, the office may be filled by the Grand Committee of the Legislature until the next annual election. In case of impeachment, inability, or temporary absence, Governor appoints a person to fill vacancy. Vacancies on Superior, Family, and district courts may be filled by Governor with advice and consent of Senate.

	Removal	Filling of Vacancy
South Carolina	By impeachment or by Governor on address of 2/3 of each house of General Assembly.	By Governor if unexpired term does not exceed 1 year; otherwise, by General Assembly to fill unexpired term.
South Dakota	Supreme Court judges and circuit court judges may be removed by impeachment. Trial by Senate, 2/3 vote for conviction. Recommendation by Judicial Qualifications Commission to Supreme Court for removal.	Supreme and circuit court judges by the Governor, for balance of term.
Tennessee	By impeachment for misfeasance or malfeasance in office; by concurrent resolution of 2/3 of each house of the Legislature when the judge is physically or mentally unable to perform his duties.	By Governor until next general election. County judge by county court; but if they do not elect to fill vacancy, Governor may do so. Judge elected fills unexpired term.
Texas	Supreme Court, and Appeals and district court judges may be removed by impeachment, Senate, 2/3 vote, or by joint address, 2/3 vote of both houses. District judges may be removed also by the Supreme Court. County judges and justices of the peace may be removed by district judges. Upon charges filed by the Judicial Qualifications Commission, all judges in the State may be involuntarily retired for disability or removed for misconduct by the Supreme Court.	Appellate, district, domestic relations, and juvenile court judges by Governor, until next general election. County courts by county commissioner's court. Municipal judges by governing body of municipality. Judge elected fills unexpired term.
Utah	By concurrent vote of 2/3 of the members of each house of the Legislature. All judicial officers except justices of peace may be impeached. Trial by Senate, conviction on 2/3 vote. Removal from office by Supreme Court upon recommendation of Commission on Judicial Qualifications for willful misconduct in office, final conviction of a crime punishable as a felony, persistent failure to perform duties, habitual use of alcohol or drugs which interferes with performance of judicial duties; retirement for disability seriously interfering with performance of duties which is, or is likely to become, of a permanent character.	By Governor, upon recommendation of Judicial Selection Commission, until next general election. Judge elected fills unexpired term.

(Table 2–3 cont'd overleaf . . .)

Table 2–3. continued

State or Other Jurisdiction	How Removed	Vacancies: How Filled
Vermont	All judicial officers impeachable. Trial by Senate, conviction on 2/3 vote. Supreme Court has disciplinary control over all judicial officers not inconsistent with constitutional powers of the General Assembly; it has power to impose sanctions, including suspension from judicial duties for the balance of the term of the judicial officer charged.	Supreme Court and superior court vacancy filled by Governor, from list of 3 or more persons selected by Judicial Selection Board. Interim vacancies of assistant judges of county courts filled by Governor.
Virginia	All judges may be impeached by House. Trial by Senate. Conviction on 2/3 vote of members present. By Supreme Court after charges against judge have been certified by Judicial Inquiry and Review Commission. By concurrent vote of majority of elected members of both houses of General Assembly.	A successor shall be elected for the unexpired term by the General Assembly. If General Assembly not in session, Governor makes appointment to expire 30 days after commencement of next session. Ad interim appointee customarily elected to full term.
Washington	By joint resolution of the Legislature, in which 3/4 of the members of each house concur, for incompetency, corruption, malfeasance, delinquency in office, or other sufficient cause stated in resolution. Any judge of any court of record may be impeached. Trial by Senate. Conviction on 2/3 vote.	Vacancies on appellate and general trial courts filled by Governor until next general election, when election to fill the unexpired term.
West Virginia	Removal by concurrent vote of both houses of the Legislature in which 2/3 of the members of each house must concur, when a judge is incapable of discharging the duties of his office because of age, disease, mental or bodily infirmity, or intemperance. By impeachment by a 2/3 vote of the Legislature for maladministration, corruption, incompetency, gross immorality, neglect of duty, or any crime or misdemeanor.	By Governor if unexpired term is less than 2 years; if more than 2 years, Governor may appoint judge until next general election when a judge is elected to fill the unexpired term.

	Removal	Appointment / Vacancy
Wisconsin	All judges subject to impeachment. Supreme, circuit, and county court judges by the address of both houses of the Legislature, 2/3 of all members of each house concurring and hearing, and by recall. Since all judges of courts of record must be licensed to practice law in Wisconsin, removal also can be by disbarment. A judge of the Supreme or circuit court may be removed for physical or mental disability upon voluntary or involuntary petition and upon hearing by a disability board.	By Governor until next regular judicial election is held, when judge is elected for a full term. At any election only one Supreme Court justice may be elected, so that appointee holds until next available election. Disabled Supreme Court justice replaced by Governor. Disabled circuit court judge may be replaced through appointment by chief justice from list of reserve judges (retired judges on assignment); if not available, Governor may fill the temporary vacancy which continues during disability of judge or until he dies or his term expires.
Wyoming	All judicial officers, except justices of peace, by impeachment. Trial by Senate, 2/3 vote for conviction. May be retired by Supreme Court on recommendation of Judicial Supervisory Commission. Justices of the peace by Supreme Court after hearing before panel of 3 district judges.	By Governor from a list of 3 submitted by Judicial Nominating Commission, for approximately 1 year, then stand for election for retention in office. Justices of the peace by appointment by county commissioners.
District of Columbia (b)	All judges shall be removed from office by the Commission on Judicial Disabilities and Tenure, upon conviction of a felony (including a federal crime), for willful misconduct in office, for willful and persistent failure to perform judicial duties, or for other conduct prejudicial to the administration of justice or which brings the office into disrepute.	By the President of the United States upon the advice and consent of U.S. Senate for a term of 15 years.
Guam	Any justice or judge may be removed by a special court of 3 judges on recommendation of a Judicial Qualification Commission for misconduct or incapacity.	By Governor for term of 5 years.

(Table 2–3 cont'd overleaf . . .)

Table 2–3. continued

State or Other Jurisdiction	How Removed	Vacancies: How Filled
Puerto Rico	Supreme Court justices by impeachment for treason, bribery, other felonies, and misdemeanors involving moral turpitude. Indictment by 2/3 of total number of House members and trial by Senate. Conviction by 3/4 of total number of senators. All other judges may be removed by Supreme Court for cause as provided by judiciary act, after hearing upon complaint on charges brought by order of the chief justice, who shall disqualify himself in the final proceedings.	By Governor, as in case of original appointment.

(a) See footnote (d) on Table 10.

(b) Reflects 1974 survey. Later information not available.

Reproduced by permission of the Council of State Governments from its publication *State Court Systems Revised 1976.*

CONTINUING JUDICIAL EDUCATION

An important development affecting the quality of justice is continuing judicial education. In the United States, unlike in some civil law countries, lawyers are not trained in law schools to serve as judges, and it has been found necessary to provide continued in-service education.

Judges, at all court levels, are going back to school. The movement began in 1956 when the Institute of Judicial Administration at New York University sponsored an annual Appellate Judges Seminar. Each year this seminar brings together twenty to twenty-five judges of the United States Courts of Appeals and state courts of last resort. They live together in the student dormitory and meet each day from 9 A.M. to 4 P.M. for two weeks. They discuss the nature of the judicial process and the responsibilities of the judge. Developments in the law and court administration are stressed. A companion project for intermediate appellate judges, the Intermediate Appellate Judges Seminar, was launched in 1959.

Other programs soon followed. The movement bringing both new and experienced trial, appellate, and special court (domestic relations, traffic, juvenile courts, for example) judges back to school is burgeoning. Such institutions as the National College of the State Judiciary in Reno, Nevada, offer courses and seminars for new and sitting judges. In-service training is now available for traffic judges, family and juvenile court judges, municipal court judges, and justices of the peace, as well as those judges serving in general, civil, and criminal trial and appellate courts.

Lectures are avoided in favor of round table discussions by small groups of judges. Emphasis is placed on participation by those judges who have been recently elevated to the bench.

Another aspect of this continuing education of the judiciary is the federal and state sentencing institutes. The object here is to discuss and formulate a policy which will avoid great disparity in sentencing for what appears to be an identical offense.

Activity in the professional training of judges of courts of special and limited jurisdiction is increasing. The National Council for Juvenile Court Judges sponsors regional and state institutes. One of the main purposes of this training program is to bridge the gap between academic knowledge and personal effectiveness in solving the problems of the young offender. The behavioral sciences are utilized to gain a better understanding of children and to explore the dilemmas of juvenile court work.

The American Bar Association conducts a large-scale program of traffic court conferences attended not only by judges, but also by prosecutors, police, and interested laymen. This traffic program, along with various training programs for justices of the peace, becomes of special significance. Affected is the lower court judiciary which, since it handles the largest number of cases, may have contact with the greatest number of people.

These lower court judges are often laymen who lack prior legal or judicial training. Usually, the personnel turnover is quite high. Such factors suggest that for these courts judicial education in this area is a necessity if they are to function effectively. New York, responding to this need, has made special training mandatory for all newly elected justices of the peace who are not lawyers. An increasing number of other states have inaugurated training programs for judges of courts of limited jurisdiction. The American Academy of Judicial Education in Washington, D.C., directs its attention to educational programs for judges of limited and special jurisdiction on a national level.

A recent report by the National Center for State Courts entitled *State Judicial Training Profile* lists Alabama, Alaska, Arizona, Colorado, Hawaii, Idaho, Illinois, Iowa, Kansas, Maryland, Michigan, Mississippi, Nebraska, New Jersey, New Mexico, New York, Oklahoma, South Carolina, South Dakota, Texas, Virginia, Washington, and Wisconsin as states having some type of mandatory judicial training programs for one or more courts.

California has a Center for Judicial Education and Research (CJER) which bears the responsibility for carrying on continuing judicial education programs and providing the necessary materials.

Legislatures are increasingly appropriating the money necessary for judges' traveling, housing, and living expenses in attending educational conferences outside their communities. The supreme courts of Minnesota, Wisconsin, and Iowa are among those which have passed rules providing for mandatory attendance at specified educational seminars.

COURT ADMINISTRATION

Managing a court system may be compared to managing a large business organization. Yet until fairly recently there was little effort in the United States to employ trained personnel to operate the courts efficiently—to facilitate the movement of cases, to keep statistical records, to hire and train personnel, to deal with the financial needs and budgets of courts, and to report regularly on the operation of the court. Because courts have budgets of millions of dollars annually, forty-six states within the last two decades have provided for statewide administrative offices.

Usually, ultimate administrative control is vested in the court of last resort or in its chief justice; and is delegated to an administrative assistant who is appointed by and serves at the pleasure of the court. Administrative assistants are variously known as the executive secretary, administrative clerk, administrative assistant, administrative director, or court administrator. Their duties and authority vary. It is now widely recognized that the performance of a court can best be judged by monitoring the activities of the judges and keeping current and meaningful statistics on the volume of judicial business the court handles. In addition to collecting statistics on the cases, some administrators are authorized to assign judges (under the direction of the chief justice) to courts where they are most needed, to prepare court budgets, to act as purchasing officers for the courts, to act as liaison between the courts and the legislature and the public, to serve as executive secretary to the judicial conference, to conduct studies, make recommendations, and perform other comparable duties as directed by the chief justice and the state supreme court.

New Jersey has one of the most efficient administrative offices. Established by Chief Justice Arthur T. Vanderbilt in 1949 following the federal model, New Jersey has an administrative judge to assist the supreme court and also trial court administrators to serve local courts of general jurisdiction. Many states have similar administrative offices.

Court Delay

The administrative office is but one attempt to deal with court congestion. Among the other solutions which have been tried or suggested are: increasing judicial manpower; a split trial, that is, the issue of liability is heard first; if liability is found, the issue of damages is decided; pretrial conferences; elimination of jury trials for certain civil cases; reducing the size of the jury in specific cases; no fault in automobile personal injury cases; and redistricting of judicial districts. Recently, courts have been experimenting with individual calendaring: a single judge will dispose of every aspect of a given case—from preliminary hearings on motions to trial. Arbitration in all types of cases has taken innumerable controversies out of the courts entirely.

Delays in criminal cases, in violation of the constitutional guarantee of the right to a speedy trial, have assumed alarming proportions. Federal and state courts have provided speedy trial rules which call for dismissal of certain charges against persons whose trials are not held within six months, and for release of defendants from jail wherever it is deemed feasible. Detention prior to trial is limited to three months, at which time a prisoner must be released on bond, or on his own recognizance. The problem of protecting the constitutional rights of the accused consistent with the safety and best interests of the public has been the subject of a ten-year-long study of the American Bar Association and the Institute of Judicial Administration. From this study have evolved the published *Standards for Criminal Justice*, which in eighteen volumes recommend basic standards for courts, lawyers, and legislatures to follow in criminal cases from arrest to final appeal.

Increasingly, electronic data processing techniques and other types of automation, including videotaping, have been introduced into the operation of courts. Court administrators and others charged with managing the courts are relying on business management tools to gain control of burgeoning court calendars. Indicative of this trend is the establishment in 1970 of an Institute for Court Management, first advocated by Chief Justice Warren E. Burger. The institute is designed to prepare prospective court executives with the necessary management skills to solve critical problems of calendaring, managing, and budgeting for the courts. The Institute for Court Management is funded in part by the Ford Foundation and sponsored jointly by the American Bar Association, the Institute of Judicial Administration, and the American Judicature Society. The program presented to students at the Institute for Court Management combines structured classroom training and a thirteen-week internship training period, during which the students participate in field work. The first class of the Institute was graduated in 1970. Many of the graduates have been placed in courts at the state and local level to employ the skills developed at the Institute for Court Management. By June 1975, 230 individuals had been trained by this Institute.

According to a 1975 report of the Council of State Governments, which serves as the Secretariat to the National Conference of Chief Justices, there were in 1975 fourteen court/judicial administration programs of one type or another, directed to court personnel other than the judges, existing in California, Colorado, Florida, Michigan, Missouri, Nevada, New York, Ohio, Pennsylvania, and Vermont, and in the District of Columbia.

The national organization formed by the state court administrators is the Conference of State Court Administrators. Many trial courts with multiple judges have similar officers called trial court administrators. Their national organization is the National Association of Trial Court Administrators. Court administration is now recognized as a full-fledged independent profession.

Table 2–4.　Selected Data on Court Administrative Offices

State or Other Jurisdiction	Title	Date of Establishment	Citation
Alabama	Court Administrator (a)	1971	Act 1503 of 1971
Alaska	Administrative Director	1959	Alas. Const., Art. IV, Sec. 16, as amended
Arizona	Administrative Director of the Courts	1960	Ariz. Const., Art. VI, Sec. 7
Arkansas	Executive Secretary, Judicial Dept.	1965	Act 496 of 1965 as amended (Ark. Stat. Ann. 22–142, et seq.)
California	Administrative Director of the Courts	1960	Calif. Const., Art. VI, Sec. 6, Govt. Code Sec. 68500–68500.5
Colorado	State Court Administrator	1959	Colo. Const., Art. VI, Sec. 5(3); C.R.S. 1973, Sec. 13–3–101
Connecticut	Chief Court Administrator	1965	Conn. Rev. Gen. Stat., Sec. 51–2
Delaware	Director, Administrative Office of the Courts	1971	Del. Code Ann., Title 10, Sec. 128
Florida	State Court Administrator	1972	Supreme Court Rules
Georgia	Director, Administrative Office of the Courts	1973	Ga. Laws 1973, p. 288
Hawaii	Administrative Director of Courts	1959	Act 259, Session Laws of Hawaii, 1959
Idaho	Administrative Director of the Courts	1967	Session Laws of 1967, Ch. 39, p. 61, as amended, 1974
Illinois	Administrative Director	1959	Ill. Const., Art. VI, Sec. 16 (1970)
Indiana	Supreme Court Administrator-Commissioner Executive Director, Div. of State Court Administration	1968 1975	Supreme Court Internal Rule 12 I.C. 1971, 33–2.1–7–1
Iowa	Court Administrator	1971	1975 Code of Ia., Ch. 685
Kansas	Judicial Administrator	1965	K.S.A. 20–318, et seq.
Kentucky (i)	Administrative Director of the Courts	1954	Ky. Rev. Stat. 22.110 & 120 (1960)

(Table 2–4.　cont'd overleaf . . .)

Table 2–4. continued

State or Other Jurisdiction	Title	Date of Establishment	Citation
Louisiana	Judicial Administrator	1954	La. Const. of 1974, Art. V, Sec. 7; La. Rev. Stat. 13.9
Maine	Administrative Assistant to Chief Justice	1970	Ch. 467, Laws of 1969
Maryland	State Court Administrator	1955	Md. Code, Courts Art., Sec. 13–101
Massachusetts	Executive Secretary, Supreme Judicial Court for the Commonwealth	1956	Gen. Laws. Ch. 211, Sec. 3A to 3F inserted by Acts of 1956, Ch. 707 & amended by Acts of 1960, Ch. 424; of 1963, Ch. 755; of 1967, Ch. 650; of 1970, Ch. 567
Michigan	Court Administrator	1952	Mich. Const., Art. VI, Sec. 3 (1963)
Minnesota	Court Administrator	1963	Ch. 758, Laws of 1963
Missouri	State Court Administrator	1970	Mo. Const., Art. V, Sec. 4, Cl. 2, as amended
Montana	State Court Administrator	1975	. . .
Nebraska	State Court Administrator	1972	Neb. Const., Art. V, Sec. 1
Nevada	Court Administrator	1971	Nev. Rev. Stat. 1.320–370
New Jersey	Administrative Director of the Courts	1948	Art. VI, Sec. VII, Par. 1, Const. of 1947, N.J. Statutes 2A: 12–1
New Mexico	Director, Administrative Office of the Courts	1959	Sec. 16–6–1, et seq., N.M. Stat., 1953 Compilation
New York	State Administrator(b)	1955(c)	Art. VII–A, Judiciary Law
North Carolina	Director, Administrative Office of the Courts	1965(d)	Ch. 310, 1965 Session Laws
North Dakota	State Court Administrator, Judicial Council(e)	1971	Sec. 27–02–05.1. N.D. Century Code
Ohio	Administrative Director of the Courts	1955	Rev. Code, Secs. 2503.05, .281, .282, Art. IV, Sec. 5, Ohio Const.

State	Title	Year	Citation
Oklahoma	Administrative Director of the Courts	1967	Art. Vii. Sec. 6. Const. of Okla. Enrolled H.B. 1208 (May 10, 1968)
Oregon	State Court Administrator	1971(d)	Ore. Laws 1971, Ch. 193, Secs. 1–4
Pennsylvania	State Court Administrator	1968	Const. of Pa., Art. V, Sec. 10(b)
Rhode Island	Court Administrator	1969	R.I. Pub. Laws 1969, c. 239
South Carolina	Court Administrator	1973	S.C. Const., Art. V.
South Dakota	Court Administrator	1974	1969, Ch. 239
Tennessee	Executive Secretary of the Supreme Court	1964	Pub. Acts 1963, Ch. 86, Secs. 16–325, et seq., T.C.A.
Texas	Executive Director, Judicial Council	1974	. . .
Utah	State Court Administrator	1973	78–3–18, et seq, UCA 1953
Vermont	Court Administrator(f)	1967	1967, No. 174, Sec. 2 (4 V.S.A. 8 & 21)
Virginia	Executive Secretary, Supreme Court	1952	Va. Code Ann., Secs. 17–111.1, 17–111.2 (supp. 1950)
Washington	Administrator for the Courts	1957	Rev. Code of Wash. 2.56.010
West Virginia	Director, Administrative Office of the Supreme Court of Appeals	1945	W.Va. Code 51–1–15, et seq.
Wisconsin	Administrative Director of the Courts(g)	1962	Wis. Stats., Sec. 257.19
Wyoming	Court Coordinator	1974	Sup. Ct. Rule
Dist. of Col.(h)	Executive Officer of D.C. Courts	1971	D.C. Code 1703; 84 Stat. 510, P.L. 91–358 (July 29, 1970)
Puerto Rico	Administrative Director, Office of Court Administration	1952	P.R. Laws Ann., Title 4, Secs. 331–34 (1965)

(Table 2–4 Notes overleaf . . .)

Table 2–4. continued (Notes)

(a) Constitutional amendment in 1973 provides for an Administrative Director of Courts to administer the entire court system with the Court Administrator administering state trial courts. Duties of Administrative Director are spelled out in Act 1205, approved October 10, 1975.

(b) State Administrator or State Administrative Judge also serves as Secretary, Judicial Conference of New York and Administrative Board.

(c) 1955, Judicial Conference and Office of State Administrator; 1962, Administrative Board; 1974, Office of State Administrative Judge and Office of Court Administration.

(d) Previous position of Administrative Assistant to the Chief Justice was created in 1951 in North Carolina and in 1953 in Oregon.

(e) Serves as Secretary to Judicial Council.

(f) Also clerk of the Supreme Court.

(g) In 1974 position of Executive Officer of Supreme Court created to administer Supreme Court and related agencies while Administrative Director is responsible for administration of trial court.

(h) Reflects 1974 survey. Later information not available.

(i) See footnote (d) on Table 10.

Reproduced by permission of the Council of State Governments from its publication *State Court Systems Revised 1976.*

Table 2–5.   Selected Data on Court Administrative Offices

State or Other Jurisdiction	Administrator			Number on Staff	Appropriation for Administrative Office	
	Appointed by	Term of Office	Salary		Amount (a)	Period
Alabama	CJ		$19,713	3	$ 75,000	10/1/73–9/30/74
Alaska	CJ (b)		48,576	30	980,000	7/1/75–6/30/76
Arizona	SC		30,240	3 (c)	95,000 (d)	7/1/75–6/30/76
Arkansas	CJ (e)	All	25,064	10	274,405	7/1/75–6/30/77
California	JC		45,504	44	1,235,448 (f)	7/1/74–6/30/75
Colorado	SC		30,600	54	1,193,284 (g)	7/1/75–6/30/76
Connecticut	(h)		38,000	48	697,325	7/1/74–6/30/75
Delaware	CJ		30,000	11	346,000	7/1/75–6/30/76
Florida	SC		32,000	32	969,168	7/1/75–6/30/76
Georgia	JC		24,500–32,500	29	172,620	7/1/75–6/30/76
Hawaii	CJ (b)	serve	40,000	20	701,676	7/1/76–6/30/77
Idaho	SC		29,000	14	250,000	7/1/75–6/30/76
Illinois	SC		45,000	26	613,000	7/1/75–6/30/76
Indiana	SC		27,000 (i)	4	(j)	(j)
			22,000 (k)	2	(j)	(j)
Iowa	SC		23,540	15	337,230 (g)	7/1/75–6/30/76
Kansas	SC		27,500	6	(j)	(j)
Kentucky (v)	SC	at	26,000	8	(j)	(j)
Louisiana	SC		39,500	5 (l,m)	124,000	7/1/75–6/30/76
Maine	CJ		24,500	5	178,000	1/1/75–1/1/77
Maryland	CJ		39,200	29	820,697	7/1/75–6/30/76

(Table 2–5. cont'd overleaf . . .)

Table 2–5. continued

State or Other Jurisdiction	Administrator			Number on Staff	Appropriation for Administrative Office	
	Appointed by	Term of Office	Salary		Amount (a)	Period
Massachusetts	SC		30,554	3	205,455(g)	7/1/75–6/30/76
Michigan	SC		40,799	92	4,079,135	7/1/75–6/30/76
Minnesota	SC		25,000–32,000	6	120,000	7/1/73–6/30/75
Missouri	SC		27,025	26	138,295	7/1/75–6/30/76
Montana	SC	pleasure	14,000	1½	30,000(g)	10/1/75–9/30/76
Nebraska	CJ		30,000	8	155,000(d)	7/1/75–6/30/76
Nevada	SC		22,500	2	33,000	7/1/71–7/1/72
New Jersey	CJ		37,770–50,993	82	1,460,516(d)	7/1/75–6/30/76
New Mexico	SC		26,400	23	(j)	(j)
New York	(n)		57,000	237	5,444,463	4/1/75–3/31/76
North Carolina	CJ	of	32,500	62	914,809	7/1/75–6/30/76
North Dakota	SC		24,000(o)	6	300,000	7/1/75–6/30/77
Ohio	SC		34,400(p)	8	(j)	(j)
Oklahoma	SC		26,000	3(m)	(j)	(j)
Oregon	CJ		32,556	27	680,000	7/1/75–6/30/77
Pennsylvania	SC		40,000	34	868,000	7/1/75–6/30/76
Rhode Island	CJ		20,584–23,478(q)	7	180,000(d)	7/1/75–6/30/76
South Carolina	CJ	appointing	27,000	3	115,000	7/1/74–6/30/75
South Dakota	SC		22,500	8	(j)	(j)
Tennessee	SC		36,052	6	420,883(r)	7/1/75–6/30/76

State	Court	Salary	Number of judges	Appropriation	Period
Texas	SC	27,500	Information not available		
Utah	SC	25,800	5	157,500	7/1/75–6/30/76
Vermont	SC	30,524	6	(i)	(i)
Virginia	SC	30,825	28	426,160	7/1/75–6/30/76
Washington	SC(s) authority		18	799,484	7/1/75–6/30/77
West Virginia	SC	30,000	4	200,000	7/1/75–6/30/76
Wisconsin	SC	38,000	22	549,306(g)	7/1/75–7/1/76
Wyoming	SC	21,000	1	(i)	(i)
Dist. of Col.(t)	(u)	36,000	68	1,551,355	7/1/73–6/30/74
Puerto Rico	CJ	30,600	208	2,419,960	7/1/75–6/30/76

Symbols: SC—the State's court of last resort; CJ—the Chief Justice or Chief Judge of the State's court of last resort; JC—Judicial Council.

(a) Appropriations for the various offices are not necessarily comparable because of variations in the time periods covered and the purposes of the appropriations. In some States amounts shown include appropriations for travel and expenses of trial court judges.

(b) With approval of Supreme Court.

(c) Arizona: in addition, a federally funded planning section which also administers Supreme Court sub-grants staff—Chief of Planning (professional), fiscal officer (professional), secretary (clerical), and financial and statistical clerk (professional).

(d) Estimate, since budget not segregated from court budget. Nebraska: includes $65,000 in federal funds. New Jersey: approximate amount for salaries, including 12 positions with assignment judges, with duties not directly related to administrative office.

(e) With approval of Judicial Council.

(f) Total appropriation for Judicial Council, including administrative office of the courts, but not including salaries of assigned judges, circuit justice court judges, and federal grant projects.

(g) Includes $559,000 in federal funds, $325,000 of which is for data processing and computer rental; also includes $81,331 in general fund money for judicial conference, nominating and qualification commission, judicial training, and retired judges' per diem. Iowa: includes $145,958 in federal funds. Massachusetts: includes $57,668 to be used as LEAA matching funds. Montana: includes $27,000 grant. Wisconsin: includes $176,900 in federal funds.

(h) Appointed by General Assembly upon nomination by the Governor.

(i) Supreme Court Administrator.

(j) Not segregated from general appropriation of court of last resort. New Mexico: $10 million for State's entire judiciary.

(*Table 2–5. Notes cont'd overleaf . . . .*)

Table 2–5. continued (Notes)

(k) Executive Director, Division of State Court Administration.

(l) In Louisiana, also executive officer of judiciary commission.

(m) Louisiana: in addition, deputy judicial administrator and secretary. Oklahoma: in addition, research assistant under federal grant.

(n) Appointed by chairman of the Administrative Board, who is the Chief Judge of the Court of Appeals, by and with advice and consent of Administrative Board.

(o) Serves as secretary to Judicial Council.

(p) Discretion of the court.

(q) Longevity payments at 7, 15, and 20 years of state service.

(r) Includes salaries of 21 law clerks for members of Supreme Court.

(s) Appointed from list of 5 submitted by Governor.

(t) Reflects 1974 survey. Later information not available.

(u) Joint Committee.

(v) See footnote (d) on Table 10.

Reproduced by permission of the Council of State Governments from its publication *State Court Systems Revised 1976.*

Table 2–6. Judicial Administration Education and Training Programs (1975)
Summary of Programs

State or Other Jurisdiction	Name of Institution	Degree Conferred			No. of Courses
		M.A. Level	*B.A. Level*	*Certif.*	
Alabama	U of AL, Birmingham	–	–	–	One
Arizona	AZ State, Tempe	–	–	–	One
Arkansas	U of Arkansas Fayetteville	M.P.A.	–	–	
California	U of Southern CA Los Angeles	M.P.A.	–	–	
	San Jose State, San Jose	–	–	–	One
Colorado	U of Denver, Denver	M.S.J.A.	–	–	
	Inst of Court Mgt, Denver	–	–	Certif.	
	CO State U, Fort Collins	–	B.A.	–	
Dist. of Columbia	American U, Washington	M.S.	B.S. & Associate	Certif.	
Florida	FL State, Tallahassee	M.S.	–	–	
Guam	U of Guam, Agana	–	–	–	Three
Illinois	Northern IL, DeKalb	M.P.A.	–	–	
Indiana	IN U, Indianapolis	–	–	Certif.	
Kentucky	Eastern KY U, Richmond	M.A.	–	–	
	Western KY U, Bowling Green	–	–	–	One
Maryland	U of MD, College Park	–	–	–	Two
Michigan	Grand Valley, State Colleges, Allendale	–	B.S.	–	
Missouri	Central MO State U, Warensburg	M.A.	–	–	
Nevada	U of NV, Reno	–	–	Certif.	
New York	City U of NY, New York	M.A.	–	–	
	Hofstra U, Hempstead	–	–	–	Two

(Table 2–6 cont'd overleaf . . .)

Table 2−6. continued

State or Other Jurisdiction	Name of Institution	Degree Conferred			No. of Courses
		M.A. Level	B.A. Level	Certif.	
New York (cont'd)	Pace U, Pleasantville	–	B.S.	–	
	Rochester Inst of Tech, Rochester	–	–	–	Two
Ohio	U of Cincinnati, Cincinnati	–	–	–	Two
Pennsylvania	Temple U, Philadelphia	–	Associate	Certif.	
Puerto Rico	U of PR, Puerto Rico	–	–	–	Three
South Dakota	U of SD, Vermillion	–	–	–	One
Vermont	Castleton State College, Castleton	–	–	–	One

Reproduced by permission of the Council of State Governments.

In a communication dated May 7, 1976, the Conference of State Court Administrators indicated that the following schools have started new programs since the publication of their monograph:

> San Diego State University
> San Diego, California 92182
> > Judicial Administration Program
> > (Eff. January, 1976)

> Mansfield State College
> Mansfield, Pennsylvania 16933
> > Criminal Justice Administration—Court
> > Management emphasis

> Valdosta State College
> Valdosta, Georgia 31601
> > B.A. with concentration in Judicial
> > Administration

BIBLIOGRAPHY

AMERICAN Bar Association. Law and the courts. Chicago, 1973. 35 p.
AMERICAN Bar Association. Commission on Standards of Judicial Administration. Standards relating to appellate courts. Chicago, 1976 (tent. draft). 124 p.

AMERICAN Bar Association. Commission on Standards of Judicial Administration. Standards relating to court organization. Chicago, 1974. 120 p.

AMERICAN Bar Association. Commission on Standards of Judicial Administration. Standards relating to trial courts. Chicago, 1975 (tent. draft). 136 p.

AMERICAN Bar Association. The selection of judges in Alaska. Judges' Journal 14:77 (1975).

AMERICAN Judicature Society. Court administration (report number 17). Chicago, 1971. 112 p.

AMERICAN Judicature Society. Judicial disability and removal commissions, courts and procedures. Chicago, 1973. 635 p.

AMERICAN Judicature Society. Judicial selection and tenure. Chicago, 1975. 58 p.

AMERICAN Judicature Society. Court studies, an annotated bibliography. Chicago, 1976. 105 p.

BARR. The limited trend toward state court financing. Judicature 58:322 (1975).

BRAITHWAITE. Who judges the judges? Chicago, 1971. 167 p.

COUNCIL of State Governments. Book of the States. Lexington, Kentucky, 1976—1977. Section II The Judiciary at 87—101.

COUNCIL of State Governments. Judicial administration: education and training programs. Lexington, Kentucky, 1975.

COUNCIL of State Governments. State court systems, prep. for Conference of Chief Justices, 1950—1976. Lexington, Kentucky, 1976. 43 p. Revised 1976.

DAHL and BOLDEN. The American judge; a bibliography. Vienna, Virginia, 1968. 330 p.

DUNN. Judicial selection in the states: a critical study with proposals for reform. Hofstra Law Review 4:267 (1974).

ELLIS. Court reform in New York State: an overview for 1975. Hofstra Law Review 3:663 (1975).

FREMLIN. Modern judicial administration, a selected and annotated bibliography. Battle Creek, Michigan, 1973. 359 p.

GLICK and VINE. State court systems. Englewood Cliffs, New Jersey, 1973. 111 p.

KARLEN. The citizen in court; litigant, witness, juror, judge. New York, 1964. 211 p.

KAUFMAN. Of juvenile justice and injustice. American Bar Association Journal 14:77 (1975).

KLEIN. The administration of justice in the courts. Dobbs Ferry, New York, 1976. 2 vols., 1,152 p.

KLEIN. Judicial administration and the legal profession, an annotated bibliography. Dobbs Ferry, New York, 1963. 650 p.

KLEIN and LEE. Selected writings of Arthur T. Vanderbilt. Dobbs Ferry, New York, 1965. 231 p.

LAW Enforcement Assistance Administration. National survey of court organization. Washington, 1973 (1975 supp.). 257 p.

LAW Enforcement Assistance Administration. Law enforcement assistance administration: a partnership for crime control. Washington, 1976. 43 p.

MARTIN. Electronic courtroom recording. Judicature 50:262 (1967).

THE MODERNIZATION of court functions: a review of court management and computer technology. Rutgers Journal of Computers and the Law 5:97 (1975).

NATIONAL Advisory Commission on Criminal Justice Standards and Goals. National strategy to reduce crime. Washington, 1973. 195 p.

NATIONAL Advisory Commission on Criminal Justice Standards and Goals. Task force on the courts. Washington, 1973. 358 p.

NATIONAL Association of Legal Assistants. Facts and findings, official publication. La Mesa, California, 1975–

NATIONAL Center for State Courts. State judicial training profile. Denver, 1974. 142 p.

NATIONAL Center for State Courts. Survey of judicial salaries in state court systems. Denver, 1976. 38 p.

NATIONAL Conference of Appellate Court Clerks. Outline of basic appellate court structure in the United States. St. Paul, 1975. 211 p.

NATIONAL Conference on the Judiciary. Justice in the states; addresses and papers. Williamsburg, 1971. 350 p.

POUND. Causes of popular dissatisfaction with the administration of justice. American Bar Association Report 29:395 (1906), republished Federal Rules Decisions 35:273 (1964).

POUND. Organization of courts. Boston, 1940. 322 p.

SHETREET. Judges on trial. A study of appointment and accountability of the English judiciary. 1976. 432 p.

STEIN. The Paralegals—a resource for public defenders and correctional services—a prescriptive package. Washington, D.C. 1976. 563 p.

SYMPOSIUM: judicial ethics. Law & Contemporary Problems 35:1 (1970).

U.S. ADVISORY Commission on Intergovernmental Relations. New proposal for 1972. Washington, 1971. 98 p.

U.S. ADVISORY Commission on Intergovernmental Relations. For a more perfect union: court reform. Washington, 1971. 22 p.

VANDERBILT. The challenge of law reform. Princeton, 1955. 194 p.

VANDERBILT. The essentials of a sound judicial system. Northwestern University Law Review 48:1 (1953).

VANDERBILT. Improving the administration of justice—two decades of development. Cincinnati, 1957. 123 p.

VANDERBILT. Judges and jurors, their functions, qualifications and selection. Boston University Law Review 36:1 (1956).

VANDERBILT. Minimum standards of judicial administration. New York, 1949. 752 p.

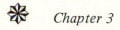 *Chapter 3*

The Grand Jury

DEVELOPMENT AND FUNCTIONS

The grand jury is called grand because of its size, to distinguish it from the petit jury. The grand jury does not act in a court setting, it is not part of a trial and does not deal in civil cases. Its functions do not include findings of guilt or innocence as does the petit jury in criminal cases. Simply stated, the grand jury's functions are twofold: (1) It has the duty with accompanying investigative powers to hear the evidence produced by the state and to find *bills of indictment* against particular individuals if it is satisfied that a crime has been committed and a trial ought to be had. Ideally, it serves to protect citizens against being unjustly accused of criminal offense. (2) It has the duty with accompanying powers to investigate wrongdoing of public officials for the purpose of preferring criminal charges. In this role it examines the functions of county government to insure honesty and judiciousness in the expenditure of public funds. It has the powers to investigate within its geographic jurisdiction all matters of public concern and to act upon its findings even without acquiescence of the prosecutor.

In his informative article, "The Grand Jury, Spirit of the Community," 15 *Arizona Law Review* 893 (1973), Dean and Professor Richard L. Braun of the University of Detroit Law School wrote:

Today's grand jury is an arm of the court. Under federal law it may be composed of from 16 to 23 members, with 12 votes necessary for indictment. Grand jury sessions are conducted in secrecy and proceedings may be reported, although certain testimony may be provided defendants when necessary at trial. Besides the witness under examination, only a prosecu-

tor may be present with the jurors during the sessions, and even he is nor-
mally excluded during deliberations and voting. A witness may not have an
attorney present with him while being questioned, but he may step outside
the chambers to consult with counsel before answering. Probable cause to
believe that the defendant has committed the crime charged is the standard for indictment.

The dual functions of the grand jury are commonly said to be "determining if there is probable cause to believe that a crime has been committed and . . . protecting citizens against unfounded criminal prosecutions."
A careful analysis suggests that a somewhat different description would be
more accurate. One purpose of the grand jury is to investigate wrongdoing
for the purpose of preferring criminal indictments where appropriate. This
function is primarily prosecutorial in nature. The jury's other purpose is to
insure that indictments are supported by evidence showing probable cause
to believe that the defendants named have committed the crimes charged.
This is basically a judicial function in which the impartial judgment of
jurors is said to be a check against prosecutorial excesses.

The advantages of the grand jury from a prosecutor's standpoint include
the power to subpoena witnesses and require them to testify or deliver
records on pain of being held in comtempt of court, and the authority to
grant witnesses immunity from prosecution in order to require them to
testify on matters which they might otherwise refuse to discuss under a
claim of the privilege against self-incrimination. The advantage of the jury
to defendants lies in the authority of its citizen-members to refuse to
indict or take other action requested by the prosecutor. In this regard the
grand jury serves as at least a potential restraint on overzealous government officials. Unfortunately, such restraining influence is often more
theoretical than actual.

The authority of the grand jury to inquire into facts and require testimony is extremely broad. More than 50 years ago Justice Pitney outlined
the almost unlimited scope of a grand jury investigation:

> (A grand jury) is a grand inquest, a body with the powers of inves-
> tigation and inquisition, the scope of whose inquiries is not to be lim-
> ited by questions of propriety or forecasts of the probable result of
> the investigation, or by doubts whether any particular individual will
> be found properly subject to an accusation of crime. . . . (T)he iden-
> tity of the offender, and the precise nature of the offense, if there be
> one, normally are developed at the conclusion of the grand jury's la-
> bors, not at the beginning.

The public, through the grand jury, has a right to "every man's evidence," and the duty to testify is limited by only a few exceptions. The
most significant of these is the privilege against self-incrimination. Neither
the grand jury nor the court can compel a witness to testify as to matters
which may incriminate him. If he is properly granted immunity, however,
the witness must answer all questions. If no immunity is given, he still may
be required to answer nonincriminating questions and to undergo nontes-

timonial identification procedures, such as fingerprinting or giving voice exemplars, which are not within the fifth amendment privilege. Courts have also recognized the right to refuse to testify as to certain privileged communications, such as those between attorney and client, husband and wife and clergyman and communicant. Furthermore, it is improper for one grand jury to gather evidence to be used against a defendant who has already been indicted for another offense.

In general, a witness has no standing to object that evidence is incompetent or inadmissible, nor does the fact that incompetent or improper evidence may have been considered by the grand jury provide a defendant with a right of relief. Hearsay is admissible and a defendant cannot object to an indictment based entirely on hearsay, or one supported by third-party testimony before the grand jury regarding otherwise inadmissible statements of the defendant.

ANALYSES AND CRITIQUE

For many decades judges, lawyers, professors, politicians, and publicists have waged a continuing debate as to the value of the grand jury and whether it should be retained. Its supporters call it the "guardian of liberty" of the individual and they substantiate its constructive influence by citing examples of grand juries protecting the public interest in rooting out evil practices by public officials. They demonstrate how individual liberties have been protected against prosecutorial abuse and personal vengeance.

Its opponents call it an antiquated, costly, archaic relic of the distant past that has outlived its usefulness. They say the grand jury is no guardian of liberty, and in many cases has been the opposite. They maintain that delegating important responsibilities to a group of nonlawyers completely untrained for the important duties they must assume has resulted in often oppressing individuals rather than in protecting them from oppression. They illustrate with examples prosecution motivated by an executive, particularly in the cases of political dissidents and members of the "watchdog" press.

Even when they opt for retaining the grand jury, critics strongly advocate changes in procedures. They point to discrimination against the poor, who usually do not have the right to appointment of counsel until arrested so that there is no lawyer to advise them while they are waiting outside the grand jury room, as happens when a witness can afford a counsel. They enumerate many procedures which operate against the witnesses who become defendants because of their inability to rebut; such as the admission of hearsay or illegally seized evidence. They point to the denial of the witness's right to the transcript of grand jury minutes in many cases. They cite examples where grand juries have been untrue to their oath and have for political or personal reasons refused to indict celebrated defendants.

Critics who advocate complete abolition urge that an information brought by one man and prosecuted in the courts is the safest, most dependable insurance against unmerited conviction. An information is defined as a procedure which begins with the issuance of a warrant by a magistrate or justice under a sworn complaint. A preliminary hearing is conducted at which the accused can summon witnesses in his behalf. After the examination the magistrate certifies that there is, or there is not, probable cause to believe a crime has been committed. If probable cause is found the district attorney or the public defender prepares and files an information in the criminal court possessing jurisdiction and the case is tried on the facts.

In the United States the reputation of the grand jury has fluctuated. It has been held in highest repute at certain periods, and it has been denigrated at others. The movement to abolish or severely limit its use in the states has gathered momentum. In many states where the grand jury functions, indictment by the grand jury is required only for serious offenses. Three states, Michigan, New Hampshire, and Connecticut, have created "the one man grand jury." It consists of a magistrate who is given the power to investigate, summon witnesses, and return an indictment. Idaho, Montana, and Washington use the grand jury for special occasions only. In Wisconsin and North Dakota the grand jury appears only when summoned by a judge. In Arizona, California, Colorado, Indiana, Kansas, Maryland, Missouri, Montana, Nebraska, Nevada, New Mexico, Oklahoma, Oregon, South Dakota, Utah, Washington, and Wyoming, prosecution may be commenced by an information in most cases. In Missouri constitutional amendments have been approved assigning grand jury duties to the district attorneys. The Advisory Commission on Intergovernmental Relations in its 1971 Report entitled *State-Local Relations in the Criminal Justice System* sums it up as follows:

> All fifty states permit the grand jury to be used for indictments in felony cases. However, the twenty-one states permit the use of "information" in such offenses, which permits the prosecutor to bring the accused to trial after a preliminary court hearing. Three more states—Connecticut, Florida, and Indiana—permit the information process in cases not involving death or life imprisonment penalties. Five others—Delaware, Maryland, Massachusetts, Oregon, and Virginia—permit the use of information when the accused waives his right to a grand jury proceeding. The grand jury has constitutional status in forty-three states, while six have constitutional provisions permitting abolition or modification of the grand jury system.

The late former Chief Justice of the United States Supreme Court, Earl Warren, designated the grand jury as an invaluable body standing between the accuser and the accused. The late chief justice of the state of New Jersey, Arthur T. Vanderbilt, wrote "what cannot be investigated in a republic is likely to be feared. The maintenance of popular confidence in government requires that there be a body of laymen who may investigate instances of wrongdoing." On the other side, Associate Justice of the United States Supreme Court William O. Douglas said, "It is indeed common knowledge that the grand jury having been conceived as a bulwark between the citizen and the Government is now a tool of the Executive."

In England the grand jury was temporarily suspended by Parliament in 1917, ostensibly due to the wartime manpower shortage. Reformers protested and in 1921 the grand jury was reinstated. But, during the depression, the expense of maintaining the grand jury became too great and in 1933 Parliament accepted the recommendations of a special commission to abolish the grand jury.

BIBLIOGRAPHY

BICKNER. The grand jury; a layman's assessment. California State Bar Journal 48:661 (1973).

BRAUN. The grand jury: spirit of the community? Arizona Law Review 15:893 (1973).

CALIFORNIA Judicial Council. A report on the grand jury's criminal law function. Annual Report of Judicial Council 1974:23.

CLARK. The grand jury; the use and abuse of political power. New York, 1975. 163 p.

DUFF and HARRISON. The grand jury in Illinois: to slaughter a sacred cow. University of Illinois Law Forum 1973:635.

EXAMINATION of the grand jury in New York. Columbia Journal of Law and Social Problems 2:88 (1966).

SPAIN. The grand jury, past and present: a survey. American Criminal Law Quarterly 2:119 (1964).

SYMPOSIUM: the grand jury. American Criminal Law Review 10:671 (1971).

YOUNGER. The people's panel: the grand jury in the United States, 1634–1941. Providence, 1963. 263 p.

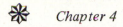 *Chapter 4*

The Petit Jury

HISTORY, DEVELOPMENT, AND USE OF THE CIVIL AND CRIMINAL JURY

The jury system is of utmost importance to the administration of justice in the United States.

The jury constitutes a branch of the court. "It is a body of adult persons possessing qualifications prescribed by law, summoned to attend a judicial tribunal and sworn to try, well and truly, the issue joined between parties litigant in civil cases or the facts adduced for and against the accused in criminal cases and to give a true verdict according to the evidence." (Funk and Wagnalls Standard Dictionary of the English Language [1951].)

The right to a jury trial for both criminal and civil cases in the federal courts is guaranteed by the sixth and seventh amendments to the United States Constitution.

The sixth amendment states:

> In all criminal prosecutions, the accused shall enjoy the right to a speedy and public trial, by an impartial jury of the State and district wherein the crime shall have been committed. . . .

The seventh amendment provides:

> In suits at common law, where the controversy shall exceed twenty dollars, the right of a trial by jury shall be preserved, and no fact tried by a jury shall be otherwise reexamined in any court of the United States, than according to the rules of the common law.

The United States Supreme Court held in *Duncan v. Louisiana,* 391 U.S. 145, 149 (1968) that the sixth amendment guarantee applies to the states; thus a jury trial must be available in state courts for criminal cases where it would be available in federal courts. The Court said "because we believe that trial by jury in criminal cases is fundamental to the American scheme of justice, we hold the Fourteenth Amendment guarantees a right of jury trial in criminal cases which — were they to be tried in a federal court—would come within the Sixth Amendment." Petty offenses which do not require a jury trial in federal courts are excluded. These are usually described as crimes carrying penalties up to six months.

In England, originally, trial by ordeal and trial by combat were used to settle disputes or to establish guilt or innocence. Gradually these methods were replaced by the custom of calling upon male neighbors, generally twelve in number, who had personal knowledge of the facts to decide disputed questions. In time those who knew the facts became the witnesses while others without knowledge became the decisionmakers. This development came in the middle of the fourteenth century. The right to trial by jury was provided in the Magna Carta.

The jury as an institution in both civil and criminal cases was established in the American colonies, but its use was hampered by the Royal governors and by the judges. For instance, the judge presiding over the Peter Zenger case ordered ". . . the jury to bring in a verdict of guilty if . . . by Zenger, but not to base a guilty verdict on whether or not the statements were libelous, reserving that decision for himself." Despite these orders, the jurors brought in a verdict of not guilty and were promptly jailed.

It is not surprising that the right to trial by jury was incorporated in the Constitution (article III) and the Bill of Rights (amendments VI, VII).

Traditionally, the jury consisted of twelve males. The origin of the number twelve has a variety of explanations. The twelve Apostles, the twelve Tribes of Israel, the twelve Patriarchs are offered. The number twelve required in ancient days was continued in the new world, as was the requirement for unanimity of verdict in criminal cases.

But some states now accept a lesser number in civil cases and in specified minor criminal cases. Unanimous verdict is also the rule in many states although in some jurisdictions less than unanimous verdicts are permitted in civil cases. Some states also permit nonunanimous verdicts in criminal cases, limited usually to lesser crimes.

Among the states which permit by constitution variations in the traditional use of twelve member juries (mostly in civil cases or in misdemeanors) are Alaska, Arizona, California, Colorado, Florida, Hawaii, Idaho, Iowa, Louisiana, Michigan, Minnesota, Mississippi, Missouri, Montana, Nebraska, Nevada, New Jersey, New Mexico, New York, North Dakota, Ohio, Oklahoma, Oregon, South Carolina, Texas, Utah, Washington, West Virginia, Wisconsin, and Wyoming. However, very few states have changed the right of a person accused of a serious crime to demand a trial by a jury of twelve.

Often, state constitutions permit the legislature to fix the number of jurors necessary for the disposition of a case. In Florida, for example, the number of jurors for both civil and noncapital criminal cases has been set at six. In Twenty-eight states a jury verdict need not be unanimous for civil cases tried in either all or specified courts. For example, the California constitution requires that only three-fourths of the jury need concur on a verdict in civil cases. In Wisconsin, five-sixths of the jury may reach a verdict in a civil case. And in Montana, a two-thirds verdict is sufficient for all civil cases and in misdemeanor cases. States that allow a verdict from three-fourths of the jury in civil cases are Alaska, Arizona, Arkansas, California, Hawaii, Idaho, Kentucky, Mississippi, Missouri (in courts of record), Nevada, Ohio, Oklahoma, Oregon, South Dakota, Texas, Utah, and Washington. Five-sixths is the number required in civil cases in Michigan, Nebraska, New Jersey, New York, Wisconsin, and Minnesota. In Montana, the number is two-thirds, as it is in Missouri in courts not of record (where no stenographic record of the proceeding is kept in the court). New Mexico provides only that the legislature may set a less than unanimous vote in specific cases. Some of the states that permit less than unanimous verdicts in criminal cases less than felonies are Idaho (five-eighths vote), Montana (two-thirds vote), Oklahoma (three-fourths vote), Oregon (five-sixths vote except in first degree murder cases), and Texas (three-fourths vote).

A six-person jury was introduced into the federal court system on January 1, 1971 for three categories of civil litigation in the district court of Minnesota. Subsequently, a majority of district courts have reduced the required number of jurors to six in specific civil cases.

Between 1970 and 1972, the United States Supreme Court decided three cases substantially affecting the size of criminal juries and the requirement for a unanimous verdict in serious cases.

In *Williams v. Florida*, 399 U.S. 78 (1970) the U.S. Supreme Court held that serious criminal cases could be tried in state courts by fewer than twelve jurors. The Court stated that the requirement of twelve was "an historical accident unnecessary to effect the purposes of the jury system and wholly without significance." In *Johnson v. Louisiana*, 406 U.S. 356 (1972) the Court held that Louisiana's use of 9−3 verdicts in major criminal cases was constitutional and in *Apodaca v. Oregon*, 406 U.S. 404 (1972) it decided that Oregon's 10−2 verdict in serious criminal cases did not violate the federal constitution.

SELECTION OF JURORS FOR THE VENIRE

All jurisdictions enumerate qualifications for service on the jury and grounds for exemption from jury service. Usually a juror is required to be physically and mentally healthy, to possess a good reputation for honesty and morality, to be able to read, write, and understand English, and to have sufficient intelligence and experience to understand problems presented in both civil and criminal litigation. These qualifications were drawn up and approved by the American Bar Association.

It has been said that for a jury to be fair and representative, no person or class of persons may be excluded from service because of race, color, religion, sex, economic status, or national origin. Selection of the venire (the panel from which attorneys choose jurors for each case) varies from county to county, city to city, and state to state. Studies have demonstrated that juries are often disproportionately male, middle aged, with above average education and employment status. From time to time, the charge is made that a particular jury does not adequately represent the race of the litigants or defendants. Women have been excluded or automatically excused in some jurisdictions.

In many communities the venire is selected on a random basis from the list of registered voters. Potential jurors are usually required to fill out required forms; in some jurisdictions personal interviews follow while in others an investigatory service looks into the qualifications of potential jurors.

Dissatisfaction with the quality and methods of selecting jurors for federal courts led to the new Federal Jury Selection and Service Act of 1968. The Act states specifically the criteria by which federal jurors must be chosen, naming the sources from which the names of potential jurors must be obtained, the methods of selecting the names and the bases for eliminating jurors from service.

One of the main features of reform was the elimination of the "key man" system, by which system prospective jurors were nominated by leading members of the community (key men). The objective of the "key man" system was to produce a cross-section of the community for jury duty because the key men (and they were usually all male) would be drawn from all classes, races, and vocations. Therefore, those they recommend would likewise be representative. However, it did not always work out that way. In practice, sometimes the "key man" system resulted in purposeful bias. It was found that the "key man" system tended to develop "blue-ribbon" juries as the key men tended to be male, white, middle or upper class leaders in the community.

The 1968 Federal Jury Selection and Service Act of 1968 has provided a fair and unbiased juror selection method for the federal courts.

Recently the American Bar Association Commission on Standards of Judicial Administration has studied these problems in the states. It reports as follows in the American Bar Association Project on Standards for Judicial Administration:

> At the time Congress was modifying the key man system, many states had already instituted similar improvements, but many states were using, and still use, out-of-date source lists and juror screening techniques susceptible to considerable subjective bias (e.g., door-to-door interviews for prospective jurors). In one attempt to remedy those defects at the state level, shortly after passage of the new federal juror selection law, the National Conference of Commissioners on Uniform State Laws developed a Uniform Jury Selection and Service Act. The Uniform Act incorporated the safeguards of the federal law. It also went further toward ensuring the broadest possible community representation in the venire by prohibiting

automatic exemption of any groups and by requiring that the registered voter list be supplemented by other lists to serve as the source list of prospective juror names.

Interest in improving juror selection in state jurisdictions is now rising rapidly. Innovations such as those of Harris County, Texas, (where a carefully developed formula yields a demographic cross-section based on the voter list) and the state of Colorado (which uses multiple lists to obtain prospective juror names) have sparked interest elsewhere.

The recommendations presented in the sections which follow are directed toward achieving a juror selection system which:

1. Reaches as many citizens as practically possible for prospective jury service;
2. Eliminates the possibility of influencing the selection or exclusion of names at each stage where a selection is made;
3. Embodies a policy with respect to screening and excusing jurors that is consistent with the attempt to achieve broad representation of the community;
4. Is in all its aspects, beginning with maintenance and supply of the source lists of names, subject to the direction of the court; and
5. Achieves the above objectives as efficiently as possible.

TRENDS

In England the use of the jury in civil cases at common law had declined in the early part of the twentieth century so that in 1917, it is reported, only about half the cases heard in the trial court of the King's Bench Division came to trial before the judge with a jury. Manpower shortages during World War I, 1917, led to further lessening of the use of the jury in civil cases. The popularity of the civil jury trial had considerably diminished. By the Administration of Justice Act, 1933, restrictions upon jury trial in King's Bench actions reduced the use of the civil jury to cases involving fraud, libel, slander, malicious prosecution, false imprisonment, seduction, and breach of promise of marriage, and even in such cases the court may dispense with the jury. With the advent of World War II similar rules concerning trials in other courts brought, virtually, an end to the jury trial in county courts, and to limited use as stated above in the King's Bench Court.

Many judges, lawyers, and other authorities in the United States advocate the same objective in state courts—to substantially limit the use and the number of juries in civil and criminal cases—even to abolish the use of the civil jury and to abandon the call for mandatory unanimous verdict in criminal cases.

De Tocqueville, in his *Democracy in America* (Bradley, ed. 1945 at 285–87), wrote: "It is especially by means of the jury in civil causes that the American magistrates imbue even the lower classes of society with the spirit of their profession. Thus the jury, which is the most energetic means of making the people rule, is also the most efficacious means of teaching it how to rule well."

Associate Justice of the United States Supreme Court (Retired) Tom Clark sums up his thoughts as follows:

> . . . it is submitted that the jury system improved the quality of justice that is dispensed by the courts. It is, therefore, the duty of every citizen to always honor the call to jury service. We of the Bench and Bar must face up to the faults in the system as now operated. We must modernize it and reduce the sacrifices incident to such service. Jury service is the only remaining governmental function in which the citizen takes a *direct* part. It is therefore, the sole means of keeping the administration of justice attuned to community standards. Daniel Webster tells us that justice is the great interest of man on earth. Let us not cut its jugular vein!

Pointing out some of the practical problems as to how civil juries have been used, former chief judge of the New York Court of Appeals Charles S. Desmond counters:

> Eminent authorities have praised the jury as a judicial and social institution and the opportunities it gives for nongovernmental people to play a significant part in the judicial processes of our democracy, opportunities for fruitful discussion, argument and exchange of ideas before decision making. These commentators tell us that the jury as an institution and its decisions have wide public acceptance in the United States and they cite polls to prove it. But in fact these considerations really treat the jury as a political institution, as a method of educating our citizens. We all know that as a judicial institution or instrument it leaves much to be desired. Its decisions being anonymous, impersonal and unpredictable suggest arbitrariness. Too often its verdicts represent not carefully worked out conclusions but mere compromises. All this is familiar to you. But what we have so far failed to face honestly and practically is the enormous cost of the civil jury system in dollars, in jurors' time and especially in court congestion and delay.
>
> I will not exaggerate these factors. There is, however, substantial evidence that a typical personal injury case tried to a judge takes only half the time the trial of the same cause would consume before a judge and jury. I have, as many of you have, sat in on non-jury trials in England and I think the one-to-two proportion is not too far from accuracy. The effect on our trial calendars of elimination of civil juries would be enormous.
>
> The other great cost of the present method is in the time of busy citizens serving as jurors and the burden of juror's fees on the public treasury. Statistics on these latter items are hard to come by but I have some pretty close estimates. For the City of New York alone, our research shows, jury service in the state supreme court and civil court of the city required that there be used and paid for several hundred thousand juror days with a total payroll of perhaps, $4,000,000. Jurors are poorly paid but the total dollar cost is enormous in our state.

In the present drive to relieve congestion in the trial courts, the jury system has been the focus of a good deal of attention. Because arguments to abolish the use of the jury in certain cases have not found an enthusiastic audience, the effort is concentrated on studies examining the operation of a six-person jury compared to that of a twelve-person jury. So-called empirical studies have been made, some concluding that there is little saving in time, and the saving in money is not worth the jeopardizing of a basic constitutional right and changing the quality of the verdict if indeed each change does occur.

At a February 16–17, 1976 meeting of the House of Delegates of the American Bar Association in Philadelphia, the delegates went on record as favoring "no trimming of the classic right of a criminal defendant to a jury trial that must reach a unanimous verdict before he can be sent to prison." And it backed a requirement for a twelve-member jury "in cases that could involve more than six months in prison."

It is suggested by some that rather than abolish the use of juries in civil cases altogether, there be limitations placed on the use of both civil and criminal juries which will speed and improve the administration of justice.

BIBLIOGRAPHY

AMERICAN Bar Association Advisory Committee on the Criminal Trial. Standards relating to trial by jury. New York, 1968. 180 p.

AMERICAN Bar Association Commission on Standards of Judicial Administration. Management of the jury system. Chicago, 1975. 39 p.

AMERICAN Judicature Society. The jury, selected readings. Chicago, 1971. 129 p.

AMERICAN Judicature Society. Lawyers speak the truth about counsel-conducted voir dire. Chicago, 1970. 17 p.

ASHMAN and McCONNELL. Trial by jury. Southwestern Law Journal 27:436 (1973).

CORNISH. The jury. London, 1968. 298 p.

DEFENSE Research Institute. The civil jury system: an essential of justice; preserve it. Milwaukee, 1971. 22 p.

DESMOND. Juries in civil cases—yes or no? Judicature 47: 219 (1964).

DEVLIN. Trial by jury. 3d impression, with addendum. London, 1966. 216 p.

EFFECT of jury size on the probability of conviction: an evaluation of *Williams v. Florida*. Case Western Reserve Law Review 22:529 (1971).

EMPIRICAL study of six- and twelve-member jury decisionmaking process. University of Michigan Journal of Legal Reference 6:712 (1973).

ERLANGER. Jury research in America. Law & Society Review 4:345 (1970).

FEDERAL Judicial Center. Guidelines for improving juror utilization in U.S. district courts. Washington, 1972. 67 p.

THE FEDERAL selection act of 1968: a critique. Columbia Survey of Human Rights Law 2:52 (1970).

INSTITUTE of Judicial Administration. Comparison of six- and twelve-member juries in New Jersey superior and county courts. New York, 1972. 58 p.

INSTITUTE of Judicial Administration. Suggestions for improving juror utilization in the United States district court for the Southern District of New York. New York, 1971. 95 p.

INSTITUTE of Judicial Administration. Suggestions for improving juror utilization in the United State district court for the Eastern District of New York. New York, 1971. 45 p.

JUDICIAL Conference of the United States. Report of the committee on the operation of the jury system. Federal Rules Decisions 26:411 (1973).

KALVIN and ZEISEL. The American jury. Boston, 1966. 559 p.

KARLEN. Can a state abolish the civil jury? Wisconsin Law Review 1965:103.

KAUFMAN. The wasted juror. Judicature 56:72 (1972).

McCART. Trial by jury; a complete guide to the jury system. Philadelphia, 1964. 204 p.

MEYER and ROSENBERG. Questions juries ask: untapped springs of insight. Judicature 55:105 (1971).

MOORE. Jury: tool of kings, palladium of liberty. Cincinnati, 1973. 202 p.

NATIONAL College of the State Judiciary. Jury. Reno, 1974. 207 p.

NATIONAL Conference of Commissioners on Uniform State Laws. Uniform jury selection and service act. Chicago, 1970. 19 p.

NEW YORK (State) Supreme Court, Appellate Division, 1st and 2d Departments, Subcommittee on the Jury System. The juror in New York City: a survey of attitudes and experiences. New York, 1973. 408 p.

PABST. Juror waiting time reduction. Washington, 1971. 107 p.

PABST. What do six-member juries really save? Judicature 57:6 (1973).

PADAWER-SINGER and BARTON. Experimental study of decision-making in the 12- versus 6-member jury under unanimous versus non-unanimous decisions. Final Report. New York, 1976. Various pagings.

POTASH. Mandatory inclusion of racial minorities on jury panels. Black Law Journal 3:80 (1973).

ROSENBLATT and ROSENBLATT. Six-member juries in criminal cases: legal and psychological considerations. New York State Bar Journal 46:259 (1974).

SIMON. The jury system in America—a critical overview. Beverly Hills, California, 1975. 254 p.

THOMPSON. What is the magic of "21"? Judges' Journal 10:88 (1971).

U.S. NATIONAL Institute of Law Enforcement and Criminal Justice. Guide to juror usage. Washington, 1974. Various pagings.

ZEISEL. And then there was none: the diminution of the federal jury. University of Chicago Law Review 38:710 (1971).

ZEISEL. The waning of the American jury. American Bar Association Journal 58:367 (1972).

 *Chapter 5*

Selected State Court Systems

ALASKA

Prior to its admission to the Union as the forty-ninth state in January 1959, Alaska was an organized territory of the United States.

Justice was administered by the U.S. District Court for the Territory of Alaska; the courts of the U.S. Commissioners acted as justices of the peace. Alaska had no court system of its own in the sense that states or the Territory of Hawaii had. Thus, the writers of the state constitution were confronted with the challenge of creating an entirely new state court system. Under the auspices of the Alaska Statehood Committee a report was submitted by the Public Administration Service on the organization of the judicial branch of Alaska. Dr. Sheldon Elliott, then the director of the Institute of Judicial Administration in New York, served as special consultant to the Public Administration Service in this phase of its work, assisting the Board of Governors of the Alaska Bar in preparing a working draft of a bill to establish the judicial system.

The state court system is partially modeled after the federal system. The court of last resort is the supreme court of the state of Alaska, comparable to the U.S. Supreme Court. The superior court is the trial court of general jurisdiction comparable to the U.S. District Court. Alaska does not have an intermediate appellate court.

The Supreme Court. The highest court in Alaska, the supreme court, sits in Juneau, the state capital. However, by court rule, one justice has an office in Juneau, one in Fairbanks, and three in Anchorage, and the justices travel around the state to hear oral argument. The court consists of four justices and a chief

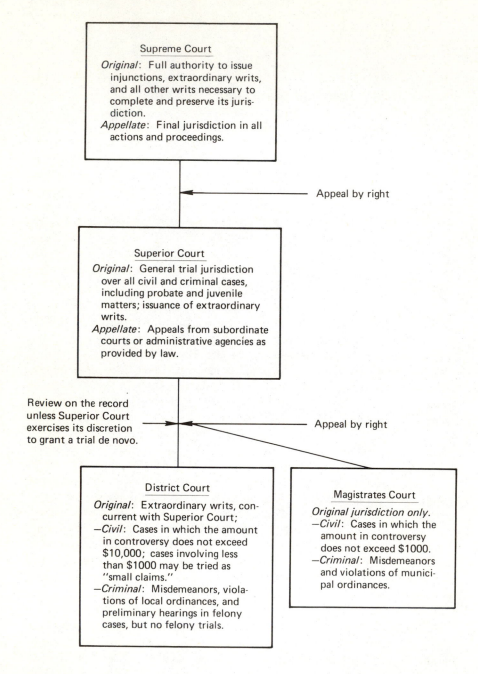

Figure 5–1. Alaska Judicial System

justice, each of whom receives $52,992. Thus, the state which ranks last in population ranks third, behind New York and California, in salaries paid to its highest appellate judges.

The number of justices may be increased by law, upon the request of the supreme court. The governor appoints supreme court justices after receiving nominations from the Judicial Council. The chief justice is selected from among the justices of the supreme court by a majority vote of the justices for a term of three years. Pursuant to constitutional amendment the chief justice may not serve two successive terms. Each justice is subject to approval or rejection on a nonpartisan ballot at the first general election held more than three years after his appointment. Thereafter, each justice is subject to approval or rejection in a like manner every tenth year. Mandatory retirement is at age seventy. Supreme court appointees must be licensed to practice law in the state and must have practiced for at least eight years prior to appointment.

The jurisdiction of the supreme court is broad. The court has final appellate jurisdiction in all actions and proceedings. The supreme court may issue injunctions, writs of review, mandamus, certiorari, prohibition, habeas corpus, and all other writs necessary or proper to the complete exercise of its jurisdiction. Each of the justices may issue writs of habeas corpus, upon petition by or on behalf of any person held in actual custody, and may make such writs returnable before him or herself or before the supreme court or before any judge of the superior court of the state. Appeals to the supreme court are a matter of right.

The Superior Court. The superior court is a statewide court divided into four judicial districts. Four superior court judges are assigned to sit in the first district, one in the second district, ten in the third district, and three in the fourth district. In addition, the chief justice may direct a superior court judge to hold court in a designated area for a specified period of time.

A presiding judge for each district is selected by the chief justice of the supreme court. In addition to regular judicial duties, presiding judges are responsible for the assignment of cases, supervision of court personnel and expedition of court business, and the appointment of magistrates within their districts.

Each superior court judge is selected in the same manner as a supreme court justice and must also face the electorate at the first general election held three years after initial appointment. The judge is thereafter subject to approval or rejection by the electorate every sixth year in a nonpartisan election. Superior court appointees must have actively engaged in the practice of law for five years prior to their appointment. Mandatory retirement is at age seventy, but a retired judge may render further service on the bench (special assignments) as provided by court rule. Superior court judges receive an annual salary of $48,576. As of September 1975, this was the second highest salary paid to general trial level court judges in the country; New York, paying its supreme court (trial) judges $48,998, ranked first.

The jurisdiction of the superior court is that of a trial court of general jurisdiction, with original jurisdiction in all civil and criminal matters. It includes all probate and juvenile matters. The superior court and its judges may issue injunctions and writs of habeas corpus, and may grant relief which was formerly available by writs of review, certiorari, mandamus, prohibition, and other writs. In addition, the superior court has jurisdiction in all matters appealed to it from subordinate courts or administrative agencies which such appeal is provided by law. In such cases the superior court may grant a trial de novo. All appeals from subordinate courts or administrative agencies are a matter of right.

Courts of Limited Jurisdiction

The District Court.   The district court is established by the Alaska Statutes. As of December 1970, the district court replaced recorders' courts, domestic relations courts, juvenile courts, mayor's courts, and justice of the peace courts, all of which were abolished. Each of Alaska's four judicial districts has branches or subdivisions of the district court in various communities as required by caseload. Judges of the district court are known as district judges. They are elected in the same manner as superior court judges; however, they serve a term of four years instead of six years. To be eligible to serve on the district court, an individual must be licensed to practice law in at least one of the states. As of 1975, the salary of a judge of the district court was $41,068.

The civil jurisdiction of the district courts extends throughout the respective judicial districts and includes civil matters where the amount in controversy does not exceed $10,000, except for the recovery of damages in vehicular tort cases where the amount claimed, exclusive of costs and attorney fees, does not exceed $15,000. Cases involving $1,000 or less may be designated "small claims" and are heard in accordance with simplified procedural rules and forms as prescribed by the supreme court. The criminal jurisdiction of the district court is statewide and includes misdemeanors, violations of local ordinances, and preliminary hearings in felony cases, but not felony trials. The district court may also issue extraordinary writs. A district court trial jury consists of six persons. Appeals of district court judgments in both civil and criminal cases may be taken to the superior court as of right.

Magistrates Court.   As of 1975, there were fifty-eight magistrates. The presiding judge of the superior court in each judicial district appoints the magistrates; they serve at the pleasure of the presiding judge. Magistrates are not required to be attorneys, and may serve on a part-time basis. The salaries for magistrates range from $5,595 to $26,160, depending upon the number of hours required in the particular geographical locations.

The jurisdiction of the magistrates is highly restricted. Criminal jurisdiction extends to misdemeanors and violations of municipal ordinances. Civil jurisdiction extends to cases in which the amount in controversy does not exceed $1,000. Jury trials are available in both civil and criminal cases. Appeals from judgments of the magistrate courts are as of right to the superior court. Review by the superior court is on the record, unless the superior court exercises its discretion to grant a trial de novo.

Administration

The chief justice of the supreme court is the administrative head of the courts and is empowered to assign judges from one court or judicial district to another for temporary service. The chief justice can appoint an administrative director of courts who serves at the pleasure of the supreme court. The present administrative director receives an annual salary of $57,716. It is the duty of the administrative director to inspect and examine the administrative methods used; collect and compile statistical and other data regarding the court; examine the state of dockets of all courts; determine the need for assistance by a court; make recommendations to the chief justice relating to the assignment or reassignment of judges where courts are in need of assistance; prepare and submit budget estimates of state appropriations necessary for the maintenance and operation of the judicial system; formulate and submit to the chief justice, the supreme court, and the Judicial Council recommendations of policies for the improvement of the council, recommendations of policies for the improvement of the judicial system; and attend to such other matters as may be assigned by the chief justice.

The Judicial Council, which is established by the Alaska constitution, is an independent body composed of three attorneys, three laymen, and the chief justice of the supreme court, who is an ex-officio member and chairman. The council functions both as a judicial selection nominating commission and as a continuing court study group. In its nominating capacity the Judicial Council is charged with submitting nominations to the governor for appointment to the supreme court, superior court, and district court. In its court study capacity the Judicial Council conducts ongoing studies for the improvement of the administration of justice, and submits periodic reports and recommendations to the supreme court and the legislature.

Pursuant to a constitutional amendment, a Commission on Judicial Qualifications has been established in Alaska for the purpose of dealing with judicial misconduct. The commission is composed of one justice of the supreme court, three judges of the superior court, two judges of the district courts, two attorneys, and two laymen; each member serves a four-year term. The commission may recommend to the supreme court that a judge of any court in the state be retired, censured, suspended, or removed upon a showing of disability, prior or pending felony conviction, or misconduct in office. If initial investigation by the commission warrants further proceedings, the case is referred to the supreme court, where the judge receives a full hearing with procedural due process before the supreme court acts on the commission's recommendation.

Since the early 1960s Alaska has employed a system of electronic recording of court proceedings in lower level trial courts. It is one of the few jurisdictions in the United States to have done so. Alaska's judicial officials have found that it saves time and money, and more accurately and faithfully records the proceedings than the stenographic recording system previously used. Interestingly, California undertook a study to determine the potential use of electronic recording in 1972, and concluded that the accuracy of such a system would depend to such an extent upon human monitoring and logging of proceedings that, in court proceedings with high transcript demands, the traditional methods of court reporting would be cheaper and more efficient. Nevertheless, electronic reporting is an acceptable means of preserving court proceedings with which a number of states have experimented.

Judicial Training

As of late 1974 Alaska had not yet established a judicial training program conducted under the auspices of the Alaska judicial system. Alaska's judges are, however, strongly urged to attend "conferences, seminars, or schools which further their legal education or professional qualifications." (Court Administrative Rules 48(b)). To encourage judges to participate in such judicial training programs, they are granted special leave and are provided with travel expenses and per diem expense allowances. Among the programs attended by Alaska's judges and magistrates are those conducted by the Institute of Judicial Administration, the National College of State Judiciary, and the American Academy of Judicial Education.

CALIFORNIA

The court system of the nation's largest state is typical of the many states which have three judicial levels: a general trial court, an intermediate appellate court, and a supreme court. California, however, does not at this time have a wholly unified court system. The Superior Court—the general trial court—has limited jurisdiction: certain cases are statutorily assigned to other lower courts, the Municipal Courts or the Justice Courts. This division of trial level jurisdiction engenders a costly and inefficient appellate procedure. A proposal for unification of the California judicial system is now under consideration by a joint committee of the legislature. California already employs a highly progressive approach to judicial training. Since the creation of the California Center for Judicial Education and Research in 1973, California has been one of the leaders in furthering continuing judicial education.

The Supreme Court. The California constitution vests the state's highest appellate authority in the supreme court. It has statewide jurisdiction and conducts regular sessions in Sacramento, San Francisco, and Los Angeles. The supreme court consists of seven justices: six associates, and a chief justice, all of

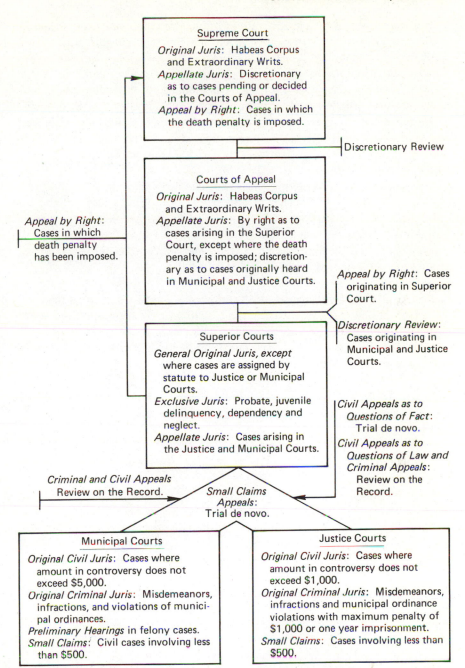

Figure 5–2. California Judicial System

whom are appointed by the governor with the approval of the Commission on Judicial Appointments. After appointment and confirmation, the justices serve until the next gubernatorial election. They are then eligible to run in a non-partisan retention election for the remainder of their predecessor's twelve-year term. In order to qualify for a seat on the supreme court, a candidate must have been a member of the state bar or have served as a judge of a court of record in the state for ten years immediately preceding his selection. The California Supreme Court justices' salary is the second highest in the country—only New York is higher. The associate justices receive $57,985 annually and the chief justice receives $61,609.

The supreme court has discretionary appellate jurisdiction to hear cases pending in or decided by the courts of appeal. In addition, the supreme court is empowered to hear direct appeals from the superior court in cases in which a judgment of death has been pronounced. Finally, the supreme court has original jurisdiction over habeas corpus proceedings and proceedings for extraordinary relief, such as mandamus, prohibition, or certiorari.

The Courts of Appeal. California's intermediate appellate court is the court of appeal. Its authority derives from the California constitution. The state is divided geographically into five appellate districts with one court of appeal in each district. Each district may have one or more divisions consisting of three or more judges. The districts are as follows:

First District:	San Francisco	Four Divisions
Second District:	Los Angeles	Five Divisions
Third District:	Sacramento	One Division
Fourth District:	San Diego	Two Divisions
	San Bernadino	
Fifth District:	Fresno	One Division

The courts of appeal have appellate jurisdiction over all cases on appeal from the superior court, except when a death sentence has been imposed. In addition, the courts have original jurisdiction over proceedings for extraordinary relief and discretionary appellate jurisdiction over certain cases arising in the municipal and justice courts, as prescribed by statute. Each division has a presiding judge and two or more associate judges. There is a total of fifty-one judges in the courts of appeal. They are selected and retained in the same manner as the supreme court justices. The annual salary for a judge of a court of appeal is $54,361. To qualify for service on a court of appeal an individual must meet the same criteria as prospective supreme court justices: ten-year membership in the state bar or service as a judge of a court of record.

Courts of General Jurisdiction

The Superior Courts. The California constitution has established the superior courts as the major trial courts in the state. There is a superior court in each of the fifty-seven counties, plus one in the city and county of San Francisco. The number of judges who sit on the superior court varies with the size of the county; each superior court, however, has at least one judge. As of 1975, there were 471 superior court judges: 171 of them served in Los Angeles County. Those superior courts which have two or more judges choose a presiding judge whose responsibility is to distribute the business of the court among the judges and prescribe an order of business. The superior court judges are elected in nonpartisan county elections and serve a term of six years. Vacancies are filled by appointment of the governor. To qualify as a judge of the superior court, an individual must fulfill the same criteria which apply to candidates for the courts of appeal and supreme court: ten years of practice in the state or as judge of a court of record. The salary of superior court judges, as of September 1975, is $45,299.

The superior courts have unlimited original trial jurisdiction of all cases except those assigned by the statutes to other courts: i.e., the municipal and justice courts. Because this division of trial level jurisdiction causes duplication, confusion, and delay, the state legislature's Joint Committee on the Structure of the Judiciary is considering a proposal to unify the trial courts. The proposal is discussed in full below (see "The Proposed Reform of the California Judicial System").

At the present time, the superior courts primarily exercise jurisdiction over felonies, civil suits where the amount in controversy exceeds $5,000, and equity and domestic relations proceedings. Superior courts have exclusive jurisdiction of probate matters, juvenile delinquency, and child neglect. In addition, the superior courts have appellate jurisdiction over all cases arising in the municipal and justice courts. Appeals from municipal courts and justice courts are heard on the record, except that civil appeals from justice courts involving questions of fact are tried de novo in the superior court. Appeals from the superior court may be taken to a court of appeal, except in cases involving a death sentence.

Although the superior court is a unified trial court with general jurisdiction, the Los Angeles County Superior Court, because of its size, is functionally subdivided into the following units: the civil court; the family law department; the conciliation court; the probate department; the civil law and discovery departments; the mental health department; the juvenile court; the criminal court; and the appellate division of the superior court, which handles appeals from the justice and municipal courts. Each of the divisions handles the genus of cases implied by its title. The conciliation court is of special interest. Established in 1954, the Los Angeles County Conciliation Court was the first of its kind in the

United States. It initiated the concept of a court-connected marriage counseling service. The function of the court is to salvage as many marriages as possible; and, where that proves impossible, to terminate marriages amicably, enabling both sides to retain their dignity. Thus the goal of this unique court is not only to preserve family harmony, but also to lessen the incidence of post-dissolution litigation. Its achievements have gained national recognition and, as a result, similar courts have been established in other counties in California and in at least fifteen other states.

Courts of Limited Jurisdiction

California has two lower level trial courts with limited jurisdiction: the municipal courts and the justice courts. Municipal courts are established in jurisdictions with a population of greater than 40,000 residents; those jurisdictions with a lesser population have a justice court. The number of judicial districts has been decreasing since California reorganized and consolidated the lower courts in 1953. The number of municipal courts, however, has increased because municipal courts have supplanted justice courts when population increased above the 40,000 limit.

Municipal and Justice Court Jurisdiction. The municipal courts have civil jurisdiction when the amount in controversy does not exceed $5,000. Claims under $500 may be filed in the small claims division. Municipal courts have original criminal jurisdiction of all misdemeanors, infractions, and municipal ordinance violations, and they conduct preliminary hearings in felony cases. Jury trials are available in both civil and criminal cases. Appeals are taken to the superior court on the record, with the exception of appeals from small claims judgments for which a trial de novo is permitted.

The justice courts have original civil jurisdiction when the amount in controversy does not exceed $1,000. They also have original criminal jurisdiction of misdemeanors, infractions and municipal ordinance violations which are punishable by not more than a $1,000 fine or a one year sentence. Jury trials are available in the justice courts. The justice courts are also empowered to hold preliminary hearings in felony cases. Appeals are to the superior court where civil appeals involving questions of fact are heard de novo and other appeals are heard on the record.

Municipal and Justice Court Judges. The number of municipal court judges is fixed by the legislature, with each municipal court having at least one judge. Municipal court judges are elected by the voters of their respective districts in a nonpartisan election; vacancies are filled by the governor. The term for a municipal court judge is six years. To qualify an individual must have been admitted to the state bar for at least five years immediately preceding designation. The salary of a municipal court judge is $41,677.

There is one judge for each justice court. Justice court judges are elected in the same manner as municipal court judges; however, vacancies are filled by the County Board of Supervisors rather than by the governor. Terms are for a period of six years. To qualify as a judge of the justice court, a person must be admitted to the state bar. This requirement was recently instituted to eliminate the need to subject candidates for the justice courts to a qualifying examination. The salary of a justice court judge ranges from $1,200 to $33,703.

The Proposed Reform of the California Judicial System

A report prepared by the Advisory Commission of the Joint Committee on the Structure of the Judiciary was submitted to the Joint Committee on October 18, 1975. The report calls for a complete unification of the trial level of the California judicial system. It recommends that the superior, municipal, and justice courts of each county be merged into a single trial court to be known as "the county superior court." The commission contends that unification offers numerous advantages: maximum flexibility in the assignment of judges to cases, and cases to judges; greater opportunities for judges to specialize in certain types of cases; elimination of confusing jurisdictional distinctions; elimination of the use of trials de novo; elimination of unnecessary duplication in administration functions; and a number of other advantages which would reduce costs and increase efficiency. This proposal, which will be considered by the California legislature in 1976, typifies the national trend toward unification of state judicial systems.

Administration

The California constitution vests administrative authority over the state judicial system in a Judicial Council. The council is required to survey judicial business, make recommendations to the courts, report annually to the governor and the legislature, and adopt rules of court administration, practice, and procedure. Other duties may be assigned to the Judicial Council by statute. The chairman of the council expedites the judicial operation of the state, equalizes the workload of judges, and is authorized to assign judges from one court to another. (The council chairman may not assign judges to a *lower* court without their consent.)

The Judicial Council appoints an administrative director of the courts who serves at its pleasure and performs functions assigned to him by the council or its chairman. The director and his staff prepare recommendations for court rules and court-related legislation for consideration by the council, issue an annual report, and prepare specialized reports for the legislature and the governor concerning the need for judicial reform. In addition, the administrative director organizes workshops for trial and appellate court judges and conducts management studies on the state judicial system. The annual salary of the administrative director is $45,504.

The membership of the Judicial Council is comprised of the chief justice of the supreme court, as chairman, one associate justice of the supreme court, three judges of the courts of appeal, five judges of the superior courts, three judges of the municipal courts, two judges of the justice courts, four attorneys, one state senator, and one state assemblyman. The chief justice appoints the judges; the Board of Governors of the State Bar appoints the attorneys; and the State Senate and Assembly designate their respective representative to the council.

The administrative director is not the only official charged with administering the California judicial system. A number of counties throughout the state have created the office of trial court administrator to supervise the operation of the superior courts. For example, the Los Angeles County trial court administrator is selected by the 171 judges of the Los Angeles superior court. As of 1973 the annual salary for the Los Angeles trial court administrator is $31,900. The position includes the following managerial responsibilities: personnel, fiscal matters, physical facilities, information services, statistics, calendar control, jury administration, and research. In addition, the Los Angeles superior court administrator performs as an intergovernmental liaison. It is clearly no understatement to suggest that the administrator enhances the overall efficiency of the superior court.

Judicial Appointments

A Commission on Judicial Appointments has been established by constitutional amendment to screen nominees to the supreme court and the courts of appeal. The commission has the power to veto nominees of the governor to the two major appellate courts. The commission may ask the state bar for a formal investigation if necessary. Members of the commission include the following: the chief justice, the attorney general, the senior presiding justice in the appellate district in which the appointment is being made, or if an appointment to the supreme court, the senior presiding justice of all courts of appeal in the state.

Judicial Qualifications

Since 1960, the Commission on Judicial Qualifications has been constitutionally authorized to investigate judges throughout the California judicial system. Where it is necessary, the commission may hold hearings and then recommend to the supreme court that a judge be removed, retired, or censured; the supreme court may then accept or reject the recommendation, or it may choose to conduct further hearings before rendering a decision. The Judicial Council has ultimate constitutional authority to promulgate rules regarding disqualification proceedings. The commission includes two judges of the courts of appeal, two judges of the superior courts, and one judge of a municipal court, all of whom are appointed by the supreme court. In addition, the state bar appoints two attorneys who have practiced law in the state for ten years, and the governor appoints two laymen subject to Senate approval. Members serve a term of four years.

Judicial Training

California's efforts to achieve a fully qualified judiciary have been among the most zealous in the country. Although California has no mandatory judicial training program, the Judicial Council sponsors several educational institutes and workshops on specialized topics for judges each year. In addition, the Conference of California Judges holds "section meetings" at its annual meeting; the individual sections deal with specific concerns of appellate court judges. The most significant development in California judicial training, however, was the creation in 1973 of the California Center for Judicial Education and Research. The "CJER" was created under the joint sponsorship of the Judicial Council and the Conference of California Judges. It is charged with the following responsibilities: producing judicial education materials, disseminating these materials, organizing orientation and continuing education programs, and coordinating and assisting other organizations in arranging judicial education programs.

The CJER is directed by an eight-judge Governing Committee appointed by the chief justice of the California Supreme Court; the committee represents both the Judicial Council and the Judges' Conference. It is the continuing responsibility of the Governing Committee to see that CJER provides a complete program of judicial education for California judges. Thus far CJER programs are designed exclusively for judges; no programs have been established for training nonjudicial personnel. The programs fall into two broad categories: continuing education programs for judges and orientation programs for new judges. The continuing education programs include institutes in criminal justice, juvenile justice, and municipal and justice court administration. There is also an institute for California Court of Appeal judges. All of the continuing education and the orientation programs are conducted on an annual basis for approximately two weeks.

Typical of the kind of programs sponsored by the CJER is the California Trial Judges 1976 College Session, which, was held July 11–23, 1976 at the Berkeley campus of the University of California. The program included both orientation lectures as well as continuing education seminars for experienced judges. This ambitious program offered twenty-one courses taught by 136 instructors; the various lectures and seminars comprised a total of eighty hours of instruction in ten days.

COLORADO

As of the date of this writing, the state of Colorado has not adopted a unified three-tiered court system. The Colorado judicial system is still characterized by a multiplicity of courts at the trial level. Although justice of the peace courts were eliminated by a 1962 constitutional amendment, there remain several distinct courts of limited and special jurisdiction, particularly within the separate courts of Denver County. A subsequent constitutional amendment in 1966 did reform the method of selection of judges by replacing the partisan ballot election with a system of merit selection and retention. In addition, the 1966 amendment established a mandatory retirement age of seventy-two and a Judicial Qualifications Commission with authority to monitor the conduct of judges. In 1973, a new constitutional amendment was proposed which would merge the Denver Juvenile and Probate Courts into the Denver District Court, and also would eliminate part-time county judges. No action was taken on this proposal.

The Supreme Court. The highest court in Colorado, the supreme court, sits in Denver, the state's capital and largest city. The court derives its authority directly from the Colorado constitution. It consists of seven justices, but that number may be increased to nine, upon request by the court and with the concurrence of a two-thirds majority of both houses of the General Assembly.

Colorado appoints its supreme court justices by means of the merit system. Each justice is appointed by the governor for a term of two years from a list of three names compiled by the Supreme Court Nominating Commission. At the end of that provisional term, the justices must submit to a retention ballot in order to qualify for a full term. If retained by the electorate, the supreme court justice serves a term of ten years, at the conclusion of which the justice may seek retention for another term. Eligibility is restricted to those persons who have been licensed to practice law in the state for not less than five years prior to their election. As of July 1976, the justices of the Colorado Supreme Court receive an annual salary of $40,000. The chief justice, who is elected by the members of the court, receives a salary of $42,500.

The original jurisdiction of the court is limited to the issuance of remedial writs, with full authority to hear and determine application for such writs. The appellate jurisdiction, however, is broad. Included in the scope of the supreme court's appellate review are: cases in which the federal or state constitutionality of a statute, municipal charter, or an ordinance is in question; summary proceedings instituted under the election code; writs of habeas corpus; and Public Utility Commission cases. All of these cases may be appealed to the supreme court as a matter of right. Moreover, the court may exercise certiorari review on cases from the court of appeals, and on county court cases that have been appealed to the district court. All appeals to the supreme court are considered on the record. To exercise its vast jurisdiction the supreme court may sit in two departments of either three or four justices. The chief justice may sit in either or both departments. To render opinions involving the United States or Colorado Constitutions, however, the justices may sit en banc.

The Court of Appeals. The State of Colorado has an intermediate appellate court known as the court of appeals. Its authority derives from the Colorado

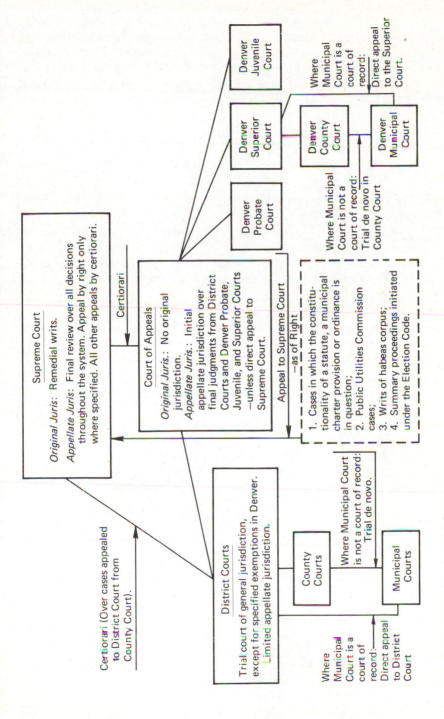

Figure 5–3. Colorado Judicial System

Statutes; it consists of ten judges. The court of appeals sits in Denver in two divisions; however, either division may sit in any county to hear oral arguments. Judges of the court of appeals are appointed in precisely the same manner as justices of the supreme court. Upon retention by the electorate, however, the term is for a period of eight years. To qualify for election to the court of appeals, the individual must have been licensed to practice law in the state for not less than five years. Judges of the court of appeals receive an annual salary of $37,000.

The court of appeals has no original jurisdiction, but it may issue appropriate writs and orders to determine cases within its jurisdiction. It does have initial appellate jurisdiction over appeals from final judgments of the district court and the Denver Superior, Probate, and Juvenile Courts. Excepted from this appellate jurisdiction are those matters which are appealable directly to the supreme court. Cases are appealed from the court of appeals to the supreme court by a writ of certiorari. In addition, the court of appeals may certify a case to the supreme court prior to final determination under certain circumstances; the supreme court may refuse to accept cases so referred. The supreme court may also order the court of appeals to certify any case before the court of appeals to the supreme court for final determination.

The District Courts. The Colordao Constitution has established the district courts, which are the major trial courts of general jurisdiction in the state. The district courts are divided into twenty-two jurisdictions with from one to seven in each of the sixty-three counties. All district courts are courts of record and possess statewide jurisdiction. There are presently ninety-four district court judges, each appointed in the same manner as justices of the supreme court and judges of the court of appeals. The elected term, however, is for a period of six years. The current salary for a district court judge is $33,000.

Colorado's District Courts have original jurisdiction over all civil, probate, and criminal cases, *except* in the city of Denver, where probate and mental health cases are heard in a separate probate court, and juvenile cases are heard in a juvenile court. Jury trials are available in all cases—civil, criminal, and juvenile.

The district courts have appellate jurisdiction which extends to all final judgments from county courts. These judgments are reviewed on the record; however, the district court has discretion to order a new trial in the county court or a trial de novo in the district court. Final judgments of the district courts in civil and criminal matters may be appealed to the court of appeals.

Courts of Limited Jurisdiction

The County Courts. The Colorado constitution has established one county court in every county of the state. Each county court has statewide geographical jurisdiction. The county courts are graded into four classes, (A, B, C, D), to correspond with the standard of judicial qualifications whether or not the judges serve full time or part time. There are 104 county court judges, with 1 to 5 in each county, except Denver, where there are 15. The number of judges is determined by state statute, again with the exception of Denver, where the number is determined by city and county charter. County court judges are appointed in the same manner as the judges of the higher courts; however, the elected term is for a period of four years. Eligibility requirements, as established by statute, vary with the particular class of the county court. Judges in classes A and B must be practicing attorneys and must serve full time; judges in class C must be attorneys, but may practice part time in other than the county court; and judges in class D must be high school graduates and must attend an institute held by the supreme court on county court practice and procedure. Salaries range from a minimum of $2,500 for part-time service to $30,000 for full-time service. This includes a 20 percent increase across the board for all part-time county judges which took effect on July 1, 1976.

The county courts do not have general jurisdiction; their jurisdiction exists only as conferred by law, and tends to overlap the jurisdiction of the district courts. The county courts have concurrent original jurisdiction with the district courts over the following: misdemeanors, preliminary hearings, bindovers in felony cases, issuance of warrants, and admission of bail in misdemeanors and felonies. In addition, the original jurisdiction of the county courts is concurrent with that of the district courts in that it extends to civil actions where the amount in controversy does not exceed $1,000. Effective October 1, 1976, the county courts will also have a small claims procedure for controversies involving no more than $500. Attorneys may not participate in this time-saving procedure.

While the county courts have no jurisdiction over juvenile or probate matters, they do have appellate jurisdiction over cases which are originally heard in municipal courts. Since the municipal courts are not courts of record, the county court conducts a trial de novo. Jury trials are available in all cases tried by the county courts. Appeals from the county courts are taken to the district court, except in the city and county of Denver where all appeals are to the superior court.

The Municipal Courts. The municipal courts in cities and towns with populations in excess of 1,000 comprise the lowest level of the Colorado court system. As of 1972, there were 189 such courts. Each municipal court has from one to four judges, appointed by the city or town council to a two-year term. Judges may serve full or part time. While it is not obligatory that municipal court judges be lawyers, efforts are made to select lawyers wherever possible. Salaries for municipal court judges range from $500 for part-time judges to $30,000 for full-time judges, depending upon the number of working hours, caseload and qualifications.

Original jurisdiction over all cases arising under the ordinances of the municipalities is vested in the municipal courts. Where the municipal court is not a court of record, an appeal may be taken to the county court (for a trial de novo), with the possibility of appeal to the district court. Where the municipal court sits as a court of record, an appeal may be taken directly to the district court on the record. The municipal courts have no appellate or juvenile jurisdiction. As a practical matter, the bulk of the municipal court caseload involves traffic violations.

Denver Courts

The Superior Court.   The Colorado legislature has established a superior court for all counties with a population of at least 300,000. Thus far the only superior court is in Denver; and it is expected that, at the next legislative session, the population limits will be revised to assure that there will be no more superior courts. The superior court's geographical jurisdiction is limited to the confines of Denver County. Only one judge sits on the bench of the superior court. Appointment is by the governor from a list of two or three names submitted by the Nominating Commission of the judicial district. The superior court judge is eligible for a term of six years if retained by the electorate. The judge of the superior court receives a salary of $28,000.

The superior court exercises exclusive jurisdiction over appeals from the county court within the city and county of Denver. These appeals are heard on the record only; there are no trials de novo. Original jurisdiction is concurrent with the district courts. It extends to civil actions where the amount in controversy is not less than $500 nor more than $5,000. Excluded from the grant of jurisdiction are all matters pertaining to probate, mental health, domestic relations, criminal prosecutions, and juvenile cases. Thus the superior court essentially possesses a small claims jurisdiction, largely in duplication of the functions of the district courts. Appeals may be taken, on the record, to the court of appeals and to the supreme court by a writ of certiorari.

The Juvenile and Probate Courts. Numerous states have separate juvenile and probate courts. What is distinctive about the Colorado system is that the juvenile and probate courts exist only in Denver. They derive their authority from the Colorado constitution and exercise countywide geographical jurisdiction.

The Denver Juvenile Court exercises exclusive jurisdiction over all juvenile matters arising in the city and county of Denver. In criminal prosecutions which are punishable by death or imprisonment, the juvenile court has exclusive jurisdiction for persons eighteen years of age or younger. The district court has exclusive jurisdiction if the individual is older than eighteen. For other felonies, the juvenile court has exclusive jurisdiction for persons under sixteen years of age and concurrent jurisdiction with the district court for persons between the ages of sixteen and eighteen. The determination of which court has jurisdiction depends on the seriousness of the offense, the number of prior offenses, and whether the district attorney desires to file directly in the district court.

Three judges serve on the juvenile court. They are appointed by the governor from a list of names submitted by the Nominating Commission and are then eligible to run for election on their record for a term of six years. They receive an annual salary of $28,000.

The jurisdiction of the probate court is original and exclusive over all probate matters and adjudications of the mentally ill arising in Denver County. In all other counties in the state, this jurisdiction is vested in the district courts. One judge sits on the probate court, but this may be increased by law. Appointment is by the governor and the term, if the judge is retained by the electorate, is for six years. The annual salary is currently $28,000. Appeals may be taken from both the probate and the juvenile courts, on the record, to the court of appeals. Further review by the supreme court is available only on certiorari.

Proposed Constitutional Amendment

In 1973, the Legislative Council Interim Committee on Courts proposed a constitutional amendment which would merge the Denver Probate and Juvenile Courts in the Denver District Court. In addition, it would eliminate part-time judges throughout the state, replacing them with full-time county judges on a circuit basis. Only members of the bar would qualify for those judgeships.

The proposed changes in the Denver courts would expand the role of the Denver District Court to encompass the same jurisdiction as other district courts throughout the state. The courts of special jurisdiction would be eliminated, and their functions would be performed by divisions of the court of general jurisdiction. Colorado would thus complete the unification of the judicial system which was initiated by the creation of the general jurisdiction district courts under the 1962 court reorganization amendment. In addition, the proposed replacement of part-time county judges with a circuit county court judge (in rural areas) would reduce the possibility of conflict of interest inherent in part-time judgeships. Furthermore, it would foster the development of a career judiciary.

As of 1976, the proposed amendment had not been adopted.

Administration

The supreme court is ultimately responsible for making and promulgating rules governing practice and procedure in all civil and criminal cases. As the executive head of the state judicial system, the chief justice has constitutional authority to assign judges to temporary judicial duties and to appoint the chief judge of each judicial district whose administrative authority is delegated by the chief justice. The chief judge of each judicial district has administrative authority over the district and county courts.

In practice, the principal administrative officer is the court administrator, who is a constitutional officer, appointed by the supreme court and responsible to the chief justice for the overall management of the system. The court administrator receives an annual compensation of $32,000. Additional, supportive personnel may be appointed by the supreme court as it deems necessary. Similarly, the judges of all lower courts throughout the judicial system have authority to appoint a clerk and other necessary personnel, pursuant to personnel rules promulgated by the supreme court.

In recent years court reformers have argued for full state funding of court systems. The major responsibility for court financing would be transferred from county boards to state legislatures. Recent surveys indicate that the shift from local to state funding has taken place at a snail's pace; Colorado, however, has led the field. The Annual Statistical Report of the Colorado Judiciary for 1973–1974 indicates that over 90 percent of state judicial expenditures were funded by Colorado's state government. This represents an increase in state funding of over 70 percent in five years. In addition, Colorado receives some federal assistance which defrays the balance of the cost of court administration.

Judicial Selection

An indispensable component of the Colorado merit selection system is the Judicial Nominating Commission. Under authority of the Colorado constitution, twenty-three such commissions have been established: one Supreme Court Nominating Commission and one in each judicial district. These commissions are responsible for submitting nominations of judges to the governor for the vacancies which arise in their respective courts. The Supreme Court Nominating Commission has eleven members; its function is to submit nominations for judges to serve on the supreme court and the court of appeals. The District Court Nominating Commissions have seven members; each of the district commissions submit nominations for all appointive judicial positions within their respective jurisdictions. All of the nominating panels must have at least one more nonlawyer member than lawyer members. Nonlawyer members are appointed by the governor and lawyer members are appointed by majority vote of the governor, chief justice, and attorney general. Each member serves a six-year term. The chief justice serves as the nonvoting chairman of the Supreme Court Nominating Commission; and an associate justice serves as the nonvoting chairman of each District Nominating Commission.

The Commission on Judicial Qualifications also plays a vital role in the Colorado judicial system. This commission is constitutionally charged with the responsibility of investigating complaints concerning alleged willful misconduct, willfull or persistent failure to perform duties, or intemperance by any member of the judiciary. Complaints concerning judicial incapacity because of physical or mental disability may also be investigated by this commission. Upon completion of a preliminary investigation, the commission may hold a hearing before its members, or before masters appointed by the supreme court, concerning the removal or retirement of a justice of the supreme court or a judge of any other court. At the close of this proceeding, the commission may recommend removal or retirement to the supreme court, which makes a final determination after reviewing the record and weighing any other evidence it deems pertinent. The Commission on Judicial Qualifications consists of the following membership: three district court judges and two county court judges appointed by the supreme court; two attorneys appointed by majority action of the governor, chief justice, and attorney general; and two nonlawyers appointed by the governor. All appointments are for a term of four years. In addition to a proceeding by the Commission on Judicial Qualifications, a judge may also be removed by legislative impeachment. Where a judge has been convicted of an offense involving moral turpitude the supreme court may act independently to remove the judge.

Judicial Training Program

Colorado is among an increasing number of states which require mandatory attendance at a Judicial Conference "to discuss such recommendations and such other business as will benefit the judiciary of the State of Colorado." A conference must be held at least once yearly and all judges' expenses are paid by the district or county which they serve. The conferences are conducted under the auspices of the state court administrator and his staff. Their purpose is to insure that judicial personnel at the various levels throughout the system receive adequate training. The programs and individual conferences are highly specialized. In addition to providing continuing education for experienced judges, the programs are geared to serve new judges, administrators, probation officers, and court clerks.

THE DISTRICT OF COLUMBIA

When Congress legislates for the District of Columbia, it acts as a state legislature. Thus, under a 1970 enacted court reorganization plan, the District of Columbia has a unified local court system, independent of the federal courts and similar to a state court system. The District now has a superior court with general and special jurisdiction and a District of Columbia Court of Appeals with appellate jurisdiction over all superior court cases.

Judges of the District of Columbia courts are appointed by the president with the advice and consent of the Senate for a term of fifteen years. Under the District of Columbia Self-Government and Governmental Reorganization Act (The Home Rule Act) enacted by Congress in 1973, a Judicial Nomination Commission, consisting of seven members, who serve six-year terms, submits to the president, within thirty days following the occurrence of a vacancy on either court, a list of three persons for each vacancy. No person may be named on a list for more than one vacancy on either court, although the president may select more than one nominee from the same list.

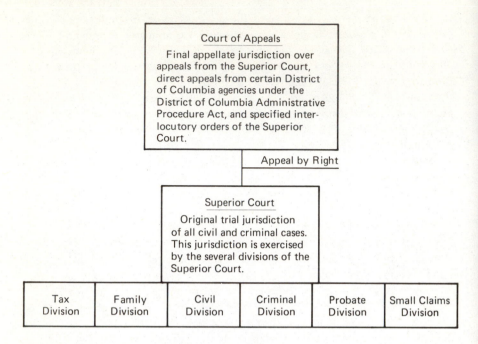

Figure 5–4. District of Columbia Local Court System

The president nominates one individual for each vacancy for Senate confirmation. In the event he fails so to do within sixty days after receiving the list, the commission itself nominates one of those on the list and appoints that person to fill the vacancy with the advice and consent of the Senate.

An incumbent judge seeking reappointment files a declaration of candidacy for reappointment with the Commission on Judicial Disabilities and Tenure at least three months prior to the expiration of the judge's term. The commission submits to the president a written evaluation covering the judge's fitness for appointment to another term. The written evaluation must be made not less than thirty days prior to the expiration of the judge's term. If the commission determines the candidate is exceptionally well qualified or well qualified, the judge's term is automatically extended for another fifteen years. If, however, the commission determines the judge to be qualified for reappointment, the president may nominate the judge, submitting the nomination to the Senate for advice and consent. If the president does not nominate the judge for another term, then the procedure previously described in which the Judicial Nomination Commission submits a list of names, follows. If the Tenure Commission finds a judge unqualified for reappointment, the name of that judge may not be submitted to the Senate for advice and consent, and he is not eligible for reappointment.

The Home Rule Act also changed the way in which a chief judge of a District of Columbia court is designated. Formerly a chief judge was designated by the President of the United States from among the active judges on the court, to serve for a term of four years. Under this legislation, a chief judge of a District of Columbia court is designated by the Judicial Nomination Commission from the judges in regular active service; a chief judge serves a term of four years or until a successor is designated. A chief judge is eligible for redesignation.

Each judicial nominee to a District of Columbia court must be an active member of the District of Columbia Bar for at least five years immediately preceding his appointment, or for the five years immediately preceding appointment must be on the faculty of a law school in the District, or employed as an attorney by the District of Columbia or United States government. The candidate must be a bona fide resident of the District of Columbia and must have resided there for ninety days preceding appointment.

A judge may continue in office until a successor is named, but he is subject to mandatory retirement at age seventy.

Judges of the District of Columbia courts may be suspended, retired, or removed by the District of Columbia Commission on Judicial Disabilities and Tenure for causes which include a felony conviction, willful misconduct in office, conduct which is prejudicial to the administration of justice or which brings the judicial office into disrepute, or for mental or physical disability. The commission is composed of seven members: two appointed by the District of Columbia Bar, both of whom must have been engaged in the practice of law in the District of Columbia for five years immediately preceding the appointment, two by the mayor, one of whom shall not be a lawyer, one by the president, one nonlawyer by the city council, and one active or retired federal judge by the chief judge of the United States District Court for the District of Columbia. All members must be bona fide residents of the District of Columbia where they have maintained a place of abode for at least ninety days prior to appointment. The Tenure Commission annually chooses its chairman and such other officers it may deem necessary. All members serve six-year terms. The members receive per diem compensation (except that a member who is a judge or a government employee may not receive compensation). The commission may hire personnel and promulgate rules for investigation and formal hearings for judges against whom complaints are filed.

Administration

The new District of Columbia court system has a Joint Committee on Judicial Administration composed of the chief judge of the District of Columbia Court of Appeals who is chairman, the chief judge of the superior court, an associate judge of the court of appeals, elected annually by the judges of that court, and two associate judges of the superior court elected annually by the judges of that court.

The Joint Committee, empowered to do so, has appointed a court executive officer who is responsible for administering the District of Columbia courts. The Annual Reports of the chief judge and the court executive have been published each year since 1971. It is well demonstrated that a system of two tiers of courts with strong centralized administrative and continuing administrative oversight is substantially beneficial to each unit, to the entire court system, to the judges themselves, and to the people of the District of Columbia whom the system serves.

The Court of Appeals. The court of appeals was established by Congress and the District of Columbia Code. It has appellate jurisdiction throughout the District over appeals from the superior court and certain District of Columbia agencies. There are nine judges, one of whom serves as the chief judge. The salary of court of appeals judges is $40,140, and that of the chief judge is $40,640.

The Superior Court. The superior court of the District of Columbia exercises sole and exclusive jurisdiction over cases of a state and local nature. It combines in a single tribunal those functions which elsewhere may be distributed among courts of two or more tiers. The jurisdiction of the court, for example, is unlimited in amount at one end of the scale in civil cases, while at the other end the court exercises small claims jurisdiction. In criminal cases the court exercises jurisdiction from felonies to traffic violations, as well as arraignments. The Family Division exercises exclusive jurisdiction over domestic relations, adoptions, commitments, and juvenile cases, as well as intrafamily matters.

From an organizational viewpoint, the court has five statutory divisions: civil, criminal, tax, probate, and family.

Other operations of the court include:

1. A Landlord and Tenant Branch and a Small Claims Branch in the Civil Division;
2. A Social Services Division divided into three branches: adult probation, intrafamily neglect and conciliation, and juvenile;
3. A Data Processing Division;
4. An Auditor-Master Division; and
5. A Central Violations Bureau that has simplified the system of processing traffic violations among the police, the courts, and the public.

The court is authorized forty-four judgeships, including the chief judge. The salary of a superior court judge is $37,800, and that of the chief judge is $38,300. The chief judge may assign a judge to sit in any division or branch, but in making assignments to the Family and Tax Division, the chief judge considers the qualifications and interests of the judges.

HAWAII

The Constitution of the nation's fiftieth state vests judicial power in one supreme court and circuit courts which serve as courts of general jurisdiction. Four circuit courts are established by statute. In addition, the Hawaii Statutes vest limited original jurisdiction in four district courts. Within the past few years Hawaii has made significant strides toward unification of its court system; however, since the trial level jurisdiction of the district courts is in some cases concurrent with the circuit courts', Hawaii's court system cannot be characterized as fully unified.

The Supreme Court. The highest court of Hawaii sits in Honolulu and is composed of five justices, including the chief justice. Associate justices receive an annual salary of $45,000; the chief justice receives $47,500. Justices are appointed by the governor, with the advice and consent of the Senate, and serve a term of ten years. To retain office at the conclusion of the initial term, the justice must be reappointed by the governor. Mandatory retirement is at age seventy. To qualify for a supreme court judgeship, the candidate must have been admitted to practice before the state supreme court for at least ten years.

The supreme court has both appellate and original jurisdiction. On the appellate level, the court hears all questions of law, or of mixed law and fact, which are properly brought before it on appeal from any other court according to law or by reservation of any circuit court or judge. Original jurisdiction includes questions arising under writs directed to lower courts. Also, the supreme court or any individual justice may issue writs of habeas corpus returnable to the supreme court, the issuing justice, or any circuit court. All cases are heard on the record. Jury trials are not available.

The Circuit Courts. There are four judicial circuits in Hawaii. The geographic jurisdictional boundary of each circuit court is coextensive with its respective county. The four circuits encompass the following counties: First—Honolulu; Second—Maui; Third—Hawaii; and Fifth (the Fourth and Third were merged)—Kauai. Each circuit may hold separate sessions at different locations within the county. Each circuit judge is appointed by the governor with the advice and consent of the Senate for a term of ten years. To retain office the circuit judge must be reappointed by the governor. Mandatory retirement is at age seventy. To qualify for circuit court service an individual must be an attorney with a minimum of ten years experience as a member of the Hawaii bar. There are presently seventeen circuit court judges; thirteen in the First Circuit, one in the Second, two in the Third, and one in the Fifth. Pending the signature of the governor, a second judge will sit in the Second Circuit, thereby bringing the total to eighteen. Circuit court judges receive an annual salary of $42,500.

The circuit court is Hawaii's court of general trial jurisdiction. Its original

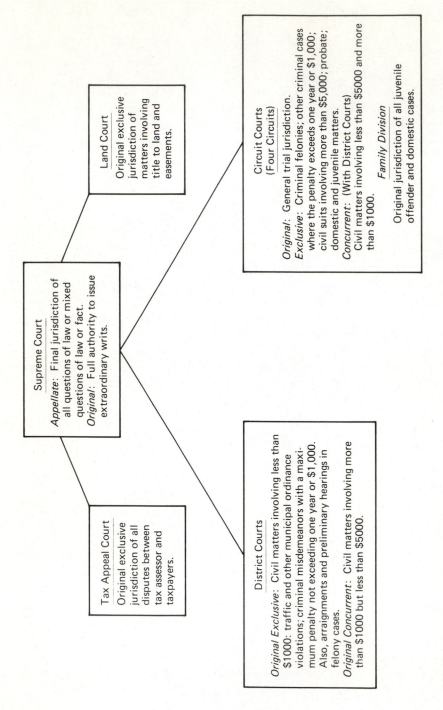

Figure 5–5. Hawaii Court System

jurisdiction includes exclusive jurisdiction over the following matters: criminal felony cases; all other criminal cases in which the fine may exceed $1,000 or imprisonment may exceed one year; civil suits involving more than $5,000; probate proceedings; and, within the Family Court Divisions, cases involving juvenile offenses, marital actions, and other family matters. In addition, the circuit courts have concurrent jurisdiction with the district courts in civil matters involving $5,000 or less but more than $1,000. Jury trials are available in the circuit courts. Appeals are to the Hawaii Supreme Court on the record.

As indicated, within each circuit court there is a separate Family Court Division which is empowered to deal with juvenile offenders and domestic matters. In the First Circuit the family court is considered entirely separate from the circuit court proper. The chief justice of the supreme court assigns two circuit court judges, who are assisted by five district family court judges, to handle family division matters. In all other circuits, however, the family court workload is integrated into the circuit court, with some assistance from district court judges provided in the Second and Third Circuits. The Hawaii family courts are unique in that they transcend a strictly adjudicatory function and provide extensive counseling, guidance, self-help, and supervisory programs for both children and adults.

The District Courts. Hawaii's district courts are established by state statute. A 1972 reorganization of the district courts significantly advanced Hawaii's court system toward the ultimate goal of a fully unified judicial system. Prior to the reorganization, there were twenty-seven district courts as opposed to the four which currently exist; there were twenty-eight magistrates in constrast to today's sixteen judges. The district courts formerly were not courts of record; as a result, time-consuming trials de novo were required in the circuit courts. Today the district courts are courts of record and appeals are taken directly to the state supreme court on the record.

The sixteen district court judges are appointed by the chief justice of the supreme court for terms of six years. Retention of office requires reappointment by the chief justice. To qualify for service on the district court, an individual must be an attorney with a minimum of five years experience as a member of the Hawaii Bar. District court judges receive an annual salary of $40,000.

The district courts exercise exclusive jurisdiction in civil matters involving less than $1,000, traffic and other municipal violations, and criminal misdemeanors which are punishable by a fine not exceeding $1,000 or imprisonment of not longer than one year. In addition, the district courts conduct arraignments and preliminary hearings in felony cases. Concurrent with the circuit courts, the district courts exercise jurisdiction in civil disputes involving more than $1,000 but not to exceed $5,000. No jury trials are available; however, defendants in criminal cases desiring a jury trial may have their cases transferred to a circuit court. Although the reorganization of the district courts has eliminated considerable waste and duplication from the Hawaii judicial system, a vastly increased case-load—which has overburdened district court personnel—has prompted new concern with the quality of justice dispensed by these courts. To remedy this situation, it is likely that efforts will be made either to expand the staffs of the district courts or to contract their jurisdictions.

Land Court. The land court, which administers the state system of land registration, is a statewide court of record located in Honolulu. It exercises exclusive original jurisdiction over all matters involving legal title to land and easement rights. Appeals may be taken directly to the supreme court. Its two judges are designated by the chief justice of the supreme court from among the judges of the First Circuit Court. These is also a three-person administrative staff.

Tax Appeal Court. The tax appeal court is a statewide court of record with original jurisdiction in all disputes between taxpayer and tax assessor. It is located in Honolulu. The tax court shares the judges and staff of the land court.

Administration
The constitution of the state of Hawaii provides that the chief justice of the supreme court shall be the administrative head of the courts. The chief justice is authorized to assign judges from one circuit to another for temporary service, and must prepare a unified budget for the state's courts. Subject to approval of the supreme court, the chief justice is empowered to appoint an administrative director who serves at the pleasure of the chief justice. This director assists the chief justice in the administration of the courts, examining the operation of the state court system, collecting data on the courts, and reporting findings to the chief justice. The director's salary is $40,000. The administrative director, with the approval of the chief justice, may appoint such assistants as may be necessary.

A Judicial Council has been established by the supreme court pursuant to statutory authorization. The chief justice of the supreme court is chairman of the council. Fourteen other members are appointed by the Supreme Court to represent a cross-section of the community. It is the function of the Judicial Council to make recommendations and advise the supreme court on needed changes in substantive law and to analyze and suggest court related programs and court administrative policy.

Judicial Qualifications
A Commission on Judicial Qualifications operates under authority conferred by the Hawaii Statutes. It is the responsibility of the commission to receive, initiate, and consider charges concerning the alleged misconduct or incapacity of a justice of the supreme court or a judge of the circuit courts. The commission

consists of five members appointed by the governor, subject to confirmation by the state Senate, from a panel of ten persons nominated by the judicial council. The term of each member is four years. If a majority of the members of the commission determine that there is probable cause for belief that a justice or judge is too incapacitated to perform necessary duties or is guilty of dereliction of duties, misconduct or intemperance, the commission certifies its finding to the governor.

Upon receipt of the commission's certification of its findings the governor refers the matter to a "Board of Judicial Removal" to adjudicate the charge. The board consists of three members appointed by the governor of which one must be either the chief justice or an associate justice who acts as chairman of the board. The board is empowered to conduct a full hearing, at which all parties must be given an opportunity to be heard and may avail themselves of the sub-poena power, right to counsel, and cross-examination of witnesses. At the con-clusion of the hearing, the board submits its findings and recommendations to the governor; two members must concur in any decision. If the board recom-mends that a judge or justice be removed from office, the governor is required to remove or retire the judge or justice within thirty days after receipt of the board's findings.

The members of both the Commission on Judicial Qualifications and the Board of Judicial Removal serve without compensation.

Judicial Training

In-state, judicial seminars are held biennially. Additional judicial training for Hawaii's judges takes place at the National College of the State Judiciary. There is no constitutional or statutory rule requiring judges to attend these sessions. The chief justice of the supreme court, however, in an exercise of administrative authority over all inferior courts, has mandated the participation of Hawaii's judges. State appropriations and grants from the U.S. Department of Justice Law Enforcement Assistance Administration cover the judges' costs.

ILLINOIS

The Illinois court system typifies the modern trend toward unification of state court systems. To eliminate the inefficiency engendered by several trial level courts with overlapping jurisdiction, Illinois restructured its court system by a constitutional amendment in 1962. Under the new Judicial Article, all trial level courts other than the circuit courts were abolished, and their jurisdiction, power, and duties were transferred to the circuit court in the respective geographical areas. Thus Illinois has eliminated the probate courts, family courts, municipal courts, justices of the peace, and other minor courts which still prevail in many other states.

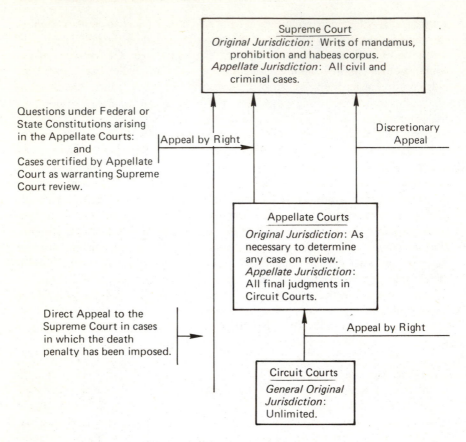

Figure 5–6. Illinois Judicial System

The Supreme Court. Illinois's highest tribunal, the supreme court, sits in the capitol, Springfield. The court is authorized by the Illinois constitution, and is composed of seven justices: six associate justices and the chief justice. Supreme court justices are initially elected in partisan elections from five districts. Three justices are elected from the First District, which includes Cook County, and one justice is elected from each of the remaining four districts. Each justice serves an initial term of ten years, after which the justice may stand for retention in a districtwide merit retention election: that is, by running on a noncompetitive, nonpartisan judicial ballot for another ten-year term. The chief justice is selected from among the elected justices themselves and serves a three-year term. A supreme court justice in the state of Illinois must be a licensed attorney. As of September 1975, all supreme court justices, including the chief justice, receive an annual salary of $50,000.

The jurisdiction of the Illinois supreme court extends to all civil and criminal appeals from the appellate court systems. An appeal may be taken directly from the circuit courts to the supreme court as of right in cases where the death penalty has been imposed. All other appeals are within the discretion of the supreme court. In addition, the supreme court has original jurisdiction to issue writs of mandamus, prohibition, or habeas corpus.

Intermediate Appellate Courts. The intermediate appellate courts constitute the primary courts of appeal within the Illinois judicial system. There are five such courts: one in Cook County, with five divisions, and four others with multicounty jurisdiction. As with the supreme court and the circuit courts, the appellate courts derive their authority directly from the Illinois constitution.

Thirty-four judges sit on the appellate courts: eighteen in the First District, and four in each of the other four districts. Procedures for election and retention of these judges are the same as those for supreme court justices. There is an initial partisan election, a ten-year term and a merit retention election for another ten-year term. Similarly, the appellate judges must be attorneys. Their annual salary is $45,000.

The appellate courts hear all appeals from the circuit courts, except those heard on direct appeal from the circuit courts to the supreme court. The constitution provides that the appellate courts are authorized to exercise original jurisdiction "as may be necessary to the complete determination of any case on review." Appeals from the appellate courts to the supreme court are a matter of right if a question under the Constitution of the United States or under the Illinois constitution arises for the first time in and as a result of the actions of the appellate court, or if a division of the appellate court certifies that a case decided by it involves a question of such importance that the case should be decided by the supreme court.

The Circuit Courts. The circuit courts are the pivotal element in the Illinois system. They are the major trial courts; their general jurisdiction is unlimited. There are twenty-one circuit court systems in Illinois, all of which are multicounty, except for Cook and Dupage Counties. In milticounty circuits, court is held in each county. As of 1975, the circuit courts comprised 610 judges who were designated circuit court judges and associate judges. Circuit court judges are elected and retained under procedures which are essentially the same as those which govern the selection and retention of supreme court justices and appellate judges. The term of the circuit court judges, however, is six years. In each circuit one judge is selected as chief judge, from among those elected, by the judges themselves. The chief judge has general administrative authority within the circuit, subject to the overall supervisory and administrative authority of the supreme court. The associate circuit judges are appointed by the circuit judges for a term of four years; continuation in office beyond the initial term is conditional upon reappointment. Both circuit judges and the associate judges must be lawyers; and both possess the full jurisdiction of the circuit court. The circuit judges receive an annual salary of $42,500, while the associates receive $37,000.

Appeals from final judgments of a circuit court may be taken as a matter of right to the appellate court in the judicial district in which the circuit court is located, except in cases appealable directly to the supreme court and in criminal cases, where there can be no appeal in case of acquittal.

Court of Claims. The Illinois Court of Claims is an administrative agency created by the legislature which is invested with permanent jurisdiction to hear all claims against the state, as specifically authorized by statute. The court of claims consists of a chief justice and two judges, appointed by the governor, by and with the advice and consent of the Senate, for a term of six years. As of February 1975, the salary for court of claims judges was fixed at $12,000. The secretary of state is the ex-officio clerk of the court. A judge may convene a session of the court at any place in the state to hear a case. Concurrence of two judges is necessary in order to decide a case.

Although the court of claims is called a "court" and is presided over by "judges," it is not really a court and is not considered a part of the Illinois judicial system. The only appeal from an adverse judgment by the court of claims is to the Illinois General Assembly.

Administration

The Illinois Supreme Court has general administrative authority over all courts in the state. Included within the ambit of its broad administrative responsibility is the right to assign judges temporarily to courts other than those to which they were elected. While the supreme court is nominally responsible for the administration of the Illinois court system, an administrative director and staff, who serve at the court's pleasure, are appointed to assist the court in its duties. The annual compensation of the administrative director is $45,000.

In addition to the state court administrator, there is also a trial court administrator for Cook County. Under authorization conferred by court rule, the trial court administrator is appointed by the chief judge of the Cook County Circuit Court. The administrator's jurisdiction is coextensive with the Cook County Circuit. Responsibilities of the position include: management of the court calendar, personnel, fiscal matters, physical facilities, and information services. In addition, the trial court administrator oversees jury administration, compilation of statistics, research, and serves as an intergovernmental liaison. As of 1975, the Cook County administrator received an annual compensation of $35,000.

Additional support personnel are available to the Supreme Court and the lower courts. The judges of the supreme court and each of the five district appellate courts appoint clerks to assist them, and one circuit court clerk is elected in each county.

It is interesting to note that when Illinois adopted its unified judicial system, the state of Illinois assumed a large financial burden which was previously borne by the counties and cities. Thus, while the costs to the state increased, the costs to the counties and municipalities sharply decreased. Nevertheless, the overall cost to the state has been modest. For fiscal year 1976, the cost of administering the judicial system was approximately $42,000,000, a mere 0.4 percent of the total state expenditure.

The Judicial Conference

Illinois has established a Judicial Conference to consider the problems pertaining to the administration of justice in the state and to make appropriate recommendations for its improvement. The Judicial Conference is conducted under authority of the Illinois Constitutional and Supreme Court Rule. It meets at least once a year, as designated by the supreme court. The participating membership of the conference includes all justices of the supreme court, judges of the appellate courts, and circuit court judges. To assist in conducting the Judicial Conference, the supreme court appoints an executive committee. The executive committee consists of the chief justice, who serves as an ex-officio member, and twelve appellate and circuit court judges: six from within Cook County and six from outside Cook County. Members of the executive committee are appointed by the supreme court for terms of three years.

Judicial Conduct

The Judicial Inquiry Board, authorized by the Illinois constitution, is convened permanently to conduct investigations, receive or initiate complaints concerning a judge or associate judge and file complaints with the Courts Commission. The board's membership consists of two circuit court judges selected by the supreme court, and three lawyers and four nonlawyers appointed by the governor. All members serve a four-year term.

Where a matter is sufficiently serious to warrant further inquiry, the Judicial Inquiry Board can file a complaint with the Courts Commission. This body, which also derives its authority from the Illinois constitution, is responsible for conducting a public hearing on any complaint filed by the Inquiry Board and, thereupon, removing a judge from office for physical or mental inability to perform his duties. Removal may also result if a judge is found guilty of willful misconduct in office, persistent failure to perform required duties, or other conduct that is prejudicial to the administration of justice or that brings a judicial office into disrepute. The membership includes the following: one supreme court justice, selected by the supreme court, who serves as commission chairman; two appellate court judges selected by the appellate courts; and two circuit court judges selected by the supreme court.

Judicial Training

Illinois has several judicial training programs, three of which mandate participation. The Annual Judicial Conference deals with developments in the law and the administration of justice, and includes specialized improvement seminars. It is attended by over 350 judges of the supreme court, appellate courts, and circuit courts. The Annual Associate Judges Seminar has a similar agenda; it is attended primarily by associate circuit judges.

The New Judges Seminar, which deals in depth with the Illinois judicial system, its structure and operation, the authority of a trial judge, and related legal developments, offers a more rigorous program. As its title suggests, it is designed for the newly designated or elected judges of all levels. The program is offered every two years for two and one-half days. It is conducted under the supervision of the state administrative director. In addition to these three principal programs, the Illinois judicial system sponsors a number of regional seminars covering such areas as criminal law, civil law and juvenile justice.

Illinois also has a statute which provides for a Judicial Advisory Council whose task it is to observe and visit any and all groups concerned with the modernization of law or procedure and the improvement of standards of civil or criminal justice. This information is made available for study by the administrative staff of the Illinois judicial system.

MASSACHUSETTS

The state of Massachusetts does not have a unified court system, but rather a number of trial courts with complex overlapping jurisdictions which are difficult to operate efficiently. Massachusetts, however, has recently made strides toward attaining a more effective judicial system. In 1972, an appeals court was established to function as the state's primary intermediate appellate court. This court serves as a "filter," thus reducing the workload of the supreme judicial court. Also, to upgrade the system of selecting judges, Executive Order #114 has established a voluntary nonpartisan Judicial Selection Committee to recommend judicial nominees to the governor.

Courts of Appellate Jurisdiction

Supreme Judicial Court. Massachusetts' highest court is the supreme judicial court. Its authority derives from the constitution and laws of Massachusetts. The supreme judicial court exercises statewide jurisdiction; it sits in Boston.

The court consists of six associate justices and a chief justice. All are appointed by the Governor, with the consent of the Executive Council. They serve during good behavior until they reach the mandatory retirement age of seventy. Although previous legal training is not officially required to qualify as a justice of the supreme judicial court, in practice, those appointed are always attorneys. In 1975, the annual salary of associate justices was $40,788, and the salary of the chief justice was $42,236.

The supreme judicial court has final appellate jurisdiction of all criminal and

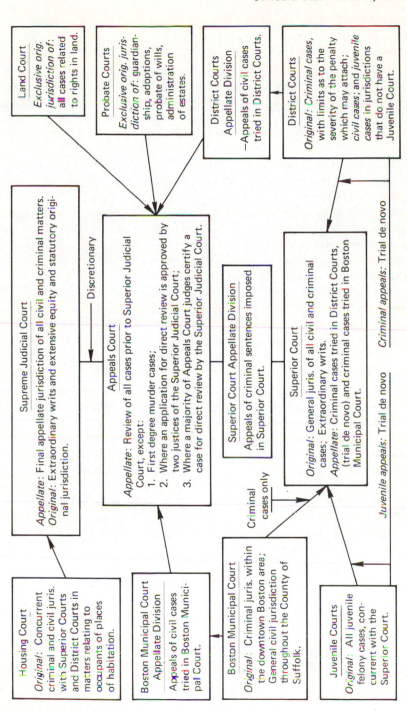

Figure 5–7. Massachusetts Judicial System

civil matters. It also has original jurisdiction of extraordinary writs concurrent with the appeals and superior courts, and extensive equity and statutory original jurisdiction.

Appeals Court. The appeals court was established (by statute) in 1972 and it went into operation on July 1, 1974. Similar to the supreme judicial court, the appeals court sits in Boston and exercises statewide jurisdiction. It is an intermediate appellate court through which most appeals must pass before they can move the supreme judicial court to render further appellate review. Specifically, appeals court jurisdiction includes the following: (1) all criminal cases; (2) all civil proceedings at law or in equity; and (3) proceedings in the superior court for the review of administrative determinations. There are, however, three situations in which the appeals court may be bypassed: (1) first degree murder cases; (2) cases in which an application for direct review by the supreme judicial court is approved by two of its justices; and (3) cases in which a majority of the judges of the appeals court certify direct review by the supreme judicial court.

The appeals court consists of a chief judge and five associate judges who are appointed for life by the governor with the consent of the Executive Council. The chief judge receives $39,220 per year; the associate judges receive $37,771.

Courts of General Jurisdiction

The Superior Court. The superior court of Massachusetts is established by state statute. Sessions of the superior court are held in each of Massachusetts' fourteen counties. In January 1975, there were forty-six justices on the superior court, including its chief justice. These justices are appointed for life in the same manner as are the justices of the supreme judicial court and the judges of the appeals court. Although legal training is not required by law, lawyers are always appointed. Salaries are $36,203 for the associate justices and $37,771 for the chief justice.

The superior court has general jurisdiction over all criminal and civil cases, except those over which some other court has exclusive jurisdiction. Trial by jury is available. In civil cases, except equity matters, jury trials are deemed waived unless claimed. In equity cases, there is no right to a jury. In criminal cases, a jury trial is provided unless waived. Appellate jurisdiction extends to all offenses tried in the district courts; such appeals are accorded a trial de novo. Appeals from the superior court may be taken to the appeals court, except in those specific cases where the appeals court can be bypassed. One interesting facet of the superior court is its Appellate Division, which consists of three superior court justices, assigned by the chief justice of the superior court to hear and rule on appeals of criminal sentences imposed by justices of the superior court.

Courts of Limited and Special Jurisdiction

District Courts. Massachusetts law authorizes district courts throughout the state with varying geographic limitations. The district courts are courts of record. In January 1975, there were sixty-seven full-time district court justices, including a chief justice appointed by the governor, and sixteen part-time justices. Most cases are heard by a single justice without a jury, except in the Central District of Worcester County where it is possible to have a six-person jury in certain civil cases.

Salaries for district court justices vary widely. The chief justice receives $31,738, the associate justices receive $30,168, and the part-time justices receive from $9,171 to $12,189, depending upon the number of hours worked. Legal training is not required for judges of the district court; they are appointed for life by the governor.

The jurisdiction of the district courts is limited. Criminal jurisdiction extends to misdemeanors and felonies carrying a maximum sentence of five years. In practice, however, since district court justices cannot commit offenders to state prisons, the maximum sentence is two and one-half years, the maximum sentence for offenders committed to county prisons. Criminal cases are tried without a jury in district courts; however, in many counties there may be an appeal to the superior court for a trial de novo. In Suffolk County, such appeals for trial de novo may be to the superior court or to the Boston Municipal Court. In appealing a district court judgment in a criminal proceeding, the defendant may waive the right to trial de novo in superior court and elect instead to be tried by a jury of six persons in the district court. The legislature has designated certain district courts to conduct "jury of six" trials. District courts also have original civil jurisdiction, and, in the absence of juvenile courts, the district courts have exclusive jurisdiction within their respective geographical areas of juvenile cases.

While most criminal appeals are taken directly to the superior court, civil appeals are generally taken to the Appellate Division of the district court in cases where the right to a jury trial has been waived. There are three such Appellate Divisions, encompassing the northeastern, southeastern, and western portions of the state. Each division consists of five justices, who are assigned by the chief justice of the district courts from among the full-time justices. Where the right to a jury trial in a civil case has been preserved, a trial de novo may be had in the superior court.

Boston Municipal Court. The Municipal Court of the City of Boston is authorized by state statute. Its geographical and legal jurisdiction is strictly limited. In criminal matters, its geographical jurisdiction is limited to a portion of downtown Boston; in civil matters, its jurisdiction extends throughout the county of Suffolk. The Boston Municipal Court has criminal jurisdiction of misdemeanors and felonies punishable by a fine or a maximum prison sentence of five years. This is similar to the criminal jurisdiction of the district courts. Civil jurisdiction includes general civil cases and domestic relations cases (excluding divorce, separation, and adoption). In Boston, landlord/tenant disputes come within the jurisdiction of the Boston Housing Court.

Jury trials are available in criminal cases only on a de novo basis. Generally, criminal appeals are to the superior court; civil appeals are to the Appellate Division of the municipal court. Cases brought before the Appellate Division are heard by three associate justices assigned by the chief justice. The municipal court has a total of nine associate justices and one chief justice. All are appointed for life by the governor. Legal training is not required, but lawyers are always appointed. Municipal court salaries are equal to district court salaries: the chief justice receives $31,738 and the associate justices receive $30,168.

Probate and Insolvency Courts. The probate and insolvency courts are authorized by Massachusetts state law. They function as one court with sessions in each of the fourteen counties of the state. The probate and insolvency courts exercise exclusive jurisdiction over guardianship, adoptions, probate of wills, and the administration of estates. These courts also have equity jurisdiction, concurrent with that of the superior court. In some probate matters the equity jurisdiction of the probate and insolvency courts is concurrent with that of the supreme judicial court. There are a total of twenty-seven judges on the probate courts, including one chief judge. The salaries are $32,994 for the chief judge and $31,738 for the associates. All judges are appointed for life by the governor.

Juvenile Courts. The juvenile courts are authorized by special legislation in the cities of Boston, Springfield, and Worcester, and the county of Bristol; geographical jurisdiction is limited to the confines of the respective cities and Bristol County. Juvenile courts have legal jurisdiction solely over juvenile cases. This jurisdiction is concurrent with that of the superior court; it extends to offenders, under seventeen years of age, accused of felonies not punishable by death or life imprisonment. The Boston Juvenile Court exercises jurisdiction exclusive of the Boston Municipal Court over cases of juvenile offenders under seventeen years of age and cases of neglected or delinquent children. Appeals are to the superior court where a trial de novo is available in a juvenile session. However, in Suffolk County, a de novo jury trial in a juvenile case is available in the Boston Juvenile Court.

The Boston Juvenile Court consists of one full-time justice and two part-time justices. The other juvenile courts each have one justice. All juvenile justices are appointed for life by the governor and must be attorneys. The Boston Juvenile Court justice receives an annual salary of $31,738; other juvenile court justices receive $30,168.

Housing Courts. Massachusetts has created a housing court in Boston and Hampden Counties. The jurisdiction of the housing courts extends to the limits of Boston County and Hampden County respectively. The housing courts have concurrent criminal and civil jurisdiction with the superior and district courts in all matters relating to the health or welfare of any occupant of any place used, or intended for use, as a place of habitation. Jury trials are generally not available, unless required by the Massachusetts constitution. Appeals from housing court judgments are to the supreme judicial court. Each housing court has a chief judge and an associate judge; both are appointed for life by the governor. The judges must be attorneys and residents of the city or county in which they will serve. Housing court justices, in both Boston and Hampden Counties, receive an annual salary of $36,203.

Land Court. The land court, which has statewide geographical jurisdiction, has exclusive original legal jurisdiction of all petitions for confirmation and registration of title to land, easements and rights in land within the state, and power to hear and determine all questions arising under such petitions. The land court has original equity jurisdiction concurrent with the supreme judicial court and the superior court in matters relating to any right or interest in land, except in suits for specific performance of contracts; and it has original jurisdiction, concurrent with the supreme judicial, superior, and probate courts, of declaratory judgment proceedings. The court sits in Boston, but may adjourn to other locations as public convenience may require.

Administration

The supreme judicial court of Massachusetts has ultimate responsibility for the administration of all courts in the state. An executive secretary is elected by the justices to supervise the court's administrative office. In effect this executive secretary performs the duties of a court administrator. The executive secretary receives an annual salary of $30,691. The justices of the supreme judicial court also appoint a "clerk of the Commonwealth" who serves as the chief appellate clerk of the court. There is also an elected clerk of the supreme judicial court for Suffolk County who serves as a clerk for the court's single justice session and, under statutory authority, as ex-officio clerk of the appeals court. Similarly, each of the courts throughout the Massachusetts judicial system has a clerk. The procedures for clerk selection vary among the different courts. In the superior court system, a clerk is elected in each county; in the district court system, however, a clerk is appointed to each district court by the governor for life. Clerks are also appointed by the governor to the Boston Municipal Court, the juvenile courts, and the housing courts. A register of probate is elected to the probate court in each county.

Massachusetts has created two judicial bodies concerned with maintaining and improving the efficiency of the state judicial system. The Judicial Council, established by legislature, is authorized to study, on a continuous basis, the organization, rules and methods of procedure and practice of the judicial system of the state. The council is composed of the chief justice of the supreme judicial court; the chief justice of the superior court; the judge of the land court; the chief justice of the municipal court of the city of Boston; one judge of the probate courts and one justice of the district court; and not more than four members of the bar. All members of the Judicial Council are appointed by the governor, with the advice and consent of the Executive Council. Tenure, not exceeding four years, is determined by the governor. The Judicial Conference, established by court rule, convenes to consider matters relating to the judicial process, the improvement of the judicial system, and the administration of justice. The justices of the supreme judicial court call conferences for the judges of the various courts and for invited members of the bar. The executive secretary of the supreme judicial court acts as secretary of the conferences.

Judicial Training

Massachusetts law does not provide for mandatory training of judges. Recently, however, a number of programs and conferences have been instituted by various courts throughout the state. The district courts, the superior court, and other courts within the Massachusetts judicial system sponsor semiannual conferences. In addition, there are seminars for new judges and clerks. There is also an education coordinator who provides support for the education programs for court personnel who do not yet have such programs. In addition, the education coordinator edits a quarterly newsletter which is distributed to all court personnel.

Judicial Selection and Removal

All Massachusetts judges are nominated and appointed by the governor for life, conditioned upon good behavior. These gubernatorial appointments require the advice and consent of the Governor's Council—an eight member body elected by the voters. However, the Massachusetts governor, Michael S. Dukakis, has established a Judicial Selection Committee by executive order. The committee consists of eleven persons: six lawyers and five nonlawyers. For all judicial vacancies the committee submits three nominees to the governor, from which he must select one.

Massachusetts has no statewide commission to oversee judicial conduct. Generally, complaints against judges are processed initially by the administrative staffs of the courts, particularly the executive secretary's staff. There is, however, a Committee on Complaints which was established in 1969 by the supreme judicial court. The committee consists of three present or former judges and two members of the bar who serve at the pleasure of the justices of the supreme judicial court. It is empowered to conduct preliminary investigations on any complaints and to submit appropriate recommendations to the chief justice or the full court. The probate courts and the district courts have similar Committees on Judicial Complaints. However, although the rule establishing the committees still exists, the committees are now moribund. In 1973, the Massachusetts Bar Association created its own Committee on Judicial Complaints in response to a substantial increase in the instances of public criticism of judical conduct. It consists of three judges and four lawyers. In its first fifteen months the committee disposed of seventy-two complaints. This represented a vast improvement over the less efficient Committee on Complaints established by the supreme judicial court, now long nonoperative. Despite this success, the Massachusetts legal community is presently considering various means of improving the supervision of judges' performances.

NEW JERSEY

Under the leadership of Chief Justice Arthur T. Vanderbilt, New Jersey became one of the first states to adopt a unified court system. New Jersey also pioneered in the use of court administrators. The constitution of 1947, the culmination of years of effort by Vanderbilt and others, radically altered and modernized the New Jersey courts by eliminating such vestiges of an antiquated system as: inconsistent procedures resulting from local custom; ineffective supervision; overlapping jurisdictions; and, most important, a distinction between law and equity that was so pronounced that, in effect, there were two separate court systems. The constitution of 1947 corrected these defects and simultaneously created a framework for a modern and efficient judicial system.

For the most part the framework established by the 1947 constitution has stood the test of time. New Jersey's judicial system remains essentially as it has been since September of 1948 when the new constitution took effect. It is a three-tiered system, with a supreme court as the court of last resort, an intermediate appellate court, and a variety of trial courts. As is typical of modern court systems, the lingering weakness in the New Jersey system is the multitude of trial courts with overlapping jurisdictions. Nevertheless, the system is generally efficient and able to meet the needs of the litigant.

The Supreme Court.   The supreme court sits in New Jersey's capital, Trenton. It has statewide appellate jurisdiction over cases appealed from lower courts. The following cases may be appealed to the supreme court as of right: (1) capital cases; (2) cases involving a question arising under the New Jersey or United States Constitutions; (3) cases in which there is a dissent in the appellate division. The supreme court may also certify cases for review. In addition, the supreme court may exercise original jurisdiction to issue extraordinary writs.

The supreme court consists of one chief justice and six associate justices. Each is nominated and appointed by the governor, subject to the consent of the

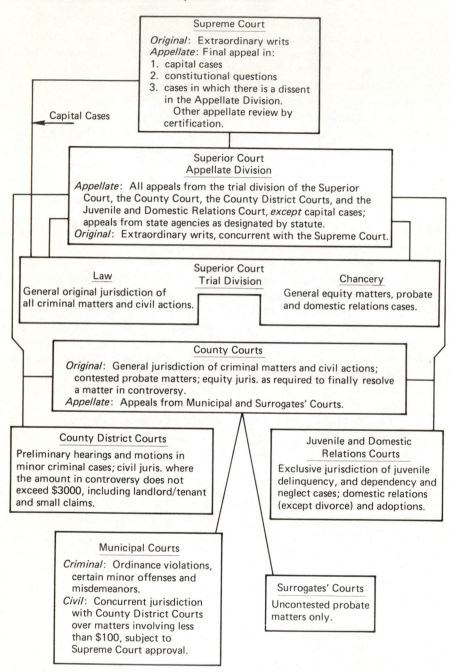

Figure 5—8. New Jersey Judicial System

Senate. The justices serve an initial term of seven years and upon reappointment hold their offices during good behavior until they reach the mandatory retirement age of seventy. Retirement is optional at age sixty-five. To qualify for service on the supreme court, an individual must have been a member of the New Jersey Bar for a minimum of ten years prior to appointment. The annual salary for the associate justices is $48,000; the chief justice receives $50,500.

The Superior Court. The superior court consists of three divisions; an appellate division and two general trial divisions. The Appellate Division of the superior court functions as an intermediate court of appeals for the entire state. It may consist of as many parts as the supreme court may designate; presently there are seven parts sitting at various locations throughout the state. The Appellate Division exercises a broad appellate jurisdiction. Except in capital cases, it hears all appeals from the trial divisions of the superior court, the county court, the county district courts and the juvenile and domestic relations court. In addition, the Appellate Division may hear appeals from state agencies, as designated by statute. It also may exercise jurisdiction, concurrent with the supreme court, to issue extraordinary writs.

The Appellate Division does not have judges of its own; rather, it consists of judges of the superior court who are assigned to the Appellate Division by the chief justice of the supreme court. Each of the Appellate Division's parts includes three such judges, with one designated by the chief justice to serve as presiding judge. As is the case with the supreme court justices, the judges of the superior court are appointed by the governor with the consent of the Senate; they serve an initial term of seven years and upon reappointment hold their offices during good behavior. They must have been members of the New Jersey Bar for ten years prior to appointment. Judges who serve in the Appellate Division receive an annual compensation of $45,000.

The general trial divisions of the superior court consist of a Law Division and a Chancery Division. The Law Division sits in each county and functions jointly with the Law Division of the county courts as a general trial court. The Chancery Division sits in twelve regions, each of which includes one or more counties. At first glance it might appear that this arrangement perpetuates the inefficiency of the old system of spearating legal from equitable causes of action. This, however, is not the case. Both the Law Division and the Chancery Division are empowered to exercise the powers and functions of the other and to grant both legal and equitable relief in any cause so that all issues may be completely determined by one court.

The jurisdiction of the Law Division extends to the following: general original jurisdiction of all criminal matters and unlimited jurisdiction of all civil actions (at law). Jury trials are available. The jurisdiction of the Chancery Division includes general equity matters, probate and domestic relations cases.

Cases tried by either division of the superior court are appealable to the Appellate Division.

As indicated above, the judges of the superior court are appointed by the governor for a term of seven years, and upon reappointment hold their offices during good behavior until retirement. Superior court judges receive an annual salary of $40,000.

The County Courts. The county courts tend to duplicate the functions of the superior court. There is one county court in each county. Each one consists of a Law Division and a Probate Division. County court jurisdiction includes general original jurisdiction of criminal matters, civil matters, and contested probate matters. Jury trials are available in both the law and probate divisions. Appeals from the county courts are to the Appellate Division of the superior court.

The county courts also have appellate jurisdiction of cases appealed from the municipal courts within the respective counties.

Each county court has at least one judge. County court judges are appointed by the governor with the advice and consent of the Senate for five year terms. After three appointments, the judge attains tenure and thereafter serves until retirement. As with the supreme court justices and the superior court judges, the county court judges must have been admitted to the New Jersey Bar ten years prior to appointment. County court judges receive an annual salary of $40,000.

Courts of Limited and Specialized Jurisdiction

County District Courts. There is one county district court in each county. The geographical jurisdiction of these courts is coextensive with the respective counties; its subject matter jurisdiction includes criminal preliminary hearings and motions, and minor offenses, concurrent with the municipal courts. In addition, county district courts have jurisdiction of civil actions where the amount in controversy does not exceed $3,000. This includes landlord/tenant matters and small claims. Jury trials are available in county district court. Appeals are taken to the Appellate Division of the superior court.

County district court judges are appointed for the several counties by the governor with the consent of the Senate. They serve five-year terms and must have been admitted to the New Jersey Bar for ten years prior to appointment. Similar to county court judges, after three appointments, a county district court judge attains tenure, and thereafter holds his office during good behavior until retirement. In those counties which do not have specific provisions for a county district court, the county court judge presides. County district court judges receive an annual salary of $37,000. A proposal to increase their salary to $40,000 is currently under consideration by the legislature.

Juvenile and Domestic Relations Courts. New Jersey's court system includes one juvenile and domestic relations court in each county. These courts have exclusive jurisdiction of juvenile delinquency and dependency and neglect cases. Additionally, they have jurisdiction of domestic relations matters (except divorce cases) and adoptions, concurrent with the Chancery Division of the superior court. Appeals are to the Appellate Division of the superior court.

Judges are either specifically appointed to the juvenile and domestic relations court or a judge of the county court fills the position. As with all judicial positions in New Jersey, the appointment is made by the governor subject to the consent of the Senate. Judges of the juvenile and domestic relations court serve an initial term of five years, and receive an annual compensation of $40,000. After three appointments, they too receive tenure and may continue to hold their offices during good behavior until retirement.

Municipal Courts. Pursuant to the New Jersey statutes, municipal courts may be established by any municipality or by a group of municipalities. (In September 1975, there were 525 municipal courts.) Municipal courts have criminal jurisdiction over ordinance violations, minor offenses, and misdemeanors where there is no grand jury indictment or no jury trial. In addition, subject to supreme court approval, municipal courts have concurrent civil jurisdiction with the county district courts in matters where the amount in controversy does not exceed $100.

Municipal courts generally have one judge, although in larger communities there may be several. Municipal court judges are appointed by the mayor or governing board of the municipality, except when serving more than one community. In such cases the judges are appointed by the governor with the consent of the Senate. Municipal court judges must be attorneys; they serve an initial term of three years and receive an annual compensation which ranges up to $27,500, depending upon the number of hours of work required.

Surrogate Courts. Finally, New Jersey has twenty-one surrogate courts, one for each county. These courts handle only uncontested probate matters. The judge of the surrogate court is known as the "surrogate" and also serves as a clerk of the probate division of the county court. The surrogates are popularly elected by the electors of each county to a five-year term; there are no requirements for legal training specified by law. Salaries for surrogates vary, but range as high as $27,000.

Administration

The earmark of an efficient court system is a modern administrative structure. New Jersey's court system meets this standard. It has a highly sophisticated administrative structure. Under the constitution, the supreme court has exclusive power to regulate the administration, practice, and procedure of all the state courts. The chief justice is the administrative head of all New Jersey courts and may, where and when necessary, assign judges from one court to another.

The chief justice is assisted by an administrative director and an administrative office. The administrative director and the staff are responsible for the enforcement of the rules and policies established by the supreme court and the chief justice. It is the function of the administrative director to collect statistical data with respect to the operation of the courts, to act as intergovernmental liaison, and generally to assist the chief justice and supreme court in the administration of the courts. The director receives an annual salary of $45,000. To assist the administrative director twelve trial court administrators serve in the twelve regions, each of which includes one or more counties. These trial court administrators are responsible for the supervision of the following areas: personnel, fiscal matters, physical plant, jury administration, statistics, calendar, and research.

Judicial Conference

A Judicial Conference has been established by the New Jersey supreme court. Its purpose is to assist the supreme court in the consideration of improvements in practice and procedure in the courts and in the administration of the judicial branch in general. The Judicial Conference has an unusually large and diverse membership, including the chief justice and associate justices of the supreme court, representative judges of the superior court and all other courts, the administrative director, legislative leaders, the attorney general, the public defender, court clerks, law school deans, bar association officials, and a number of practicing attorneys from different fields. All members serve a term of one year, except those who are ex-officio members; and all serve without pay.

Judicial Training

New Jersey's Supreme Court requires that a Conference of Judges be held at least once each year. The purpose of this conference is to raise the standards of judicial performance and to coordinate the operations and administration of the courts of the state. The conference includes all justices and judges in the state, except judges of the municipal courts. Those judges participate in a separate annual municipal court conference. Participation in these conferences is mandatory for all judges. To expose judges to judicial thinking and procedures of other areas, New Jersey also sends some judges to out-of-state programs, such as the National College of the State Judiciary.

Finally, New Jersey provides orientation seminars, usually lasting four days, for its newly appointed judges. In addition, one- or two-day seminars on specific topics are conducted for both newly appointed and sitting judges, as well as for other judicial personnel such as trial court administrators, court reporters, and court interpreters.

Judicial Misconduct

Pursuant to statutory authority, any judge in New Jersey may be removed from office by the supreme court for "misconduct in office, willful neglect of duty, or other conduct evidencing unfitness for judicial office, or for incompetence." A removal procedure may be initiated by the filing of a complaint with the clerk of the supreme court, by majority action of either house of the legislature or by the governor. In addition, the supreme court may institute such a proceeding on its own motion. The supreme court may suspend a judge with or without pay pending the disposition of the proceeding.

The removal proceeding is prosecuted before the supreme court sitting en banc, or before three supreme court justices or other judges as designated by the chief justice. The right to counsel and the right to compel the attendance of witnesses and the production of evidence is available for both the prosecuting attorney (usually the attorney general) and the judge. Removal may result if the supreme court finds beyond a reasonable doubt that cause exists. A removal proceeding does not preclude the possibility of impeachment pursuant to constitutional and statutory authority. Justices of the supreme court and judges of the superior and county courts are all subject to impeachment.

NEW YORK STATE

Until 1962, twenty-one different types of courts had existed under the New York State court system. Patterned originally after the English system, the New York courts were overhauled under the 1846 constitution to meet the needs of that day. While they were then considered a model for other states to follow, 116 years had since passed. During that time economic developments and the automobile age have brought into existence a great many new courts which were created to meet special needs. As a result of the 1961 constitutional amendment, there are now the following courts:

Court of Appeals
Appellate Division of
  the Supreme Court
  (Four Departments)
Appellate Term of the
  Supreme Court
Supreme Court
Court of Claims
County Courts
Surrogate's Courts
New York City Criminal
  Court

New York City Civil
  Court
Family Court of the
  State of New York
District Courts of Nassau
  and Suffolk Counties
City Courts
City Justice Courts
City Police Courts
Town and Village Jus-
  tice Courts
Court on the Judiciary

Author's Note: This section on New York's court system includes the history of court reform because the struggle for court reform has been long and continuous. The information is offered to illustrate a classic example of piece by piece change, not altogether effective in bringing the desired results.

The late Arthur T. Vanderbilt once said that "it is characteristic of an immature system of law that it is beset by a multiplicity of courts." Prior to 1962, New York had more than 1,500 separate and distinct courts. It became clear that the fragmented and conflicting jurisdiction of these numerous courts resulted in inconvenience to litigants, duplication of services and facilities, the inadequacies of the part-time judge system, and the impossibility of adjusting the judicial work load through easy transfer of judges and cases. In 1953, the New York Temporary Commission on the Courts was created to study these problems and to make recommendations. Its efforts and those of other groups interested in the urgently needed simplification of the judicial structure culminated in the Court Reorganization Amendment, which was approved by the electorate on November 1, 1961. The amendment and implementing legislation became effective on September 1, 1962.

The present organization of the New York courts will be outlined according to the geographic scope of their jurisdiction.

Statewide Courts

Appellate Courts

Court of Appeals. The highest court of New York, a statewide constitutional court, having final jurisdiction in civil and criminal cases, sits in Albany, the state capitol. It consists of a chief judge and six associate judges elected for fourteen years. If the office of chief judge is vacant, the governor may appoint as a successor either an associate judge of the Court of Appeals or a justice of the supreme court. A candidate for a Court of Appeals judgeship must have been admitted to the practice of law for at least ten years. While a member of the court, a judge is forbidden to hold any other public office or engage in the practice of law. When there is an excessive accumulation of cases and the court so certifies, the governor may designate up to four supreme court justices to sit temporarily on the Court of Appeals. However, no more than seven judges may hear an appeal. Five judges constitute a quorum, and four must agree to reach a decision. The first term usually begins in January and lasts three weeks; the subsequent terms are fixed by the court. At the close of each term, the date for the next term is announced. The salary of the chief judge of the Court of Appeals is $63,143. Associate judges receive $55,266. Mandatory retirement is required of judges at age seventy. They may continue to serve as supreme court justices until age seventy-six upon certification by the Administrative Board every two years that they are in good health. In fiscal year 1974, the Court of Appeals disposed of 574 cases and 1,098 motions.

The Court of Appeals reviews only questions of law, with the following exceptions:

1. death sentence cases,

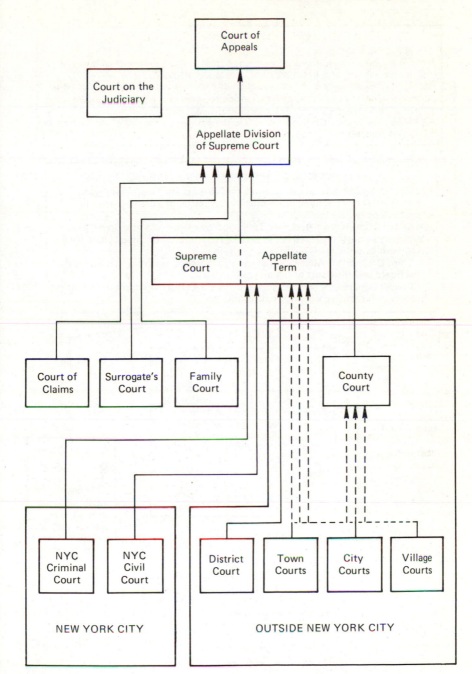

Figure 5-9. Outline of New York State Court Structure

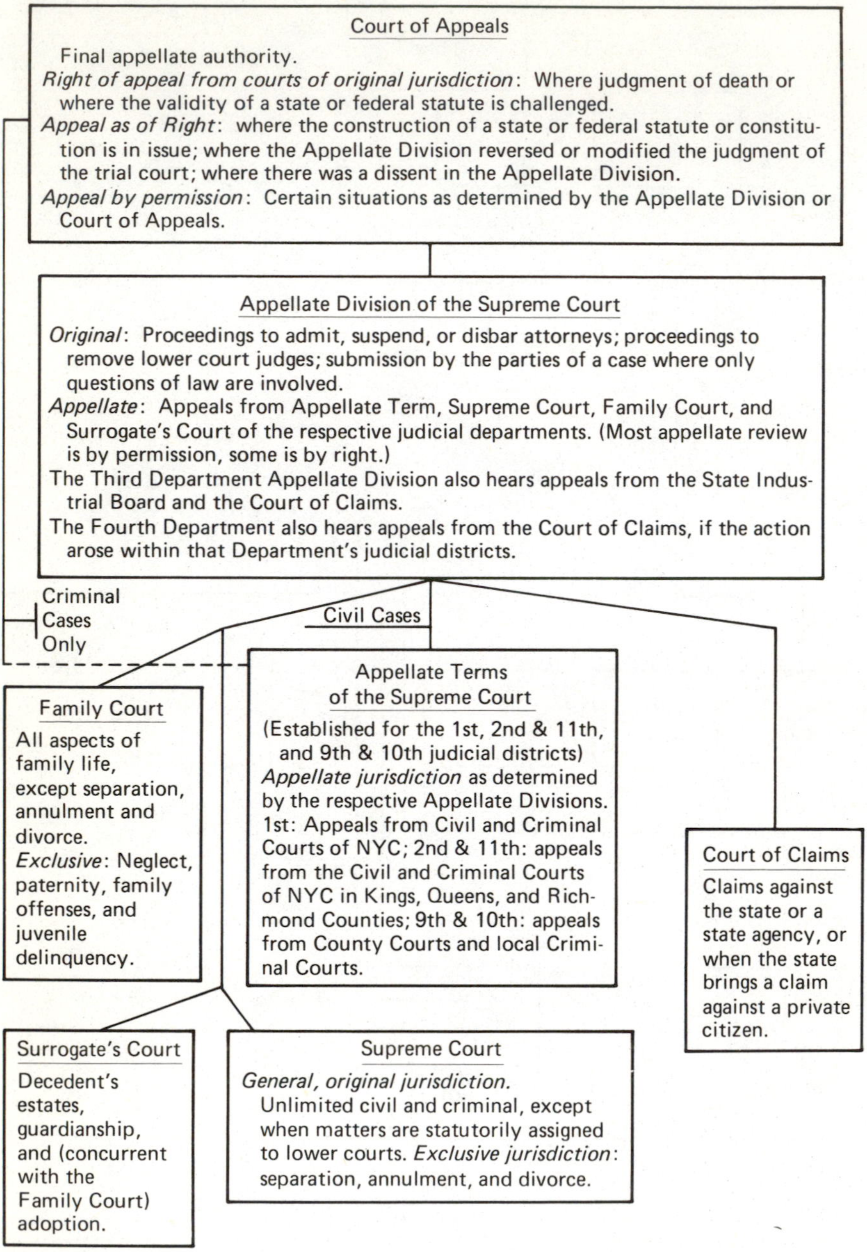

Court of Appeals

Final appellate authority.

Right of appeal from courts of original jurisdiction: Where judgment of death or where the validity of a state or federal statute is challenged.

Appeal as of Right: where the construction of a state or federal statute or constitution is in issue; where the Appellate Division reversed or modified the judgment of the trial court; where there was a dissent in the Appellate Division.

Appeal by permission: Certain situations as determined by the Appellate Division or Court of Appeals.

Appellate Division of the Supreme Court

Original: Proceedings to admit, suspend, or disbar attorneys; proceedings to remove lower court judges; submission by the parties of a case where only questions of law are involved.

Appellate: Appeals from Appellate Term, Supreme Court, Family Court, and Surrogate's Court of the respective judicial departments. (Most appellate review is by permission, some is by right.)

The Third Department Appellate Division also hears appeals from the State Industrial Board and the Court of Claims.

The Fourth Department also hears appeals from the Court of Claims, if the action arose within that Department's judicial districts.

Criminal Cases Only

Civil Cases

Family Court

All aspects of family life, except separation, annulment and divorce.

Exclusive: Neglect, paternity, family offenses, and juvenile delinquency.

Appellate Terms of the Supreme Court

(Established for the 1st, 2nd & 11th, and 9th & 10th judicial districts)

Appellate jurisdiction as determined by the respective Appellate Divisions. 1st: Appeals from Civil and Criminal Courts of NYC; 2nd & 11th: appeals from the Civil and Criminal Courts of NYC in Kings, Queens, and Richmond Counties; 9th & 10th: appeals from County Courts and local Criminal Courts.

Court of Claims

Claims against the state or a state agency, or when the state brings a claim against a private citizen.

Surrogate's Court

Decedent's estates, guardianship, and (concurrent with the Family Court) adoption.

Supreme Court

General, original jurisdiction.

Unlimited civil and criminal, except when matters are statutorily assigned to lower courts. *Exclusive jurisdiction*: separation, annulment, and divorce.

Figure 5–10. New York State General Court Structure

2. cases in which the Appellate Division has found facts different from the trial court and enters a judgment or an order on such newly found facts.

A party has the right to appeal directly to the Court of Appeals from a trial court where:

1. a judgment of death has been rendered,

2. a New York or United States statute is claimed to be unconstitutional and that is the only issue in the case,

3. the Appellate Division has granted an interlocutory judgment or denied a motion for a new trial, or affirmed such a final judgment, but in these cases the Court of Appeals will only review the prior determination of the Appellate Division.

A party has the right to appeal to the Court of Appeals from a final judgment of the Appellate Division if:

1. the construction of the state or federal constitution is directly involved or the validity of a state or federal statute under the state or federal constitution is involved. (On such an appeal only the constitutional question can be considered.),

2. the Appellate Division reversed or modified the judgment of the trial court,

3. there was a dissent in the Appellate Division,

4. from an Appellate Division order granting a new trial where the appellant stipulates that, upon affirmance, judgment absolute shall be rendered against him.

An appeal may be taken to the Court of Appeals by permission:

1. from a final judgment or order of the Appellate Division, or of the trial court which is not appealable as of right (by permission of the Appellate Division or the Court of Appeals).

2. from a nonfinal order of the Appellate Division in a proceeding involving a public office or agency (by permission of the Appellate Division or the Court of Appeals).

3. from a nonfinal judgment of the Appellate Division, or from a judgment of the Appellate Division in an action originating in a court other than the supreme, county, surrogate's court, or the court of claims (only by permission of the Appellate Division).

The Court of Appeals, in addition to its constitutional and statutory appellate duties, promulgates rules governing qualifications for attorneys seeking admission to the state bar, supplemented by rules of the four Appellate Divisions.

For the 1976 proposed constitutional amendment to change the method of selecting Court of Appeals judges, see the section on "Court Administration."

Appellate Division of the Supreme Court. The constitution of the state of New York establishes an Appellate Division of the supreme court. The state is divided into four judicial departments, each of which contains an Appellate Division of the supreme court. The First Department includes only the First Judicial

District. The Second Department consists of the Second, Ninth, Tenth, and Eleventh Judicial Districts. The Third Department includes the Third, Fourth, and Sixth Judicial Districts. The Fourth Department consists of the Fifth, Seventh, and Eighth Judicial Districts. Justices of the Appellate Division are compensated $51,627, with presiding justices receiving $55,266.

Appellate Division justices are appointed to the court for a period of five years. They are designated by the governor from among the supreme court justices. A majority of those appointed, including the presiding justice, must be residents of the department. The presiding justice is appointed for the balance of his or her term as a supreme court justice, the others for five years or for the remainder of their unexpired terms, if less than five years. Appellate division justices must retire upon reaching the age of seventy. They may continue to serve as temporary or additional justices of the Appellate Division until the age of seventy-six upon certification every two years that they are in good health. When the volume of appeals warrants it, the governor may appoint one or more supreme court justices to sit temporarily as Appellate Division judges. The normal complement of Appellate Division justices is seven for the First and Second Departments and five in the Third and Fourth Departments. In the First and Second Departments, however, no more than five may hear an appeal.

Original jurisdiction is exercised by the Appellate Divisions in all departments in the following cases:

1. proceedings to admit, suspend, or disbar attorneys,

2. proceedings to remove lower court judges (up to September 1, 1976. (See the section on "Judicial Conduct.")

3. submission by the parties of a case where only questions of law are involved—i.e., there are no disputed facts.

The Appellate Division of the First Department, located in Manhattan, reviews cases arising in the following courts:

1. Appellate term of the supreme court of the First Judicial District (civil cases). Criminal cases go directly from the appellate term to the Court of Appeals, by law,

2. Supreme court of the First Judicial District,

3. Family court (First Department).

4. Surrogate's court (First Department).

The Appellate Divisions of the Third and Fourth Departments review cases from lower courts, within their respective departments. The Third Department Appellate Division in Albany also hears appeals from the State Industrical Board and from the court of claims (to be described hereafter). The Appellate Division of the Fourth Department is located in Rochester.

The Appellate Division may hear an appeal taken by right from an action originating in the supreme court or a county court, involving:

1. a final judgment incorporating actionable issues,

2. an order concerning a provisional remedy, an application to resettle a tran-

script or statement on appeal, an order granting a new trial, the merits of the case, the substantial rights of the parties, or a finding that a state statute is unconstitutional.

A party may bring an appeal to the Appellate Division by permission of the court when the case concerns:

1. an order made pursuant to an administrative proceeding, or requiring or rejecting a more definite statement in a pleading, or resulting from a request that scandalous or prejudicial matters be stricken from the pleadings,

2. a matter not otherwise appealable by right,

3. a judgment or order from a court of original instance and lesser jurisdiction,

4. an order of the appellate term which determines an appeal from a judgment or order of a lower court.

In addition, the Appellate Division or any justice of that court may vacate or modify an ex parte order issued by a supreme court justice.

Provision is made for the transfer of appeals from an overburdened department to another department by majority vote of the four presiding justices. During the year 1973—1974, the First Department disposed of 1,663 appeals, the Second Department disposed of 2,287 appeals, the Third Department, 1,175 appeals, and the Fourth Department, 847 appeals.

Appellate Terms. The Judiciary Article of the constitution provides that the Appellate Division of each department may establish an appellate term of the supreme court. There are three appellate terms, one for the First Judicial District (Bronx and New York Counties), one for the Second and Eleventh Judicial Districts (Kings, Richmond, and Queens Counties) and one for the Ninth and Tenth Judicial District (Rockland, Westchester, Nassau, Suffolk, Orange, Putnam, and Dutchess Counties).

The appellate terms of the supreme court have appellate jurisdiction in cases as specified which would otherwise be heard by the Appellate Divisions. The appellate term of the First Judicial District hears appeals from the civil and criminal courts of the city of New York. The appellate term for the Second and Eleventh Judicial Districts hears appeals from the civil and criminal courts of New York City in the counties of Kings, Richmond, and Queens. The appellate term of the Ninth and Tenth Judicial Districts hears appeals in criminal misdemeanor cases from the county courts and from local criminal courts within the seven counties of these districts. Appeals from rulings of the appellate terms in criminal cases are to the Court of Appeals and to the Appellate Divisions in civil cases.

Five supreme court justices in the above mentioned judicial districts sit in the appellate terms. The appellate terms of the supreme court disposed of 2,475 appeals in the 1973—1974 judicial year.

Trial Courts

Supreme Court. The highest state court of original and general jurisdiction in law and equity is the supreme court of the state of New York, established by the constitution of the state of New York. As indicated above, the state is divided into eleven judicial districts, each consisting of one or more counties. In multicounty districts, the supreme court is located in each of the counties in the district (with the exception of Hamilton County in District 4). The city of New York and the five counties which comprise it are served by three judicial districts—the First Judicial District with court locations in New York and Bronx Counties: the Second Judicial District with court locations in Kings and Richmond Counties, and the Eleventh Judicial District in Queens County. The supreme court has jurisdiction by law over all crimes; however, in counties outside the city of New York, this jurisdiction is commonly exercised by the county court with the supreme court having an occasional criminal term, as needed. In the five counties which comprise the city of New York, the supreme court has and exercises jurisdiction over all felonies and misdemeanors prosecuted by indictment. The supreme court has unlimited original civil jurisdiction in law and equity and has exclusive jurisdiction over separation, annulment, and divorce proceedings. Jury trials are available in both civil and criminal cases. Appeals are to the Appellate Division of the supreme court and are heard on the record.

Supreme court justices are elected by the people for terms of fourteen years. To be eligible for election, a supreme court justice must have been admitted to the practice of law for at least ten years. For purposes of election, the state is divided into eleven judicial districts. Each judicial district, with the exception of the new Eleventh District, which consists only of the county of Queens, contains more than one county. A supreme court justice may hold court in any county and may be temporarily assigned by the Appellate Division of his department to the supreme court in any judicial district. While on the bench, supreme court justices are forbidden to hold another public office or engage in the practice of law.

Justices of the supreme court in the First to the Eleventh Judicial Districts are paid $48,998. Supreme court justices must retire upon reaching age seventy. However, they may continue to serve as justices of the supreme court until the age of seventy-six upon certification by the Administrative Board every two years that they are in good health.

On June 30, 1974, there were 257 supreme court trial justices in New York State. This represents an increase of almost 107 authorized judgeships since 1960. While the constitution authorizes the creation of one judgeship for every 50,000 people in a judicial district, such a uniform ratio has not been established. Thus, there exists one judge for 50,000 persons in the First Judicial District (Manhattan and the Bronx), while in the Eleventh Judicial District (Queens) there is one judge for every 100,000 residents. Most of the justices sit in trial or special term. Trial term refers to the trial of law cases, jury and nonjury. Civil jury cases tried in the supreme court may be decided by a verdict of five-sixth of the panel. A party to an action may demand either a jury of twelve or a jury of six members, the latter for one-half the costs of a twelve-man jury. Equity cases and motions are heard at special term. Reference must be made to the rules of the various courts to ascertain their specific practices.

Court of Claims. The state is sovereign and, therefore, cannot be sued without its consent. By legislation, and ultimately by constitutional provision, the state has waived its immunity for liability for certain claims. In general, when a private citizen has a claim against the state, or against certain state agencies, or when the state of New York wishes to bring a claim against a private citizen, suit must be brought in the court of claims. The attorney general represents the state in all proceedings by or against it in the court of claims. Appeals from the court of claims are taken to the Appellate Division of the Third Department except that appeals in claims arising in the Fourth Department are taken to the Fourth Department. The procedure and jurisdiction of the court of claims are governed by the Court of Claims Act and the New York Civil Practice Act, the former prevailing if there is an inconsistency between the two. The judges are appointed by the governor with the consent of the state Senate. They are appointed for a nine-year term, subject to the same qualifications and restrictions as justices of the supreme court. Each judge receives the same salary as justices of the supreme court, $48,998, with $1,627 extra for the presiding judge appointed by the governor.

The court of claims can hear cases arising anywhere in the state. Generally, no more than four judges of the court of claims will hear a claim while sitting in one of the court's nine districts. The office of the central clerk is located in Albany, where the court of claims has a regularly assigned courtroom. In addition, the court maintains chambers in New York City. Elsewhere, the sheriff of each county is required to provide necessary courtroom facilities. During the 1973–1974 judicial year, the court of claims had seventeen authorized judges and held 1,578 daily sessions. One thousand and thirty new claims were filed and 1,266 claims were disposed of. Eight hundred and fifty-two of the dispositions were by dismissal and 414 resulted in award. In addition, the court disposed of 936 motions.

An emergency Dangerous Drug Control Program was established by statute dated June 11, 1973 to cope with increasing violations of the criminal law respecting the sale, purchase, and use of enumerated narcotics. The law included a provision for up to 100 additional criminal court parts in the supreme court and up to 68 additional court of claims judges to handle the anticipated caseload. By July 1, 1974, the governor with the advice and consent of the Senate had appointed thirty-six one-term judges of the court of claims to serve in the supreme court for a period of nine years. (This measure was taken because while the governor appoints court of claims judges, new supreme court judgeships created by the legislature must be filled by election.) These judges may not be reappointed; the judgeships expire when they become vacant. Although there were not as many narcotics arrests as expected, these judges are serving in the supreme court mainly in the processing of all felony cases.

Family Court. There is one family court in each of the counties outside of the city of New York and one family court for New York City in each of the five counties. There are 132 family court judges. The family court of the state of New York replaced the domestic relations court of the city of New York, the girl's term court of the city of New York and the children's court in other counties. The family court has jurisdiction over all aspects of family life, except for separation, annulment and divorce. Its jurisdiction is exclusive over cases involving neglect, paternity, family offenses, and juvenile delinquency. While the supreme court is given exclusive jurisdiction over matrimonial actions (separation, annulment, and divorce), the family court is given jurisdiction to hear and determine the support and custody aspects of these actions when such matters are referred to it by the supreme court.

A juvenile delinquent is defined as a person over the age of seven and under the age of sixteen who commits an act which, if done by an adult, would constitute a crime. The family court also has jurisdiction over "persons in need of supervision." These are males under sixteen and females under eighteen who are habitual truants or who are incorrigible, ungovernable, or habitually disobedient and beyond lawful control of parental or other lawful authority. The opportunity to adjust problems on a voluntary basis without a formal court appearance is afforded by an "intake" service. A program of law guardians, or counsel appointed to represent children at delinquency and neglect proceedings, has been established.

Although under the Reorganization Amendment the family court was to exercise exclusive jurisdiction over adoption proceedings, the surrogate's court retains concurrent adoption jurisdiction. Appeals from the family court are taken to the Appellate Division of the supreme court for the department in which the family court is located.

The judges of the former domestic relations court became family court judges for the remainder of their terms. At present, thirty-nine judges are authorized for the New York City Family Court. They receive an annual salary of $42,451 and are appointed by the mayor for the term of ten years. Family court judges serve subject to the same restrictions applicable to other judges in New York City.

The Surrogate's Court. There is a surrogate's court in every county including the five counties comprising New York City. There are six surrogates in New York City (two in New York County). There are thirty-five surrogates (including the six in New York City) in New York State. In addition, outside New York City, there are nine county court judges who are also surrogates and twenty-seven county court judges who are surrogate and family court judges. In New York City the surrogates receive $48,998 annually. Outside New York City they receive from $36,000 to $48,998.

Surrogates in New York City are elected by the voters to a fourteen-year term. Outside of New York City surrogates are elected on a county basis for a ten-year term. To be eligible for election as surrogate, an attorney must have practiced for at least five years. Surrogates are forbidden to hold any other public office, or to practice law during their terms.

Surrogates have jurisdiction of decedent's estates, guardianship and, under special legislation, concurrent jurisdiction with the family court over the adoption of children. Appeals from the surrogates' decision are taken to the Appellate Division of the appropriate department.

Courts in New York City

New York State voters approved a sweeping Court Reorganization Amendment in 1961. Although county, city, and other local courts throughout the state were affected, the most significant changes embodied in the Amendment and subsequent implementing legislation affected New York City. New York City includes within its borders five counties and five boroughs. Technically, the counties are divisions of the state and the boroughs are divisions of the city; but in fact, each county is coterminous with one of the boroughs. The names of the counties (and the names of the borough, in parentheses) are: New York County (Manhattan); Kings County (Brooklyn); Bronx County (The Bronx); Queens County (Queens); and Richmond County (Richmond or Staten Island). The court structure in New York City is best understood in terms of courts exercising concurrent borough and county jurisdiction.

Under legislation effective September 1, 1962, implementing the Court Reorganization Amendment, New York City's court system was simplified with the creation of a single citywide court with civil jurisdiction up to a maximum of $10,000 and a single citywide court with criminal jurisdiction over violations of law other than those prosecuted by indictment and over actions not within the exclusive jurisdiction of the supreme court. These two courts may be merged by the state legislature at the request of the mayor and the city council. The court of general sessions of New York County and the county courts of Bronx, Kings, Queens, and Richmond have been abolished, and their judges, cases, personnel, and facilities transferred to the supreme court, which presently exercises county-wide jurisdiction in New York's five counties.

The courts as presently constituted in New York City are as follows:

Criminal Court of the City of New York. The courts of special sessions and city magistrate's courts have been abolished and replaced by this single court.

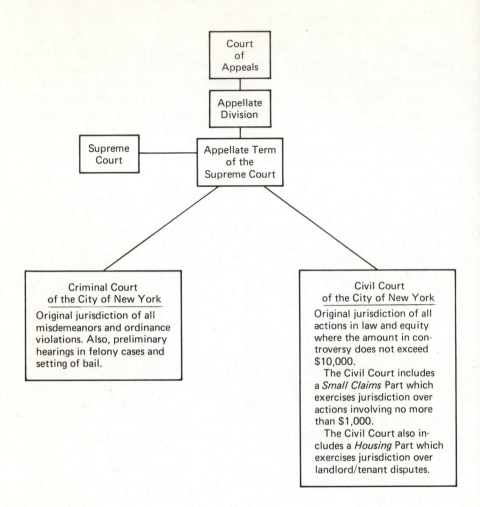

Figure 5–11.   Courts of Limited Jurisdiction *Within* New York City

The judges of the New York City Criminal Court hear, try, and determine all charges of misdemeanors, except charges of criminal libel. They also determine all offenses of a grade less than misdemeanor, but in no case can a judge try an action presented by an indictment. The judges of the criminal court exercise powers formerly vested in magistrates, including the power to set bail and punish for contempt. This court is the arraignment court for felonies.

Practice and procedure in the criminal court are governed by the Criminal Procedure Law. Trial of a misdemeanor is by a single judge without a jury where the term of imprisonment is not more than six months; where the term may be more than six months, the trial is by a jury of six unless the defendant waives the jury. Appeals are taken to the appellate term for the First and Second Departments. There are ninety-eight criminal court judges.

The twenty-four justices of the former court of special sessions and the fifty-four magistrate's courts justices became judges of the New York City Criminal Court for the remainder of their terms. Since then, judges have been appointed to the criminal court by the mayor for terms of ten years. Judges so appointed must reside in New York City and must have been admitted to the practice of law in New York State for at least ten years. Criminal court judges may not hold any other public office or engage in the practice of law while on the bench. They receive a salary of $42,451 per annum. Mandatory retirement for criminal court judges is at age seventy.

For the calendar year 1973–1974, there were 185,853 arrest cases, 431,071 summons cases (traffic and others), making a grand total of 636,924 cases in this court. Of the arrest cases, 29,130 were violations, 76,352 misdemeanors, 74,627 felonies, and 5,744 others.

When Robert Wagner was mayor of New York City in 1954–1965, he initiated the Mayor's Committee on the Judiciary, which screens potential judicial candidates for judgeships. The committee composed of laymen and lawyers, simply recommends or fails to recommend persons interviewed for judicial office. The mayor is not bound to make appointments solely from those recommended, however. Mayors in recent years have promised not to appoint a person not recommended. The mayor may and does recommend persons to the committee for screening.

Traffic Violations. Up to July 1, 1970 traffic violations were handled in the criminal courts. Thus persons accused of committing a traffic violation were subject to criminal procedures and time-consuming and costly processes. The stigma and delays associated with criminal courts were suffered by even minor traffic offenders. In July 1970 a unique new program was inaugurated, said to be the first of its kind in the nation, to handle all traffic cases other than misdemeanors occurring in New York City. The Administrative Adjudication Bureau of the New York State Department of Motor Vehicles hears cases involving moving traffic violations while the Parking Violations Bureau of the New York City Transportation Administration hears parking, stopping, standing, and jaywalking violations. Other offenses (including traffic misdemeanors) and certain nontraffic violations are heard in the criminal court.

By emphasizing an educational rather than a punitive approach to the handling of traffic violations, the administrative adjudication system is designed to improve driver safety by providing efficient administration and convenience to the public. Individual rights are preserved and effective enforcement of traffic laws maintained.

By removing from the criminal court the nearly one million traffic summonses issued for moving violations in New York City each year, this program aids the administration of criminal justice and permits the release of eighteen judges so that they may spend their full time on serious criminal matters.

Since the program is self-supporting, persons who do not receive traffic summonses do not have to share in the cost of operating this new administrative adjudication program.

Experienced lawyers, appointed by the commissioner of motor vehicles, trained by professional highway safety administrators, serve as hearing officers in cases involving pleas of guilty with explanation or not guilty.

Every summons issued for a moving traffic violation in New York City specifies the date of appearance for hearings or not guilty pleas. That date is approximately one month after the summons is issued.

Testimony in each case is electronically recorded and penalties are determined upon a determination of guilty only after review of the motorist's driving record, which appears on a visual display unit on the hearing officer's desk.

The booklet explaining the new system for dealing with traffic violations states:

> Guilty pleas may be made by mail, except in cases of excessive speeding or where conviction may result in suspension or revocation of a motorist's driver's license. In those instances, a notice of required appearance will be mailed to the motorist informing him of when and where to appear for a hearing. Also, guilty pleas, with explanation, may be made at any of the five Hearing Office locations. All guilty pleas must be made on or before the Date of Appearance indicated on the summons.
>
> Not guilty pleas may be made by mail or in person at any of the Hearing Office locations indicated below, within ten days after the issuance of a Summons. Hearings will be held on the Date of Appearance and at the time designated on the Summons. . . .
>
> A first adjournment will be granted for reasonable cause and may be arranged by a motorist, prior to the Date of Appearance, in person or by mail or by telephone at the Hearing Office Location at which the hearing was to be held. A second or subsequent adjournment may be granted only at the discretion of a Hearing Officer, and the request must be made in person.
>
> An appeal from an adverse decision of a Hearing Officer may be made, within 30 days, to the Appeals Board of the Bureau. There is a $10 fee required upon filing an appeal. Any suspension or revocation of a driver's license which has been imposed may be stayed during the period of appeal. Where a transcript has been submitted with an administrative appeal, judicial review of the Appeals Board's decision may be sought in the New York State Supreme Court.

In 1972, the supervising referee reported in substance as follows:

> Of 629,000 complaints written by the police, 119,000 were paid by mail directly to Albany, 57,000 were paid in New York City, and 232 pleaded

guilty with an explanation. Of the 34,000 contested, almost 18,000, or fifty-two percent, were convicted after a hearing. Of the remaining cases, some were transferred to the criminal court, and others constituted the twenty percent scofflaw rate.

Civil Court of the City of New York. The city court and municipal court have been abolished and replaced by a single court, the civil court of the city of New York with branches in each of the five counties. This court is given jurisdiction over actions and proceedings for the recovery of money where the amount in controversy does not exceed $10,000, or where the value of property sought to be recovered does not exceed that amount. A jury verdict may be rendered by five-sixths of the panel and a jury panel is composed of six persons. The civil court also has jurisdiction over certain equity actions involving realty, provided the property is not valued at over $10,000.

Small Claims Part of the Civil Court. The informal procedure employed in small claims actions, which formerly existed in the municipal court, is retained, with the jurisdictional amount being increased to $1,000 for the small claims part of the civil court. In that part, the court clerk serves the summons by mail. Corporations may not commence actions in the small claims part. Trial may be had within two weeks of service of summons. Unpaid arbitrators (in certain counties arbitrators receive a minimum fee), who are lawyers who have been practicing for at least five years and who have been approved by the court, help adjudicate small claims, serving as judge only if parties to the action consent. There is no appeal from the arbitrator's decision. Arbitrators receive special training, attend seminars, and are members of the National Association of Trial Judges. Sessions of the small claims part are held exclusively in the evening. During the judicial year July 1, 1973 to June 30, 1974, over 60,000 small claims were disposed of while a total of 85,631 cases were terminated by the major parts of the civil court.

The twenty-seven justices of the city court and sixty-eight municipal court justices became judges of the civil court for the remainder of their terms. There are now 120 civil court judges. They must be admitted to the bar in New York State for at least ten years. Civil court judges are not permitted to hold any other public office while serving on the bench, nor may they engage in the practice of law. The judges of the civil court—all of whom must reside within New York City—are each paid a salary of $42,451 per year. They must retire upon attaining the age of seventy.

Housing Part of the Civil Court. In October 1973 a housing court was established in the city of New York as part of the civil court. Its objective is to treat all problems arising in a residence in one "single unified continued legal proceeding." These had formerly been distributed among the criminal court and a number of city departments. In the words of the administrative judge, Supreme Court Justice Edward J. Thompson:

> The objective of this landmark legislation was to retard the deterioration of residential buildings followed by their abandonment. The mode of enforcement of city housing maintenance codes was changed drastically in order to conserve and improve existing housing and to encourage new vitally-needed housing investment by meting out justice to *both* tenants and owners. Rehabilitation was to be the new order of the day.
>
> Prior to the enactment of this statute, the traditional method of enforcing housing standards was by prosecution in the Criminal Court. Minimal fines imposed by judges to whom these cases were essentially non-criminal in nature. A minority of irresponsible owners treated fines as one more small cost of doing business. Moreover, a minority of tenants incited by publicity seeking crusaders fomented plans which served only as a roadblock to housing rehabilitation. The serious decline in older housing served as mute testimony to the futility of then existing methods of enforcing housing code standards.
>
> By legislative enactment, the fragmented jurisdiction which formerly impeded satisfactory disposition of all matters affecting housing was ended. Instead, *all* actions and proceedings relating to housing in any building must now be brought and consolidated in the Housing Court. A mandated cross-index system lists all such cases by street address, thus outlining for use by the court the total profile of a building including the owners, occupants, violations and finances where known. Actual court inspections of premises are encouraged and frequently performed. The court is obliged to exercise meaningful continuing supervision over problem buildings. Regardless of the relief originally sought, the court is empowered to employ *any remedy, program or sanction authorized by law, including the expenditure of monies appropriated by the City unless vetoed, in order to enforce housing standards and protect the public interest.*

An Advisory Council, made up of fourteen nonlawyers, serving without compensation and representing the real estate industry, tenant organizations, civic groups, and the bar associations, is entrusted to review the operations of this court. Twelve members were appointed by the administrative judge, one each by the mayor and the governor.

Sixteen hearing officers have been appointed by the administrative judge. These were selected after screening by the Advisory Council. All are qualified lawyers who are given a thirty-day orientation course. Their determinations are final and are appealable on the record to the appellate term. In equity cases, the hearing officers hear and report on such matters as are referred to them by the judge presiding in the housing court. Hearings are recorded mechanically unless reporters are available to produce a record manually.

The 1974 report of the civil court of the city of New York entitled *Civil Jus-*

tice in a Dynamic City, states that the housing court has considerably "expanded its dimensions, targets and aims by means of legislative enactment, administrative directives and judicial determination." Its operation has led to rent strike settlements and to judgments to the city of New York for monies it had expended for emergency repair programs. Civil penalties were imposed on landlords and, in a few rare sentences, jail sentences plus fines were ordered. It is reported that the work of this court in settling disputes between landlord and tenant and in preserving property rights has proven effective and worthwhile.

The housing court, however, is not without its critics. In an article appearing in the New York Times of August 6, 1976, at page 44, an investigatory reporter enumerates the shortcomings as described by lawyers, landlords, and tenants who use the court. Although it is agreed that the housing court is better than the chaotic system it replaced, it is "beset with delays, poor coordination with other housing agencies and seriously inadequate staff and quarters in some of its busiest branches . . . Not surprisingly the real estate and tenant advocates often disagree on why it is allegedly defective, with each side insisting that the court is unfairly oriented in favor of the other."

A response to the critics of the housing court procedures by Justice Edward Thompson, deputy city administrative judge for the civil branches of the supreme court and administrative judge of the civil court appears in the New York Law Journal of August 25, 1976, at page 1. He points out that those difficulties which exist are due mainly to failure of lawyers to follow required procedures and the great care the housing judges must exercise to conform to the statutes.

Courts Outside of New York City

County Courts. There are fifty-seven counties in New York State outside of New York City, each of which has at least one county judge. County court judges are elected by the residents of the county for a term of ten years, except special county judges, who are elected for six-year terms. County court judges receive an annual salary of from $36,000 to $48,998, depending on the county in which they serve. County court judges must have been admitted to the New York State Bar for at least five years prior to their election, and while in office they are forbidden to practive law or hold any other public office.

County courts exercise civil jurisdiction (often concurrently with other courts of lesser jurisdiction) where the amount sought to be recovered or the value of the claim does not exceed $6,000, or where proceedings are brought to recover possession of real property, or to remove a tenant therefrom. However, if the local legislative body so requests, the jurisdictional limit may be raised to $10,000 for cases in which the defendant resides in, or conducts business within, the county limits. In general, county court civil jurisdiction extends to all cases not within the exclusive jurisdiction of the supreme court. County courts also exer-

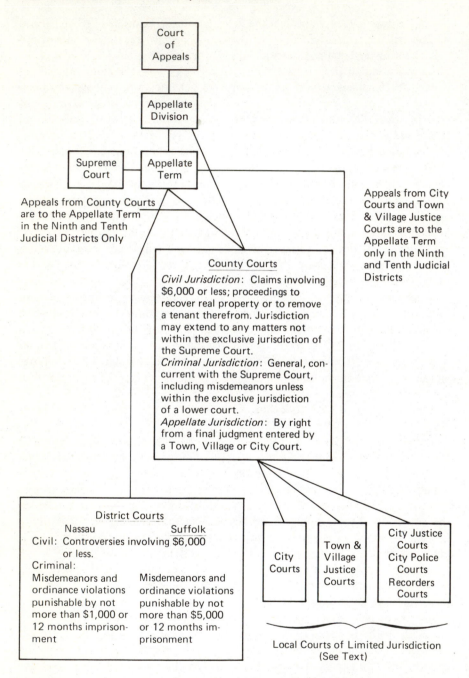

Court of Appeals

Appellate Division

Supreme Court   **Appellate Term**

Appeals from County Courts are to the Appellate Term in the Ninth and Tenth Judicial Districts Only

Appeals from City Courts and Town & Village Justice Courts are to the Appellate Term only in the Ninth and Tenth Judicial Districts

County Courts

Civil Jurisdiction: Claims involving $6,000 or less; proceedings to recover real property or to remove a tenant therefrom. Jurisdiction may extend to any matters not within the exclusive jurisdiction of the Supreme Court.
Criminal Jurisdiction: General, concurrent with the Supreme Court, including misdemeanors unless within the exclusive jurisdiction of a lower court.
Appellate Jurisdiction: By right from a final judgment entered by a Town, Village or City Court.

District Courts

Nassau   Suffolk
Civil: Controversies involving $6,000 or less.
Criminal:

| Misdemeanors and ordinance violations punishable by not more than $1,000 or 12 months imprisonment | Misdemeanors and ordinance violations punishable by not more than $5,000 or 12 months imprisonment |

City Courts

Town & Village Justice Courts

City Justice Courts
City Police Courts
Recorders Courts

Local Courts of Limited Jurisdiction (See Text)

Figure 5–12.   Courts of Limited Jurisdiction *Outside* New York City

cise considerable equity jurisdiction, as provided by law, although a claim against which a counterclaim for more than $6,000 is entered may be removed to the supreme court.

County courts have general criminal jurisdiction concurrent with the supreme court over all crimes prosecuted by indictment (i.e., felonies) as well as misdemeanors and offenses not within the exclusive jurisdiction of other lower courts. They are the major trial courts for criminal cases outside the city of New York.

Appeals from some of the courts of lesser jurisdiction may be taken to the county court by right from a final judgment entered by a town, village, or city court. Appeals may be taken to county courts, as provided by law, from interlocutory judgments or orders. Appellate jurisdiction of the county court is subject to alteration by the legislature, since the legislature may provide than an appellate term of the supreme court will assume the appellate jurisdiction of the county court. Appeals from the county court are to the Appellate Division of the supreme court in the Ninth and Tenth Judicial Districts or to the appellate term of the supreme court.

As of June 30, 1974, there were 100 county court judges outside of New York City, 56 of whom are full-time judges in the county court only, 9 of whom serve also as surrogates, 8 of whom serve also as family court judges, and 27 of whom are surrogates and family court judges as well as county judges.

District Courts. Under the New York State constitution a district court may be established by the legislature at the request of the Board of Supervisors of a county and with the approval of the electors at a general election. There are two such district courts, the Nassau County District Court and the Suffolk County District Court.

An entire county or a portion of a county may lie within the jurisdiction of the district court. The geographic area within the court's jurisdiction is divided into various districts.

Nassau County and Suffolk County District Courts. Criminal jurisdiction of the Nassau County District Court embraces misdemeanors and ordinance violations punishable by not more than $1,000 fine or twelve months in jail.

The Suffolk County District Court has original criminal jurisdiction of felonies, misdemeanors, and ordinance violations punishable by not more than $5,000 fine or twelve months in jail.

Both district courts have jurisdiction of civil cases of up to $6,000. Jury trials are available in both civil and criminal cases. Appeals are to the appellate term. If a district court were to be established in a county that has no appellate term, an appeal from the district court would go to the county court.

There are presently twenty-six judges including the presiding judge in Nassau County District Court and twenty-three judges including the presiding judge in Suffolk County. Judges are elected for six years, the presiding judge on a county-wide basis, the others from the towns comprising each district. District court judges must be admitted to practice law in New York for at least five years. The presiding judge in Nassau County is paid $44,500; the twenty-five associates receive $42,000. In Suffolk County, the presiding judge receives $43,170, while the associate judges are paid $39,030.

City Courts. The New York State constitution provides for the continuing existence of inferior civil and criminal courts in towns, villages, and cities outside the city of New York. There is a city court operating in each of the sixty-one cities outside the city of New York.

City courts have original criminal jurisdiction of crimes punishable by not more than $1,000 fine and twelve months in jail. City courts may also conduct preliminary hearings in felony cases. City courts have original civil jurisdiction in civil actions at law (including small claims), where the amount in demand is less than $6,000. Jury trials are available in city courts. Appeals are to the county court. In cities within the Ninth and Tenth Judicial Districts, appeals are to the appellate term of the supreme court for those districts.

Most city courts have one or two judges, with the city courts in the larger cities having more. City court judges are elected by the electors of their city on a partisan ballot for terms as established by local law. The salaries are also set locally. For city court judges whose salaries are over $30,000, $10,000 thereof is furnished by the state. There are no requirements for legal training. (See the section on "Judicial Seminars and Training Programs.")

City Justice Courts, City Police Courts, Recorders Courts

The constitution of New York State provides continuing inferior civil and criminal courts in towns, villages, and cities outside of the city of New York. Variously named local courts are currently operating in cities outside of the city of New York.

City police (seven courts) and recorders courts (four courts) exercise original criminal jurisdiction over crimes (mainly traffic violations) punishable by not more than $1,000 fine or twelve months in jail. City justice courts (seven courts) exercise limited civil jurisdiction (mostly small claims) where the amount in demand does not exceed $500 or $1,000. The limit in civil cases for recorders courts is $3,000. Jury trials are available in all of these courts. Appeals are to the county court.

There are one to two judges in each of the above named courts. Judges may be elected by the electors of the city or appointed by the city officials. There are no requirements for legal training. (See the section on "Judicial Seminars and Training Programs.") Salaries and terms are set locally.

Town and Village Justice Courts. Town and village justice courts are organized in towns and villages throughout the state. There are 2,240 justices of town and village justice courts who perform judicial functions.

Justice courts exercise original criminal jurisdiction (mostly traffic violations) over crimes punishable by not more than $1,000 fine or twelve months in jail. Justice courts also exercise original civil jurisdiction (generally small claims) where the amount in demand does not exceed $1,000. Jury trials are available in justice courts. Appeals are to the county court. In towns and villages within the Ninth and Tenth Judicial Districts, appeals are to the appellate term of the supreme court for those districts.

There are two justices of the peace authorized for town justice courts and one justice of the peace for village justice courts, although the village justice may be, and frequently is, a town justice as well. Town justices are elected by the electors of the town at the annual town meeting. Village justices may be elected or appointed by village officials. Justices of the peace serve four-year terms. There are no requirements for legal training. (See the section on "Judicial Seminars and Training Programs.") Salaries are set locally. There is no fee system for these justices in the state of New York.

Judicial Seminar and Training Programs

In New York, the need for training judicial and nonjudicial employees has been recognized for a number of years. Programs extending over a period of at least one week to orient newly elected judges have been offered for the past ten or twelve years. Judges from supreme, county, family, surrogate's, civil, criminal, and city courts throughout the state have received such orientation. A wide variety of substantive and procedural subjects are discussed with lawyers, professors, and judges who are experts in the various fields.

Since 1962, the Office of Court Administration (formerly the Judicial Conference) has conducted seminars and training programs for over 13,970 New York State judges and justices, designed to acquaint judges with new legislation affecting the courts and to update them on developments in the law. Mandated by statute, the Office of Court Administration conducts training for town and village justices, designed to give a basic education to incumbents not admitted to practice. They must take a prescribed course for certification to act as judges.

Since March 1972, the Administrative Board has required reelected or reappointed justices to attend an advanced training course to maintain their certification. The types of programs offered, in addition to the seminars for newly elected or appointed judges, are sentencing institutes to discuss in workshops, the developments in New York law relating to sentencing, sentencing alternatives, the role of probation, and the role of the Department of Correctional Services.

There are family court workshops, civil court seminars, conferences of supreme court justices criminal term and judges of the criminal court, state trial judges, surrogates' seminars, and town and village justices programs, mentioned above. There have been two-week seminars for newly appointed court of claims judges, designated to serve under the "Dangerous Drug Program." Annually, there is a Conference of New York State Trial Judges "to enable trial judges in courts of superior jurisdiction to better perform the function of their office by keeping abreast of everchanging law." In 1975, 765 judges and 1,424 town and village justices attended Office of Court Administration sponsored programs.

In 1974, a separate office was established within the Office of Court Administration, named the Education and Training Office, to plan, develop, and administer an effective and comprehensive educational and training program for judicial and nonjudicial personnel within the New York State court system. This is in addition to continuing to administer the ongoing Office of Court Administration training programs described above. There is a director of education and training in charge.

The director of education and training has, also, the responsibility for developing nonjudicial training programs. Pilot programs for clericial and other nonjudicial staff were offered in October and November 1975. After being evaluated, the full eight-day or sixty-four-hour program was offered in December 1975, attended by court officers and aides from county, supreme, and family courts in Suffolk County.

The Education and Training Office sponsors and coordinates selective attendance of judicial and nonjudicial personnel at nationally recognized, out-of-state educational programs. In 1975, twenty-five judges attended intensive programs of two weeks duration or longer and thirteen nonjudicial personnel attended two-, four-, and five-week programs outside the state.

Twenty judges attended, mostly during the summer months, one of four different programs, varying in length from two to four weeks at the National College of the State Judiciary in Reno, Nevada. Five family court judges attended the two-week fall course of the National College of Juvenile Justice. In addition, in 1975, 370 justices and judges attended three special evidence seminars to expand their knowledge on the New York law of evidence, specifically how to handle objections to evidence.

On the nonjudicial side, thirteen nonjudicial personnel attended three programs in 1975 at the Institute for Court Management.

New York Court of Appeals judges from time to time attend the Institute of Judicial Administration's Appellate Judges Seminars at New York University School of Law and Appellate Division judges go to interstate Appellate Judges Seminars.

Another interesting development in judicial learning were the New York School of Psychiatry seminars held in New York City in 1975. A small group of judges and psychiatrists met one night a week for thirteen weeks to discuss such topics as: what is mental illness; psychiatrists—what are they and how do they function; fitness to stand trial; the insanity defense; involuntary civil commitment standards; commitment procedures; and the right to receive or resist treatments.

Court Administration—History and Present
Organizational Structure

Prior to the Court Reorganization Amendment of 1962, the only agency providing court administration in the state had been the Judicial Conference, created in 1955, consisting of the chief judge of the Court of Appeals, the presiding justices of the Appellate Divisions and one supreme court justice from each judicial department. In addition, chairmen and ranking members of certain legislative committees could attend meetings of the Judicial Conference and make recommendations. Unfortunately, the conference's powers had been largely those of an advisory group. Except for some control that each Appellate Division had over the supreme court in its judicial district, the courts had been basically autonomous.

The Reorganization Amendment and implementing legislation were designed to provide more effective administration by bringing into the new unified court system all the courts in the state and by giving to the courts the power to administer themselves in such a way that a fully integrated court system would come into being.

The Court Reorganization Amendment placed the ultimate power of statewide court administration in a new body, the Administrative Board of the Judicial Conference, consisting of the chief judge of the Court of Appeals and the presiding justices of the four Appellate Divisions. The board, in consultation with the Judicial Conference, is responsible for the promulgation of standards and policies for general application throughout the state. The Administrative Board is given power to appoint a state administrator, who, in addition to the duties assigned to him by the board, acts as secretary to the board and to the Judicial Conference.

The constitution further provides that the Appellate Divisions shall supervise the administration and operation of the courts in their respective departments in accordance with the standards and administrative policies established by the Administrative Board. A director of administration was appointed by each Appellate Division to assist the division in performing its administrative duties and to serve as secretary to the departmental committee for court administration. There are four departmental committees, each composed of judges and justices serving within the department and members of the bar. The departmental committees are charged with the duty to examine periodically practice and procedures in the department. Each of the Appellate Divisions is empowered to designate as an administrative judge or judges to assist it in the task of administration, one or more judges of any court in its department. An administrative judge would supervise such court or group of courts in the department as the Appellate Division would direct. The legislative grant of powers is broad and includes personnel practices, fiscal practices, administrative methods, assignments and transfers of judges and cases, investigation of complaints, purchase of supplies, and supervision of the preparation of the budgets. Ultimate responsibility for the administration of the courts lies with the presiding justice of each of the Appellate Divisions.

After the Court Reorganization Amendment was approved by the voters, there was concern that separate administration by each Appellate Division could create a problem in New York City, where the new family, civil, and criminal courts are situated within both the First and Second Departments. It was objected that the split administration of these courts by two departments would lead to costly duplication of personnel and services, different procedures, fiscal rivalry between the two parts of the same court for available funds, and general inconvenience and confusion. As a corrective measure, the legislature provided that the Appellate Divisions for the First and Second Departments or the Administrative Board of the Judicial Conference could decide whether there should be joint or separate supervision of each of the New York City courts. Supreme court justices were appointed to serve as administrative judges of the New York City Civil and Criminal Courts, as well as the supreme ·courts for each of the city's counties. In addition, the family court in New York City was given an administrative judge.

Although this change resulted in substantial improvement in the administration of courts in New York, it fell short of accomplishing the desired oversight of the courts.

The illusion of centralized administration was created, but in actuality, division of administrative responsibility was highly fragmented. Responsibility was given—unclearly and sometimes inconsistently—to the Judicial Conference and to the chief judge of the Court of Appeals and to the presiding justices of the Appellate Divisions. No individual or even body of persons could exercise top level administrative authority. No individual or group could be held responsible— the state administrator least of all—because he clearly had no administrative authority.

The Dominick Commission, in its report mentioned above, recommended a complete change in administration. It suggested a constitutional amendment which would abolish both the Judicial Conference and the Administrative Board. In its place there should be a chief administrative judge responsible for the administration of the entire state court system, with power to carry out this responsibility. The chief administrative judge should be appointed, not necessarily from among incumbent judges, by the chief judge of the Court of Appeals for a term of four years.

Before the introduction of a proposed constitutional amendment by the legislature, Chief Judge Charles D. Breitel, acting with the advice and consent of the Administrative Board, appointed state Supreme Court Justice Richard J. Bartlett, who now functions as the state court administrator. This arrangement was then sanctioned by the legislature when it passed, in 1974, a statute permitting a judge to "exercise the functions, powers and duties of the State Administrator." Each chief justice of the four Appellate Divisions named the state administrative judge as the departmental administrative judge for its own department to oversee and coordinate the activities of the other administrative judges of the department. The state court administrator, who is paid $57,000, has administrative authority, under the chief judge of the Court of Appeals, over all the courts in New York State.

The Appellate Divisions in New York City subsequently jointly designated Supreme Court Justice David Ross as the New York City administrative judge "with the responsibility for supervising and coordinating the orderly operation of and the administration of justice" in the courts in New York City. He is paid $51,627 annually.

The legislature also empowered the state administrative judge to establish the Office of Court Administration (OCA). "The primary roles of this office are to recommend policies to the Chief Judge, the Administrative Board and the state administrative judge and to assist them in administering the unified court system." The Office of Court Administration was established in 1974.

Efforts to establish a more centralized administrative arrangement continued. A proposed constitutional amendment failed in 1974 when the electorate rejected the amendment which would have centralized administration and a state takeover of the judicial budget. Early in 1976 New York's Governor Hugh Carey appointed a Task Force on Court Reform. This group prepared a proposed constitutional amendment to the constitution, the essential features being:

1. Replacing the present method of electing judges with a merit selection appointive system;

2. Integrating the multiplicity of trial courts into one single statewide trial court in most areas of the state—the supreme court;

3. Improving the method of disciplining judges by abolishing the cumbersome court on the judiciary, with ultimate authority given to the Court of Appeals and the Appellate Divisions. (The latter for judges other than those on the supreme court or Court of Appeals). A Commission on Judicial Conduct created pursuant to constitutional amendment approved November 1975 could recommend censure, removal, or retirement of a judge or justice to the Court of Appeals;

4. In place of the diffuse method of court administration with authority divided among the four Appellate Divisions, the presiding justices, and the chief judge of the Court of Appeals, the unified court system would be administered by the chief judge of the Court of Appeals through the chief administrator of the courts in consultation with the Administrative Board. The chief administrator would be appointed by the chief judge of the Court of Appeals with the advice of the Administrative Board and would serve at the pleasure of the chief judge;

5. Providing that the state shall pay the cost of operating and maintaining the unified court system, but that a portion of the court budget, as determined by the legislature, would be charged back to the local municipalities. The amount to

be charged back to the municipalities and the determination of problems arising from unequal salaries and other details to be solved by legislation.

Discussion among the various political factions following the submission of Governor Carey's Task Force proposals ranged from complete rejection to innumerable counter suggestions and alterations. Finally, after last minute compromises, on August 5, 1976 at an Extraordinary Session of the Senate and the Assembly, a constitutional amendment was passed.

The proponents of court reform had to accept an amendment in three parts rather than three separate amendments originally proposed. The amendment, as is, must be passed by the 1977 legislature and approved by the voters in November 1977. Voter approval of a three-part amendment is more difficult than it would be if there were three separate amendments.

As adopted by both the Senate and the Assembly, the constitutional amendment has these three parts:

1. *Appointment of Judges.* It creates a twelve member Committee on Judicial Nominations to recommend persons to the governor for appointment to the Court of Appeals as vacancies occur. The appointments would be subject to Senate confirmation. Four members of the commission will be appointed by the governor, four by the chief judge, one each by the Speaker, the temporary president of the Senate, the minority leader of the Senate, and the minority leader of the Assembly. Of the four appointed by the governor and the chief judge, no more than two may be members of the same party, and two must be members of the bar, while two must not be members of the bar. No date is set when this provision is to take effect.

2. *Judicial Conduct.* The present Commission on Judicial Conduct is expanded into an eleven-member body to investigate complaints about judges. The commission may *determine* that a judge or justice be admonished, censured, or removed from office for cause, including, but not limited to, misconduct in office, persistent failure to perform his duties, habitual intemperance, and conduct, on or off the bench, prejudicial to the administration of justice. The commission may recommend retirement for mental or physical disability preventing the proper performance of judicial duties. The functions of the present court on the judiciary will be taken over by the Court of Appeals which may take whatever action it deems proper when it reviews a determination of the commission. The Court of Appeals may review both the commission's findings of fact and conclusions of law.

3. *Court Administration.* The chief judge is the chief judicial officer of the unified court system. There is to be an Administrative Board of the Courts consisting of the chief judge as chairman and the presiding justice of the Appellate Division of the supreme court of each judicial department. The chief judge of the Court of Appeals, with the advice and consent of the Administrative Board, shall appoint a chief administrator of the courts who shall serve at his pleasure. The chief administrator, on behalf of the chief judge, will supervise the adminis-

tration and operation of the unified court system, that is, all courts in the state except the village and town tribunals upstate. The administrator will have such powers and duties as the chief judge may delegate to him and other additional powers and duties as are provided by law. The chief judge, after consultation with the Administrative Board, shall establish standards and administrative policies for general application throughout the state, which must be submitted by the chief judge to the Court of Appeals for approval. Temporary assignments of judges and justices are to be made by the chief administrator in accordance with standards and administrative policies established by the Court of Appeals.

Previously, in 1975, an effort had been made to specifically clarify the administrative structure of the New York City courts. The Administrative Board adopted a resolution which contains the following provisions, effective January 1, 1976:

1. The New York City Administrative Judge administers the trial courts of New York City subject to the supervisory direction and control of the State Administrative Judge, who exercises such supervisory direction in consultation with the presiding justices of the First and Second Departments;

2. The New York City Administrative Judge has the power with the approval of the two presiding Appellate Division justices and the State Administrative Judge to designate two New York City judges to assist him as Deputy Administrative Judges;

3. Reporting and responsible directly to the New York City Administrative Judge are four administrative judges, one for Kings and Richmond Counties and one each for New York and Bronx Counties, Nassau and Suffolk Counties and Queens County, who administer judicial activity in the criminal and civil terms of the Supreme Court, the Criminal Court and the Civil Court in their respective counties; their administrative function includes preparation of assignment schedules of judges in the courts administered by them subject to the approval of the New York City Administrative Judge;

4. There is a Deputy New York City Administrative Judge for the Family Court who is responsible for judicial activity in the Family Court to the New York City Administrative Judge. The Deputy New York City Administrative Judge for the Family Court has the power with the approval of the two presiding Appellate Division Justices and the New York City Administrative Judge to delegate administrative responsibility to four Family Court judges, one for Kings and Richmond Counties and one each for New York and Bronx Counties, Nassau and Suffolk Counties and Queens County;

5. All administrative orders or directives originating within the New York City trial courts that relate to judicial activity may be issued only by the New York City Administrative Judge who may not delegate the authority;

6. The State Administrative Judge in consultation with the two presid-

ing justices, acting with the Deputy State Administrator for New York City, is responsible for all nonjudicial activity in the New York City trial courts.

Court Financing

A necessary ingredient for achieving a fully unified administration of all the courts in a state is financing of such courts by the state. The submission of numerous separate budgets by the various divisions, without comparing the needs of the communities they represent, brings a wide variance in appropriations by local appropriating bodies. The extent and quality of services by the courts and auxiliary agencies depend upon the financing, which, in turn, depend upon the wealth of the community. Or worse, it may depend upon the persuasiveness of a particular political figure. Courts having extensive political patronage will fare better in securing what is needed and often more than is needed in staff and facilities than a court with less patronage to dispense.

This was the case in New York before 1962. The constitutional amendment of 1961 sought to bring improvement. It provided that each court was to submit itemized estimates of its needs to the Administrative Board. After study, the Administrative Board would forward the proposed budget with comment and recommendations to the appropriating bodies for final decision. However, only the expenses of the statewide courts and certain supplemental agencies were to be paid by the state. The Dominick Commission found in 1972 that only 20 percent of the total cost of the court system was paid by the state.

The Dominick Commission recommended that

> a single comprehensive budget would be prepared by the chief administrative judge and transmitted to the governor for submission to the state legislature. An appropriation from state funds would be made for all court operations. This procedure—whereby the state mandates the cost of the court system—is referred to as a "unified court" budget or "unified financing." The change to a unified budget should take place immediately, even though there may be a limited period thereafter during which the state charges back a portion of the cost to municipalities in order to cushion the impact of state finances. . . . The state should assume the total cost of the state court system as rapidly as possible, in no event over a period longer than ten years.

Some changes in budgeting in line with these recommendations were instituted by the Office of Court Administration, but no legislative action was taken until the legislature approved a constitutional amendment in 1974, and again in 1975.

The voters, however, rejected the amendment in 1975 by the narrow margin of 17,000 votes; thus it never became a part of the New York State constitution. The amendment would have centralized the administration and budgeting of the court system. Under its provisions, a unified court budget would be prepared by the chief administrator for submission to the governor for inclusion in the state budget, without revision, but with such recommendations as the governor deemed proper. However, the state would not have assumed the cost of operating the state court system. The amendment limited the responsibility of the state to "pay the cost of operating and maintaining such courts of the unified court system as may be provided by law; provided, however, that political subdivisions shall reimburse the state for a portion of such costs as may be provided by law."

Now, finally, the state takeover of court costs is provided for in a bill passed by the legislature on August 5, 1976. Beginning April 1, 1977, the state will assume all costs of county and city courts (the supreme court, the county courts, family courts, surrogate's courts, New York City Civil and Criminal Courts, and local district and city courts. Town and village courts are not included). The takeover will occur over a period of four years with the state assuming 25 percent of the cost the first year and an additional 25 percent of the court costs each year until complete state funding is accomplished by April 1, 1980. Unified state funding will permit the most efficient allocation of funds and manpower without regard to local, political boundaries. It should in the end save money and improve the quality of justice.

To illustrate the present system of financing the New York Courts, the following is extracted from the Special Six-Month Report of the Administrative Board of the Judicial Conference, the Judicial Conference, and the Office of Court Administration, (1975):

For the New York State fiscal year ending March 31, 1975, the estimated cost of operating all the courts in the State will be $274.55 Million. Of this total, the State will pay $69.99 million (25 percent), and local units of government will pay $204.56 million (75 percent).

—State Support:		
Statewide Courts & Services		$ 44.99 million
State Assistance to Local Courts		8.82
Special Programs (includes Emergency Dangerous Drug Control Program, Emergency Felony Case Processing Program, and the Emergency Narcotics Programs)		16.18
	Total	$ 69.99 million
—Local Support		
New York City		$127.66 million
Counties outside NYC		76.90
	Total	$204.56 million

The State pays directly for the costs of the Office of Court Administration, the Court of Appeals, and the Court of Claims, as well as a portion of the salaries of the justices of the Supreme Court and the operations of the Appellate Divisions. The Legislature also appropriates funds for the Appellate Divisions and the Supreme Court in the first instance; these funds are repaid to the State proportionately by the various counties and New York City. The cost of all other courts is the responsibility of the counties, cities, towns or villages which they serve, although there is some state aid for salaries of judges in County, Surrogate's, Family, some upstate City, and New York City courts. In addition, local personnel provide some service to the Supreme Court.

Judicial Conduct

Before 1948 there was no method of removing unfit judges other than the constitutional provisions involving the legislature—impeachment, concurrent resolution of both houses, and vote of two-thirds of the Senate upon recommendation of the governor. These procedures are slow, burdensome, and political. They have rarely been used. Concurrent resolution was never used; the other two approaches were used once each.

In 1948, New York citizens, alerted to the fact that the procedures involving constitutional means for dealing with judicial inadequacy and misconduct were slow, burdensome, political, and rarely used, voted for a constitutional amendment which created the court on the judiciary. Under the 1948 amendment, the court on the judiciary consisted of the chief judge of the Court of Appeals and the senior associate judge of the court; also one Appellate Division justice from each department selected by the justices of that department.

One of the chief difficulties with the operation of the court on the judiciary is its ad hoc nature. It does not have a continuing function with a continuing investigative office. It must be called into action for each specific case, each Appellate Division electing one of its own judges on such occasion. In addition, the court can be convened only by the chief judge or at the request of the governor, the presiding justice of each Appellate Division, or the executive committee of the New York State Bar Association. This court does not handle minor cases and it has no disciplinary power short of removal, although it has censured two judges in closing a proceeding prior to a hearing; also this court acts both as a trial and appellate court, there being no further review, except possibly by the United States Supreme Court on a writ of certiorari. (Twice in the history of the court on the judiciary was this tried without success.)

When the chief judge of the Court of Appeals convenes the court on the judiciary, he is obliged to inform the governor and the legislature. The latter may take the matter into its own hands, preempting the court, by bringing its own removal proceedings.

The disadvantages of these ad hoc proceedings have been made evident by the infrequency with which this court has acted. Between 1948 and 1971 it was called into action only three times. From the moment the court is convened, there is front page reporting on the alleged charges, bringing criticism and disrepute on all judges—to say nothing of the accused, who has not yet been heard. The court acts slowly—in view of the fact that busy judges are called from their heavy burdens of judicial work to hear the charges. To add to these shortcomings, the system of having a judge's case evaluated by an all-judge panel leads the public to believe that judges are more bent on protecting each other than on taking drastic action, except in cases of blatant criminal activity.

The constitution also provided that inferior court judges be removed for cause or retired for disability by the appropriate Appellate Division of the four judicial departments. The Appellate Division had authority to remove for cause "in the manner provided by law" and after due notice and hearing, judges of the civil and criminal courts of New York City, the district courts and various city, town, and village courts; the Appellate Divisions can retire these judges for disability.

Criticism of the disciplinary procedures caused the presiding justice of the First Department in 1968 to turn to the Administrative Board of the Judiciary Conference, which has the power to investigate criticisms, complaints, and recommendations with regard to the administration of justice and to delegate to each Appellate Division the responsibility for receiving and making initial review of complaints. The First Department was authorized to and did establish a standing Judiciary Relations Committee to "process and take action" upon the complaints received with respect to the "qualifications, conduct or fitness to perform or the performance of official duties" of any judicial officer serving the First Department. The committee can discuss the charges, issue a reprimand or recommend to the Appellate Division that the court on the judiciary be convened. Since 1973, the Second Department also has had a Judiciary Relations Committee. The Third and Fourth Departments have had no such committees but have used more informal procedures. Reliance has been mainly on the director of administration to handle the complaints with the presiding justice talking to the judge in question.

Despite the efforts of the Appellate Divisions to supplement the responsibilities of the court on the judiciary, criticism of New York's system of dealing with malfeasance and misfeasance continued.

An analysis of all cases referred to the Judiciary Relations Committee (First Department) since April 1968 (the date of the committee's inception) was completed in June 1972. The analysis follows:

I.   Number of complaints presented to Judiciary Relations Committee from June, 1968 to July, 1972:   22

    Action by Committee:
      Dismissed: 4

Subcommittee admonition (not at Appellate
Division):   3
Full Committee admonition: 6[a]
Referred to Administrative Judge for Admonition: 1
Admonition in letter: 1
Referred to Appellate Division: 3[b]
Referred to Court on Judiciary by Presiding
    Justice: 1
Abated due to death: 2
Abated due to retirement: 1

II.   Number of complaints against judges screened
     (and dismissed) by Executive Secretary: 60

III. (a) Hearings held by Committee:
          Formal hearing: 1
          Preliminary Investigations (consisting
      of (i) inquiry by staff and (ii) testimony
      of complainants):   5
          Preliminary Investigation and sworn
      testimony of judge: 13

    (b) Other (no sworn testimony taken);
        State Senate Committee Investigation
      reviewed:
        Dismissed without testimony: 2
        Informal admonition without testimony: 1

The Dominick Commission recommended a system similar to California's (see section on California in this chapter). It proposed that there be a Commission on Judicial Conduct to investigate and report to a newly created continuing, permanent court on the judiciary instead of to the state's highest court, as is done in California.

Following this, the New York Legislature in 1974 passed an act which established a Temporary State Commission on Judicial Conduct. The legislation authorizes the commission, acting on complaint or on its own initiative, to conduct hearings, subpoena witnesses and records, confer immunity. It may cross-examine witnesses at a formal adversary hearing during which the judge may appear with counsel, to present evidence and call and cross-examine witnesses. Although the commission has no power to remove judges, it may, with or without a hearing, make "suggestions and recommendations" to the judge or it may recommend to those having authority over the judge that a disciplinary proceeding be instituted to determine whether the judge should be removed. The nine-

[a]One of the six judges was admonished for two separate incidents represented by two separate (current) complaints.

[b]Of the three, one resulted in formal censure, one criticized in report, one admonished.

member commission is made up of one lawyer and two lay persons appointed by the governor, two judges appointed by the chief judge of the Court of Appeals, and four members appointed by the president pro tem and majority and minority leaders of the House and of the Senate. The four appointed by the legislative leaders may be either lawyers or laymen. An administrator is appointed by the commission who serves at its pleasure and the administrator may select a staff. An annual report must be filed by the commission.

All proceedings before the commission are confidential unless the judge in question wants them published. There has, as yet, been no ruling on how far the confidentiality should go. It is being urged by the commission itself that, at the least, the complainant ought to know what action is being taken. At the same time this legislation was passed, a constitutional amendment was proposed and later adopted by the citizens in November of 1975. The amendment established a permanent State Commission on Judicial Conduct with power to recommend to the chief judge of the Court of Appeals that the court on the judiciary be convened to determine whether a judge should be removed. Following such recommendation the chief judge must convene the court on the judiciary. The commission itself can censure, suspend, or retire a judge for disability, but in that case the judge has the right to ask, within thirty days, that the court on the judiciary be convened to hear the charges. Effective September 1, 1976, the Appellate Division's power will be limited to asking the court on the judiciary to convene when the situation warrants. It will have no sanction powers.

Those who supported this amendment praised the statewide jurisdiction of the permanent commission over every judge in the state, brining for the first time complaints of this type all over the state to one continuing permanent body with staff and facilities to receive all their complaints and to carry on the necessary investigations. Offices have been established in New York City, Albany, and Buffalo. The principal objection to the amendment is that it fails to make the court on the judiciary a permanent continuing body and does not change the fact that its constituency would continue to be all judges. The same objections as to the time consuming, cumbersome, expensive procedures used to summon the court and adding burdens to the judges already busily engaged in judicial work are argued. The further criticism is raised that once the Permanent Commission has fully reviewed the facts, it is senseless to have the court on the judiciary hear all the facts de novo.

Thus critics of the amendment argue that the court on the judiciary should be abolished and that the Court of Appeals should act in these judicial conduct cases as an appellate court of last resort—similar to the California system.

Governor Hugh Carey's comprehensive proposal for court reform, put forth in May of 1976, espouses this point of view. The proposed new judiciary article of the New York constitution would abolish the court on the judiciary and give ultimate disciplinary authority to the Court of Appeals and the Appellate Divisions. Pursuant to a recommendation for censure or removal by the Commission on Judicial Conduct, the Court of Appeals would render the final decision based upon the commission's record. And the legislature could delegate this task to the Appellate Divisions in cases in which judges other than those of the supreme court or Court of Appeals are involved. The assignment of this responsibility to established courts, rather than reliance upon the creation of an ad hoc court on the judiciary, should vastly expedite the judicial disciplinary process.

The constitutional amendment passed August 5, 1976 does abolish the court on the judiciary, establishes a permanent Commission on Judicial Conduct with power to recommend final action to the Court of Appeals. (See the section on "Court Administration.")

The Commission on Judicial Conduct, as it is presently constituted, functioned actively during the year 1975. The following is extracted from the First Report of the Temporary State Commission, dated October 1975.

Cases Received and Investigated

The commission received 285 complaints as of August 30, 1975. Of these, 163 were dismissed after preliminary review. One hundred and twenty six of the dismissed complaints concerned the merits of particular cases. Thirty-four complaints alleged misconduct by attorneys or non-judicial officers. Other complainants wrote that they believed that they had been denied due process, but very few related their complaints to alleged misconduct by a judge. The rest of the complaints which were dismissed contained totally unsubstantiated allegations of corruption or bias or were founded on administrative problems, such as minor court delays. Some complainants were worried about the leniency or harshness of the courts, as noted earlier. In 14 of the dismissed cases, the Commission was able to refer the complainants to a more appropriate agency.

A total of 82 cases were earmarked for investigation. Of these, 51 complaints were directed at poor judicial demeanor. These allegations, from various parts of the state and in various courts, included instances of rudeness to litigants, lawyers and jurors and judicial pressure to settle cases. A few reports suggested mental or physical impairment. Other complaints which appeared to have merit concerned bias, corruption or conflict of interest. A few complaints were closed after investigation. Other cases are in various stages of investigation.

The investigations begun in the past year have concerned many different types of misconduct. The press drew out attention to middle-of-the-night court proceedings which resulted from requests by attorneys who were fortunate enough to know personally the judges involved. Another investigation initiated by the press concerned a judge who allegedly ordered that a person be brought before him in handcuffs so that the judge could berate him for conduct not associated with any case before the judge. One investigation revealed that a judge accepted gifts from a law firm that regularly appeared before him.

The part-time judges who were investigated were alleged to have mixed their law practices with their judicial functions. Intensive investigations by the Commission indicated that these judges presided over cases of former clients. One of the judges acknowledged having presided over cases involving parties he was then representing in other matters. In the cases examined by the Commission, the judges appeared to have extended favorable treatment to their clients.

A judge was characterized as habitually rude. Many lawyers, litigants and witnesses who had appeared before the judge were interviewed. They related incidents of intemperance, injudiciousness, partiality, rudeness, impatience and shouting by the judge, both in open court and in private conferences. The judge in open court frequently accused attorneys, litigants and witnesses of what he considered to be fraud, perjury or other misconduct.

One Commission investigation revealed that a judge sought sexual favors from female litigants who appeared before him; another judge was suspected of similar misconduct. Departure from the bench rendered both investigations moot.

The following reflects other alleged misconduct investigated by the Commission:

—a judge engaged in partisan political activities;

—a judge descended from the bench to confront a defendant who had just cursed him and a fight ensued;

—a judge repeatedly used vulgar and insulting language in addressing attorneys during the course of a hearing;

—a judge who was not permitted to purchase a ticket to a high-priced political dinner, but could go as an "invited guest" (according to rules no longer in force), went as the "invited guest" of his wife;

—a part-time judge regularly appeared as an attorney before another part-time (lawyer) judge in the same county, in violation of an Administrative Board rule;

—a judge repeatedly ridiculed an attorney in front of a jury for what the judge alleged was lack of competence;

—a judge addressed black youths in his courtroom in their "dialect";

—a judge assigned his law secretary to preside daily in court from the bench over calendar calls and rule on contested applications.

Action by the Commission

Once a complaint is investigated, the Commission may act upon it in different ways. In some cases, the Commission advised judges that it disapproved of particular actions. Admonitions are often appropriate when there is no serious impropriety, especially since it is our policy to follow up and determine whether the admonitions have been instrumental in effecting change.

When the Commission identifies misconduct it may recommend that the

Court on the Judiciary be convened or a hearing commenced by an Appellate Division. The Court on the Judiciary has jurisdiction over judges of the Court of Appeals, Court of Claims, Supreme Court, Surrogates Court, County Court and Family Court. Judges of all other courts are subject to the jurisdiction of their respective Appellate Divisions. Hearings before the Court on the Judiciary, the Appellate Divisions or hearing officers assigned by these courts are commonly known as "removal" proceedings, although even if the evidence establishes misconduct the action taken may be less severe than removal.

A total of five "removal" proceedings have been recommended recently by the Commission. The recommendations were made after extensive investigations revealed serious improprieties that might render the judge unfit for judicial office. In each instance the Commission submitted a full report, proposed charges, and transcripts of investigatory proceedings before the Commission. In three of the five cases the proposed charges included giving false testimony under oath before the Commission. One other investigation has been completed and the Commission believes that false testimony was given by the judge involved. Appropriate disciplinary action will be sought.

PUERTO RICO

When Puerto Rico attained its present status as a commonwealth in voluntary association with the United States on July 25, 1952, it assumed complete autonomy over its local affairs. Both the constitution of Puerto Rico and a judiciary act went into effect, establishing what at that time was considered the most modern and efficient judicial system yet devised. Puerto Rico distinguished itself by adopting the first unified court system in terms of jurisdiction and administration. Even by today's standards Puerto Rico's court system is a model which many states would do well to emulate. The constitution provides that: "The Courts of Puerto Rico shall constitute a unified judicial system for purposes of jurisdiction, operations and administration."

The Judiciary Act of 1952 put that constitutional mandate into practice. The Act vests judicial power of the Commonwealth of Puerto Rico in a general court of justice which is composed of a supreme court and a court of first instance. The latter court is divided into a superior court and a district court, which together exercise the general trial level jurisdiction in Puerto Rico. The court of first instance replaced a complex system of various trial courts with overlapping jurisdictions—a principal cause of much costly and wasteful litigation. In terms of judicial administration, the constitution and the Judiciary Act established a streamlined system by vesting full administrative authority in the supreme court and the chief justice; in addition, the Judiciary Act created an Office of Court Administration under the constitutional office of the administrative director to assist the chief justice and to insure the efficiency in the management of the court system.

Recently, Puerto Rico reaffirmed its commitment to a progressive system of judicial administration. In 1973, Governor Rafael Hernàndez Colòn established the Council for the Reform of the System of Justice to integrate and coordinate government resources in a renewed effort to modernize the Puerto Rico judicial system. The council's broad goal was to formulate ways of combating the court backlog, the high crime and delinquency rate, and other maladies which currently afflict court systems throughout the United States. The council included the following members: the chief justice of the supreme court, the president of the Senate, the Speaker of the House, the secretary of justice (Puerto Rico's attorney general), and a private citizen. In addition, there was input from eighteen auxiliary commissions composed of more than 125 lawyers, judges, legislators, journalists, labor leaders, and other members of the community—all of whom served without pay.

As a result of the reforms suggested by the council, the governor proposed the enactment of fifty-one bills to improve the system of justice. Forty-eight of them were adopted in 1974 and several others during 1975 and 1976. They included various acts to improve the quality of justice dispensed by the courts, to strengthen judicial authority and to attain complete administrative autonomy. In addition, several acts were designed to expedite judicial proceedings and several were geared toward substantive reform of the laws of Puerto Rico. Among the most significant changes were improved methods of judicial selection; higher standards of judicial behavior; the creation of an appellate division of the superior court in order to reduce the backlog of criminal cases; and the creation of a municipal judge system to replace justices of the peace. Each of these modifications will be discussed below.

Supreme Court. The constitution of Puerto Rico establishes a supreme court as the final repository of appellate power. The constitution also confers original jurisdiction on the supreme court, or any of its justices, over petitions for habeas corpus. In addition, the supreme court may exercise original jurisdiction over petitions for extraordinary writs and other matters, as provided by law.

The supreme court consists of a chief justice and six associate justices, all appointed for life (during good behavior and until the compulsory retirement age of seventy), by the governor, with the advice and consent of the Senate. The chief justice receives an annual compensation of $32,600 and the associates receive $32,000. To qualify for appointment to the supreme court of Puerto Rico, an individual must be a citizen of the United States and Puerto Rico, must have been admitted to the practice of law in Puerto Rico at least ten years prior to appointment and must have resided in Puerto Rico at least five years immediately prior to appointment.

Appellate review by the supreme court is afforded as a matter of right to final judgments rendered by the superior court in civil cases involving constitutional questions and in all criminal cases. Other civil cases are brought through the writ

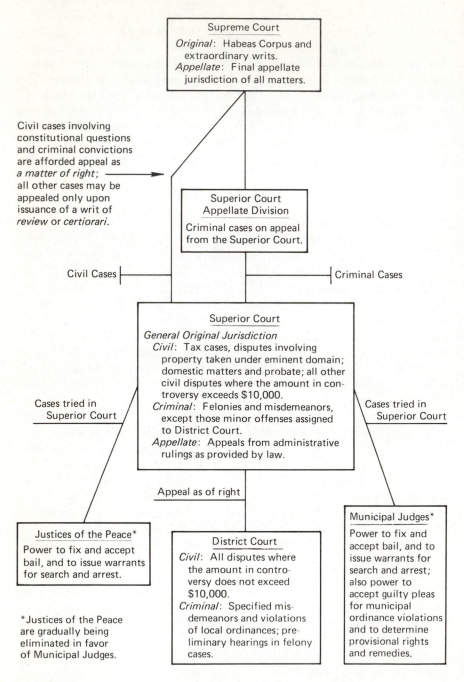

Supreme Court

Original: Habeas Corpus and
extraordinary writs.
Appellate: Final appellate
jurisdiction of all matters.

Civil cases involving
constitutional questions
and criminal convictions
are afforded appeal as
a matter of right;
all other cases may be
appealed only upon
issuance of a writ of
review or *certiorari*.

Superior Court
Appellate Division

Criminal cases on appeal
from the Superior Court.

Civil Cases

Criminal Cases

Superior Court

General Original Jurisdiction
Civil: Tax cases, disputes involving
property taken under eminent domain;
domestic matters and probate; all other
civil disputes where the amount in controversy exceeds $10,000.
Criminal: Felonies and misdemeanors,
except those minor offenses assigned
to District Court.
Appellate: Appeals from administrative
rulings as provided by law.

Cases tried in
Superior Court

Cases tried in
Superior Court

Appeal as of right

Justices of the Peace*

Power to fix and accept
bail, and to issue warrants
for search and arrest.

*Justices of the Peace
are gradually being
eliminated in favor
of Municipal Judges.

District Court

Civil: All disputes where
the amount in contro-
versy does not exceed
$10,000.
Criminal: Specified misdemeanors and violations
of local ordinances; pre-
liminary hearings in felony
cases.

Municipal Judges*

Power to fix and
accept bail, and to
issue warrants for
search and arrest;
also power to
accept guilty pleas
for municipal
ordinance violations
and to determine
provisional rights
and remedies.

Figure 5–13. Puerto Rico Judicial System

of review, granted at the discretion of the court, upon the grounds set forth in the petition. In addition, the supreme court may certify a case pending on appeal before the superior court on petition of a party if it deems that public importance justifies a deviation from the regular procedure. Finally a writ of certification procedure between any federal or state court of the United States and the supreme court of Puerto Rico was established in 1974 as a mechanism to strengthen the Commonwealth's judicial system. This procedure enables the supreme court to initially interpret a local law which is determined in a cause of action being considered in a state or federal court.

Superior Court. The superior court is the higher division of the court of first instance. It consists of 89 judges appointed by the governor, with the advice and consent of the Senate, for a term of twelve years, and thereafter until a successor qualifies. The governor makes the appointment based upon the recommendation of an Advisory Committee on Judicial Nominations which operates in coordination with a Bar Association Committee in judicial nominations. Superior court judges are paid an annual salary of $26,000. To qualify for service on the superior court, an individual must be twenty-five years of age, must have been admitted to the bar by the supreme court of Puerto Rico, and enjoy good repute. In addition, pursuant to a recommendation of the Council for the Reform of the System of Justice, which was adopted by the legislature, a requirement of five years of legal experience has been established. The number of superior court judges may be increased to 114 upon request of the chief justice, accompanied by a certificate of need supplied by the administrative director of the courts.

The civil jurisdiction of the superior court extends to the following: appeals from orders and rulings of administrative agencies as provided by law, except those matters which are initially cognizable by the supreme court; all tax cases, disputes involving compensation for property taken under eminent domain, domestic matters, and probate; and all civil disputes where the amount in controversy exceeds $10,000. The criminal jurisdiction of the superior court includes felonies and misdemeanors, except those within the jurisdiction of the district courts.

Final judgments in civil cases involving or deciding a substantive constitutional question under the United States or Puerto Rico Constitutions may be appealed to the supreme court as a matter of right. All other cases may be directly appealed from the superior court only upon the issuance of a writ or review or certiorari by the supreme court. Under one of the 1974 reform acts, an Appellate Division of the superior court was created; all criminal appeals must pass through this division. Once a criminal case which originated in the superior court has been reviewed by the Appellate Division, further review is granted by the supreme court upon writ of certiorari.

District Courts. The district courts are the lower of the two courts of general trial jurisdiction. They are also part of the court of first instance. The civil jurisdiction of the district courts extends to all cases involving disputes in which not more than $10,000 is in controversy. However, the following categories of cases are excluded from the district court's jurisdiction: land condemnation matters; domestic suits; probate; and extraordinary proceedings, such as petitions for mandamus, prohibition, and injunction. Criminal jurisdiction is limited to misdemeanors and other minor matters. Preliminary hearings on felony cases are originally held at district court level. Appeals may be taken from final judgments of the district courts to the superior court as a matter of right. Further review, by the supreme court, is only available upon writ of certiorari. All appeals are on the record; however, there is one unique twist. Puerto Rico permits the use of recording devices in the district courts, under the auspices of the Office of Court Administrator. The judge of the district court may use the recording in preparing a statement of what transpired during the trial. The underlying reason for this innovation is the shortage of court reporters in Puerto Rico. When it is alleged that the statement prepared by the district judge is inaccurate, the superior court can use the recording to decide the appeal or to order a new trial in the district court. There are, however, serious dangers inherent in the use of recording devices. Careless or intentional failure to record all testimony may lead to incomplete or distorted trial records—which in turn may engender a substantial denial of justice. In general, such cases are infrequent and the recording experiment has proved itself to be a successful means of expediting appeals.

The district courts include 98 judges appointed by the governor, with the advice and consent of the Senate. The number of judges of the district court may be increased to 126 upon request of the chief justice, accompanied by a certificate of need from the administrative director. As with other judges throughout the Commonwealth, district judges may be assigned as needed to conduct any division of the court. To qualify as a judge of the district court, a person must be at least twenty-one years of age, admitted to the bar of Puerto Rico by the supreme court, and enjoy good repute. Also, as a result of the recent reforms, an individual must have at least three years of legal experience. The term is for a period of eight years and thereafter until a successor is chosen. Judges of the district court receive an annual salary of $19,300.

Justices of the Peace and Municipal Judges. In 1974 there were fifty-five justices of the peace appointed by the governor, with the advice and consent of the Senate, for a term of four years. They exercise all functions and powers to fix and accept bail and to issue warrants for arrest and search warrants, except that they may not adjudicate cases cognizable by the district or superior courts. Gradually, however, the justices of the peace are being phased out in favor of a municipal judge system; this is another reform which was effectuated in 1974.

The municipal judges will supplant the justices of the peace as the justices' terms expire; at present thirteen municipal judges have been appointed. In addition to exercising the same responsibilities which justices of the peace have exercised, the municipal judges are empowered to accept guilty pleas for municipal ordinance violations and to establish provisional legal rights and relations between parties. When necessary, they may, upon designation by the chief justice, be authorized to perform as judges of the district court. Whereas it was not required that the justices of the peace be trained lawyers, it is required of municipal judges. They are appointed by the governor with the advice and consent of the Senate for a term of five years. Municipal judges receive an annual salary of $12,000 which may be increased to $13,000.

Special Judges and Honorary Magistrates. Two institutions were created in 1975 to increase judicial manpower within the prevailing budgetary limitations: special judges and honorary magistrates.* The former are retired judges appointed either by the supreme court or, in the case of those retired before the enactment of the Act, by the governor with the advice and consent of the Senate. Honorary magistrates are selected from distinguished members of the bar, must have at least five years of legal experience, and enjoy good repute. The Act authorizes fifty appointments by the governor with the advice and consent of the Senate for a term of four years.

While in office they are vested with the same power and prerogatives as any other regular judge of the court assigned, exercise identical functions, and are subject to the same constitutional and ethical limitations.

Neither receive compensation for their services, but are entitled to the same *per diems* which are given to regular judges.

The first group of special judges and honorary magistrates have recently been named and will be appointed to various courts, as the chief justice deems necessary.

Administration

The supreme court of Puerto Rico is empowered to make rules for the administration of the courts; however, the chief justice actually directs the administration of the general court of justice and is responsible for the efficient operation of its various parts and divisions. The chief justice may make assignments of judges within the court of first instance as need arises. An Office of Court Administration under an administrative director of the Office of Court Administration has been established to assist the chief justice in the exercise of administrative duties. The administrative director is appointed by the chief justice and holds office only at the will of the chief justice. The administrative director receives an annual salary of $30,600.

*Honorary Magistrates were created by Act. No. 17, August 17, 1975 and Special Judges were created by Act. No. 19, October 30, 1975.
Both statutes were approved in Special session of the Legislature.

The administrative director assists the chief justice in administering the courts by examining administrative methods, evaluating efficiency through compilation of data and statistics, overseeing the financial accounting, and by submitting estimates and making the necessary requisitions for public funds required for the operation of judicial system. In addition, the administrative director makes recommendations to the chief justice for the improvement of the court operation, the assignment and transfer of judges and other personnel, and generally takes steps as the chief justice directs for better administration of the courts.

The Puerto Rico judicial system has achieved almost total administrative autonomy. Since 1975, all its officials and employees, except judges, are selected and appointed by the chief justice or the administrative director upon the basis of a merit system adopted by the supreme court. The annual budget request for the operating expenses of the judicial system is automatically submitted by the governor to the legislature, without modification. Any increase in the budget request is submitted directly by the Office of Court Administration to the legislature. The chief justice is in charge of the expenditure of funds, without any interference from the two other branches of government. The tendency in most recent legislation is to grant complete administrative authority to the chief justice.

Disciplinary Procedures

Charges made against any judge of the court of first instance, against any justice of the peace, or any municipal judge, are filed with the administrative director of the Office of Court Administration, who reports the charges to the supreme court. The supreme court can order the dismissal of the charges or may order an investigation as deemed necessary and may require the secretary of justice (Puerto Rico's attorney general) or any officer of the general court of justice to investigate and to report to the supreme court. In addition, the supreme court may, on its own motion, order an investigation to be made of the conduct of any judge. After the investigation has been made, the supreme court may refer the case to one of its justices for determination of cause. If the justice determines that there is cause for further proceedings, the court may request the secretary of justice or any other member of the general court of justice to prosecute the case. Such a prosecution may also be initiated by the secretary of justice or at the request of the governor. In such cases, the secretary of justice acts as prosecutor.

Prosecution must be by complaint returnable to the supreme court charging the judge with immoral, improper, or reprehensible conduct. As a result of a proposal of the Council for the Reform of the Judicial System, the legislature has amplified the grounds for disciplinary action by adding "manifest professional incompetence in judicial duties." Furthermore, the new law provides for a "separation" of a judge due to "relative or absolute physical or mental incapacity." Such a "separation" is tantamount to a voluntary resignation.

Judicial Conference

The Judiciary Act established a Judicial Council. The function of the Judicial Council is to maintain a continuous study of the entire judicial system of Puerto Rico, of its organization and regulation, and of the advisability of introducing new methods of practice and procedure. Despite the fact that the Judiciary Act established such a council, in the last two decades, the continuous study of the entire judicial system of Puerto Rico, its organization and regulation, and the advisability of introducing new methods of practice and procedure has been performed by various Judicial Conferences summoned by the supreme court.

BIBLIOGRAPHY

Alaska

ALASKA Court System. 1975 Annual report of the administrative director. Anchorage, 1976. 146 p.

California

CALIFORNIA Center for Judicial Education and Research. Annual report. Berkeley, 1974—

CALIFORNIA Commission on Judicial Qualifications. Annual report to the governor. San Francisco, 1962—   .

CALIFORNIA Judicial Council. 1976 Annual report to the governor and the legislature. San Francisco, 1976. 225 p.

CALIFORNIA Judicial Council. California lower court study. San Francisco, 1971. 125 p.

CALIFORNIA Judicial Council. California unified trial court feasibility study. San Francisco, 1971. 111 p.

COOK. The judicial process in California. Belmont, 1967. 122 p.

FRANKEL. Judicial ethics and discipline for the 1970's. Judicature 54:18 (1970).

KLEPS. State court modernization in the 1970's: forces for reform in California. Judicature 55:292 (1972).

LOS ANGELES Superior Court. Executive officer's annual report. Los Angeles, 1959—

LOS ANGELES Superior Court. Recording and transcription of Los Angeles superior court proceedings. Los Angeles, 1972. 56 p.

NATIONAL Center for State Courts. The California courts of appeal. San Francisco, 1974. 318 p.

REPORT of the advisory commission to the joint legislative committee on the structure of the judiciary. Sacramento, 1975. 72 p.

Colorado

COLORADO Judicial Department Office of the State Court Administrator. Annual statistical report 1973—1974. Denver, 1974. 134 p.

COLORADO Supreme Court. Annual report of the chief justice of the Colorado Supreme Court. Denver, 1974. 18 p.

District of Columbia

DISTRICT OF COLUMBIA. Joint committee on judicial administration annual report. Washington, 1971–

DISTRICT OF COLUMBIA Courts. Annual report, 1974. Washington, 1975. 33 p.

DISTRICT OF COLUMBIA Superior Court. Annual review of operations, 1974. Washington, 1975. 57 p.

THE MODERNIZATION of justice in the District of Columbia. American University Law Review 20:237 (1971).

Hawaii

HAWAII Judiciary Office of the Administrative Director. Annual report 1973–1974. Honolulu, 1975. 64 p.

Illinois

COOK County Circuit Court. 1973–1974 Report. Chicago, 1975. 36 p.

FINS. Illinois court practice under the new judicial article. Chicago, 1964. 164 p.

ILLINOIS Courts—Administrative Office. Annual report to the supreme court of Illinois, 1974. Springfield, 1975. 163 p.

ILLINOIS Supreme Court Committee on Criminal Justice Program. Some functional problems of criminal justice in Courts of Illinois—the circuit court of Cook County, criminal division and municipal district one. Chicago, 1972. 19 p.

NATIONAL Center for State Courts, Appellate Justice Project. The appellate process and staff research attorneys in the Illinois appellate court. Denver, 1974. 175 p.

ROLEWICK. A short history of the Illinois judicial system. Springfield, 1968. 40 p.

Massachusetts

AMERICAN Judicature Society. Financing Massachusetts courts. Chicago, 1974. 157 p.

CENTER for the Study of Constitutional Government. The selection and discipline of judges. Worcester, 1975. 80 p.

MASSACHUSETTS District Courts. Report of the special committee on trial de novo. Boston, 1976. 24 p.

MASSACHUSETTS Supreme Judicial Court. Eighteenth annual report. Boston, 1974. 86 p.

NATIONAL Center for State Courts. A study of the Boston housing court. Boston, 1974. 70 leaves.

New Jersey

McCONNELL. A brief history of the New Jersey courts. New Jersey Digest 7:349 (1954).

McCONNELL. A blueprint for the development of the New Jersey judicial system. Chicago, 1969. 45 p.

NATIONAL Center for State Courts. The appellate process and staff research attorneys in the appellate division of the New Jersey superior court. Denver, 1974. 93 p.

NEW JERSEY Administrative Office of the Courts. Annual report. Trenton, 1948– .

SEILER. Judicial selection in New Jersey. Seton Hall Law Review 5:721 (1974).

New York

ASSOCIATION of the Bar of the City of New York, Committee on State Courts of Superior Jurisdiction. Governor Carey's judicial reform proposals. New York, 1976. 6 p.

ELLIS. Court reform in New York State: an overview for 1975. Hofstra Law Review 3:663 (1975).

GASPERINE, ANDERSON and McGINLEY. Judicial removal in New York. Fordham Review 40:1 (1971).

JUDICIAL removal in New York: a new look–revisited. The Record of the Association of the Bar of the City of New York 28:217 (1973).

KARLEN. Judicial administration in New York: developments in the last twenty-five years. Buffalo Law Review 15:319 (1965).

NEW YORK (State) Temporary Commission on the State Court System. . . . And justice for all. New York, 1973. Various pagings.

RUTZICK and HUFFMAN. The New York City housing court: trial and error in housing code enforcement. New York University Law Review 50:738 (1975).

Puerto Rico

NEGRON-GARCIA. Puerto Rico updates its courts. Judicature 58:350 (1975).

PUERTO RICO Office of Court Administration. Annual report of the administrative director, 1972–1973. (In Spanish). San Juan, 1973. 83 p.

SNYDER. New Puerto Rico judicial system is modern and efficient. Judicature 36:134 (1953).

Chapter 6

The United States Courts System

HISTORICAL BACKGROUND

As has been related in Chapter 1, while the thirteen colonies united to obtain their independence from England, reluctance to give up their individual powers to a central government resulted initially in a feeble federal judicial power. The weaknesses of the confederation led to consideration of a stronger national government, and reasons for a separate federal judicial power were persuasive. Federal laws passed by Congress had to be uniformly interpreted. Impartial disposition of disputes between citizens of different states and between the states themselves was considered improbable in the state courts. If the federal government was to have the power to levy taxes on the people, this power had to be secured. As finally adopted in 1788, article III, section 1 of the Constitution created a Supreme Court with limited original and broad appellate jurisdiction, and permitted Congress to create inferior courts.

In 1789 Congress passed the Judiciary Act which established the federal judiciary. It provided for a Supreme Court consisting of a Chief Justice and five Associate Justices. The country was divided into thirteen judicial districts. A district court was established in each judicial district and one judge was authorized for each district. The thirteen districts constituted three circuits designated as the Southern, Middle, and Eastern. Each circuit had a circuit court which was made up of two Supreme Court justices and a district court judge.

The jurisdiction of the district courts and circuit courts was very limited. Both had original jurisdiction in different types of cases. In addition, the circuit courts reviewed decisions of the district courts.

The United States Supreme Court justices performed their own duties at the nation's capital and also rode the circuit. That is, they traveled to outlying areas to help with the work of the circuit courts. With territorial expansion and the admission of new states the appeals brought to the Supreme Court increased considerably, making more onerous the duties of the Supreme Court justices in their own Court. To relieve the Supreme Court justices of their circuit travel, Congress authorized the appointment of circuit judges in 1869, with Supreme Court justices then having to ride circuit only once in two years. Then in 1891 nine intermediate appellate courts of appeal were established with their own judicial personnel. These were then known as the circuit courts of appeal.

In 1911, with the enactment of the Judicial Code, the three-tier system of federal courts as it now exists was established. At the top is the United States Supreme Court; then comes the intermediate appellate courts, now known as the United States Courts of Appeals, and last the trial courts called the United States District Courts.

Specialized courts, whose function will be described later, were also created.

CASES THE UNITED STATES COURTS
CAN DECIDE

The cases which may be decided by the United States courts are set forth in article III, section 2 of the United States Constitution. They are:

1. Controversies to which the United States itself is a party.
2. Controversies between two or more states; between a state and citizens of another state; between citizens of different states; between citizens of the same state claiming lands under grants of different states.
3. Cases affecting ambassadors, ministers, consuls; cases between a state or its citizen and foreign states, its citizens, or subjects.
4. All cases in law and equity arising under the United States Constitution, laws of the United States, treaties, and cases of admiralty and maritime jurisdiction. Under these provisions the United States courts decide cases involving the Constitution, laws enacted by Congress, treaties, or laws relating to navigable waters.

THE SUPREME COURT OF THE UNITED STATES

At the apex of the federal judicial system, and in certain cases the ultimate appelate tribunal in the United States, is the Supreme Court of the United States. Since 1935, it has conducted its sessions in an impressive marble building near the Capitol in Washington, D.C. One annual term is held beginning on the first Monday of October and usually lasting until the following June. While about 5,000 cases were disposed of in the October 1974 term, the United States District Courts and the circuit courts of appeal disposed of over 164,000 cases. Thus, the Supreme Court disposed of only about 3 percent of all cases disposed

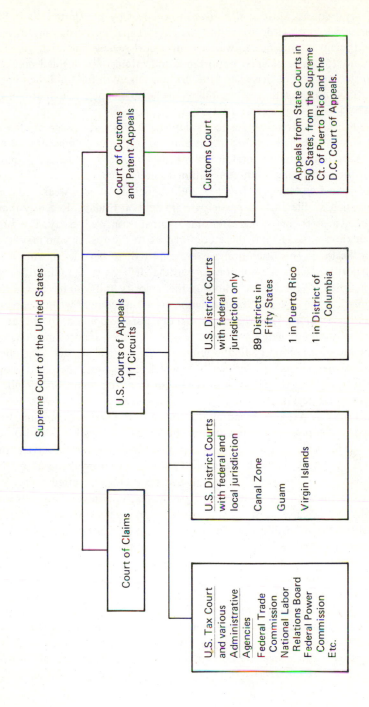

Figure 6–1.   The United States Court System

Reproduced by permission from *The United States Courts: Their Jurisdiction and Work*, by Joseph F. Spaniol (1975).

of in the federal courts. Most of the cases disposed of by the United States Supreme Court are by a brief decision that the subject matter is either not proper or not of sufficient importance to warrant full Court review. But each year between 200 and 250 cases of great importance and interest are decided on their merits. A little over half of these decisions are announced in full published opinions. Some 1,200 applications of various kinds are filed each year that can be acted upon by a single Supreme Court Justice.

Before a decision is given, the Justices study the record and written briefs and hear oral arguments. Usually each party is allowed one hour to present its case. There are exceptions in which oral argument may be heard for longer periods, even days, if the issue is one of unusual national significance.

Cases are argued on Monday, Tuesday, and Wednesday of each week and conferences in which all the Justices participate are held on Fridays. Recently there has been added a short conference after oral arguments on Wednesday. The writing of the opinion is assigned at these conferences to the Justice who may have expertise in the field. This discretion is exercised by the Chief Justice who, if he is in the majority, assigns the opinion for writing. If he is in the minority, the opinion is assigned by the Justice who is in the majority and who has served the longest term. However, even without assignment, a Justice may write a concuring or dissenting opinion. When there is a final draft of the opinion, the writer of the majority opinion circulates it among the other Justices. Justices may change their vote at any time before the final opinion for the Court is written. The opinion may be further revised, sometimes a dozen or more times, before it is approved as the opinion of the Court or of the majority of the Court. Six members of the Court constitute a quorum.

The Court's decision is announced by the author of the majority opinion. It is then released to the press and often appears in the New York Times and other newspapers on the following day as well as in an unofficial looseleaf service, the United States Law Week. Later the decision is published in official and unofficial reports. Unlike justices of some of the highest state courts, United States Supreme Court Justices are not permitted to give advisory opinions. The Court is bound by the word "cases" and "controversies" used in article III of the United States Constitution, and will not act unless an actual case involving parties with adverse interests is before it. Precisely what constitutes a "case" or "controversy," and when the controversy is ripe for adjudication, is a continuing subject of much litigation. Such questions are said to be issues of justiciability. Very few litigants carry their cases to the Supreme Court, for both the original and appellate jurisdiction are of limited nature.

Since 1869 the Supreme Court has been made up of nine justices: one Chief Justice and eight Associate Justices. They are appointed by the president of the United States with the advice and consent of the Senate. The Chief Justice receives a salary of $65,600. The Associate Justices receive $63,000 annually.

Tenure is for life during good behavior as with all federal court judges; they can be removed only by impeachment, and their salary may not be decreased during term of office. Retired federal judges may assume the status of "senior judge," thereby making them available for judicial service on federal courts other than the United States Supreme Court. It is often said that these provisions tend to insure the independence of federal judges. Without the necessity of contemplating a future election or retention procedure, federal judges are not subject to political pressures. While it is recognized that the president may appoint judges who are politically acceptable to him, there can obviously be no control by the Executive or any political leader over such an appointee because he or she will hold office for life depending only on proper conduct. A Justice may, if he or she so desires, retire with full salary at age seventy after serving ten years as a federal judge, or at age sixty-five after fifteen years of such service.

Original Jurisdiction

The original jurisdiction of the Supreme Court, rarely exercised, is substantially as follows:

1. Exclusive Jurisdiction. The following cases must be initiated in the Supreme Court:
   a. disputes between two or more states
   b. disputes in which a foreign ambassador or minister or one of their domestic servants is being sued.
2. Concurrent Jurisdiction. While the following cases may be brought in the Supreme Court originally, the Court's jurisdiction is not exclusive and Congress may permit these cases to be brought in the lower federal courts:
   a. a suit by a foreign ambassador or minister
   b. disputes between the United States and a state
   c. disputes between a state and citizens of another state or against aliens.
3. Appellate Jurisdiction. The appellate jurisdiction of the Supreme Court of the United States is subject to the regulation of Congress, which has provided three methods of review. The first is by *appeal*, which is a matter of right where a lower federal court has held a state statute invalid as repugnant to the Constitution, treaties, or law of the United States. Appeal as a matter of right may also be used where the highest court of a state has rendered a decision in which there was drawn in question the validity of a treaty or statute of the United States and the decision was in favor of its validity. The second method of review is by the writ of *certiorari*, which is not a matter of right, but which the Supreme Court can grant in its discretion if it feels that there is an important federal question involved in a case. The third method of review is by *certification* of any question of law by a U.S. Court of Appeals requesting instructions on the legal issues in a particular case.

Special writs may also be granted by the Supreme Court. Some are considered "extraordinary" writs in that they compel a lower court judge to act or prohibit him from acting. The most popular of the special writs in habeas corpus used where a person is being illegally detained.

Any party may appeal to the Supreme Court from an order of a three-judge court that grants or denies an injunction in any civil action required by any act of Congress to be heard by that court, or a decision restraining the enforcement, operation, execution of a state statute or order of a state administrative agency on the grounds of unconstitutionality; or final judgments of civil actions brought by the United States under antitrust laws and Interstate Commerce laws. (See section on "Three-Judge District Courts.")

The nature and volume of the Court's work are reported regularly in the November issue of the Harvard Law Review. As has been stated, while about 5,000 cases came before the Court in the October 1974 term, only 148 full opinions were written, that is an opinion in which reasons for the Court's decision was set out and the opinion was prepared by one of the Justices presenting the majority. "Per Curiam" opinions, or opinions by the whole Court rather than by one member for the Court, are usually short. The majority of cases, about 80 percent, are disposed of by denial or dismissal of the petition for certiorari. The problems of this Court and the courts of appeals in facing increasing appeals are discussed in the section on "The Workload of the Appellate Courts in the Federal Court System."

The Supreme Court has done much to shape the social, economic, and political life of our country. Its role as arbiter has been twofold. The Court marks the boundary between central power of the federal government and local power of the states. The Court protects the individual from the unconstitutional exercise of governmental power.

Some view the Supreme Court of the United States as giving effect to the promptings of the national conscience when change cannot find expression through normal channels of representative institutions. Rulings on civil rights, reapportionment, and school segregation cases illustrate this perspective.

UNITED STATES COURTS OF APPEALS

The United States Courts of Appeals are the intermediate appellate courts below the Supreme Court of the United States created in 1891 to relieve the Supreme Court of considering all appeals in the cases originally tried in the federal trial courts. These courts are empowered to review all final decisions and certain interlocutory decisions of the district courts within their circuit except in those very few cases where the law provides direct review by the Supreme Court. They are also empowered to review decisions of the tax court and to review and enforce orders of many federal administrative bodies such as the Securities and Exchange Commission and the Labor Relations Board.

There are eleven circuits. Each circuit includes three or more states, except the District of Columbia Circuit. The states of Alaska and Hawaii and the Territory of Guam are included in the Ninth Circuit. Puerto Rico is included in the First Circuit, the Virgin Islands is in the Third Circuit, and the Canal Zone is in the Fifth Circuit. The number of judges per circuit ranges from three in the First Circuit to fifteen in the Fifth Circuit. Circuit judges are appointed by the president of the United States with the advice and consent of the Senate. Their salaries are $44,600 per year, and cannot be diminished during term of office.

In 1967, Congress established a Commission on Executive, Legislative and Judicial Salaries. The commission is composed of nine members: three, including the chairman, appointed by the president, and two members appointed by the vice president (or president pro tem of the Senate), the Speaker of the House, and the Chief Justice. The commission convenes every four years, with the members serving for a period of one year. The commission is responsible for reviewing and reporting to the president on salaries for personnel in the three branches of the federal government. The president must then make recommendations to Congress regarding salary adjustments based on the commission report. These recommendations will then become law if Congress does not pass contrary legislation within thirty days. Thus, salaries were raised for all federal judicial officers in 1969; this was their last raise until October 1, 1975 when they received a token 5 percent cost of living increase. Early in 1976 a suit was brought in the United States Court of Claims by at least forty-four federal district and court of appeals judges, claiming that their salaries had been unconstitutionally diminished by the failure of the president and Congress to offset the impact of inflation on their salaries. This is an unprecedented action.

In 1939, Justice Felix Frankfurter, writing the opinion in *O'Malley v. Woodrough*, 307 U.S. 277, in a 7 to 1 ruling upheld the right of the government to assess federal income taxes against a judge's salary, declaring that the tax was not a diminution of a judge's compensation in violation of the Constitution, and did not encroach on the independence of the judiciary. Some constitutional experts analogize the 1976 judges' suit to this case, claiming that inflation affects everyone as does taxation. Others support the issues raised by the judges. Whether the 1976 suit raises a triable issue has not yet been determined.

The judge less than seventy years of age with the longest years of service as a circuit judge becomes the chief judge. Judges of the circuit court may retire at full salary after fifteen years of service at age sixty-five and at age seventy after ten years on the bench. They may become senior circuit judges and continue to perform judicial duties as directed by the chief judge of the circuit. They may be removed by impeachment only as is provided in the United States Constitution. There are now ninety-seven circuit court judges. Usually the judges of these courts sit in panels or divisions of three to hear appeals so that the work of the court is thus distributed among different combinations of judges. Occasionally, district court judges may be asked to sit temporarily with the court of appeals to speed disposition of pending appeals.

Table 6–1. United States Courts of Appeals

Courts of Appeals	Number of Authorized Judgeships	Location and Postal Address
District of Columbia Circuit (District of Columbia)	9	Washington, DC 20001
1st Circuit (Maine, Massachusetts, New Hampshire, Rhode Island, and Puerto Rico	3	Boston, MA 02109
2d Circuit (Connecticut, New York, and Vermont)	9	New York, NY 10007
3d Circuit (Delaware, New Jersey, Pennsylvania, and the Virgin Islands)	9	Philadelphia, PA 19107
4th Circuit (Maryland, North Carolina, South Carolina, Virginia, and West Virginia	7	Richmond, VA 23219
5th Circuit (Alabama, Florida, Georgia, Louisiana, Mississippi, Texas, and the Canal Zone)	15	New Orleans, LA 70130
6th Circuit (Kentucky, Michigan, Ohio, and Tennessee)	9	Cincinnati, OH 45202
7th Circuit (Illinois, Indiana, and Wisconsin)	8	Chicago, IL 60604
8th Circuit (Arkansas, Iowa, Minnesota, Missouri, Nebraska, North Dakota, and South Dakota)	8	St. Louis, MO 63101
9th Circuit (Alaska, Arizona, California, Hawaii, Idaho, Montana, Nevada, Oregon, Washington, and Guam)	13	San Francisco, CA 94101
10th Circuit (Colorado, Kansas, New Mexico, Oklahoma, Utah, and Wyoming)	7	Denver, CO 80202

Reproduced by permission from *The United States Courts: Their Jurisdiction and Work*, by Joseph F. Spaniol (1975).

A majority of the court of appeals judges may decide that all judges on the court should sit for a particular case when, for example, the court wishes to prevent inconsistency within the circuit, or the case is particularly significant. The court is then sitting "en banc."

Supreme Court justices are assigned to the circuits, although they rarely participate in the work of these courts. A listing of present assignments follows:

	Appointed	Assignment as Circuit Justice
Chief Justice of the United States:		
Warren E. Burger	June 23, 1969	D.C. & 4th Cir.
Associate Justices:		
William J. Brennan, Jr.	Oct. 15, 1956	1st & 3rd Cir.
Potter Stewart	Oct. 14, 1958	6th Cir.
Byron R. White	Apr. 12, 1962	10th Cir.

		Assignment as
Associate Justices (cont'd)	*Appointed*	*Circuit Justice*
Thurgood Marshall	Aug. 30, 1967	2nd Cir.
Harry A. Blackmun	June 9, 1970	8th Cir.
Lewis F. Powell, Jr.	Dec. 9, 1971	5th Cir.
William H. Rehnquist	Dec. 15, 1971	9th Cir.
John Paul Stevens	Nov. 28, 1975	7th Cir.

When Associate Justice William O. Douglas resigned from the Supreme Court, Mr. Justice John Paul Stevens was appointed to his place November 28, 1975 and assigned to the Seventh Circuit.

THE WORKLOAD OF THE APPELLATE COURTS
IN THE FEDERAL COURT SYSTEM

In recent years intensive studies have been conducted analyzing the workload of the Supreme Court and the courts of appeals. These studies were undertaken to determine what recommendations should be made to meet the increasing difficulties in giving adequate attention to each appeal because of the marked escalation of cases. For instance, 1,200 cases were brought to the Supreme Court in 1951, 4,000 cases in 1971, and about 5,000 recently reported.

A study group appointed by Chief Justice Warren E. Burger in 1971, in its report (The Freund Report), described the functions of the Supreme Court:

> The cases which it is the primary duty of the Court to decide are those that, by hypothesis, present the most fundamental and difficult issues of law and judgment. To secure uniform application of federal law, the Court must resolve problems on which able judges in lower courts have differed among themselves. To maintain the constitutional order the Court must decide controversies that have sharply divided legislators, lawyers, and the public. And in deciding, the Court must strive to understand and elucidate the complexities of the issues, to give direction to the law, and to be as precise, persuasive, and invulnerable as possible in its exposition. The task of decision must clearly be a process, not an event, a process at the opposite pole from the "processing" of cases in a high-speed, high-volume enterprise. The indispensible condition for the discharge of the Court's responsibility is adequate time and ease of mind for research, reflection, and consultation in reaching a judgment, for critical review by colleagues when a draft opinion is prepared, and for clarification and revision in light of all that has gone before.

The study group found there was lacking uniformity of holdings on federal law because of disparate decisions made by the various circuit courts—"intercircuit conflicts." It demonstrated statistically that because of mounting cases in all the federal courts resulting in appeals, the Supreme Court was unable to perform its function of unifying federal law and of resolving many important cases involving constitutional questions. The Freund study group made a number of recommendations. The most controversial was the recommendation to create a National Court of Appeals under the Supreme Court that would screen all petitions for review now filed in the Supreme Court and hear and decide on the merits in many cases where there was a conflict of holdings in the circuits. This new court would select those petitions deemed important enough for certification to the Supreme Court, denying review to the others. The recommendation received a mixed reception and no action on it was taken.

In October 1972, Congress created a Commission on the Revision of the Federal Court Appellate System, with Senator Roman L. Hruska as chairman and Professor A. Leo Levin of the University of Pennsylvania Law School as director. This commission was asked to study the workload of the circuits and to recommend such changes in the "geographical boundaries which would be more appropriate for the expeditious and effective disposition of the business." The commission found that the caseload in these courts had also increased overwhelmingly. On December 18, 1973 its first report was issued. It was limited to a discussion with recommendations as to change in the circuit boundaries.

In Phase II the commission was to study the "structure and internal procedures of the federal courts of appeals system and to report its recommendations for such additional changes in structure or internal procedures as may be appropriate for the expeditious and effective disposition of the caseload of the federal courts of appeals. After intensive research, including interviews with Supreme Court and other justices and judges and participants in the system as well as public hearings, the Commission, in June 1975, filed its final report.

Again it stressed that the real needs of the country for definitive adjudication of national issues were not being met because of rapidly multiplying litigants and appeals.

The commission found that due to increases in the number of cases filed, coupled with the Supreme Court's inability to increase perceptively the number of cases it accepts for review, many important cases are not given plenary review by the Court. Eventually, it suggested, as the probability of review by the Supreme Court declines, litigants will be discouraged from seeking to obtain review by the Supreme Court. Such developments would essentially change the role of the Supreme Court.

The final report includes a number of suggestions for improving the internal functions of the courts. It also proposes the creation of a National Court of Appeals between the courts of appeals and the Supreme Court. The report states:

1. The Commission recommends that Congress establish a National Court of Appeals, consisting of seven Article III judges appointed by the President with the advice and consent of the Senate.

2. The court would sit only en banc and its decisions would constitute precedents binding upon all other federal courts and, as to federal questions, upon state courts as well, unless modified or overruled by the Supreme Court.

3. The National Court of Appeals would have jurisdiction to hear cases (a) referred to it by the Supreme Court (reference jurisdiction), or (b) transferred to it from the regional courts of appeals, the Court of Claims and the Court of Customs and Patent Appeals (transfer jurisdiction).

(a) *Reference Jurisdiction.* With respect to any case before it on petition for certiorari, the Supreme Court would be authorized:
   (1) to retain the case and render a decision on the merits;
   (2) to deny certiorari without more, thus terminating the litigation;
   (3) to deny certiorari and refer the case to the National Court of Appeals for that court to decide on the merits;
   (4) to deny certiorari and refer the case to the National Court, giving that court discretion either to decide the case on the merits or to deny review and thus terminate the litigation.

The Supreme Court would also be authorized to refer cases within its obligatory jurisdiction, excepting only those which the Constitution requires it to accept. Referral in such cases would always be for decision on the merits.

(b) *Transfer Jurisdiction.* If a case filed in a court of appeals, the Court of Claims or the Court of Customs and Patent Appeals is one in which an immediate decision by the National Court of Appeals is in the public interest, it may be transferred to the National Court provided it falls within one of the following categories:
   (1) the case turns on a rule of federal law and federal courts have reached inconsistent conclusions with respect to it; or
   (2) the case turns on a rule of federal law applicable to a recurring factual situation, and a showing is made that the advantages of a prompt and definitive determination of that rule by the National Court of Appeals outweigh any potential disadvantages of transfer; or
   (3) the case turns on a rule of federal law which has theretofore been announced by the National Court of Appeals, and there is a substantial question about the proper interpretation or application of that rule in the pending case.

The National Court would be empowered to decline to accept the transfer of any case. Decisions granting or denying transfer, and decisions by the National Court accepting or rejecting cases, would not be reviewable under any circumstances, by extraordinary writ or otherwise.

4. Any case decided by the National Court of Appeals, whether upon ref-
    erence or after transfer, would be subject to review by the Supreme
    Court upon petition for certiorari.

These recommendations, it may be seen, vary from the Freund recommendations in at least one essential—the Supreme Court is, for the most part, the final
arbitrator in selecting the cases it will hear. In the 94th Congress, 1st Session,
S. 2762, a bill to establish a National Court of Appeals was introduced. The
House took similar action, H.R. 11218. The National Court of Appeals bill calls
for a seven-member court with its seat in Washington, D.C. The court would receive its cases either by reference from the Supreme Court or by transfer from
any U.S. Court of Appeals, the court of claims, and the court of customs and
patent appeals. In both instances the decision to review would be within the discretion of the new court, unless directed by the Supreme Court to decide the
case. Although the Supreme Court would still have the right to review opinions
of the National Court, there would be no appeal or review of an order granting
or denying a transfer to the new court.

Professor Levin describes its functions:

> The National Court of Appeals would be comprised of seven judges, ap-
> pointed by the President and confirmed by the Senate. It would hear cases
> which came to it either by reference from the United States Supreme
> Court ("reference" jurisdiction); or by transfer from one of the regional
> courts of appeals, the Court of Claims or the Court of Customs and Patent
> Appeals ("transfer" jurisdiction).
>
> The court would sit only en banc and its judgments—unless reversed or
> overruled by the Supreme Court—would constitute precedents binding on
> all other federal courts and, with respect to issues of federal law, on all
> state courts as well.
>
> The new tribunal is intended to increase the capacity of the federal judi-
> cial system to provide clarity and uniformity in the federal law. It is de-
> signed to assure that a social security claimant, a taxpayer, or a defendant
> in a criminal prosecution in Georgia is treated no differently than one in
> Oregon solely because of an accident in geography.

Several members of the United States Supreme Court and many active federal
appellate judges and legal scholars have gone on record to oppose a National
Court of Appeals as unnecessary, unconstitutional, and inimical to the cherished
status of the United States Supreme Court. The disadvantages, it is said, outweigh any possible advantages. A primary effect would be the "diminution of
authority and prestige of the Courts of Appeals; it would tend to denigrate if
not emasculate the present Courts of Appeals." Another objection is that the
"proposed court would create a fourth tier of review and new areas of potential
litigation on areas of jurisdiction." The additional expense and delay are undesir-

able—particularly in criminal cases. Delay there would be in cases referred to the National Court by the United States Supreme Court. In a recent article published in the Brooklyn Law Review, the Honorable Wilfred Feinberg of the Second Circuit, after pointing up numerous objections to the proposal, concludes:

> What is most striking about the Commission's proposal for a National Court of Appeals is that it makes no adequate attempt to assess the costs, in all senses, of the new institution. These costs would be substantial in terms of the diminution of authority and prestige of the courts of appeals; the creation in many cases of a fourth tier of courts, with attendant additional expense and delay for litigants; the significant initial and continuing financial cost of the new court; and the diversion of judicial reform effort from more pressing matters.
>
> The case made by the Commission for a National Court with a capacity of deciding 150 cases a year must be weighed against these costs. A careful analysis, however, shows that the need is not sufficient to warrant such a drastic and costly step as that proposed by the Commission. The Report admirably serves "the larger purpose of furthering discussion and debate," and the Commission has done a great service by pointing to a problem which has previously received little attention. But a more appropriate response to that problem would be to try any of a number of more limited alternatives before proceeding to the radical changes the Commission proposes.

The commission's proposal for a National Court of Appeals has been received with approval by other equally capable authorities. They regard the creation of the new court as a necessity, particularly in the light of ever increasing litigation in the federal courts and projections into the future.

UNITED STATES DISTRICT COURTS

Cases falling within federal jurisdiction are initially tried and decided in the district courts. There are ninety-four such courts, eighty-nine in the fifty states and one each in the District of Columbia, the Canal Zone, Guam, Puerto Rico, and the Virgin Islands.

Each state has at least one district court; the most populous states, New York, California, and Texas, have four district courts. In some states a division of the district court hears cases in several locations within the state. Each district has from one to twenty-seven judges, according to the volume of cases. Each district has a clerk's office, a United States Marshal's office, one or more bankruptcy judges, United States Magistrates, probation officers, and court reporters. There is a United States Attorney's office in each district and at present each district has a plan whereby lawyers are provided to indigent defendants in criminal cases. Full-time public defenders are appointed where the criminal caseload is heavy.

Four hundred district judgeships are authorized by law. The salary of district court judges is $42,000 a year. In districts where there are two or more judges, the judge senior in service, not over seventy years of age, is the chief judge. The district courts currently hear approximately 103,500 civil cases, 38,000 criminal cases, and 189,000 bankruptcy cases every year.

District courts have jurisdiction over local cases as well as those arising under federal law in the Canal Zone, Guam, and the Virgin Islands. In these places the federal government does not share the judicial power as it does with the state governments, and with the local government in the District of Columbia and in the Commonwealth Government of Puerto Rico. In other words, these courts are not limited in their jurisdiction to the types of cases described in the Constitution as part of the federal judicial power. Rather, they decide all types of cases. Judges serving in the Canal Zone, Guam, and the Virgin Islands are appointed by the president with the consent of the Senate for a term of eight years; and they are not protected against diminution of their salaries during their tenure.

Territorial courts are known as "legislative courts," to distinguish them from "constitutional courts." They have been created "not under the judiciary article of the Constitution, but under powers in the legislative article over the territories and other fields of Federal authority."

Jurisdiction of District Courts

The question of when a case may be brought into the United States District Court is so complex that it has become the basis for a separate subject taught in law schools.

Briefly, federal district courts have exclusive jurisdiction over such matters as:

1. admiralty and maritime cases
2. bankruptcy proceedings
3. cases arising under the patent or copyright laws
4. cases involving a fine, penalty or forfeiture under federal law
5. proceedings against consuls or vice consuls of foreign states
6. seizures on land or upon the waters, not within admiralty and maritime jurisdiction.

These and other principal grants of jurisdiction are set out in the United States Code.

In some instances federal district courts have concurrent jurisdiction with state courts. Two important examples are:

1. Where the controversy arises under the Constitution, laws, or treaties of the United States and more than $10,000 (exclusive of interest and costs) is involved. This is often referred to as "federal question" jurisdiction, and various tests have been applied by the courts to discover if there is really a federal ques-

tion involved, or whether the federal aspects of a case are of a more indirect nature.

2. Where the dispute is between: (a) citizens of different states, (b) citizens of one state and foreign states or the citizens or subjects of foreign states, or (c) citizens of different states and a foreign state (or where its citizens or subjects are additional parties), and more than $10,000 is in controversy, exclusive of interest and costs of the proceeding. The latter is called "diversity" jurisdiction. The word "state" includes the District of Columbia and the territorial possessions of the United States. Thus, if a New York State citizen sues a citizen of the District of Columbia and more than $10,000 is in controversy, excluding interest and any costs of the proceeding, suit may be brought in a United States District Court. The diversity required is that of complete diversity. For example, if two citizens, one from New York and one from New Jersey, join to sue a citizen from New Jersey, there is no diversity, since one of the plaintiffs is a citizen of the same state as the defendant. Where a party is joined in the suit who need not be a party of it (that is, the suit can proceed without him), that party may be dropped by the court in order to effect complete diversity. For diversity purposes a corporation is considered to be a citizen of the state in which it is incorporated and of the state where it has its principal place of business.

Summarizing, original jurisdiction exists in a suit between citizens of different states, between a citizen of a state and an alien, or between citizens of the District of Columbia or a territory and a citizen of a state, foreign country, or another territory.

The original jurisdiction of the federal district courts also includes cases in which the United States or a national bank or the Internal Revenue Service is a party, and may extend to cases involving civil rights and election disputes, as well as various other instances spelled out by federal legislation.

If a plaintiff brings suit in a state court which could have been brought in a federal district court, the defendant may remove the case to the federal district court when the case involves:

1. "diversity"
2. a "federal question"
3. an action against United States officials
4. cases in which a state court is not properly enforcing a law providing for equal civil rights
5. cases against members of the armed forces.

The purposes behind removal jurisdiction are similar to those or original jurisdiction—uniformity of interpretation of federal statutes and avoidance of local prejudice. Attorneys also consider such factors as crowded state court calendars and more effective federal court procedures.

Criminal Cases. The district court has broad criminal jurisdiction, exclusive of the state courts, over all offenses against the laws of the United States. There are no common law crimes against the United States. Only those acts which Congress forbids with penalties for disobedience are federal crimes.

Where an act is a violation of both federal and state law, different crimes are involved, and the defendant is not protected by the prohibition against double jeopardy, but is subject to prosecution in both state and federal courts for separate crimes, at least under the decisions to date. The United States Constitution requires that persons be given a jury trial in civil and criminal cases. To deal with increased case backlogs many district courts have provided for juries of six in civil cases rather than the traditional twelve and in the recent case of *Williams v. Florida*, 399 U.S. 78 (1970), the Supreme Court of the United States approved a Florida statute authorizing trial of most criminal cases by a jury of six.

Procedure. In 1934 the Congress gave the Supreme Court of the United States power to establish general rules of procedure for the federal district courts subject to congressional disapproval. The procedure followed in the federal district courts is provided by the Federal Rules of Civil Procedure and Federal Rules of Criminal Procedure, and the Supplemental Rules for Admiralty and Maritime Claims. The civil rules were adopted in 1935, the criminal rules in 1944 and the admiralty rules, first established in 1911, were substantially revised in 1966 when they were combined with the Federal Rules of Civil Procedure. By virtue of a 1958 Act of Congress, the Judicial Conference of the United States has been authorized to submit to the Supreme Court for its consideration and adoption modification or rejection changes in and additions to these rules. As a result of a study by the Judicial Conference, working in full cooperation with bench, bar, and law schools, amendments to the Civil and Admiralty Rules and General Orders and Forms in Bankruptcy were adopted by the Supreme Court in 1961. Further amendments were approved in 1953, 1966, 1968, 1970 and they currently appear as amended up to 1975. Under the Federal Rules of Civil Procedure pleadings are simplified, emphasis being placed upon liberal pretrial devices to obtain information which will clarify issues, shorten the trial, and save time and money. Surprise is eliminated to a great extent and the trial of a civil lawsuit becomes, theoretically, a search for the truth rather than a battle over legal technicalities. Comparable improvements in criminal procedure were effectuated by the Federal Rules of Criminal Procedure, although pretrial exchange of information is not as extensive.

Several states have adopted major portions of the Federal Rules of Civil Procedure. Rhode Island and Arizona have adopted them substantially unchanged.

The Chief Justice of the Supreme Court as chairman of the Judicial Conference of the United States appointed a Standing Committee of the Conference on Rules of Practice and Procedure and advisory committees which report to the Standing Committee, each working in a separate field of procedure. There are

Table 6—2. United States District Courts

District Court	Number of Authorized Judgeships[1]	Location and Postal Address
Alabama:		
Northern District	4	Birmingham, AL 35202
Middle District	2	Montgomery, AL 36101
Southern District	2	Mobile, AL 36602
Alaska	5	Anchorage, AK 99501
Arizona	2	Phoenix, AZ 85025
Arkansas:		
Eastern District	2	Little Rock, AR 72203
Western District	2	Fort Smith, AR 72902
California:		
Northern District	11	San Francisco, CA 94102
Eastern District	3	Sacramento, CA 95841
Central District	16	Los Angeles, CA 90012
Southern District	5	San Diego, CA 92101
Canal Zone	1	Ancon, C.Z.
Colorado	4	Denver, CO 80201
Connecticut	4	New Haven, CT 06505
Delaware	3	Wilmington, DE 19899
District of Columbia	15	Washington, DC 20001
Florida:		
Northern District	2	Tallahassee, FL 32302
Middle District	6	Jacksonville, FL 32201
Southern District	7	Miami, FL 33101
Georgia:		
Northern District	6	Atlanta, GA 30301
Middle District	2	Macon, GA 31202
Southern District	2	Savannah, GA 31402
Guam	1	Agana, GU 96910
Hawaii	2	Honolulu, HI 96803
Idaho	2	Boise, ID 83702
Illinois:		
Northern District	13	Chicago, IL 60604
Eastern District	2	East St. Louis, IL 62202
Southern District	2	Springfield, IL 62705
Indiana:		
Northern District	3	Hammond, IN 46325
Southern District	4	Indianapolis, IN 46204
Iowa:		
Northern District	1½	Cedar Rapids, IA 52405
Southern District	1½	Des Moines, IA 50309
Kansas	4	Wichita, KS 67201
Kentucky		
Eastern District	2½	Lexington, KY 40501
Western District	3½	Louisville, KY 40202
Louisiana:		
Eastern District	9	New Orleans, LA 70130
Middle District	1	Baton Rouge, LA 70801
Western District	4	Shreveport, LA 71102

(Table 6—2 cont'd overleaf . . .)

Table 6-2. continued

District Court	Number of Authorized Judgeships[1]	Location and Postal Address
Maine	1	Portland, ME 04112
Maryland	7	Baltimore, MD 21202
Massachusetts	6	Boston, MA 02109
Michigan:		
Eastern District	10	Detroit, MI 48226
Western District	2	Grand Rapids, MI 49502
Minnesota	4	St. Paul, MN 55101
Mississippi:		
Northern District	2	Oxford, MS 38655
Southern District	3	Jackson, MS 39205
Missouri:		
Eastern District	4	St. Louis, MO 63101
Western District	4	Kansas City, MO 64106
Montana	2	Butte, MT 59701
Nebraska	3	Omaha, NB 68101
Nevada	2	Reno, NV 89502
New Hampshire	1	Concord, NH 03302
New Jersey	9	Trenton, NJ 08605
New Mexico	3	Albuquerque, NM 87103
New York:		
Northern District	2	Utica, NY 13503
Eastern District	9	Brooklyn, NY 11201
Southern District	27	New York, NY 10007
Western District	3	Buffalo, NY 14202
North Carolina:		
Eastern District	3[1]	Raleigh, NC 27602
Middle District	2	Greensboro, NC 27402
Western District	2	Asheville, NC 28802
North Dakota	2	Fargo, ND 58103
Ohio:		
Northern District	8	Cleveland, OH 44114
Southern District	5	Columbus, OH 43215
Oklahoma:		
Northern District	1-2/3	Tulsa, OK 74103
Eastern District	1-2/3	Muskogee, OK 74402
Western District	2-2/3	Oklahoma City, OK 73102
Oregon	3	Portland, OR 97205
Pennsylvania:		
Eastern District	19	Philadelphia, PA 19107
Middle District	4[1]	Scranton, PA 18501
Western District	10	Pittsburgh, PA 15219
Puerto Rico	3	San Juan, PR 00905
Rhode Island	2	Providence, RI 02903
South Carolina	5	Columbia, SC 29201
South Dakota	2	Sioux Falls, SD 57101
Tennessee:		
Eastern District	3	Knoxville, TN 37901
Middle District	2	Nashville, TN 37203
Western District	3	Memphis, TN 38103

Table 6—2. continued

District	Number of Authorized Judgeships[1]	Location and Postal Address
Texas:		
Northern District	6	Dallas, TX 75221
Eastern District	3	Beaumont, TX 77704
Southern District	8	Houston, TX 77601
Western District	5	San Antonio, TX 78206
Utah	2	Salt Lake City, UT 84101
Vermont	2	Burlington, VT 05402
Virginia:		
Eastern District	6	Norfolk, VA 23510
Western District	2	Roanoke, VA 24006
Virgin Islands	2	St. Thomas, VI 00801
Washington:		
Eastern District	1½	Spokane, WA 99210
Western District	3½	Seattle, WA 98104
West Virginia:		
Northern District	1½	Elkins, WV 26241
Southern District	2½	Charleston, WV 25301
Wisconsin:		
Eastern District	3	Milwaukee, WI 53202
Western District	1	Madison, WI 53701
Wyoming	1	Cheyenne, WY 82001

1. The use of fractions indicates that a judge is authorized to serve in more than one district. Included in these figures are two temporary judgeship positions which will expire as vacancies occur. Under the law creating these positions it was provided that the first vacancies occuring thereafter may not be filed. These temporary positions are located in the eastern district of North Carolina and the middle district of Pennsylvania.

Reproduced by permission of the Administrative Office of the United States Courts.

advisory committees on civil, criminal, appellate, admiralty, and bankruptcy rules. The process of revision of procedural rules is continuous.

Federal Rules of Appellate Procedure were adopted late in 1967 and became effective 1968. In March 1965, Chief Justice Earl Warren appointed an Advisory Committee to formulate Rules of Evidence for the federal courts composed of federal and trial attorneys and other legal scholars. The committee prepared a preliminary draft entitled Rules of Evidence for the United States District Courts and Magistrates, circulated in 1969. By order entered November 20, 1972, the Supreme Court prescribed Federal Rules of Evidence to be effective July 1, 1973. Chief Justice Warren E. Burger on February 5, 1973 transmitted the rules to Congress, which promptly enacted legislation deferring the effectiveness of the rules until expressly approved by Congress. The Congress then amended the rules in various respects and enacted them into law approved January 2, 1975. Congress has thus used its power to disapprove and change rules of evidence approved by the Supreme Court of the United States.

The present United States Criminal Code, partially updated in 1909 and 1948, is admittedly "an archaic collection of laws, replete with contradictory redundancies."

In 1966 a National Commission on Reform of Criminal Laws was appointed by President Johnson. The commission, known as the Brown Commission (former Governor Pat Brown was its chairperson), submitted its final report to President Nixon and Congress in January 1971. President Nixon requested his attorney general, John Mitchell, succeeded by Richard Kleindienst, to rewrite the bipartisan commission's final report and on March 14, 1973 he asked Senators McClellan and Hruska to introduce the administration's "Criminal Code Reform Act of 1973." It was introduced subsequently as S.1 at the 94th Congress, 1st Session (1975).

Senate Bill 1 has caused ongoing public controversy. Its critics urge that many of its provisions violate constitutional protections, among them fair trial and free speech. They assert that the Nixon program contradicts the recommendations of the National Commission on Reform of the Federal Criminal Laws appointed by President Johnson.

It is claimed that, despite some constructive elements, the 799-page proposed legislation is so badly flawed that the many amendments proposed would not cure it.

THREE-JUDGE DISTRICT COURTS

Early in this century, the U.S. Supreme Court upheld a federal trial judge who had enjoined a state officer from performing his duties pursuant to a state law which the federal judge declared unconstitutional. Protest ensued over the ease with which a single federal judge could block a state's machinery for enforcing its laws. In response, Congress established a special procedure for use when an injunction is sought to restrain enforcement, operation, or execution of a state statute by a state officer or administrative agency. The procedure was extended to encompass injunctions sought to restrain enforcement of federal statutes alleged to be unconstitutional.

As a result, an application for an injunction restraining enforcement of a statute by a state or federal officer on constitutional grounds had to be heard and determined by a district court composed of three judges. The district judge who received the application served as one member of the three-judge court, and the chief judge of the circuit appointed the two other judges, at least one of whom had to be a judge of the court of appeals.

After a three-judge court determined whether an injunction should be granted, the losing party appealed directly to the Supreme Court. If, however, the three-judge court determined that the special procedure should not have been invoked—e.g., because there was no claim that the federal Constitution has been contravened—then appeal went to the court of appeals for the circuit.

In 1974 the Congress modified the statutes relating to three-judge courts, reducing their availability to specified types of cases. However, criticism continued and in August 1976 a bill was passed by Congress, signed into law by the president, which abolishes the general requirements for three-judge courts in most instances. Under the new law a single judge may rule on the constitutionality of state and federal laws. The act repeals those sections of the United States Code creating the general right to the three-judge court injunctive procedure where constitutional issues are raised. The three-judge court procedure remains applicable (1) where, under a special statute elsewhere in the laws, a three-judge court procedure is otherwise specially required. Such statutes include various three-judge court provisions of the Voting Rights Act of 1965 and the Civil Rights Act of 1964; (2) where an action is filed challenging the constitutionality of the apportionment of congressional districts; or (3) where an action is filed challenging the constitutionality of the apportionment of any statewide legislative body.

SPECIAL COURTS OF THE UNITED STATES

Special courts have been created by Congress to deal with particular types of cases.

United States Court of Claims

This court was established in 1855 to permit an individual citizen or a corporation to sue the federal government for money damages in a variety of claims in which the Congress has waived the sovereign immunity of the United States. Aliens and their governments may bring suit here provided their courts give our citizens the same privilege. The court has come to be known as the "keeper of the nation's conscience" and the official seal of this court describes it as "For the Republic and its Citizens."

The court is provided for in the United States Constitution; its jurisdiction is nationwide and the court is located in the Capitol. Its chief judge and six associate judges are appointed for life by the president with the Senate's approval. They receive $44,600 annually. In addition, there are fifteen commissioners who serve as trial judges and sit in any section of the country convenient to the parties. These commissioners act as individual trial judges in the same way as federal district court judges when conducting a trial without a jury. The trial commissioner prepares findings of fact and an opinion. He makes recommendations for conclusions of law which, on exception by either party, are reviewed by a panel of three judges of the court, as authorized by law or by the court sitting en banc. Final judgments of the court are subject to review by the Supreme Court on writ of certiorari. In cases where there is no legal right to recover, either the Senate or the House may refer the claim to the chief commissioner of the court to find if there is an equitable basis for the claim upon which Congress should compensate the claimant.

A pamphlet issued by the United States government, prepared by Joseph F. Spaniol of the Administrative Office of the United States Courts for use of the

Committee on the Judiciary, House of Representatives, describes this court as follows:

> This is a busy court with a heavy docket of cases, and a large volume of decisions is handed down annually. The usual case is a technical one involving complicated issues and large amounts of money, for there is no monetary ceiling on the court's jurisdiction.
>
> Suits against the Government for money damages must be tried in the Court of Claims if the amount exceeds $10,000 except in tax refund claims where the district courts have concurrent jurisdiction, and in tort claims where district courts have exclusive jurisdiction. The court has appellate jurisdiction over the district courts in tort cases by agreement of the parties. It also has appellate jurisdiction over the Indian Claims Commission and jurisdiction to make a determination of excessive profits made by government contractors who are subject to the Renegotiation Act.
>
> The Federal Government is the nation's largest contractor, purchaser and employer. The complexity of its operations and their impact on individual citizens is nowhere better illustrated than in the litigation in this court.
>
> Citizens who pay Federal taxes under formal protest may sue in the Court of Claims for refunds with interest. Citizens may bring suits for damages for the taking of private property for public use without just compensation in violation of the Fifth Amendment to the Constitution. Constitutional and statutory rights are constantly in issue. Often they involve personnel of the military services, active and retired, and their dependents. Civil service employees seek back pay for alleged illegal dismissal from office. Contractors sue for breach of contract. Oyster growers have sought compensation for damages to their beds by dredging operations for harbor or channel improvements. Farmers blame the Army Engineers for building structures in rivers that allegedly cause floods upon their lands. Inventors find this court the only one where they can claim patent infringements by the Government. Citizens appear on a wide variety of matters, many reflecting the nation's involvement in procurement of sophisticated weapons systems for national defense.
>
> This special court hears the largest claims in the world. But, the court prides itself on giving the same careful consideration to small claims. In most instances it is the court of first and last resort for the citizen who challenges the might of the State. In the Court of Claims the Federal Government is just another litigant with no more nor fewer rights than those of the humblest citizen.

United States Customs Court

When certain merchandise is imported into the United States, customs duties have to be paid to the United States government. Customs collectors at various ports in the United States classify merchandise and appraise it. Importers may bring complaints regarding the rate of duty or the exclusion of merchandise to the United States Customs Court. The court is divided into three divisions, each

Table 6−3. Special Courts

Court	Number of Authorized Judgeships	Location and Postal Address
Court of Claims	7	717 Madison Pl., N.W. Washington, D.C. 20005
Court of Customs & Patent Appeals	5	717 Madison Pl., N.W. Washington, D.C. 20005
Customs Court	9	1 Federal Plaza New York, N.Y. 10007

Reproduced by permission of the Administrative Office of the United States Courts.

consisting of three judges. Its judges may be assigned to any port in the United States to hear cases.

The president appoints nine judges to this court with the Senate's approval, but no more than five may be from one political party. The judges receive salaries of $42,000 per year, and they serve for life. The court's main offices are located in New York City because it has long been the nation's leading port.

United States Court of Customs and Patent Appeals

Appeals from the United States Customs Court are taken to the court of customs and patent appeals. This court also reviews certain decisions of the Patent Office and of the United States Tariff Commission, as well as findings of the secretary of commerce.

A chief judge and four associate judges are appointed by the president with the Senate's approval. They hold office during good behavior and receive $44,600 per year.

Table 6−3 gives the location, number of authorized judgeships, and postal address of these three special courts.

TAX COURT OF THE UNITED STATES

Although it is technically an independent executive agency, the tax court functions in a judicial capacity. When the Commissioner of Internal Revenue has determined a deficiency in tax, the taxpayer may litigate his liability in the tax court prior to payment.

Appeals are taken to the United States Court of Appeals for the prescribed circuit, or, by agreement, to the United States Court of Appeals for the District of Columbia. Final appeals are to the United States Supreme Court by certiorari.

The court conducts trial sessions at various locations within the United States as reasonably convenient to taxpayers as is possible. Sixteen judges are appointed by the president with the consent of the Senate for fifteen-year terms. Each receives a salary of $42,000 per year. A chief judge is elected biennially from among the judges. The following description of the tax court is excerpted from *The United States Courts: Their Jurisdiction and Work*, by Joseph F. Spaniol.

Originally established in 1924 in the Executive Branch of the Government as the "United States Board of Tax Appeals," the court became officially known as the "Tax Court of the United States" in 1942 and its name was changed to the "United States Tax Court" in 1969. During World War II the Tax Court also made final determinations of excessive profits in renegotiable government contract cases—a function transferred to the Court of Claims in 1971. . . . Other judicial officers of the Court are retired judges who may be recalled by the Chief Judge. There are presently five commissioners, appointed by the Chief Judge, who serve under rules and regulations promulgated by the Court. They form the Small Tax Division which is headed by a judge appointed by the Chief Judge. The Court is organized into divisions, each of which is headed by a judge. For other assignments the commissioners serve under the Chief Judge.

The Tax Court conducts trials at approximately 110 cities within the United States and each trial session is conducted by a single judge or commissioner. The offices of the Court and all of its judges and commissioners are located at 400 Second Street, N.W., Washington, D.C. 20217.

Sec. 957 of the Tax Reform Act of 1969 (83 Stat. 733), as amended, provided for simplified procedures for the trials of tax disputes involving $1,500 or less, at the option of the individual taxpayers, and provided also that in a case conducted under these procedures the decision of the Court would be final and not subject to review by any other court. All other decisions are subject to review by the United States Court of Appeals for the District of Columbia, and thereafter by the Supreme Court of the United States upon the granting of a writ of certiorari as above stated.

UNITED STATES EMERGENCY COURT OF APPEALS

The Emergency Court of Appeals was created by Congress during World War II to review the legality of administrative decisions concerning price, rent, and other business regulations relating to war. The Chief Justice of the United States Supreme Court is empowered to appoint at least three judges from the district courts and the courts of appeals to act as judges in this court. During that war and for several years following, the court sat usually at the place of the controversy, thus serving the convenience of the parties. At the end of 1957, there were no cases pending. By its own order, the court ceased to function as of April 19, 1962.

Temporary Emergency Court of Appeals

Under the Economic Stabilization Act Amendment of 1971, a special court known as the Temporary Emergency Court of Appeals of the United States was created. The court has exclusive jurisdiction of all appeals from the district courts of the United States in cases or controversies arising under the economic stabilization laws. It consists of eight district and circuit judges appointed by the Chief Justice. The court has been in operation since February 1972 with the principal office located at the United States Courthouse in the District of Columbia.

The court operates under its own rules and under the Federal Rules of Appellate Procedure. Hearing divisions sit when necessary at Washington, D.C.; St. Paul, Minnesota; Atlanta, Georgia; Houston, Texas; and San Francisco, California, and such other places as the chief judge of the court may designate.

UNITED STATES COURT OF MILITARY APPEALS

Court martial decisions arising in the armed services are referred to a Board of Review by the judge advocate general of the branch of service involved. Appeals from the Boards of Review are heard by the court of military appeals. This court was established in 1951 as part of the Department of Defense, and sits in Washington, D.C. It consists of three judges, a chief judge, and two associate judges appointed by the president of the United States from civilian life to serve for terms of fifteen years. Judges of the military court of appeals receive $44,600 per year. Review by this court is discretionary in some cases, mandatory in others. Death penalty cases must be reviewed.

Judicially independent, although it operates as a part of the Department of Defense for administrative purposes, this court exercises jurisdiction as to questions of law in cases certified to the court by the judge advocates general of the armed services, and by the general counsel of the Department of Transportation acting for the Coast Guard.

The court may also be petitioned by convicted defendants who have received sentences of a year or more confinement, or a punitive discharge.

In these cases, the decisions of the court are final—there is no further direct review.

In addition, the court is required by law to work jointly with the judge advocates general of the armed services and the general counsel of the Department of Transportation and to report annually to the Congress on the progress of the military justice system under the Code, and to recommend improvements therein wherever necessary.

UNITED STATES MAGISTRATES

Until 1968, the United States commissioners comprised the frontline ranks of the federal court system. These judicial officers functioned on a full-time or a part-time basis and received compensation based on a fee system. Although theirs were not courts of record and decisions by commissioners were subject to a trial de novo on appeal, the commissioners were often called upon to referee civil and admiralty claims; take and certify depositions; issue attachments; dispose of tax matters and seamen's wage claims; discharge or bind over accused persons to answer charges in a district court; admit accused persons to bail; file sworn, written complaints; grant or deny formal, written applications for search warrants; conduct proceedings for the discharge of indigent prisoners; and try and sentence persons accused of petty offenses.

The Federal Magistrates Act, passed by Congress in 1968, was aimed at sweeping reform of the Office of U.S. Commissioner. The commissioners were to be phased out of existence and replaced by United States magistrates after a three-year transitional period. Unlike the commissioners, magistrates receive a salary fixed by statute for full-time magistrates and there is a maximum salary for those serving on a part-time basis. Federal magistrates must be members of the bar—a qualification lacking for U.S. Commissioners.

The federal magistrates perform many judicial duties. They are empowered to administer oaths and affirmations, try misdemeanors in all but a few exceptional cases, set conditions of release other than bail for accused persons, and perform such duties as the district court may specify. The latter may include assisting a district judge in the conduct of pretrial or discovery proceedings and preliminary review of habeas corpus petitions. The Federal Rules for U.S. Magistrates became effective in May 1969 and prescribe procedure for the magistrates.

At the end of fiscal year 1974, there were 541 U.S. magistrates positions including 112 full-time positions, 411 part-time positions, and 18 combination positions whereby clerks and deputy clerks of courts or part-time bankruptcy judges performed magistrate duties. The direction now is to convert part-time to full-time magistrates, reducing the number of part-time magistrates.

ADMINISTRATION OF THE UNITED STATES COURTS

Judicial Conference of the United States, Circuit Judicial Council, Circuit Judicial Conference

The judicial branch of the United States government includes several organizations for its own administration. The Judicial Conference of the United States consists of the Chief Justice of the United States, the chief judges of the ten circuits and District of Columbia circuit, the chief judge of the court of customs and patent appeals, the chief judge of the court of claims, and a district judge from each circuit chosen for a term of three years by the judges of the circuit at an annual meeting of the Judicial Conference of the Circuit. The Chief Justice is required by law to summon annually the Judicial Conference of the United States, and may also call special sessions of the Judicial Conference as required. At present the Judicial Conference meets twice a year to resolve administrative problems affecting all the circuits, to make recommendations to Congress concerning legislation affecting the federal judicial system, and to examine generally the conduct of the federal judiciary. In addition, because lack of sentencing uniformity has been a chronic problem, institutes and joint councils on sentencing practices are conducted for federal district judges under the auspices of the Judicial Conference, for the purpose of achieving standardized sentences and sentencing criteria in the federal courts.

Each circuit has a Judicial Council consisting of the judges of its court of appeals which has the power to take such steps, such as the assignment of judges, as may be required to dispose efficiently of the cases in each district. Semiannual meetings are mandated by statute.

The Judicial Conference of the Circuit consists of all the district and circuit judges in that circuit and invited members of the bar who meet annually to discuss common problems, make recommendations for the improvement of the administration of justice within the circuit, and conduct seminars for newly-appointed judges in the circuit.

Administrative Office of the United States Courts

An Administrative Office of the United States Courts was established in 1939. Its director is appointed by the Supreme Court to perform the administrative duties for the federal court system. The administrative office prepares and submits to Congress the budget for the federal courts; receives reports from, and exercises some degree of supervision over the clerical staffs of the courts, probation officers, referees in bankruptcy, reporters and other court personnel; audits and disburses money for the operation of the courts; compiles and publishes—quarterly and annually—statistical reports on the volume and distribution of business in the federal courts, and recent procedural and legislative developments having some bearing on the courts; supplies professional, legal, and statistical services to committees of the Judicial Conference of the United States; and conducts studies of court procedures under the direction of the Judicial Conference and other interested federal authorities, including congressional committees.

The Federal Judicial Center

The Federal Judicial Center, created by Congress in 1967 at the behest of the president and the Chief Justice, functions as the planning and research arm of the Administrative Office of the United States Courts and the Judicial Conference of the United States. Supervised by a board of directors which includes the Chief Justice of the United States, judges of the district courts and the courts of appeals, and the director of the Administrative Office of the United States Courts, the Federal Judicial Center and its director are charged with responsibility for educating and training federal judges and court personnel; conducting and stimulating research in the field of judicial administration; developing and presenting recommendations for court reforms at the request of the Judicial Conference; staffing and aiding the Judicial Conference; and initiating and adopting data processing and other computerized techniques to improve the administration of justice.

Circuit Court Executive

Recognizing the need to further the modernization of the administration of the federal courts, Congress in 1971 promulgated legislation establishing the office of circuit court executive. Eleven positions have been created, one in each circuit, including the District of Columbia Circuit, to be filled by a court executive, a person particularly familiar with court problems and capable of providing solutions based on court management techniques. The Judicial Council of each circuit has the power to appoint a court executive, delegating specific duties to him, subject to the general supervision of the chief judges of the circuit. Such circuit executives have been appointed in nine circuits. Included are the D.C., Second, Third, Fourth, Fifth, Sixth, Eighth, Ninth, and Tenth Circuits.

Each circuit executive serves at the pleasure of the judicial council of the circuit and receives a salary of $37,800 annually. Exercising administrative authority over the operation of the United States Court of Appeals and the federal district courts located in the circuit, the court executive performs a wide range of tasks, including the assignment and direction of nonjudicial personnel, budgeting, and accounting; the conduct of management studies for the circuit and the Judicial Conference of the United States; liaison with government agencies and state courts within the geographical boundaries of the circuit; and the establishment of procedures for calling and compensating jurors.

Administrative Assistant to the Chief Justice

In 1972 the Congress provided an administrative assistant to the Chief Justice of the Supreme Court of the United States to ease the way of the Chief Justice in his many administrative duties as head of the entire United States court system. The administrative assistant serves at the pleasure of the Chief Justice and receives a salary of $42,000.

BIBLIOGRAPHY

ABRAHAM, DOHERTY and DOHERTY. The judiciary; the supreme court in the governmental process. Boston, 1973. 158 p.

AMMERMAN. Three-judge courts: see how they run! Federal Rules Decisions 52:293 (1971).

BABBIT and MORRIS. Introduction to the tax court of the United States. Tax Law 21:615 (1968).

BENNETT. The United States court of claims, a 50-year perspective. Federal Bar Journal 29:284 (1970).

BRENNAN. United States supreme court: reflections past and present. Marquette Law Review 48:437 (1965).

CANNON. Administrative change and the supreme court. Judicature 57:334 (1974).

CLARK. The federal judiciary; 50 years of progress. Federal Bar Journal 29:245 (1970).

CLARK. The new federal judicial center. American Bar Association Journal 54: 743 (1968).

DRENNEN. New status of the tax court. New York University Institute of Federal Taxation 29:1017 (1971).

FRANK. The Warren court. New York, 1964. 200 p.

GENDELMAN. Court of customs and patent appeals and 35 U.S.C. 103. Journal of the Patent Office Society 45:645 (1963).

GINSBERG and STEIN. Due process and the tax court. Kentucky Law Journal 53:336 (1964/1965).

HARRELL. Equal justice under law. The supreme court in American life. Washington, D.C. (1975). 151 p. (Federal Bar Foundation).

KIPPS. Unique national court: the United States court of claims. American Bar Association Journal 53:1025 (1967).

McDERMOTT. The court of claims: the nation's conscience. American Bar Association Journal 57:594 (1971).

McKAY. Supreme court as an instrument of law reform. St. Louis University Law Journal 13:387 (1969).

MARGOLIS. Federal magistrates: relief for the federal courts. Judges Journal 12:85 (1973).

POWELL. Myths and misconceptions about the supreme court. New York State Bar Journal 48:6 (1976).

SCHWARTZ. A basic history of the U.S. supreme court. Princeton, 1968. 191 p.

SHAFROTH. Off with the old, on with the new. American Bar Association Journal 55:32 (1969).

SYMPOSIUM: the United States Court of Claims. Georgetown Law Journal 55: 393 (1966/1967).

THREE-JUDGE court act of 1910: purpose, procedure and alternatives. Journal of Criminal Law 62:205 (1971).

THREE-JUDGE district court: scope and procedure under section 2281. Harvard Law Review 77:299 (1963).

U.S. ADMINISTRATIVE Office of the Courts. Management statistics for the United States Courts. Washington, 1974. 120 p.

U.S. ADMINISTRATIVE Office of the United States Courts. Annual report of the director. Washington, 1940–

U.S. ADMINISTRATIVE Office of the United States Courts. Quarterly report of the director. Washington, 1951–

U.S. CONGRESS House Committee on the Judiciary. The United States courts; their jurisdiction and work. Washington, 1975. 16 p. By Joseph F. Spaniol.

VINES. The role of circuit courts of appeal in the federal judicial process: a case study. Midwest Journal of Political Science 7:305 (1963).

WIECEK. Origin of the United States court of claims. Administrative Law Review 20:387 (1968).

WILSON. The United States customs court. Utah Bar Journal 2:11 (1974).

WRIGHT. The federal courts: a century after Appomattox. American Bar Association Journal 52: 742 (1966).

The Work Load of the Appellate Courts

ALLAN. Demarche or destruction of the federal courts: a response to Judge Friendly's analysis of federal jurisdiction. Brooklyn Law Review 40:637 (1974).

AMERICAN Bar Foundation. Accommodating the workload of the United States Courts of appeals; report of recommendations. Chicago, 1968. 8 p.

BICKEL. A reply to Arthur J. Goldberg: the overworked court. New Republic 168:17 (1973).

BICKEL. The caseload of the supreme court, and what, if anything, to do about it. Washington, 1973. 37 p.

BLACK. The national court of appeals: an unwise proposal. Yale Law Journal 83:883 (1974).

BRENNAN. The national court of appeals: another dissent. University of Chicago Law Review 40:473 (1973).

BURGER. Observations on the report of the study group on the caseload of the supreme court. Washington, 1973. 14 p.

BURGER and WARREN. Retired chief justice Warren attacks, chief justice Burger defends Freund study group's composition and proposal. American Bar Association Journal 59:721 (1973).

CARRINGTON. Crowded dockets and the courts of appeals: the threat to the function of review and the national law. Harvard Law Review 82:542 (1969).

CASPER and POSNER. A study of the supreme court's caseload. Journal of Legal Studies 3:339 (1974).

FEDERAL Judicial Center. Study group on the caseload of the supreme court (Freund Report). Washington, 1972. 65 p. Reprinted in Federal Rules Decisions 57:573 (1973).

FEINBERG. A national court of appeals? Brooklyn Law Review 42:1 (1976).

FREUND. Why we need the national court of appeals. American Bar Association Journal 59:247 (1973).

FRIENDLY. Federal jurisdiction: a general view. New York, 1973. 199 p.

FRIENDLY. Averting the flood by lessening the flow. Cornell Law Review 59:634 (1974).

GOLDBERG. One supreme court: it doesn't need its cases "screened." New Republic 168:14 (1973).

GRESSMAN. The national court of appeals, a dissent. American Bar Association Journal 59:253 (1973).

GRESSMAN. The Constitution v. the Freund report. George Washington Law Review 41:951 (1973).

HAYNSWORTH. A new court to improve the administration of justice. American Bar Association Journal 59:841 (1973).

HUFSTEDLER. New blocks for old pyramids: reshaping the judicial system. Southern California Law Review 44:901 (1971).

JUSTICE Brennan calls national court of appeals proposal "fundamentally unnecessary and ill-advised." American Bar Association Journal 59:835 (1973).

KURLAND. Jurisdiction of the United States supreme court: time for change? Cornell Law Review 55:616 (1974).

LEWIN. Helping the court with its work: a response to Goldberg and Bickel. New Republic 168:15 (1973).

POL, SCHMIDT and WHALEN. A national court of appeals: a dissenting view. Northwestern University Law Review 67: 842 (1973).

REHNQUIST. The supreme court: past and present. American Bar Association Journal 59:36 (1973).

REHNQUIST. Whither the courts. American Bar Association Journal 60:787 (1974).

U.S. COMMISSION on Revision of the Federal Court Appellate System. The geographical boundaries of the several judicial circuits: recommendations for change. Washington, 1973. 32 p.

U.S. COMMISSION on Revision of the Federal Court Appellate System. Structure and internal procedures: recommendations for change. Washington, 1975. 188 p.

WARREN. Let's not weaken the supreme court. American Bar Journal 60:677 (1974).

Appendixes

Appendix A

Legal Research

Edward J. Bander

TABLE OF CONTENTS

	Paragraph
Legal Research Books	3–13
Authority	14–18
Reports	20–27
Digests	28–36
Annotations	37–40
Loose-Leaf Services	41–45
Encyclopedias	46–48
Treatises	49–53
Restatements	54
Law Reviews	55–58
Case Citators	59–69
Transition	70
Constitutions	71–72
Statutes and Regulations	73–87
Legislative History	88–94
Bowling v. Sperry	95
Shepard's Citations, specimen pages	96
American Law Reports Chart	97
Alphabetical Appendix (Index and Bibliography)	

I would like to express my appreciation to Professor Fannie J. Klein for her advice and counsel in the preparation of this chapter.

1   The purpose of this appendix is to familiarize the reader with the tools of legal research and to provide specific aids to legal research by subject.

2   As an introduction, it is necessary to discuss some basic texts with which every legal researcher should be familiar. The annotations accompanying each book will be useful in suggesting additional sources to complement this appendix as well as to indicate the nature of legal research. The law, it has been said, is a "seamless web," but there is a simplicity to it that is within the grasp of the diligent.

LEGAL RESEARCH BOOKS

3   Andrews, Joseph L. et al. *The Law in the United States of America; A Selective Bibliographical Guide.* (New York University Press 1965).

A dated bibliographic guide that is geared to indicate to the foreign law librarian a basic American law collection. More conveniently than elsewhere, you get a bird's-eye view of just which sets are in a standard law library. There is an annotated listing of books by subject from Accounting to Zoning.

4   Cohen, Morris L. *Legal Research in a Nutshell.* 2d ed. (West 1971).

Chapters on Judicial Reports, Case-Finding, Statutes, Legislative History, Administrative Law, Loose-Leaf Services, Treaties, Secondary Materials (Encyclopedias, Restatements Periodicals, Citators, etc.), Foreign and International Law. A 259-page summary of the more complete texts, such as *How to Find the Law*, Pollack, Price and Bitner, etc. Referred to as *Cohen* in this appendix.

5   Cohen, Morris L., ed. *How to Find the Law.* 7th ed. (West 1976).

The chapter on Analysis of the Problem effectively describes how a factual problem can be solved with legal research tools. There are also chapters on Legal Encyclopedias, Digests, American Court Reports, Stattutes, Administrative and Executive Publications, Loose-Leaf Services, Periodical Literature, Treatises, Restatements, Uniform Laws, Dictionaries, Citators, English and Canadian Materials, Non-Legal Materials (government documents, biography, etc.), the writing of letters, opinions, memoranda, and appellate briefs. Each chapter is written by a law librarian. There are also chapters on multimedia (microforms, computers, etc.), research in the social sciences, and international, foreign, and comparative law. Referred to as *How to* in this appendix.

6   Farnsworth, E. Allan. *An Introduction to the Legal System of the United States.* (Oceana 1963, 1975).

A brief introductory text on the legal system. Its chapters on the judicial system, case law, the legislative system, statutes, and secondary authority form a cohesive and well-written commentary for an American student, as well as the foreign student for whom it was designed. There are also bibliographical essays on civil procedure, criminal procedure, evidence, conflict of laws, contracts, torts, property, family law, commercial law, business enterprises, constitutional law, trade regulation, labor law, tax law, and criminal law. While the book is dated, particularly as to current texts it is superior in oversight and insight to the other texts.

7   Jacobstein, J. Myron and Roy M. Mersky. *Pollack's Fundamentals of Legal Research.* 4th ed. (Foundation Press 1973).

Chapters on Glossary of Terms used in Legal Research, the Legal Process. Preliminary Procedure in Legal Research, Court Reports, Federal Court Decisions, State Court Decisions and the National Reporter System, Digests, Annotated Law Reports, Constitutions, Federal Legislation, Legislative History, State and Municipal Legislation, Court Procedure, Administrative Practice, Citations, Encyclopedias, Legal Periodicals and Indexes, Treaties, Restatements, Model Codes, Uniform Laws, International Law, English Legal Research, Summary of Research Procedure, Citation Style, Abbreviations. Referred to as *Pollack* in this appendix.

8   Lloyd, David. *Finding the Law; A Guide to Legal Research.* (Oceana 1974).

Chapters on Researching the Common Law, Using the Statutes, Persuasive Authority, Researching in Specific Fields of Law (Environmental Law, Consumer Law, Bankruptcy, Criminal Law, Constitutional Law, Commercial Law, Family Law, Taxation, Business Organizations, Natural Resources Law, International Law, Torts, Trade Regulation, Property Law, Estate Planning), Citation Style, Abbreviations, Citators. An inexpensive beginner's text that has some excellent features.

9   New York University School of Law. *Moot Court Handbook; Introduction to Legal Research, Brief Writing and Oral Argument.* 4th ed. (New York University Moot Court Board 1975).

The chapter on Researching the Brief presupposes a knowledge of legal research, but nevertheless is a fine summary of legal research materials and citation style. Although designed to assist students in writing a brief, it can be helpful to the neophyte, particularly as the entire book is offset from typewritten copy and the student can observe the form in typed copy rather than printed copy. There is also a bibliography of books on legal writing and oral argument.

10   Price, Miles O. and Harry Bitner. *Effective Legal Research; A Practical Manual of Law Books and their Use.* (Prentice-Hall 1953).

Also published in a 1962 student edition (Little, Brown). Chapters on Legislation, Federal Legislation, Treaties, Legislative Histories, Indexes and Tables, Work with Federal Statutes, State Legislation, Rules of Courts and Administrative Agencies, Law Reports, Administrative Law, Index and Search Books, Digests, Encyclopedias, Treatises, Legal Periodicals, Restatements, Dictionaries, Words and Phrases, Maxims, Form

Books, Loose-Leaf Services, Citators, English and Canadian Materials, Tables of Cases, Citation Style. The Appendices include lists of American, British and Canadian material, Standard Form of Appellate Brief, Memorandum of Law and a list of commonly used Anglo-American abbreviations. While both editions are obviously dated, this is a standard text in the field and indispensable in any legal reference collection. Referred to as *Price* in this appendix.

11 Research Group, Inc. *Basic Legal Research Techniques.* (American Law Pub. Service, P.O. Box "U," San Mateo, CA 94402 (1976).

An innovative text on legal research by an organization engaged in legal research for lawyers with offices in Charlottesville, Va., Cambridge, Mass., Ann Arbor, Mich., and Berkeley, Calif. The discussion of the "back-door approach," is a novel and satisfactory way of leading into secondary sources. This organization also published "Researchers" which they claim provides digests of cases more recent than West. Appendices include legal writing information, citation form and spacing guide, citation style for state codifications, an extensive list of abbreviations, footnote terms such as "Cf.," general abbreviations and a short list of treatises by subject. Referred to as *Research Group* in this appendix.

12 Rombauer, Marjorie D. *Legal Problem Solving: Analysis, Research and Writing.* 2d ed. (West 1973).

Chapters on How to Brief a Case, How to Analyze an Opinion, How to Interpret Legislation, How to Use Legal Research Material, How to Write a Memorandum, How to Argue Orally (sample oral argument). While not as exhaustive as books such as *Pollack* or *Price*, this is basically a book on how to do legal research.

13 Werner, O. James. *Manual for Prison Law Libraries.* (Rothman 1976).

Chapters on the Prison Law Library, Library Quarters and Equipment, Law Books and their Use, Library Acquisitions and Records, Cataloging and Shelving Books, Lending and Borrowing Books, etc. While designed for a specialized clientele, with the emphasis on criminal law, the information on legal research is concise and informative.

AUTHORITY

14 All the previous mentioned books are designed to inform the user where to locate and how to apply authority, i.e., what the courts believe they are obligated to obey in deciding a case before them. In general this means researching for applicable laws, regulations, decisions of courts (also called cases, opinions, reports) and, obviously, state and federal constitutions.

15 This authority can be a law (National Labor Relations Act), the United States Constitution (Fifth Amendment on the right against involuntary self-incrimination), a regulation (tax deductions for moving expenses), and cases

interpreting the above. Cases have assumed such an important part of our legal system that it can safely be said that no one knows what a law means until the courts interpret it through decided cases.

16   What about cases in such areas of the law as contracts and torts that are not based on the passage of a law (which involves approval by a legislature and signing by the executive)? The long answer is to read a treatise on the common law (the heartbeat of our legal system), consult the American Law Institute Restatements (See paragraph 54), and find a good treatise on the topic (See Alphabetical Appendix). The short answer is to find the relevant cases.

17   The previous paragraph may mislead the reader into believing that all legal research leads to litigation. Most research, in fact, safeguards the individual from litigation. It is called preventive law. Also, most litigation ends at trial (that is, an appeal is not taken), and it may be heartening to know that for the myriad cases that come before the courts, few are recorded in the official reports and thus are of little use to researchers.

18   As you read this section keep in mind that our system of jurisprudence is determined to a great extent by what courts have written in the past. We are guided by precedent (See paragraph 26 and Alphabetical Appendix: Precedent). All the material pertaining to legal research is designed to lead one to precedent (unless the situation is governed by statute) or to try and establish a precedent. For a fuller explanation of this concept (and such related terms as *stare decisis*, *res judicata*, *ratio decidendi*), consult the texts mentioned earlier and the following:

Comment, Diverse Views of What Constitutes the Principle of Law of a Case, 36 *Colo. L. Rev.* 377 (1964).

Cross, *Precedent in English Law.* 2d ed. (Clarendon Press 1968).

19   It may also be instructive as you read about legal research in this appendix to keep in mind the order of research that one law professor recommended for state law: (1) local encyclopedia, (2) annotated statutes, (3) state digest, (4) *American Jurisprudence 2d*, (5) *American Law Reports* series, (6) *Corpus Juris Secundum*, (7) treatises, (8) *Words and Phrases*, (9) loose-leaf services, (10) *Restatements*, (11) law reviews, (12) *Shepard's Citators.* See Emery, *A Streamlined Briefing Technique for States with Encyclopedias* (1970), p. 10.

REPORTS

Official Reports

20   Most states publish official reports of their cases, including the reports of the highest court of the state and its intermediate appellate court. For example, Massachusetts publishes the *Massachusetts Reports* and *Appellate Decisions.* The former contains the opinions of the Supreme Judicial Court,

the highest court in Massachusetts; the latter contains the reports of the intermediate court—that is, the court that is appealed to from the trial court. About a third of the states have made the West Publishing Company the official reporter for their decisions. For example, *Oklahoma Decisions*, although published by West, is certified as the official reporter for that state. The units of the National reporter System (See paragraph 23) are unofficial reports and provide a parallel citation, except for states like Oklahoma which have contracted with West to do their printing. In fact, *Oklahoma Decisions* are taken directly from the *Pacific Reporter*, a unit of the National Reporter System. The significance of official and unofficial reports has become blurred with current practice. Legally, if a discrepancy occurs between the official and unofficial report the former holds; practically, the only difference is in the order of citation (official citation first). *Martindale-Hubbell Law Directory*, published every year, has a law digest volume which conveniently keeps abreast of this information. For each state digest there is a category for Courts and another for Reports. The former gives the official name of all the courts in the state, including federal courts; the latter lists what reports are currently published for that state and where they are digested. This volume also digests the substantive law of all states and many foreign countries by subject.

21   The federal government publishes the official United States Supreme Court Reports (*United States Reports*). Lower federal court decisions are published by West: *Federal Reporter*, *Federal Supplement*, *Federal Rules Decisions*. It is imperative that you cite this material properly (See Alphabetical Appendix: Citation Style).

22   Most libraries get advance sheets of official reports only for their own state and the United States Supreme Court (See paragraph 25). These reports are mailed within a week of the date of decision. For other jurisdictions they rely on the unofficial reports which take about two months from the date of decision.

Unofficial Reports

23   The Uniform System of Citation (11th ed. 1967; 12th ed. has been announced for Summer of 1976) is a valuable research tool, as well as setting the style for legal footnoting. It requires that official state citations be complemented by the National Reporter citation, if both are available. The *National Reporter System* is published by West and it reprints (or prints in a state that has designated West as its official reporter) the highest court decisions in all fifty states as well as the aforementioned federal material. The West complete system is as follows:

Atlantic Reporter (A.)
(Conn., Del., Me., Md., N.H., N.J., Pa., R.I., Vt.)

North Eastern Reporter (N.E.)
    (Ill., Ind., Mass., N.Y., Ohio)
North Western Reporter (N.W.)
    (Iowa, Mich., Minn., Neb., N. Dak., S. Dak., Wis.)
Pacific Reporter (P.)
    (Alaska, Ariz., Cal., Colo., Hawaii, Idaho, Kan., Mont., Nev., N.M.,
    Okla., Ore., Utah, Wash., Wyo.)
South Eastern Reporter (S.E.)
    (Ga., N.C., S.C., Va., W. Va.)
South Western Reporter (S.W.)
    (Ark., Ky., Mo., Tenn., Tex.)
Southern Reporter (So.)
    (Ala., Fla., La., Miss.)

These reporters encompass all fifty states' highest court opinions and some intermediate court opinions. Other state units are:

California Reporter (Cal. Rptr.)

New York Supplement (N.Y.S.)

These units accommodate the needs of attorneys who want all the reported opinions of California and New York. The *North Eastern Reporter* and the *Pacific Reporter* presently have only the opinions of the highest courts of New York and California respectively.

The federal units of the *National Reporter System* are as follows:

Supreme Court Reporter (S. Ct.)
    (United States Supreme Court reports beginning with 106 U.S.)
Federal Reporter (F.)
    (Opinions of the United States Courts of Appeals).
    1st Circuit (1st Cir.)
        (Me., Mass., N.H., Puerto Rico, R.I.)
    2d Cir.
        (Conn., N.Y., Ct.)
    3d Cir.
        (Del., N.J., Penn., Virgin Islands)
    4th Cir.
        (N. Car., S. Car., Va., W. Va.)
    5th Cir.
        (Ala., Canal Zone, Fla., Ga., La., Miss., Tex.)
    6th Cir.
        (Ken., Mich., Ohio, Tenn.)
    7th Cir.
        (Ill., Ind., Wis.)
    8th Cir.
        (Ark., Iowa, Minn., Miss., Neb., N. Dak., S. Dak.)

9th Cir.
  (Alaska, Ariz., Cal., Guam, Hawaii, Idaho, Mont., Nev., Ore.,
  Wash.)
10th Cir.
  (Colo., Kan., N. Mex., Okla., Utah., Wyo.)
D.C. Cir.
U.S. Court of Claims
U.S. Court of Customs and Patent Appeals.
Federal Supplement (F. Supp.)
  (United States District Courts, United States Customs Court,
  Special Court-Regional Rail Reorganization Act, and Rules of the
  Judicial Panel on Multidistrict Litigation)
Federal Rules Decisions (F.R.D.)
  (Opinions, decisions, and rulings involving the Federal Rules of
  Civil and Criminal Procedure. Also contains articles on these
  topics.)

It is important to note that a "2d" after any unit (this applies to all legal publications) means a new series of volumes. For example, volumes 1–200 of the *North Eastern Reporter* covers cases from 1885–1936; volume one of the *North Eastern Reporter 2d Series* (N.E.2d) began in 1936 and continues to the present day. It is the publisher's prerogative to designate the volumes as he pleases (the British practice of emphasizing the year is much preferable as it eliminates the need for the cumbersome "2d."

24   All West Reports are published as follows: a weekly pamphlet for each unit (200–300 pages) that contain (1) the opinions, (2) headnotes, (3) an alphabetical arrangement by topic and key number of these headnotes, (4) special features that can easily be understood by checking the pamphlet. These pamphlets are eventually replaced by bound volumes containing the same pagination (thus the pamphlet can be cited).

25   The Lawyers Cooperative Publishing Company (LCP) is another printer of reports. *Lawyers' Edition* reprints the reports of the United States Supreme Court and includes notations to indicate precisely where each page of the official *United States Reports* begins and ends (the *Supreme Court Reporter* also does this). The accepted and logical practice is to cite only to the *United States Reports* (Example: *In re Winship* 397 U.S. 358 (1970)). If you question the need for these unofficial reporters remember that *Lawyers' Edition* provides annotations and the *Supreme Court Reporter* is keyed into West's *National Reporter System.* The unofficial reports also reach the user before the official reports.

26   Let us discuss an actual case before we go to the Digests. Larry Bowling, a teenager, purchased a car from Sperry Ford, a dealer. He disaffirmed the contract ostensibly because of his infancy and refused to make further payments. Mr. Sperry sued for the balance due and won the case. On appeal to

the Indiana Appellate Court, the trial court was reversed and Mr. Bowling now has no legal obligations to Mr. Sperry. This court held that a minor can disaffirm a contract unless an exception can be found to this rule, such as that the purchase was a necessity (which the court did not find after reviewing the facts). For this principle of law or precedent, the Indiana Appellate Court cited the highest court of Indiana, the Indiana Supreme Court (theoretically only the highest court of a state can establish precedent in that state).

27   How is this information made available? Information on the trial can be found only in the archives for the trial court under the name of the case: *Sperry v. Bowling*. Sperry was the plaintiff or person seeking redress at law, and Bowling the defendant (a much misspelled word), or the person being sued. The appellate opinion can be found in *Bowling v. Sperry*, 133 Ind. App. 692, 184 N.E.2d 901 (1962). Bowling, who lost at trial and is appealing, is now the appellant; Sperry is the appellee. 133 stands for volume 133 of the *Indiana Appellate Reports*. 692 is the page where the case begins. 184 is the volume of the *North Eastern Report, 2d Series* and 901 is the page where this case is reprinted verbatim, but with the West headnotes that make up their digests. 1962 is the year the case was decided (this case is reprinted at paragraph 95).

DIGESTS

28 The headnotes referred to in the previous paragraphs are the reason that West has a virtual monopoly on unofficial reporting. The headnote(s) or abstract(s) that precede the opinion refer to points of law or factual situations discussed in the case. The headnotes are numbered consecutively and when this number appears in the opinion in brackets it relates to that portion of the opinion that is summarized in the headnote (the order of headnotes also has use when Shepardizing cases). This topic-key number is not only relevant to the case at hand but will also lead you to other cases in the entire *National Reporter System*.

For instance, a headnote in the *Bowling* case reads as follows:

1. Infants, key number 47
    Contracts of minors are voidable and may be disaffirmed.

That proposition is obviously applicable to the *Bowling* case, but by consulting any West Digest unit you can find other cases holding similar propositions. And remember that while an Indiana court cannot consider the reports of other states as precedent it can use their reasoning to set its own precedent.

29   Obviously these topics and key numbers do not tell us enough. The topic and key number lead to cases which must be read to determine their relevancy.

30   The overall method West uses to assemble these headnotes is the American Digest System. Theoretically (there are always qualifying factors to every legal proposition), we can find every federal and state case on the proposition that "contracts of minors are voidable and may be disaffirmed" by utilizing "Infants, key number 47" in the following units of the American Digest System:

Century Digest (to 1896)

Decennial Digests (1896–1966: six units)

General Digest (1966 to date: 45 units to date)

This translates into 52 units that will have to be consulted to locate every case that West has on any topic-key number. Usually, the researcher works backwards beginning with the latest volumes first.

31   If you wish to localize your search, consult a state digest (*Indiana Digest* in the *Bowling* case) or the *Federal Digest*, *Modern Federal Practice Digest*, and *Federal Practice Digest 2d* for all federal material in the *National Reporter System*. For United States Supreme Court cases, consult the *Supreme Court Digest*. There are also regional digests corresponding to the *National Reporter System*.

32   The advantage of a state digest is that you can completely research the topic and key number in one volume and the pocket part to that volume (at times it can be a separate volume—each volume or pocket part will tell you what reports have been digested). Remember that each volume of the regional reporter and each weekly pamphlet has the same key number breakdown as the digest units.

33   There are three methods of search that can be utilized to locate a desired key number, which will lead one to cases. (This analysis is abstracted from West's *Law Finder*, available from the publisher):

1. Descriptive Word Index

Each digest unit has an exhaustive listing of terms that include parties (infants), places and things (automobiles), basis of action or issue (contract), defense (infancy), relief sought (disaffirmance of contract).

2. Topic Method

There are 400 topical breakdowns in the digests from Abandonment to Zoning. By going directly to the topic, (if one is certain regarding the basis of the cause of action), consulting the scope note, and then the key number breakdown to that topic, one can bypass the Descriptive Word Index.

3. Table of Cases

If one has the name of a case said to be in point, each digest unit has a table of cases, arranged alphabetically, that provides the citation to the case, the history of the case, and the topics and key numbers used to digest the case. There are also Defendant/Plaintiff (the reverse of the general order of case name) listings for units other than the American Digest.

34   The first method is the most practical, the second comes with experience,

and the third gives the citation and parallel citation to the case whose name you have.

35   The critical thing to remember is that digests lead to cases. Digests cannot be cited, they cannot be relied on for precedent, and only constitute a beginning point in one's research. The cases must be read, briefed, and analyzed in the context of the problem.

36   The West key number system is copyrighted by West; however, digests are a common device for a subject breakdown of material by law publishers. Other publishers who employ this device (using their own logical subject breakdown of the material) are *United States Patent Quarterly* (BNA), *Uniform Commercial Code Reporting Service* (Callaghan), *Negligence and Compensation Cases Annotated* (Callaghan), and all the annotated codes.

ANNOTATIONS

37   The most comprehensive set of annotations is published by the Lawyers Cooperative Publishing Company (LCP). Their *American Law Reports* (*A.L.R.*, *A.L.R. 2d*, *A.L.R. 3d*) and *A.L.R. Federal* are organized as follows: significant cases are reprinted with headnotes and also a summary of briefs of counsel. This is followed by a signed annotation that explores thoroughly an issue raised in the reprinted case. The editors provide an index to the annotation, a breakdown by jurisdiction (state or federal), and a checklist of LCP publications that treat aspects of the annotation (such as forms, encyclopedic references, practice, etc.). *A.L.R.* is updated by the *Blue Book of Supplemental Decisions*. *A.L.R. 2d* is updated by the *Later Case Service*, and a pocket part updates *A.L.R. 3d* and *A.L.R. Fed.* (see paragraph 97). There are *Quick Index* volumes that lead to annotations in these sets as well as a table of cases reprinted and a list of annotations that have been superseded. The *Federal Quick Index* leads to references in United State Code Service as well as annotations. Many publications, including *American Jurisprudence, Second Series* (*Am. Jur. 2d*), law review articles, treatises, and *Shepard's Citations*, will refer one to these annotations.

38   LCP also publishes the *Lawyers' Edition*, Supreme Court Reporter (L.Ed.), which reprints United States Supreme Court Reports and also annotates them. Marginal markings provide parallel citations to the *United States Reports* (U.S.), making it unnecessary to cite to anything but the official *United States Reports*. There is also a *Lawyers' Edition Digest* (similar to the West *Supreme Court Digest*), which has a volume that indexes all the annotations as well as the usual table of cases and topic index.

39   An annotation "in point" can save the researcher a good deal of work. It will not only provide an overview of a narrow legal topic but cite one to precedents in all jurisdictions, including the jurisdiction he or she is researching.

40   One research approach to locate annotations is as follows: if one reads the *Bowling* case, *supra* (*supra* means that the case has been mentioned previously, *infra* means that it will be subsequently mentioned) he will find that the court cites (not as authority but to illustrate its position) 27 *Am. Jur.* Infants, Section 17. *Am. Jur.* has been superseded by *Am. Jur. 2d*, and a table in front of the volume containing the topic Infants advises the user that 42 *Am. Jur. 2d* Infants, Section 70 now covers this topic. By consulting this citation and the pocket part one will have cases bearing on the rule as to disaffirmance by infants when motor vehicles are involved. One is also told that there is an annotation in 56 *A.L.R. 3d* 1335 (1974) on "Automobile or Motorcycle as Necessary for Infant." The *Bowling* case is discussed and distinguished at 56 *A.L.R. 3d* 1350 (1974). In effect, one has brought the 1962 *Bowling* case up to date. The lesson to be learned is that research tools complement each other, particularly if issued by the same publisher.

LOOSE-LEAF SERVICES

41   This term is applied to publishers who supply a weekly, biweekly, or monthly service that involves updating by means of adding and removing pages. Commerce Clearing House (CCH), Prentice-Hall (P–H), and the Bureau of National Affairs (BNA) are the best known of this genre. An example is the *CCH Standard Federal Tax Reporter.* The publisher supplies the subscriber with the following: (1) relevant statutory material, (2) a reprinting of each section of the Code followed by regulations, digests of cases, an annotation or explanation of key sections of the Code, (3) full text of cases, some of which are not included in the *National Reporter System*, (4) finding lists, (5) special releases containing new laws and bills, explanations of new laws, committee reports and studies, (6) a short review of significant developments since the last release, and (7) instructions as to what pages to remove and what pages to insert.

42   These services are made available in fields where the subscriptions can support the service, such as criminal law, tax, labor, environment, trade regulation, patents, etc. The subject listing in the Alphabetical Appendix to this chapter will supply specific references.

43   Some loose-leaf services such as the *BNA Criminal Law Reporter*, provide analysis but limit themselves to full text only of pertinent United States Supreme Court cases and significant lower federal court and state cases. Other services, such as *Standard and Poor's Review of Securities Regulation*, limit themselves to a thirty- or forty-page monthly review of the field.

44   The BNA *United States Law Week* (*U.S.L.W.*) deserves special mention. It publishes all United States Supreme Court cases (CCH *Supreme Court Bulletin* also does this) within a week of decision day and provides a calendar of all activity of the Supreme Court, such as a list of pending cases,

certiorari matters, etc. In its General Section it quotes selectively from significant state and lower federal court opinions. It also reviews the work of the court each summer, prints significant new laws, and on occasion prints oral arguments before the court.

45 Although they are not strictly loose-leaf services, a word should be included here about those sets that provide for loose-leaf updating. Many publishers put out loose-leaf treatises that are updated annually (more frequently if the occasion warrants) by providing instructions for removing and replacing pages.

ENCYCLOPEDIAS

46 Legal encyclopedias, in many ways, perform the same function as treatises. The advantage of the encyclopedia is that it attempts to be a complete compendium on the law, it is exhaustively indexed, and it is supplemented annually. The major encyclopedias are *Corpus Juris Secundum* (*CJS*) and *American Jurisprudence* (*Am. Jur. 2d*). There are also state encyclopedias such as *New York Jurisprudence* (also *California Jurisprudence 2d* and *3d*, *Florida Jurisprudence*, *Florida Law and Practice*, *Michigan Law and Practice*, *Ohio Jurisprudence*, *Summary of Pennsylvania Jurisprudence*, *Texas Jurisprudence*, *Michie's Jurisprudence of Virginia and West Virginia*) and the previously mentioned multivolume treatises such as White on *New York Corporations*, Wigmore on *Evidence*, and Wright and Miller on *Federal Practice and Procedure* that treat their subject matter in encyclopedic fashion.

47 A few caveats about encyclopedias. They will generally give you the law on all sides of an issue. You will not find them opinionated as you will a law review article or treatise. The reason is that their primary purpose is to provide the researcher with cases—and encyclopedias have copious footnotes citing the user to cases, usually by jurisdiction. Encyclopedias are case finders; they are not authorities. No research should be limited to encyclopedias, and it is a weak researcher who cites an encyclopedia.

48 One further word about encyclopedias that applies to all legal research tools. Legal research texts of necessity go to interminable lengths to describe the features of legal tools. A careful inspection of each tool can be more productive. Peruse a subject in an encyclopedia. Is there an index to the subject as well as to the set? Is there a table of cases? (There is none.) Is it supplemented? (Practically all law material is supplemented or promised as such.) You will learn more about research by using the material than reading about it.

TREATISES

49 Treatises and hornbooks can be good secondary authorities. Prosser on *Torts* is a reliable and opinionated text, but it is dated. Wigmore on *Evi-*

dence is a venerated name in law, but Mr. Wigmore died long ago and the set is kept up to date by many others.

50   A West treatise is called a hornbook; West has also recently been publishing mini-treatises or "nutshell" volumes.

51   Akin to treatises are casebooks which are designed specifically for classroom use but can be helpful to the researcher as they include the text of opinions, author's notes, references to other material, etc.

52   In recent years, there has been a growth of continuing legal education among lawyers. Organizations providing this service publish many books that vary from authentic texts through how-to-try-it manuals to compilations of various legal materials and outlines.

53   Current issues of the *Harvard Law Review* contain an alphabetical arrangement of current casebooks and treatises. Sloane, *Recommended Law Books* (American Bar Association 1969), contains a listing designed for law firms. The Farnsworth, Lloyd, and *How to Find the Law* books listed in the beginning of this chapter have selective listings, and the Alphabetical Appendix to this chapter lists this material by subject.

RESTATEMENTS

54   The *Restatement* is an attempt to "codify" case law in those areas where case law rather than state statutes predominate; agency, conflict of laws, contracts, judgments, property, restitution, security, torts, and trusts (there is also a *Restatement* for *Foreign Relations Law*). It is the work of a prestigious body of scholars and practitioners under the aegis of the American Law Institute. The set is constantly being reappraised and there is an *Agency 2d*, *Torts 2d* as well as tentative drafts currently being published to *Contracts 2d* and *Torts 2d*. While the *Restatement* is a secondary authority it is most persuasive and cited frequently by the courts. *Restatement in the Courts* provides annotations to cases that have cited the *Restatement*. Each *Restatement* is indexed and there is an index for *Restatement I*. *Restatements* have been published for individual states, they can be Shepardized for some states and are not neglected by authors of treatises and law review articles. The Alphabetical Appendix to this chapter includes them in the subject listings.

LAW REVIEWS

55   Most law schools publish at least one law review. Law reviews are student-run publications that feature lead articles by law professors and practitioners, comments, student notes, case notes on current significant cases, and book reviews. Although this characterization may not be strictly accurate a

comment is narrower in scope than an article and usually concerned with an issue just emerging rather than one ready to be laid to rest. A student note can range from a full investigation by the law reviewers of state-court jurisdiction to a discussion of right to counsel in a particular jurisdiction. Case notes are abbreviated comments on current cases of significance. Many reviews publish annual surveys of the law in a particular jurisdiction (for instance, New York University School of Law publishes *Annual Survey of American Law*, *Harvard Law Review* publishes a survey of the work of the United States Supreme Court, *Syracuse Law Review* publishes a review of New York Law, and *St. John's Law Review* publishes a review of New York practice). The articles can provide valuable information on burgeoning legal topics, and the case notes may provide fresh perspective on current cases. It takes a degree of sophistication in research to determine whether an article should be cited in a finished piece of legal research or in a court opinion.

56   Many law reviews are indexed in the *Index to Legal Periodicals* by subject and author, case comments (by name of case), and book reviews. This index is published nine times a year (with cumulations) and is cumulated annually and triannually. References to law review articles can be found in treatises, annotated codifications and Shepard's citators. Readers should be cautioned that the *Index to Legal Periodicals* has its limitations. Not all law reviews are included, few bar journals are included, and the indexing is too broad for effective use (See 69 *Law Lib. J.* 125 (1976) for a rationale for this). Wypyski, *Legal Periodicals in English* (Glanville 1976) is a loose-leaf volume that lists periodicals and indicates if they appear in the *Index to Legal Periodicals*, as well as providing other information.

57   There are other legal periodicals besides the law reviews published by law schools. Private publishers offer them in the following areas: securities, criminal law, corporation law, real estate, banking, etc. (See the subject listing in the Alphabetical Appendix to this chapter). Bar associations (federal, state, county and city) publish periodicals that vary in content. The *American Bar Association Journal* is the best known of this genre. Associations of the trial bar, the defense bar, the insurance bar, law professors, and law librarians also publish periodicals dedicated to the perpetuation of their interest in the law.

58   Another source of related information is provided in legal newspapers. The *New York Law Journal*, for instance, besides covering current legal events, reporting docket information, and being the only source for many lower New York court opinions, carries an array of articles by members of the legal profession. The *New York Law Journal's* reported cases are digested in *Clark's Digest-Annotator*, which also includes an index of the articles published in the *New York Law Journal* as well as other features.

CASE CITATIONS

59   Shepard case citators. Basically, and with qualifications, this set will tell one every time a case he is researching has been subsequently cited. In the publisher's language, "The case divisions . . . is to make available to the lawyer every instance in which a reported decision has been cited in a subsequent case." (From *How to Use Shepard's Case Citations*, available from the publisher.)

60   By using the state citation (193 Mass. 364), the researcher can locate every case in a state that has cited his or her case; by using the regional citation (79 N.E. 745), the researcher can also locate every citation to his or her case throughout the fifty states. If your case is not listed, it has never been cited.

61   By adding symbols to this simple compilation of cases by citation of the case, the publisher can quickly let the reader know whether his case has been overruled, distinguished, followed, or in any way characterized. It is imperative that one check the prefatory pages to the citator so that all the abbreviations are understood. By use of the superscript the user can also determine which headnote in the cited case is being considered in the citing case (paragraph 96 contains sample pages from a Shepard citator and explanatory captions).

62   There is a Shepard citator for every state. Besides providing the above information, the user can get parallel citations (i.e., to the unofficial National Reporter), references to the cited case in selected law reviews, annotations, *Restatement* references, federal citations, and other information. As with all secondary sources, Shepard's is neither final nor infallible. The researcher must read the cases.

63   Shepard's regional citators provide a means of determining if one's state case has been cited in other jurisdictions as well as the jurisdiction of the cited case.

64   Besides the state and regional citators, there are federal citators for the United States Supreme Court and other federal courts (including administrative courts such as the Securities and Exchange Commission), and a labor citator.

65   This does not exhaust the Shepard repertoire. There is also a law review citator and there are statutory citators, basically arranged by sections of the state code or *United States Code* which will inform the user if the statute cited has been amended by the legislature or cited by a court. If you write to Shepard's Citations (See Alphabetical Appendix under Publishers for a list of addresses), they will send you a lengthy pamphlet that gets into all ramifications of this unique and useful (and expensive) set. Pages from that pamphlet are reproduced in this appendix.

66   The advantage and disadvantage of Shepard's is that it indiscriminately

tells you every time "your" case is subsequently cited. Librarians are often asked, "Do I have to check each citation?"—to which one facetious answer is "Only if your client can afford it." The nonfacetious answer is "Yes."

67   Shepard's is not the only publisher who provides a citation service. Prentice-Hall and Commerce Clearing House tax services include a citator factor in their table of cases. Any analysis of a case, your own included, updates a case, particularly if it is accepted by the court to which the analysis is given.

68   You must also remember that in doing your research you are your own citator. There is no law stating that a case that does not expressly consider a cited case does not affect it. If that were so, the law could well be a static system of jurisprudence. There are times when the power of reasoning before a court is far more persuasive than research by rote. Even more important, courts can overrule precedents—examples can be given for every court in the land.

69   The previous paragraph cannot pass without a mention of Louis Brandeis, a great Justice of the United States Supreme Court and a magnificent lawyer. Prior to the year 1890, no English or American court had ever granted relief based expressly on a right to privacy. After Warren and Brandeis wrote an article on the subject (4 *Harv. L. Rev.* 193 (1890)), this right came to be accepted in many jurisdictions (see Prosser on *Torts* §117 4th ed. 1971). Another example of this Justice's ability to fashion the law is "the Brandeis brief." In *Muller v. Oregon*, 208 U.S. 412 (1908), he submitted a brief containing two pages of legal argument and over 100 pages of sociological data. It was the latter that won the day. The significant point to be made is that all books on legal research and finding the law suffer from the fatal flaw of equipping the researcher to locate the illusive while it is the artist who discerns the obvious.

TRANSITION

70   The concluding part of this chapter is theoretically the most vital. In the order of things, the Constitution is paramount to the United States Supreme Court (the United States Supreme Court ruled that an income tax was unconstitutional; the seventeenth amendment made it constitutional), and state legislation has priority over state court decisions (no-fault legislation has wiped out hundreds of automobile personal injury precedents). But it should be kept in mind that legislation, rather than putting courts out of business, usually results in an increase of judgeships.

CONSTITUTIONS

71   Probably every state code carries a copy of the United States Constitution as well as its state constitution. If it is an annotated set, the state constitution will carry all state and federal cases interpreting the state constitution.

72   The United States Constitution can also be found in the *United States Code* (*U.S.C.*), *United States Code Annotated* (*U.S.C.A.*) and the *United States Code Service* (*U.S.C.S.*). The Constitution is annotated in the latter two sets. *United States Constitution: National and State* (Oceana) provides an index-digest to all state constitutions.

STATUTES AND REGULATIONS

UNITED STATES

73   *Statutes at Large* (sample citation: 84 *Stat.* 1943 (1971)). A chronological arrangement of laws and resolutions as promulgated by Congress and signed by the president (when necessary). This is the primary source of all law unless Congress enacts certain titles of the *United States Code* into positive law (such as the Internal Revenue Code).

74   *United States Code Congressional and Administrative News* (West) is published monthly while Congress is in session and contains all current laws, selected regulations and committee reports, and other primary material. It publishes the laws in the same form as the *Statutes at Large* and its pamphlets are usually the earliest source for current legislation.

75   *United States Code* (sample citation: 15 U.S.C. §13 (1970). The official compilation of all laws in force, arranged by title (approximately fifty: the Internal Revenue Code is Title 26). This code is derived from the *Statutes at Large* and the appropriate citation is provided after each section. A cumulative supplement is provided after each session of Congress to keep the set up to date. *Supplement IV* brings the 1970 edition up to January 2, 1975. A new edition is published every six years. The set includes a popular-name table (Taft-Hartley Act) and a conversion table from a *Statute at Large* citation to the *United States Code*; also an index.

76   *United States Code Annotated* (*U.S.C.A.*). Basically the same as the *United States Code* except that it contains extensive case annotations following each section. It is not published in an edition, but volumes are supplemented with pocket parts or recompiled when warranted. There are also pamphlet supplementations to the pocket parts. *U.S.C.A.* contains a popular-name table, a conversion table from the *Statutes at Large* to the *United States Code*, plus additional features.

77   *United States Code Service.* Basically the same as the *U.S.C.A.*, but this set provides citations to Lawyers Cooperative Publishing Company and occasionally prints committee reports and excerpts from the Congressional Record (see the volume on the Federal Rules of Evidence).

78   *Administrative Law.* When Franklin D. Roosevelt introduced the New Deal to the American society, he advertently revolutionized legal research. The executive branch of government undertook the onerous task of policing

the business community so as to prevent such abuses as monopolies, impure foods, anti-union practices, and a host of other relationships between the powerful and the weak. To implement President Roosevelt's program, administrative agencies proliferated (Federal Communication Commission, National Labor Relations Board—See the *United States Government Manual* for a complete listing) which naturally resulted in regulations to carry out the laws that created these agencies, decisions of administrative courts to resolve differences between the agency and those they sought to regulate, and many reports and studies issued by these agencies. Once the pride of reformers, these agencies are now being given second thoughts by a new breed represented by Ralph Nader.

79   In the Alphabetical Appendix (under Executive Orders) there are references that fully explore the ramifications of this development. It should be kept in mind that most agencies issue decisions, that there is a *Shepard's United States Administrative Citations* that Shepardizes many of them, and the agencies themselves put out helpful publications. Most important, looseleaf services (paragraphs 41–45), in many instances, reprint administrative materials (check the Alphabetical Appendix by subject; for example, Commercial Law and Trade Regulation for specific mention of applicable services.

80   *Federal Register* (citation style: 22 *Fed. Reg.* 8910 (1964)). Published five times a week, this is the official receptacle for all agency regulations, cease and desist orders, proposed regulations, etc. It is indexed monthly and annually and has tables that indicate which sections of the *Code of Federal Regulations* have been affected by current regulations.

81   *Code of Federal Regulations* (citation style: 11 *C.F.R.* §37 (1975)). A compilation of all regulations by title (similar to *U.S.C.* titles) that have appeared in the *Federal Register.* Title 3 accumulates all Executive Orders, and the set has an index to each title and an index to the set. It is currently being recompiled each year on a staggered basis.

82   The regulations are promulgated by administrative agencies to implement the laws. They have the effect of law. Federal regulations are not easy to fathom, cannot be Shepardized, and in certain subject areas, such as tax and labor, are more easily accessible in loose-leaf services.

STATES

83   Codes and Session Laws. Each state publishes session laws (public laws, acts, etc.) that are the equivalent of the *Statutes at Large* (see para. 73). Codifications are published by the states and also by publishers with the permission of the states. The latter are extensively annotated and contain features as dictated by the publisher. While all provide annotations, a West publication will invariably refer you to key numbers, and a Lawyers Coop-

erative publication will refer you to annotations. On occasion, law review articles are also provided. All codifications refer the reader to where the codification section originally appeared in the session laws (or whatever nomenclature the state uses for its laws). The sets are indexed, usually contain numerous tables, and are supplemented by pocket parts and for some states, by monthly pamphlets. There is a *Shepard Citator* for each codification. The *Uniform System of Citation* provides the recommended style of citation, and the *Harvard Law Review* produces a mimeographed listing of suggested citation style for each state's codification. Always put the name of the state first in any citation to a codification. Another safe rule is to ignore all publishers' recommended styles of citation.

84   Not all state laws are part of the code. In New York, for instance, rent control legislation is not part of the consolidated code but is included under the title of Unconsolidated Laws. Appropriations are not part of the *United States Code* and can only be found in the *Statutes at Large*.

85   Rules of Court. The West codification include the state rules of court with their subscriptions. Local publishers also publish them, usually with their practice volumes. (See Alphabetical Appendix: Civil Procedure).

86   State Administrative Agencies. New York, Florida, and California are three states that publish administrative regulations in a formal manner. If not available in a formal publication, it is suggested that the particular state agency be written to.

87   Cities and Towns. There is no consistent pattern for the publication of laws, rules, and regulations for cities and towns. In New York City there is an eight-volume *Charter and Code* as well as the *City Record*. For a citator to city and town material consult:

> *Ordinance Law Annotations; A Comprehensive Digest of American Cases that Interpret or Apply City and County Ordinances.* (Shepard's Citations 1969 to date. 6 v.)

This set is arranged by subject with references to case law.

LEGISLATIVE HISTORY

88   Sutherland on *Statutes and Statutory Construction* is a multi-volume set that exhaustively covers the vagaries and intracies of legislative history (See also Alphabetical Appendix: Legislation).

89   Constitutional Provisions and Amendments. *The Constitution of the United States Annotated* (1973) is a one-volume, indispensable source. The *U.S.C.*, *U.S.C.A.*, and *U.S.C.S.* provide annotations to the legislation and the amendments. Classical sources such as the *Federalist Papers* and *Farrand's Records of the Federal Constitution* are compelling.

90   Federal Legislation. Legislative histories for important federal enactments have been compiled in the tax, labor, atomic energy, and securities areas.

Check the card catalog in law libraries by subject to determine what legislative histories are available. *The Monthly Catalog of United States Government Publications* is another good source. A good deal of this material is being compiled on microfilm and microfiche (the Securities Acts of 1933 and 1934 are available in this form).

91   The *United States Code Congressional and Administrative News* (see paragraph 74) is an invaluable aid in legislative history despite the fact that the material it reprints is available elsewhere. It selectively publishes presidential messages, proclamations, executive orders, administrative regulations, the Statutes at Large, House and Senate reports. All public laws are printed, but only selected House and Senate reports. It does provide information as to legislative history which it does not reprint. It is published monthly while Congress is in session and is usually the first available source for the material it publishes. This publication does not contain hearings of the various House and Senate committees which are available through the Government Printing Office, through the committee holding the hearing, or at depository libraries which are required to provide the general public access to all government documents.

92   The last volume of the *Congressional Record* (for each session of Congress) has a history of bills and resolutions that will also assist one in compiling legislative histories. *U.S.C.A.* and *U.S.C.S.* may provide you with citations or actual text of legislative material such as committee reports and, in a few instances, of debates from the *Congressional Record* and testimony given at congressional hearings (compare their treatment of the Federal Rules of Evidence). The *CCH Congressional Index* loose-leaf service is a complete index for current bills in that it will provide information as to the status of bills and tell whether Committee Reports and Hearings have been held. It does not print the material. Many large libraries and universities have the bills on file for the current session of Congress. This is a vast and complicated field, which is covered more fully in the *Price, Pollack*, and *How to Find the Law* books.

93   State Legislation. There is no uniform method of collecting legislative histories of state enactments. There are research books on California, Florida, Pennsylvania, and Texas law that provide detailed information for those states. In New York, legislative documents are published by commissions, but they are generally related to the work of the commission rather than specific legislation. These legislative documents are available at the State Law Library in Albany and in designated depository libraries throughout the state. Transcripts of hearings are usually not available but application for information as to hearings must be made to the commission conducting the hearing. *McKinneys' Session Laws of New York* publishes the Law Revision Commission Report and the governor's covering memoranda for certain pieces of legislation. The New York Judicial Conference *Reports* does dis-

cuss pending legislation relating to its function. The *Empire State Report* (Jan. 1975, p. 40) contains an excellent summary of material published relative to legislation in New York.

94   Case Research for Statutes. All that we have said about research in case law applies to statutes and constitutions. State digests will provide cases interpreting statutory material; the *Federal Digest*, *Modern Federal Practice Digest*, and *Federal Practice Digest 2d*, while overlapping, provide case coverage for all federal statutory material; the *Supreme Court Digest* and *Lawyers Edition Digest* does the same for United States Supreme Court cases.

BOWLING V. SPERRY CITE AS
184 N.E.2d 901 (1962)*

95   Action to disaffirm and set aside the purchase of a used automobile on grounds of infancy of the buyer. The Circuit Court, Noble County, Lowell L. Pefley, Special Judge, rendered judgment for defendant, and plaintiff appealed. The Appellate Court, Myers, J.; held, inter alia, that sixteen-year-old high school boy was entitled to disaffirm and set aside purchase of used automobile, though he was accompanied by grandmother and aunt at time of purchase and borrowed money from aunt to make final payment, and regardless of whether certificate of title was delivered in blank or bore buyer's name, and that the evidence was insufficient to meet seller's burden of showing that the automobile sold and delivered was a necessary within statute, Burns' Ann. St. §58–102, requiring payment of reasonable price for necessaries sold and delivered to a minor.

Judgment reversed and cause remanded with directions.

Topic Key Number:

1. Infants 47
Contracts of minors are voidable and may be disaffirmed.

2. Infants 58 (2)
Other party to contract disaffirmed by minor need not be placed in statu quo and minor need not tender back money or property he has received before suing for value or possession of money or property given by him.

3. Infants 58 (1)
Voidable contracts of minor in regard to personalty may be avoided at any time during minority or upon attaining majority.

4. Infants 58 (1)
Minor was entitled to disaffirm purchase of used automobile and recover back purchase money paid therefor, even though he was accompanied by

*Reprinted by permission of West Publishing Company.

aunt and grandmother at time of purchase and borrowed money from aunt to make final payment, and regardless of whether certificate of title was delivered in blank or bore name of minor.

5. Infants 58(1)

That burned-out bearing was caused by minor's operation of automobile and failure to put oil in crankcase would constitute no defense to action by minor to disaffirm and set aside purchase of used automobile.

6. Infants 50

As used in statute requiring payment of reasonable price for "necessaries" sold and delivered to minor or other person incompetent to contract, quoted word means such things as are necessary to his support, use or comfort, including such personal comforts as comport with his condition and circumstances in life, provided he is in actual need of such things at time and obliged to procure them for himself. Burns' Ann. St. §58−102.

> See publication Words and Phrases for other judicial constructions and definitions.

7. Infants 102

Whether goods are necessaries for which minor under statute may be required to pay reasonable price is a question of law, and if deemed necessaries, their quantity, quality and reasonable value are matters of fact. Burns' Ann. St. §58−102.

8. Infants 98

Seller had burden of proving that used automobile sold and delivered to minor, seeking to disaffirm and set aside transaction, was a necessary for which under statute minor should be required to pay reasonable price. Burns' Ann. St. §58−102.

9. Infants 100

Evidence was insufficient to meet seller's burden of showing that used automobile sold and delivered to sixteen-year-old high school boy was a necessary for which under statute minor should be required to pay reasonable price. Burns' Ann. St. §58−102.

———————

John C. Hagen, Ligonier, for appellant.
Albert J. Kuster, Ligonier, for appellee.

MYERS, Judge.

This is an appeal from a judgment of the Noble Circuit Court in a civil action brought by appellant, Larry Bowling, by Norma Lemley as next friend, hereinafter referred to as Larry, against appellee, Max E. Sperry, d/b/a Sperry Ford Sales, to disaffirm and set aside a contract for the purchase of an automobile on the grounds of infancy.

Larry was a minor, sixteen years of age. On June 29, 1957, he purchased from appellee a 1947 Plymouth automobile for the sum of $140 cash. He paid $50 down on that day and returned on July 1, 1957, to pay the balance of $90 and take possession of the car. Appellee delivered to him a certificate of title and a written receipt. This receipt stated that as of June 29, 1957, Max Sperry Ford Sales sold to Larry Bowling a 1947 Plymouth for the amount of $140, cash, paid in full.

Larry drove the car several times during the following week and discovered that the main bearing was burned out. He had the car brought back to appellee's place of business where he was informed that it would cost him from $45 to $95 to make repairs. He declined to pay this amount and left the car on appellee's lot. Subsequently, he mailed a letter to appellee to the effect that he disaffirmed the contract of purchase and demanded the return of his money. Upon appellee's refusal to pay back the $140, this lawsuit followed.

Larry's complaint is based upon the fact that appellee sold him a car knowing that he was a minor; that he tendered back the car, rescinded the contract, and demanded the sum of $140. Appellee's answer was in two paragraphs, the first being in the nature of a general denial. pursuant to the provisions of Supreme Court Rule 1–3, and the second being an allegation that Larry was accompanied by his grandmother and aunt at the time of the purchase, and that the aunt paid appellee the sum of $90 of the purchase price. Upon trial of the case by the court, judgment was rendered in favor of appellee and against Larry.

[1–3] It has been the rule in Indiana for many years that the contracts of minors are voidable and may be disaffirmed. It is not necessary that the other party be placed in *statu quo*, nor is it necessary that the minor tender back the money or property he has received before suing for the value or possession of the money or property given by him to the adult. All such voidable contracts by a minor in regard to personal property may be avoided at any time during his minority or upon his arrival at full age. Shipley v. Smith (1904), 162 Ind. 526, 70 N.E. 803; McKee v. Harwood Automotive Co. (1932), 204 Ind. 233, 183 N.E. 646; Wooldridge, by Next Friend, v. Hill (1953), 124 Ind. App. 11, 114 N.E.2d 646.

The evidence showed that Larry's grandmother and aunt accompanied him to appellee's used car lot on June 29, 1957, when he selected the automobile, and that his aunt drove the car around the lot at that time. Furthermore, it was revealed that his aunt had loaned him $90 in order to make final payment on the car and that he had commenced to pay this back at $10 a week thereafter.

[4] These facts, however, do not change the general rule. In so far as the agreement and sale is concerned, there was sufficient evidence to show that it was made between appellee and Larry, and no one else. It is of no consequence that his aunt and grandmother accompanied him at the time of purchase; and the fact that his aunt made payment of the $90 balance due could have no effect upon Larry's right to take advantage of his minority in an action to recover such payment. Story, etc., Piano Co. v. Davy (1918), 68 Ind. App. 150, 119 N.E. 177. Appellee was fully aware of Larry's age when the sale was negotiated. The written receipt was in Larry's name alone. This contract was squarely between an adult and a minor and falls within the rule pronounced above. Larry had every right to disaffirm it and set it aside.

Appellee claims there is doubt as to whether Larry received a certificate of title from appellee with his name on it. It is contended that the certificate was delivered in blank. As was said in the case of Wooldridge, by Next Friend, v. Hill, supra (at page 14 of 124 Ind. App., at page 648 of 114 N.E. 2d): "It is of little consequence whether title to the property involved had passed to the infant or not." The certificate of title is only evidence of ownership, and in this case it would make no difference whether Larry had received a certificate in blank or with his name on it. Automobile Underwriters v. Tite (1949), 119 Ind. App. 251, 85 N.E.2d 365.

[5] Appellee argues that an inference may be drawn from the evidence to show that the burned-out bearing was caused by Larry's operation of the car and his failure to put oil in the crankcase. Even if this were true, it is no defense to this action. There is no requirement in Indiana that before a disaffirmance is effected the parties must be placed in *statu quo*. Story, etc., Piano Co. v. Davy, supra.

The question of whether or not the automobile was a necessary was injected into the trial of the case although appellee did not plead it as a defense. Some argument on this subject was made by the parties in the briefs. Section 58—102, Burns' Ind. Stat., 1961 Replacement, reads as follows:

"Capacity to buy and sell is regulated by the general law concerning capacity to contract, and to transfer and acquire property.

"Where necessaries are sold and delivered to an infant, or to a person who by reason of mental incapacity or drunkenness is incompetent to contract, he must pay a reasonable price therefor.

"Necessaries in this section means goods suitable to the condition in life of such infant or other person, and to his actual requirements at the time of delivery."

[6] In the case of Price et al. v. Sanders et al. (1878), 60 Ind. 310, 314, the following is stated:

" 'Necessaries,' in the technical sense, mean such things as are necessary to the support, use or comfort of the person of the minor, as food, raiment, lodging, medical attendance, and such personal comforts as comport with his condition and circumstances in life, including a common school education; but it has been pithily and happily said, that necessaries do not include 'horses, saddles, bridles, liquors, pistols, powder, whips and fiddles.' "

[7] Whether the goods are necessaries is a question of law, and if they are deemed as such, their quantity, quality and reasonable value are matters of fact. Garr et al. v. Haskett et al. (1882), 86 Ind. 373.

It has been stated in 27 Am. Jur., Infants, §17, pp. 760, 761, as follows:

"Aside from such things as are obviously for maintenance of existence, what are or what are not necessaries for an infant depends on what is reasonably necessary for the proper and suitable maintenance of the infant in view of his social position and situation in life, the customs of the social circle in which he moves or is likely to move, and the fortune possessed by him and by his parents. It has been said that articles of mere luxury or adornment cannot be included, but that useful articles, although of an expensive and luxurious character, may be included if they are reasonable in view of the infant's circumstances. The necessities to be procured by the contract must be personal necessities, that is, for the living or personal well-being of the infant.

"What is furnished to the infant must be suitable, not only to his condition in life, but also to his actual requirements at the time—in other words, the infant must not have at the time of delivery an adequate supply from other sources. To be liable for articles as necessaries, an infant must be in actual need of them, and obliged to procure them for himself."

The evidence revealed that at the time of this transaction, Larry was living with his grandmother in Cromwell, Indiana, where he had lived for the past fifteen years; that his mother was dead and his father resided in Fort Wayne; that he was a student at Cromwell High School, but was on vacation; that he had a summer job working at a restaurant in the town of Syracuse, Indiana, which was eight or nine miles away from his home; that his usual means of transportation back and forth was with the cook; that on occasion he could "bum" rides with other people.

The acting manager for appellee, who had dealt with Larry, testified that when Larry's aunt and grandmother came to the sales lot on June 29, 1957, "they" said Larry needed something for him to get back and forth to work. He said it was his "understanding" that the car was needed for that purpose.

Larry stated that during the short period of time he had possession of it, he only used it for pleasure, and did not drive it to work.

[8,9] We are well aware of the overwhelming increase in the use and number of automobiles in this country since World War II. What once was a great luxury for only the wealthy has become a matter of common necessity for the ordinary workingman, farmer and businessman. The automobile is as important to the modern household as food, clothing and shelter. The problem here is whether the car in question was so needed by Larry, in view of his situation in life, his social status and his financial position, that he could not be maintained properly or suitably without it. The burden of showing this was upon appellee. Robertson v. King (1955), 225 Ark. 276, 280 S.W.3d 402, 52 A.L.R.2d 1108. From the evidence presented, we do not think appellee met this burden. While every high school boy today wants a car of his own, and many of them own automobiles which under given circumstances may be considered as necessaries, we do not consider the car in this case so vital to Larry's existence that it could be classified as a necessary.

Judgment reversed, and cause remanded with instructions that the trial court sustain appellant's motion for a new trial on the ground that the judgment is contrary to law.

Cooper, P.J., and AX and Ryan, JJ., concur.

SPECIMEN PAGE—Shepard's Massachusetts Citations, Case Edition, 1967

Vol. 193							
			MASSACHUSETTS REPORTS				
317Mas²432	d283Mas³561	341Mas¹642	230Mas⁷190	**—392—**	219Mas¹506	264Mas²109	311Mas⁷370
326Mas²147	284Mas⁴607	269F²782	234Mas²602	(79NE739)	301Mas³327	270Mas¹173	'03-22EC64
184F¹220	297Mas³273	293F²406	234Mas⁴604	(9Lns695)	167F¹81	312Mas¹289	90AR755n
216F¹507	304Mas²642	324R1316n	234Mas⁵609	201Mas¹540	53AR145n	320Mas¹626	55A324n
248F²263	d314Mas²682	155AR643n	241Mas¹528	237Mas²398	**—419—**	321Mas¹675	**—464—**
f258F¹299	322Mas³219	41A1304n	242Mas³32				(79NE784)
263F²1014	322Mas³227	**—351—**	f242Mas⁶34	*Followed with reference to paragraph six of syllabus*			95Mas⁸109
j39F2d540	328Mas³534	(79NE790)	245Mas8				42Mas¹534
6BUR234	d339Mas²728	cc222F349	f250Mas⁵60				250Mas¹457
8BUR151	343Mas³779	203Mas²130	250Mas⁸71	280Mas¹330	f208Mas²566	(79NE797)	250Mas¹535
8BUR210	182F⁴127	203Mas²424	255Mas⁸171	**—400—**	210Mas¹552	(7Lns148)	319Mas¹308
11BUR142	252F³516	241Mas²474	257Mas¹153	(79NE774)	213Mas¹294	197Mas³396	10BUR39
24MQ(1)2	245F2d³447	250Mas²314	264Mas¹87	203Mas¹327	f236Mas¹223	202Mas²446	10BUR168
24MQ(4)9	50AR1366n	281Mas²166	270Mas¹524	217Mas¹32	256Mas²56	205Mas³171	35AR963n
59AR157n		343Mas¹371	286Mas¹618	244Mas¹306	257Mas¹50	208Mas³157	**—470—**
—324—	**—336—**	343Mas²723	286Mas²618	250Mas¹87	262Mas¹580	215Mas²470	(79NE878)
(79NE734)	(79NE771)	4BUR30	289Mas⁴185	256Mas¹153	319Mas²314	216Mas³180	247Mas¹203
196Mas483	242Mas¹392	39BUR494	315Mas⁷342	270Mas¹39	319Mas¹599	d216Mas214	333Mas¹777
d197Mas	282Mas376	40BUR228	323Mas¹650	284Mas¹9	326Mas¹460	217Mas³95	34AR49n
[¹178	101AR237n	78AR1040n	323Mas⁴650	308Mas¹405	335Mas²700	223Mas¹184	8A965n
200Mas¹35	**—339—**	45A119n	324Mas¹⁰448	47ABA602		230Mas²391	**—479—**
206Mas²389	(79NE733)	45A143n	328Mas¹676	(79NE776)	22AR578n	236Mas¹14	(79NE787)
207Mas¹501	197Mas¹292	45A183n	333Mas⁴778	f195Mas¹128	11A434n	d236Mas³538	**—482—**
d216Mas	d197Mas	45A250n	339Mas208				(79NE794)
[¹322	[¹422	46A160n	f41F2d¹938	*Cited by lower federal court*			284Mas¹521
216Mas²339	201Mas¹57	46A191n	6AG182				339Mas¹710
220Mas¹30	5A815n	46A219n	6AG440	305Mas⁴44	(79NE735)	254Mas⁴189	**—486—**
220Mas¹299	**—341—**	46A265n	7AG451	317Mas¹566	211Mas¹485	d263Mas¹75	(79NE763)
273Mas²29	(79NE815)	46A385n	6BUR166				201Mas158
273Mas²476	(118A8516)		6BUR306	*Cited in Boston University Law Review*			204Mas337
326Mas¹795	(7Lns729)	**—359—**	8BUR79				208Mas510
—327—	f194Mas⁵459	(79NE742)	10BUR322			321Mas¹45	205Mas¹461
(79NE818)	d195Mas	(9Lns874)	10BUR324	74A998n	(79NE748)	327Mas¹73	221Mas¹320
199Mas¹11	[¹318	202Mas¹495	18BUR92	74A1011n	202Mas²204	341Mas¹699	308Mas¹545
202Mas⁴113	196Mas¹71	207Mas¹131	21BUR650			⁵18	**—488—**
222Mas⁵261	201Mas⁴70	209Mas¹88	22BUR381	*Cited in Harvard Law Review*			(80NE588)
266Mas⁴546	205Mas¹3	214Mas²541	37HLR842				cc191Mas441
292Mas⁴550	d205Mas²36	224Mas²360	13MQ(6)72				c198Mas580
299Mas⁴3	206Mas486	245Mas¹10	43MQ(3)61	*Cited in Massachusetts Law Quarterly*			194Mas573
299Mas⁵4	207Mas¹498	265Mas³412	48MQ(4)492				198Mas¹582
321Mas⁵198	d207Mas	272Mas³220	34AR46n				276Mas¹286
174F8³455	[²563	295Mas²55	8A965n	*Cited in annotations of Annotated Reports System*			**—495—**
—331—	208Mas³447	339Mas²250	58A1088n				(79NE738)
(79NE749)	210Mas²456	266F²198					198Mas¹531
194Mas¹446	212Mas²309	28F8²157	**—378—**	315Mas⁴345	201Mas¹265	46MQ(3)245	d203Mas¹261
199Mas¹541	213Mas⁵329	46F8¹957	(79NE777)	319Mas²674	f202Mas³10	48MQ(3)318	204Mas¹201
220Mas¹581	f213Mas²597	46F8²958	233Mas¹253	32AR215n	202Mas¹65	171AR369n	205Mas¹274
—332—	f217Mas²421	41AR127n	32AR215n	**—383—**	204Mas²229	**—453—**	229Mas¹44
(79NE765)	217Mas¹517	44AR1068n		(79NE737)	209Mas349	(79NE775)	335Mas¹427
(7Lns1076)	223Mas²494	126AR1095n		**—412—**		310Mas¹555	345Mas¹41
196Mas²31	d227Mas	126AR1097n		*Same case reported in Northeastern Reporter, American State Reports and Lawyers Reports Annotated, New Series*		Mas¹335	**—498—**
199Mas²44b	[²115	**—364—**				Mas¹286	(79NE796)
199Mas²475	d229Mas⁸67	(79NE745)					194Mas³575
201Mas²185	f232Mas²551	(118A8523)				**—455—**	1MQ311
203Mas396	d233Mas	(23Lns1160)		*Affirmed by United States Supreme Court*		(79NE770)	**—500—**
204Mas²68	[²350	a214US91				212Mas²109	(79NE781)
206Mas⁸388	238Mas²231	a53LE923				227Mas²51	201Mas²607
d207Mas⁸29	239Mas¹227	a29SC567				237Mas²507	205Mas⁴328
207Mas⁸448	239Mas¹567	f193Mas⁸476	218Mas¹191	246Mas⁴389	206Mas⁸3	274Mas²501	210Mas280
217Mas⁸118	244Mas²452	198Mas	260Mas¹385	285Mas⁸543	304Mas¹222	284Mas²506	241Mas³544
220Mas⁸31	d245Mas	[¹¹256	260Mas¹397	305Mas⁴440	304Mas¹470	292Mas¹193	254Mas279
220Mas⁴32	[¹122	200Mas¹484				300Mas²88	267Mas⁴101
224Mas²407	d248Mas	d203Mas⁸29	*Distinguished with reference to paragraph eight of syllabus*			309Mas²531	30AR1164n
241Mas⁴79	d250Mas	203Mas¹155				313Mas²416	
245Mas⁴121	[²245	206Mas¹432	310Mas660			337Mas²546	**—507—**
246Mas⁸521	d251Mas²59	f206Mas⁷433	312Mas¹645	**—415—**	**—444—**	6MQ(2)27	(79NE764)
260Mas¹337	252Mas¹274	208Mas¹622	323Mas¹567	(79NE821)	(79NE769)	16MQ(5)218	195Mas⁴160
263Mas⁴218	d259Mas	208Mas⁷630	f337Mas¹30	f196Mas²551	204Mas²354	**—458—**	196Mas¹128
266Mas⁴543	[³328	219Mas	339Mas¹14	200Mas¹93	208Mas²403	(79NE807)	196Mas²486
287Mas⁸366	264Mas²368	[¹¹197	339Mas¹16	200Mas³343	224Mas¹584	216Mas¹143	198Mas²571
f269Mas⁴63	297Mas¹195	220Mas¹275	4AG279	202Mas⁸224	h234Mas¹23	216Mas223	200Mas²543
270Mas⁴266	303Mas¹244	222Mas	8AG474	204Mas¹481	d239Mas	222Mas⁸82	201Mas384
276Mas⁸384	d316Mas²619	[¹¹580	3AR1456n	205Mas²179	[¹232	236Mas¹347	f203Mas³584
277Mas²365	322Mas⁸294	225Mas	23AR249n	205Mas¹370	h247Mas	240Mas¹370	206Mas⁴545
279Mas⁴345	338Mas¹128	[¹¹196	73AR825n	f212Mas⁸170	[¹213	256Mas⁷470	208Mas⁴118
		228Mas⁸374	86A2675n	216Mas³498	248Mas¹289	262Mas¹53	*Continued*

For later citations see any subsequent bound supplement or volume, the current issue of the periodically published paper-covered cumulative supplement and any current issue of the advance sheet

Source: *How to Use Shepard's Citations*. Colorado Springs, Shepard's Citations, 1971. Reprinted with permission.

STATE REPORTS

Illustration

Let us assume that by reference to a digest, encyclopedia, text book or other unit of legal research or the statute law of the state, you have located the case of Welch v. Swasey, reported in Volume 193 Massachusetts Reports at page 364.

The specimen page *opposite* contains a reproduction of page 726 in the 1967 Case Edition of Shepard's Massachusetts Citations. Note the number of the volume of reports "Vol. 193" in the upper left corner of the page.

An examination of the bold face type numbers appearing in the column locates the page number "—364—" in the third column of citations. This is the initial page of the case under consideration. Following this page number you will find the citations "(79 NE 745)", "(118 AS 523)", "(23 Lns 1160)" indicating that the same case is also reported in 79 Northeastern Reporter 745, 118 American State Reports 523 and 23 Lawyers Reports Annotated, New Series 1160.

In obtaining the history of this case, you will observe that upon appeal to the United States Supreme Court it was affirmed "a" in 214 United States Reports "US" 91, 53 Lawyers' Edition, United States Supreme Court Reports "LE" 923 and 29 Supreme Court Reporter "SC" 567.

It is also to be observed by examining the abbreviations preceding the citations that this case has been followed "f" and distinguished "d" in subsequent cases in the Massachusetts and federal courts.

In the citation "f 193 Mas ^{8}476", the small superior figure "8" in advance of the citing page number 476 indicates that the principle of law brought out in the eighth paragraph of the syllabus of 193 Mas 364 has been followed in 193 Mas 476.

You will note that other citations which contain the superior figure "8" in advance of the citing page number and which deal with this point in particular are 203 Mas 29, 228 Mas 374 and 250 Mas 71.

In addition to the citations in point with paragraph eight of the syllabus, note the numerous citations in point with other paragraphs of the syllabus or other headnotes of this case by the Massachusetts and federal courts. The cases dealing with a point of law in any particular paragraph of the syllabus or headnote may thus be referred to instantly without examining every citing case listed.

This case has also been cited in the Harvard Law Review "HLR", Boston University Law Review "BUR" and Massachusetts Law Quarterly "MQ".

The citations appearing in annotations of the Annotated Reports System are grouped together for convenience of use.

By examining this same volume and page number in any subsequent bound supplement or volume, the current issue of the periodically published paper-covered cumulative supplement and any current issue of the advance sheet of Shepard's Massachusetts Citations, all subsequent citations to this case will be found.

In this instance, as in every instance, Shepard's Citations to cases will enable the lawyer in a very short time to collect the entire body of case law that revolves around and about a given case.

SPECIMEN PAGE—Northeastern Reporter Citations. Volume 1, 1945

NORTHEASTERN REPORTER

Vol. 79

142NE¹694	127NE⁴528	161SE80	105NE¹985	N D	178NE¹542	113NE¹202		**–776–**
Ind	135NE³876	N H	105NE²987	137NW416	181NE¹219	h124NE431		(193Mas402)
96NE¹977	136NE²339	141At145	127NE¹432	Nebr	d186NE¹671	d131NE¹855		f80NE¹807
107AR23n	136NE⁴339	Okla	140NE¹594	180NW560	188NE¹391	h142NE¹90		81NE¹911
W Va	139NE382	192P353	189NE2593	N H	8NE17n	142NE¹799		130NE³206
73SE268	f145NE²264	So C	26?	Cited in annotations of the American				177NE²823
–741–	145NE²268	150SE275	j70	Law Reports				22NE¹46
(193Mas545)	150NE⁴897	Va						129AR13n
–742–	153NE⁵356	67SE376	164So569	Okla	252F¹516	186F¹754		Conn
Case 1	161NE¹899	134SE916	Calif	138P155	N Y	**–770–**		92At681
(193Mas398)	170NE¹391	192SE888	258P139	Ore	166NE¹174	(193Mas455)		Idaho
182NE¹583	191NE¹35	Wis	Del	206P297	50AR1366n	98NE¹696		26P2d122
Iowa	193NE815	147NW28	197At384	S D	Ark	116NE¹544		Me
179NW528	f41F2d¹938	194NW161		Followed with reference to para-			NE¹112	104At228
–742–	Ill	196NW455		graph one of syllabus			NE¹79	**–777–**
Case 2	e94NE⁴924	W Va	S4NE1090	118GE120	20P2d752	197NE¹888		(193Mas378)
(193Mas359)	133NE⁵270	149NE¹789	s92NE61	Vt	Conn	d14NE¹154		124NE¹21
89NE¹133	149NE¹789	84SE107	81NE¹914	130At767	85At636	36NE¹413		32AR215n
92NE¹1031	180NE¹773	94SE498	f83NE¹1019	Wis	Del	48NE¹44		**–779–**
95NE¹400	193NE¹134	**–748–**	84NE¹8	196NW766	197At486			Case 1
102NE²66	Ind	(193Mas431)	88NE¹696	W Va		**–771–**		(194Mas44)
112NE²952	d92NE⁵650	88NE³591	9		Idaho	(193Mas336)		104NE¹467
139NE³383	172NE¹312	f116NE¹899		Cited by the lower federal courts		190		107NE²58
164NE376	172NE⁴312	56F2d²811				387		165NE²903
172NE¹215	N Y	Ill				237n		167NE¹679
3NE⁴27	118NE³792	104NE¹675	**–757–**	**–763–**	Minn	**–772–**		197NE²103
266F²198	150NE¹123	177I1A181	(75OS355)	(193Mas486)	217NW375	(193Mas551)		N Y
28FS²157	154897	Ind	119NE¹416	s87NE189	Mo	99NE¹415		38S2d300
46FS¹957	216S311	f104NE¹61	142NE²691	s90NE578	236SW20	100NE¹62		Ga
41AR127n	220S660	N Y	3NE³354	s94NE752	Okla	102NE¹420		23SE418
44AR1068n	258S890	119NE¹558	30A496	92NE¹47	159P1013	137NE¹375		**–779–**
126AR1095n	148S2d593	217S59	90A22	108NE¹1086	Va	137NE¹694		Case 2
126AR1097n	28S2d318	Me	Ind	33NE¹269	63SE448	156NE¹744		(193Mas540)
Ala	Ohio	108At194	e89NE¹517	**–764–**	86SE66	161NE¹621		877NE762
70So728	149NE433	Mo	e89NE³517	(193Mas507)	128SE541	192NE¹630		21AR1445n
169So719	34AR46n	164SW641	**–762–**	80NE¹508	162SE20	10NE¹126		**–780–**
Ark	Ala	**–749–**	(193Mas556)	80NE¹697	Wash	36FS¹925		Case 1
65SW15	52So945	Case 1	102NE¹67	81NE²888	5P2d986	36FS¹928		(193Mas593)
Calif	Calif	(193Mas331)	d155NE¹443	82NE¹497	**–766–**	Ill		106NE²852
55P2d228	134P973	80NE¹610	165NE¹513	84NE¹842	(193Mas419)	101NE¹945		138NE²7
Ga	Conn	85NE¹847	j169NE¹493	86NE²936	88NE¹836	N Y		138NE¹816
86SE328	111At357	108NE¹364	181NE¹716	87NE613	f93NE¹605	288S440		144NE²764
Miss	111At902	**–749–**	15NE¹487	f89NE¹1041	f95NE¹94	Ohio		196NE860
80So282	162At29	Case 2	232F²559	92NE²720	96NE¹1095	142NE¹896		199NE²896
Tenn	165At605	(193Mas438)	296F²375	94NE¹390	100NE¹557	Me		42NE¹562
192SW169	179At200	79NE¹751	Ill	104NE¹381	f128NE¹14	145At398		21AR1459n
–744–	Del	87NE¹475	241I1A17	107NE450	152NE¹78	N J		60AR385n
(194Mas14)	129At518	f8		Cited in all units of the National Re-		569	8A2d569	Ala
121NE¹31	Fla			porter System with state of citing		8	**–774–**	161So551
158NE¹799	65So284	98		case shown			(193Mas400)	Pa
Vt	94So689	157So655	117NE¹311	108AR411n	84	22AR578n	89NE¹546	162At344
13A2d208	157So655	Iowa	136NE¹104	108AR419n	(193Mas332)	Ala	104NE¹450	Tex
Wyo	126NW917	19AR1372n	108AR421n	81NE¹895	81So21	138NE¹551	252SW268
120P2d597	184NW830	Iowa	Ala	85NE¹571	Ark	145NE¹54	**–780–**
–745–	273		Cross references to state reports		NE¹573	179SW818	152NE¹229	Case 2
(193Mas364)		46P			NE¹490	Conn	169NE¹517	(193Mas534)
a214US91		Ky			NE²564	181At209	187NE¹107	106NE¹633
a53LE923		f9SW975	Minn	101P2d715	90NE¹534	Iowa	32NE¹271	108NE¹471
a29SC567		Md	Iowa	90NE¹548	186NW442	**–775–**	127NE¹517
f79NE¹879		Md	202NW240		Affirmed "a" by the United States		8NW277	(193Mas453)	137NE¹295
84NE⁵456	70At114		Supreme Court		Ky	97NE¹100	144NE¹404
86NE¹917	95At1063		Kan	67SW228	110NE¹962	146NE¹687
d89NE¹146	Me	85NE¹573	171P6	107NE¹377	N D	135NE¹139	177NE¹270
89NE³180	69At629	93NE¹840	Md	112NE¹1025	147NW785	Utah	e31NE¹554
92NE¹708	128At185	95NE¹752	96At518	134NE²376	R I	220P699	235F¹653
f92NE⁴709	137At400	120NE¹591	Me	139NE¹822	129At804	**–775–**	65F2d¹868
94NE³1045	140At387	142NE¹904	138At71	141NE¹587	So C	Case 2	N Y
95NE³932	Minn	148NE1632		157NE652	76SE699	(193Mas518)	290S212
106NE⁵853	158		Citations analyzed to paragraph of		98	Wis	f83NE²324	56AR65n
107NE379			syllabus of cited case		59	228NW507	92NE506	Vt
111NE⁵412	25				634	**–769–**	94NE²266	146At74
114NE⁵289						(193Mas444)	97NE¹021	**–781–**
117NE²589	256SW491	97NE²103	135SW73	f168NE172	90NE¹590	190NE²737	(193Mas500)
119NE³689	N C	100NE²545	N C	169NE¹781	94NE¹466		88NE¹334
127NE¹527	122SE472	e104NE¹344	195SE808	177NE¹580			*Continued*

For later citations see any subsequent bound supplement or volume, the current issue of the periodically published paper-covered cumulative supplement and any current issue of the advance sheet

NATIONAL REPORTER SYSTEM

Illustration

To illustrate the use of Shepard's National Reporter Citations we will use the same case, Welch v. Swasey, that was selected to demonstrate the use of the state publication. This time we will make our search in terms of its Northeastern Reporter reference, 79 NE 745. The mechanics are the same as in the preceding illustration dealing with a state reports edition.

Let us further consider this Reporter citator in light of its use as a case finder. By a check of the specimen page (opposite) we find every Massachusetts case that cites 79 NE 745 in terms of their Northeastern Reporter references; cases from other states within the scope of the Northeastern Reporter, namely Illinois, Indiana, New York and Ohio. In addition, we find every other state citing reference to our case (nineteen states in addition to those within the Northeastern Reporter area). Add to this the references to annotations and you can see that exhaustive national research is instantly available, opening avenues of investigation that would have required countless hours of search using other methods.

The use of the Northeastern Reporter publication with respect to the evaluation of our material is also exactly the same as in the state reports example as is the ability to pinpoint research by use of the small superior figures immediately to the left of the page reference.

When research in depth is desired the careful investigator will use both the state and the Reporter citation units in searching his problem. The state units being intrastate in their orientation will emphasize local citing references, including statutory material and law reviews. The Reporter units, with their interstate frame of reference in addition to state case coverage, also lead to regional and national citing references.

NOTE: To obtain regional and national citing references for cases reported prior to the first units of the National Reporter System use your Shepard "State" edition.

AMERICAN LAW REPORTS ANNOTATED (ALR)

A Quick Command Of All Case Law In Point

With Additional References To Law Reviews And Other Legal Authority

	ALR	ALR 2d	ALR 3d	ALR FED
LAW FINDERS	ALR Quick Index Alternates: Word Index – 4 vols. Digest – 12 vols. AmJur 2d	ALR 2d–3d Quick Index, Second Edition (Supplemented by Paperback for ALR 3d, vol. 51 –) Alternates: ALR 2d Word Index – 3 vols. ALR 2d Digest – 7 vols. AmJur 2d	Alternates: AmJur 2d	ALR Federal Quick Index, Second Edition Alternates: AmJur 2d U.S. Code Guide
THE LAW	First Series 1919–1948 Vols. 1–175	AMERICAN LAW REPORTS ANNOTATED Second Series 1948–1965 Vols. 1–100	Third Series 1965–Present Vols. 1–	ALR Federal 1969–Present Vols. 1–
		Annotation History Table for ALR, ALR 2d, ALR 3d, ALR FED (located in the back of Quick Index for ALR 3d)		
UPDATING TOOLS	ALR Blue Book of Supplemental Decisions 5 Volumes plus Paperback Supp. published annually	ALR 2d Later Case Service 16 Volumes Supplemented on an annual basis by pocket parts	ALR 3d Pocket Part Supps. Published annually for each volume	ALR FED Pocket Part Supps. Published annually for each volume

THE LAWYERS CO-OPERATIVE PUBLISHING CO.
Rochester, New York 14603

BANCROFT-WHITNEY CO.
San Francisco, California 94107

September 1976

ALPHABETICAL APPENDIX

Abbreviations.

A *Uniform System of Citation* lists abbreviations of frequently used words, states, reports, publications, legal actions, etc. It also has abbreviations for English, United Nations, international, and foreign law materials. Probably the most convenient list of citation abbreviations is in Lloyd (see paragraph 8). Abbreviations of reports and legal terms can be found in the current edition of Black's Law Dictionary (West), Ballantine's Law Dictionary (LCP), and in *Price* and *Research Group*.

Administrative Law (see paragraphs 78−82).

Davis. *Administrative Law Text.* 3d ed. (West 1972).

Davis. *Administrative Law Treatise.* 4 v. (West 1958). 1970 bound supplement.

Gellhorn. *Administrative Law and Process in a Nutshell.* (West 1972).

Pike and Fischer. *Administrative Law.*

4 loose-leaf volumes. 38 volumes of cases.

Schwartz. *Administrative Law.* (Little, Brown 1976).

United States Government Manual 1975/1976.

Volz et al. *West's Federal Practice Manual.* 2d ed. 7 v.

Provides text and forms for federal actions, particularly as regards federal agencies. Current pocket parts.

See also *Cohen*, pp. 139−157; *How to*, pp. 219−247.

Advance sheets (see Slip decisions).

Agency.

Restatement of Agency 2d. (1958).

Seavey. *Handbook of the Law of Agency.* (West 1964).

Seavey. *Studies in Agency.* (West 1949).

Sell. *Agency.* (Foundation Press 1975).

case book.

American Digest System (see paragraph 30).

For explanatory pamphlets write to West (See Publishers for address).

See also *Cohen*, p. 31; *How to*, pp. 53−63; *Pollack*, p. 107; *Price*, p. 183.

American Law Reports (see paragraphs 37−40).

For explanatory pamphlets write to Lawyers Cooperative Publishing Co.

See also *Cohen*, p. 31; *How to*, pp. 39−48; *Pollack*, p. 107; *Price*, p. 143; *Research Group* p. 11.

Antitrust (see Trade Regulation).

Bankruptcy (see Commercial Law).

Bibliographies (see paragraphs 3—13).

Henke. *California Legal Research Handbook—State and Federal* 387—714.
(1971, 1976 supplement).

Law Books in Print. (Oceana 1976).

See also *How to*, pp. 203, 305; *Research Group*, pp. 47—53.

Briefs and Records.

Official papers submitted to a court in a pending case. The Association of the
Bar of the City of New York is one depository for the briefs and records of
the United States Supreme Court. These briefs are also available from Information Handling Services and Law Reprints on microfiche. All briefs and
records are a matter of public record and must be made available by the court
that required them. *Lawyers Edition* and *American Law Reports* also give
summaries of briefs of cases they reprint.

Business Organizations (see also Agency, Securities).

Bromberg. *Crane and Bromberg on Partnership.* (West 1968).

Cavitch. *Business Organizations with Tax Planning.* (M. Bender).
loose-leaf. v.1—10 covers corporations, partnership; v. 11 securities; v. 12
trade secrets; v. 13—13B corporate acquisitions and mergers; v. 14 patent
licensing transactions; v. 15 franchising; v. 16 antitrust and trade regulation; v. 17—17D professional corporations and associations; v. 18 labor
law.

Corporation Manual 1975. (U.S. Corp. Co.).
contains uniform arrangement of the laws of all states as they relate to corporations.

Fletcher. *Corporation Forms Annotated.* 10 v. (Callaghan).
current pocket parts.

Fletcher. *Cyclopedia of Corporations.* 25 v. (Callaghan).
loose-leaf.

Henn. *Law of Corporations.* 2d ed. (West 1970).

Hornstein. *Corporation Law and Practice.* 2 v. (West 1959).

Israels. *Corporate Practice.* 2d ed. (PLI 1969).

The Lawyer's Basic Corporate Practice Manual (ALI/ABA).
loose-leaf—supplemented to 1973.

Model Business Corporation Act Annotated. 2d ed. (West 1971).

O'Neal. *Close Corporations.* (Callaghan, 1971, 1974).

Prentice-Hall. *Corporations.* 6 v.
loose-leaf service.

Rohrlich. *Organizing Corporate and other Business Enterprises.*
5th ed. (M. Bender 1975).

Soboloff. *Tax and Business Organization Aspects of Small Business.*
(ALI/ABA 1974).

Citation Style.

The following is a guide to commonly used footnote citations as adapted from *A Uniform System of Citation* (commonly known as "Blue Book"). The 12th edition of this publication was published in 1976. For capitalization, spacing, and type styles when preparing a manuscript for law review publication consult the Blue Book.

NEW YORK CITATIONS

Constitution

N.Y.CONST. art. 1, sec. 6
  Note: A symbol for section is required by Blue Book.

Code

N.Y. CIV. PRAC. sec. 302(a) (1) (McKinney 1972).
N.Y. BUS. CORP. sec. 1314 (Consolidated Law Service Supp. 1975).
  Note: The Blue Book cites only to McKinney, but either set will do.

Session Laws

Ch. 167, [1975] N.Y. Sess. Laws secs. 100−601.

Bills

S.2824, N.Y. State Senate (1975); A.2543, N.Y. State Assembly (1975).
  See 1 N.Y. LEGISLATIVE RECORD AND INDEX S274, A237 (1975).

Court of Appeals

pre 1956

People v. Manfredi, 309 N.Y. 898, 131 N.E.2d 576 (1955).

post 1955

Cohen v. Boyland, 1 N.Y. 2d 8, 132 N.E.2d 890, 150 N.Y.S. 2d 5 (1956).

use of *id* and citing to page

68 People v. Sandoval, 34 N.Y.2d 371, 314 N.E.2d 413, 357 N.Y.S.2d 849,
     aff'g 337 N.Y.S.2d 994 (2d Dep't 1972) (mem.).
69 . . .
70 The record shows otherwise. 34 N.Y.2d at 373, 314 N.E.2d at 415, 357
     N.Y.S.2d at 852.
71 *id* at 375, 314 N.E.2d at 417, 357 N.Y.S.2d at 853.
 . . .
74 34 N.Y. 2d at 375, 314 N.E.2d at 416, 357 N.Y.S.2d at 854.

Appellate Division

Brown v. Lavine, 45 App.Div.2d 858, 358 N.Y.S.2d 530(1974) (mem.).

Tappis v. New York State Racing and Wagering Bd., 46 App.Div.2d 613, 359 N.Y.S.2d 780(per curiam), *rev'd*, 36 N.Y.2d 862, 331 N.E.2d 697, 370 N.Y.S.2d 922(1975).

Miscellaneous

Heath v. Diamond, 82 Misc.2d 217, 368 N.Y.S.2d 440(Sup.Ct. 1975).

FEDERAL AND OTHER CITATIONS

Baird v. Day & Zimmerman, 390 F.Supp. 883(S.D.N.Y. 1974), *aff'd mem.*, 510 F.2d 968(2d Cir. 1975).

United States Reports

Jenkins v. Delaware, 395 U.S. 213(1969).

Law Reviews

vom Bauer, Some Fundamentals of Looking Up Law, 18 Prac. Law. 63(1972).

Books

W. PROSSER, LAW OF TORTS sec. 47 (4th ed. 1971).

Annotations

Annot., 12 A.L.R.2d 382 (1950).

Civil Procedure.
Am. Jur. *Pleading and Practice Forms.* (LCP).
multi-volume. 1975 pocket parts. Forms and text designed to be helpful in a multitude of actions. The arrangement is by topic.
Bender's Federal Practice Forms. 13 v.
loose-leaf.
Federal Rules Digest. (Callaghan).
loose-leaf. Bound volumes of reprinted cases on the Federal Rules are part of the set.
Moore's Federal Practice. 2d ed. 25 v. (M. Bender).
loose-leaf.
Moore, Vestal and Kurland. *Moore's Manual—Federal Practice and Procedure.*
2 v. (M. Bender).
1975 update.
Stern and Gressman. *Supreme Court Practice.* 4th ed. (BNA 1969).
West's Federal Forms. 10 v.
1975 pocket parts. loose-leaf.
Wright. *Law of Federal Courts.* 2d ed. (West 1970).
1972 pocket part.

Wright and Miller. *Federal Practice and Procedure.* (West 1969).
multi-volume. 1975 pocket parts.

Court Rules

Court rules are to be distinguished from rules of civil and criminal procedure which apply to practice before the courts. Court rules, in some respects, are the minutiae of rules of procedure. See Peterfreund, The Essentials of Modern Reform in the Litigative Process, 287 *Annals* 154 (1953). See also *How to*, ch. IV L. Court rules have to do with admission to the bar, judicial conduct, and professional responsibility, and generally govern the conduct of the court as procedural rules govern the conduct of lawyers before the court. These rules appear in bar association journals, in addenda to the reports of the particular court, as separate pamphlets, as loose-leaf services, and as part of West Publishing Company's service to subscribers to their annotated statutes. A selective list follows:

Alaska Rules of Court Procedure and Administration. (Washington Book Publishing Co., 1974).
4 v. loose-leaf.

Arkansas Rules of Criminal Procedure. (Bobbs-Merrill 1976).
Part of Arkansas Statutes Annotated.

California Rules of Court. (West 1976).
Includes both California and federal court rules for 9th Circuit.

District of Columbia Courts. Court Rules. (West 1976).
Part of District of Columbia Code Encyclopedia.

———. United States Courts. (West 1976).
Part of District of Columbia Code Encyclopedia.

Florida Rules of Court. (West 1976).
Includes both Florida and federal court rules for 5th Circuit.

Illinois Practice Act and Rules. (West 1976).
Includes both Illinois and federal court rules for 7th Circuit.

Louisiana Court Rules. (West 1976).
Includes both Louisiana and federal court rules for 5th Circuit.

Maine Rules of Court. (West 1976).
Includes both Maine and federal court rules for 1st Circuit.

Massachusetts Rules of Court. (West 1976).
Includes both Massachusetts and federal court rules for 1st Circuit.

New Jersey. *Rules Governing the Courts of the State of New Jersey.* (West 1975).
Includes both New Jersey and federal court rules for 3d Circuit.

New York Court Rules. (West 1975).
Includes both New York and federal court rules for 2d Circuit. It should be kept in mind that in New York the New York Civil Practice Law and Rules are enacted by the legislature whereas the New York courts are

limited to supplementary rule-making power to create court rules. (The legislature can, at any time, step in and change the court rules.)

Ohio. *Rules Governing the Courts of Ohio.* (W.H. Anderson 1975).
    Part of Page's Ohio Revised Code.

Oklahoma Court Rules and Procedure. (West 1975).
    Includes both Oklahoma and federal court rules for 10th Circuit.

Pennsylvania Rules of Court. (West 1976).

United States. *Federal Local Court Rules.* (Callaghan).
    loose-leaf. An up-to-date collection of rules for all Federal District Courts.

United States Code Annotated. (West).
    Title 28 carries the court rules for the United States Supreme Court, Bankruptcy, Court of Claims, Court of Customs, Federal Rules of Appellate Procedure, United States Court of Appeals, and Federal Rules of Evidence. It does not contain the rules for the Federal District Courts. It should be added that Title 28 also carries the Federal Rules of Civil Procedure and Title 18 carries the Federal Rules of Criminal Procedure. The *United States Code Service* carries the same material.

See also Researching a Federal Rules Problem in *Research Group* pp 58–62.

Code of Federal Regulations (see paragraph 81).
    See also *Cohen*, p. 142; *How to*, pp. 156–159; *Pollack*, p. 240; *Price*, p. 166.

Commercial Law.

American Bar Association. *Section of Insurance, Negligence and Comparative Law.*
    annual volume.

Appleman and Appleman. *Insurance Law and Practice.* (West).
    multi-volume. current pocket parts.

Benders Uniform Commercial Code Service. (Bender).
    loose-leaf. Secured transactions, commercial paper, sales, forms, reporter-digest, index.

Boston College Industrial and Commercial Law Review.
    v. 16 published in 1975.

Collier on Bankruptcy. 14th ed. (M. Bender).
    19 loose-leaf volumes. 6 v. of bankruptcy cases.
    This publisher also has a 3 v. loose-leaf manual.

CCH. *Bankruptcy Law Reporter.* 3 v.
    loose-leaf.

CCH. *Consumer Credit Guide.* 5 v.
    loose-leaf.

CCH. *Secured Transactions Guide.* 4 v.
    loose-leaf.

Couch. *Cyclopedia of Insurance Law.* 2d ed. (LCP).
  multi-volume. current pocket parts.
Ezer. *UCC Bibliography.* (ALI/ABA 1972).
Gilmore. *Security Interest in Personal Property.* 2 v.
  (Little, Brown 1965).
Gilmore and Black. *The Law of Admiralty.* 2d ed. (Foundation 1975).
Healy and Sharpe. *Cases and Materials on Admiralty.* 2d ed. (West 1974).
Insurance Counsel Journal. (International Association of Insurance Counsel).
  v. 42 published in 1975.
Insurance Law Journal. (CCH).
  1975 volume.
Kripke. *Consumer Credit, Text-Cases-Materials.* (West 1970).
Nordstrom. *Law of Sales.* (West 1970).
Patterson. *Essential of Insurance Law.* 2d ed. (McGraw-Hill 1957).
Remington. *Treatise on the Bankruptcy Law of the U.S.* 5th-6th ed. (LCP).
  current pocket parts.
Uniform Commercial Code Journal. (Warren, Gorham & Lamont).
  v. 8 published in 1976.
Uniform Commercial Code Reporting Service. (Callaghan).
  17 volumes of reported cases. 2 volumes of loose-leaf current commentary
  and cases. 6 volume digest.
Uniform Laws Annotated. *Uniform Commercial Code.* (West 1973).
  current pocket parts. This set also includes Uniform Partnership Act, Uniform Limited Partnership Act and uniform laws on family, health, matri-
  mony, criminal and civil procedure, and Model Penal Code.
White and Summers. *Uniform Commercial Code.* (West 1972).
Williston on Sales by Squillante and Fonseca. 3 v. (LCP).
  current pocket parts.

Common Law. (See para. 3–12 for additional books).
Cross. *Precedent in English Law.* 2d ed. (Clarendon Press 1968).
Levi. *An Introduction to Legal Reasoning.* (Univ. of Chicago 1949, 1963).

Computers.
  There are two "working" computers for legal research. LEXIS is based on
quick word retrieval (a sophisticated method of feeding words such as "last
clear chance" and "motor vehicles" into a bank of opinions and locating
opinions utilizing these words); and WESTLAW has a data bank of West headnotes. For a survey on this topic see Dee and Kessler, The Impact of Computerized Methods on Legal Research Courses . . . , 69 *Law Lib. J.* 164 (1976).
See also *How to*, pp. 459–464.

Conflict of Laws.
Ehrenzweig. *Conflicts in a Nutshell.* 3d ed. (West 1962).
Leflar. *American Conflicts Law.* (Bobbs-Merrill 1968).

Lowenfeld. *International Private Trade.* (M. Bender 1975).
Restatement on the Law of Conflicts 2d. (1971).

Congressional Record.   (See para. 92).
See also Cohen, p. 122; Pollack, p. 183; Price, p. 61; *How to*, pp. 199, 204.

Constitutional Law.
Constitution of the United States, Analysis and Interpretation. (G.P.O. 1973).
Cushman. *Cases in Constitutional Law.* 4th ed. (Prentice-Hall 1975).
   excellent one-volume compilation of cases.
Emerson, Haber and Dorsen. *Political and Civil Rights in the United States.*
   4th ed. v. 1 by Dorsen, Bender and Neuborne. (Little, Brown 1976).
   cases and text.
Freund. *The Supreme Court of the United States.* (World 1961, 1965).
Schwartz. *Constitutional Law.* (Macmillan 1972).
   Professor Schwartz has also published a multi-volume set on this topic.
Supreme Court Review. (University of Chicago Press).
   annual volume since 1960.

Contracts.
Calamari and Perillo. *Contracts.* (West 1970).
Corbin on *Contracts.* (West).
   multi-volume. 1971 pocket parts. Also in one v. ed. (1952).
Murray on *Contracts.* (Bobbs-Merrill 1974).
   A revision of Grismore.
Restatement of Contracts. (1933).
   Tentative drafts for Contracts 2d currently being published.
Restatement of Restitution. (1937).
Schaber and Rohwer. *Contracts in a Nutshell.* (West 1975).
Simpson. *Handbook on the Law of Contracts.* 2d ed. (West 1965).
Williston. *A Treatise on the Law of Contracts.* 3d ed by Jaeger (LCP).
   multi-volume. 1975 pocket parts. Also in one v. ed. (1938).

Court Rules (see Civil Procedure).

Criminal Law and Procedure.
American Bar Association. Project on Standards for Administration of Criminal Justice. (1966–).
   Pretrial, discovery, pleas of guilty, fair trial, trial by jury, speedy trial,
   Judge's role, electronic surveillance, police, sentencing, post conviction
   remedies, Appellate review of sentences, providing defense services,
   founder and severence, probation, prosecution function, defense function,
   appeals and *index.* Shepard's *Criminal Justice Citations* cites to cases citing
   these standards.
American Criminal Law Review. (A.B.A.).
   v. 13 published in 1975.

Amsterdam et al. *Trial Manual 3 for the Defense of Criminal Cases.*
(ALI/ABA 1975).
bibliography.
Bailey and Rothblatt. *Complete Manual of Criminal Forms.* (LCP 1968,
1974).
1975 supplement.
Bailey and Rothblatt. *Investigation and Preparation of Criminal Cases.*
(LCP 1970).
1975 supplement.
Bernstein, *Criminal Defense Techniques.* 5 v. (M. Bender 1970).
1975 supplement. loose-leaf.
BNA. *Criminal Law Reporter.*
loose-leaf. v. 18 published in 1975. published weekly.
Criminal Law Bulletin. (Warren, Gorham & Lamont).
v. 12 published in 1976.
Fox. *Juvenile Courts in a Nutshell.* (West 1971).
Hermann and Haft. *Prisoners' Rights Sourcebook.* (Clark Boardman 1973).
Israel and Lafave. *Criminal Procedure in a Nutshell.* (West 1971).
Journal of Criminal Law and Criminology. (Williams & Wilkins).
v. 66 published in 1975.
Krantz. *Law of Corrections and Prisoners' Rights in a Nutshell.* (West 1976).
LaFave and Scott. *Criminal Law.* (West 1972).
Loewy. *Criminal Law in a Nutshell.* (West 1975).
Model Penal Code. (West 1974).
v. 10 of Uniform Laws Annotated. Also published by ALI.
Nedrud. *The Criminal Law.* (LE Publishers).
loose-leaf. published monthly.
Orfield. *Criminal Procedure under the Federal Rules.* 6 v. (LCP 1966).
1975 supplement.
Packer. *Limits of Criminal Sanction.* (Stanford Univ. P. 1968).
Torcia. *Wharton's Criminal Evidence.* 13th ed. 4 v. (LCP).
1975 pocket parts.
Torcia. *Wharton's Criminal Law and Procedure.* 12th ed. 3 v. (LCP 1957).
1976 pocket parts.

Dictionaries.

Ballentine's Law Dictionary. 3d ed. by William S. Anderson. (LCP 1969).
includes abbreviations.
Bander, *Law Dictionary of Practical Definitions.* (Oceana, 1966).
Black's Law Dictionary. Rev. 4th ed. (West 1968).
Oran. *Law Dictionary for Non-Lawyers.* (West 1975).
Includes abbreviations, current terms ("plea bargaining" is in Oran but not
in Black or Ballentine).

Stroud. *Judicial Dictionary of Words and Phrases.* 4th ed. by J.S. James (Sweet and Maxwell 1971–).

an English publication. multi-volume.

Words and Phrases. (West).

A set of over one hundred volumes that extracts direct quotes from National Reporter System cases. The state digests include a volume that performs a similar function. Annual pocket parts.

See also *How to*, pp. 296, 298.

Digests (see paragraphs 28–36).

See also *Cohen*, p. 40; *How to*, pp. 51–84; *Pollack*, p. 70; *Price*, p. 158.

For a critique of digests, see *Research Group*, p. 41.

Directories.

Directory of Law Teachers. (West 1974).

1975 supplement.

Martindale-Hubbell Law Directory. 6 v. (1976).

Arranged alphabetically by state and then by city for lawyer listings. There are two listings for each state. The first listing is open to all lawyers; the second is solicited for by the publisher. The last volume has a state and foreign law digest. There is also a directory of American Bar Association functions and leaders, cannons of professional responsibility, and other material. See also paragraph 20 of this appendix. See also *How to*, pp. 300–301.

Encyclopedias (see paragraphs 46–48).

See also *Cohen*, p. 56; *How to*, pp. 264–284; *Pollack*, p. 310; *Price*, p. 213, *Research Group*, p. 14.

English and Canadian Material.

Consult books listed in paragraphs 3–12, particularly *How to*, pp. 366–388.

Environment Law.

Annual Survey of American Law. (New York University School of Law).

Currently carries a survey article on this subject.

BNA. *Energy Users Report.*

loose-leaf.

BNA. *Environment Reporter.*

13 loose-leaf volumes, 7 volumes of cases.

Clark, ed. *Water and Water Rights.* (Allen Smith 1967–).

Ecology Law Quarterly. (Univ. of Calif., Berkeley).

v. 4 published in 1975.

Environment Law Review. (Clark Boardman).

v. 6 published in 1975. Reprints of law review articles.

Environmental Affairs. (Boston College).

v. 4 published in 1975.

Environmental Law Reporter. (Environmental Law Institute).

loose-leaf.

Grad. *Treatise of Environmental Law.* (M. Bender 1975).

Yannacone et al. *Environmental Rights and Remedies.* 2 v. (LCP 1972).

Evidence.

Am. Jur. *Proof of Facts.* 30 v.

Am. Jur. *Proof of Facts 2d.* 8 v.

1975 pocket parts. Includes medical glossary. Topics range from Auto-mobiles to Zoning. Includes testimony at trial.

Quick Index volume.

McCormick. *Handbook on the Law of Evidence.* 2d ed. (West 1972).

Torcia. *Wharton's Criminal Evidence.* 13th ed. 4 v. (LCP).

Weinstein and Berger. *Weinstein's Evidence.* (M. Bender 1975).

This is a loose-leaf text that covers the new Federal Rules of Evidence.

Wigmore. *A Treatise on the Anglo-American System of Evidence.* 3d ed.

(Little, Brown).

pocket parts and update by various authors. multi-volume.

Executive Orders.

Code of Federal Regulations (see paragraph 81).

Title 3 has a compilation of executive orders.

Federal Register (see paragraph 80).

Executive orders can be located through indexes.

Loose-leaf services (see paragraphs 41–45).

Presidential Papers. A Weekly Compilation of Presidential Documents, 1965–.

United States Code Annotated (see paragraph 76).

The Tables volume lists executive orders as cited by U.S.C.A. section.

U.S.C.C.A.N. (see paragraphs 74, 91).

Tables list orders for the period covered.

See also *Cohen*, p. 140; *Pollack*, p. 241; *How to*, pp. 241–242; *Price*, p. 144.

Family Law.

BNA. *Family Law Reporter.*

loose-leaf. weekly.

Clark, *Domestic Relations.* (West 1968).

Foster and Fried. *Law and the Family.* 2 v. (Lawyers Cooperative Publishing Co. 1972).

Lindey, *Separation Agreements and Ante-Nuptial Contracts.* 2 v. (M. Bender).

loose-leaf. updated.

Federal Cases.

A thirty volume set of Federal District Court and Circuit Court cases ar-ranged alphabetically. It covers the years from 1789 to 1880 and effectively replaces the many reports put out by the individual federal courts during those years. The *Federal Reporter* begins where this set leaves off. Citation

style: Salmon v. Burgess, 21 F. Cas. 254 (No. 13, 262) (C.C.E.D.Va. 1875).
See also *Cohen*, p. 24; *How to*, pp. 37−38; *Pollack*, p. 38; *Price*, p. 108.

Federal Register (see paragraph 80).
See *Cohen*, p. 140; *How to*, pp. 224−228; *Pollack*, p. 239.

Federal Reporter (see paragraph 23).
See also *Cohen*, p. 24, *How to*, p. 35−38; *Pollack*, p. 39; *Price*, p. 109.

Federal Rules Decisions (see paragraph 23; see also Civil Procedure).
A competitor to this set is Pike and Fischer, *Federal Rules Service.* (Callaghan). Both these sets report the opinions interpreting the Federal Rules of Civil and Criminal Procedure.
See also *Cohen*, p. 25; *Pollack*, p. 231, *Price*, p. 110.

Federal Supplement (see paragraph 23).
The *Federal Supplement* publishes only those opinions submitted to it by Federal District Court Judges. Many loose-leaf services (particularly tax and labor) publish opinions that do not appear in the *Federal Supplement.* There is an average of a two-month lag between the date a court hands down an opinion and the date West publishes the opinion in its National Reporter series (except for the *Supreme Court Reporter*).
See also *Cohen*, p. 25; *How to*, pp. 37−38; *Pollack*, p. 39; *Price*, p. 109.

Foreign and Comparative Law.
Consult books listed in paragraphs 3−12, particularly *How to*, ch. XV.

Forms.
Forms are also included in this Alphabetical Appendix by subject.
The following is only a sampling as most states are inundated with practice books that contain forms (see, for instance, *California County Law Library Basic List* issued by California State Library, May, 1976).
Am. Jur. Legal Forms Annotated 2d. (LCP).
23 v. current pocket parts. Federal tax guide to forms included.
Jones. *Legal Forms Annotated.* 10th ed. 3 v. (Bobbs-Merrill 1962).
Modern Legal Forms. (West).
17 v. 1975 pocket parts.
New York Forms. 5 v. (LCP).
1975 pocket parts.
Nichols. *Cyclopedia of Legal Forms Annotated.* 16 v. (Callaghan).
1975 pocket parts.
Rabkin and Johnson. *Current Legal Forms with Tax Analysis.* 22 v. (M. Bender).
loose-leaf. updated.

Insurance (see Commercial Law).

International Law.
Consult books listed in paragraphs 3—12, particularly *How to*, pp. 412—445.

Labor Law.
BNA. *Government Employee Relations Report.* 2 v.
  loose-leaf.
BNA. *Labor Relations Reporter.*
  loose-leaf. weekly. similar to CCH described *infra*.
CCH. *Labor Law Reporter.*
  loose-leaf. weekly. Includes labor relations (5 v.), wages and hours (2 v.), state laws (3 v.), union contract arbitration (1 v.), employment practices (3 v.), unemployment insurance (4 v.).
  There are also bound volumes of cases (*Labor Cases, N.L.R.B.*).
Jenkins. *Labor Law.* 4 v. (Anderson).
  loose-leaf. updated.
Labor Law Journal. (CCH).
  v. 26 was published in 1975.
Larson. *Workmen's Compensation.* 7 v. (M. Bender).
  loose-leaf. updated.
Law Reprints. *Labor Series.*
  briefs and records of current labor cases. v. 9 was published in 1975/76.
N.Y.U. *Annual Conference on Labor.* (M. Bender).
  v. 28 published in 1975.
Prentice-Hall. *Labor Relations Guide.* 3 v.
  loose-leaf.

Legal Writing.
Consult books listed in paragraphs 3—12, particularly *How to*, ch. XVIII—XX. For a bibliography of books pertaining to brief writing, memoranda, etc., see paragraph 9.

Legislation (see paragraphs 73—77, 83—85, 87).
Davies. *Legislative Law and Process in a Nutshell.* (West 1975).
Statsky. *Legislative Analysis: How to Use Statutes and Regulations.*
  (West 1975).
Sutherland on Statutory Construction. 4th ed. by C. Dallas Sands. 6 v.
  (Callaghan).
See also *How to*, pp. 184—218, 331—332.

Loose-Leaf Services (see paragraphs 41—45).
See also *Cohen*, p. 27; *How to*, pp. 248—263; *Pollack*, p. 61.

Microforms.
Microforms come in reels, microcard, and microfiche. All the state reports prior to the National Reporter System are on microfilm (Oceana). West has

issued its first series of the National Reporter System on ultrafiche. Many legislative histories are available in this form. Microforms make it possible for law libraries to expand without building additional stack space. See Tzeng, *Complete Guide to Legal Materials in Microform* (University Publications 1976).

See also Briefs and Records, this chapter, and *How to*, pp. 447–456.

National Reporter System (see paragraph 23).
See also *Cohen*, p. 27; *How to*, pp. 21–39; *Pollack*, p. 61.

Parallel Citations (see paragraph 23).
It is proper citation style to cite to the official state report and to the West regional reporter. All the *Digests* have case tables that provide this information, if available. *Shepard's Citators* can be used for this purpose. The West *Blue Books* and *Blue and White Books* have tables for this purpose. There is also a Shepard's *Acts and Cases by Popular Names—Federal and State* that can be useful. If you know the subject matter, try the case tables to treatises and case books.

See also *How to*, pp. 25–29.

Partnership (see Business Organizations).

Periodicals (see paragraphs 55–68).
For a list of law reviews and other legal publications with complete cataloging, see Wypyski, *Legal Periodicals in English* (Oceana 1976). Citation style: Bander, How to Protect Yourself from Legal Experts, 1 *Obiter Dictum* 24 (Fall 1975).

See also *Cohen*, p. 197; *How to*, pp. 306–326; *Pollack*, p. 332.

Precedent (see paragraph 18).
The common law requires courts to follow the reasoning of their prior decisions. One must therefore expose the court to its past. Cases, like fingerprints, are never the same, and one must balance fact patterns, analogous situations (which digests do not reveal), the temper of the times, and even the temper of the judge with the agility of a juggler. For a collection of writings, see Aldisert, *The Judicial Process* (West 1976). See also *Cohen*, p. 40; *How to*, pp. 4–11.

Products Liability (see Torts).

Property.
Anderson. *American Law of Zoning—Zoning, Planning, Subdivision Control.* 4 v. (LCP 1968).
1975 pocket parts.
Bernhardt. *Real Property in a Nutshell.* (West 1975).
Bogert. *Handbook on the Law of Trusts.* 5th ed. (West 1973).
Bogert. *Law of Trusts and Trustees.* 2d ed. (West).
multi-volume. 1975 pocket parts.

Brown. *The Law of Personal Property.* 3d ed. by Raushenbush. (Callaghan 1975).

Burby. *Handbook on the Law of Real Property.* 3d ed. (West 1965).
4th ed. announced in 1976.

Casner, ed. *American Law of Property.* 8 v. (Little, Brown 1953).

Cribbet. *Principles of the Law of Property.* (Foundation 1962).

Land Use Law and Zoning Digest. (American Society of Planning Officials).
v. 28 no. 4 published in 1976.

Powell, *The Law of Real Property.* 10 v. (M. Bender).
loose-leaf. updated. Also in one volume edition (1968).

Prentice-Hall. *Wills, Estates and Trusts.* 5 v.
loose-leaf.

Rathkopf. *The Law of Zoning and Planning.* 4th ed. 4 v. (Clark Boardman).

Real Estate Law Journal. (Warren, Gorham & Lamont).
v. 4 published in 1975.

Real Property Probate and Trust Journal. (A.B.A.).
v. 10 published in 1975.

Restatement of Property. (1936–44).

Restatement of Security. (1941).

Restatement of Trusts 2d. (1959).

Rohan and Reskin, *Real Estate Transactions.* (M. Bender). 10 v.
Includes condominium law, cooperative housing, condemnation, real estate financing, and forms. loose-leaf. 1975 supplement.

Scott. *The Law of Trusts.* 3d ed. (Little, Brown 1967).
6 v. 1975 pocket parts.

Simes. *Handbook on the Law of Future Interests.* 2d ed. (West 1966).

Simes and Smith. *The Law of Future Interests.* 2d ed. 4 v. (West 1956).
1973 pocket parts.

Smith and Boyer. *Survey of the Law of Property.* (West 1971).

Thompson. *Commentaries on the Modern Law of Real Property.* 23 v.
(Bobbs-Merrill).
1975 pocket parts.

Yokley. *Zoning Law and Practice.* 3d ed. 4 v. (Michie 1965).
1974 pocket parts.

Publishers.

American Bar Association or American Bar Foundation (A.B.A. or A.B.F.)
1155 E. 60th St.
Chicago, Ill. 60637
312 493–0533

American Law Institute (A.L.I. or ALI/ABA)
4025 Chestnut St.
Philadelphia, Penn. 19104

Allen Smith
1435 North Meridian St.
Indianapolis, Indiana 46202

W.H. Anderson Co.
646 Main St.
Cincinnati, Ohio 45201
513 421—4142

Banks-Baldwin Law Pub. Co.
1904 Ansel Road
Cleveland, Ohio 44106
216 721—7373

Bancroft-Whitney Co. (same as LCP)
301 Brannan St.
San Francisco, Calif. 94107
415 986—4410

M. Bender & Co.
P.O. Box 658
Albany, N.Y. 12201

or

235 E. 45 St.
New York City, N.Y. 10017
212 661—5050

Bobbs-Merrill Co., Inc.
4300 W. 62d St.
Indianapolis, Indiana 46206
317 291—3100

Bureau of National Affairs (BNA)
1231 25th St., N.W.
Washington, D.C. 20037
202 223—3500

Callaghan & Co.
6141 N. Cicero Avenue
Chicago, Illinois 60646
312 566—6920

Claitor's Books
3165 S. Acadian at I—10
Box 239
Baton Rouge, La. 70821
504 344—7631

Clark Boardman Co.
435 Hudson
New York City, N.Y. 10014
212 929—7500

Commerce Clearing House (CCH)
4025 Peterson Ave.
Chicago, Illinois 60646
312 689—5233

Dennis & Co.
251 Main Street
Buffalo, N.Y. 14203
716 852—2309

Environmental Law Institute
1346 Conn. Ave. #620
Washington, D.C. 20036
202 452—9600

Foundation Press
170 Old Country Road
Mineola, N.Y. 11501
516 248—5580

Wm. W. Gaunt & Sons
3011 Gulf Drive
Holmes Beach, Florida 33510
813 778—5211

Wm. S. Hein & Co.
1285 Main St.
Buffalo, N.Y. 14209
716 882—2600

Information Handling Services
P.O. Box 1154
Englewood, Colo. 80110
303 771—2600

Law Reprints
37 W. 20th St.
New York City, N.Y. 10011

Lawyers Cooperative Publishing Co.
  (LCP)
Aqueduct Building
Rochester, N.Y. 14603
715 546—5530

Little, Brown & Co.
34 Beacon St.
Boston, Mass. 02106
617 227−0730

Lofit Publications
Box 297
Saugerties, N.Y. 12477

Martindale-Hubbell
1 Prospect St.
Summit, N.J. 07901

Michie Co.
P.O. Box 7587
Charlottesville, Va. 22906
703 295−6171

Oceana Publications
Dobbs Ferry, N.Y. 10522
914 693−1320

Pike and Fischer
2000 L St. N.W.
Wash., D.C. 20036

Practicing Law Institute (PLI)
810 Seventh Ave.
New York City, N.Y. 10019
212 765−5700

Prentice-Hall
P.O. Box 21X
Englewood Cliffs, N.J. 07663
212 687−7660

Fred B. Rothman & Co.
57 Leuning Street
South Hackensack, N.J. 07606
201 489−4646

Shepard's Citations
P.O. Box 1235
Colorado Springs, Colo. 80901
303 633−5521

Standard & Poor
345 Hudson St.
New York City, N.Y. 10014

Sweet & Maxwell Spon Ltd.
Northway
Andover Hampshire
England

Charles C. Thomas
301−327 E. Lawrence Ave.
Springfield, Ill. 62703
217 789−8980

U.S. Corporation Co.
70 Pine St.
New York City, N.Y. 10005

U.S. Government Printing Office
  (GPO)
Washington, D.C. 20402
202 783−3238

Warren, Gorham & Lamont
210 South St.
Boston, Mass. 02111
617 423−2020

West Publishing Co. (West)
50 Kellogg Boulevard
St. Paul, Minn. 55102
612 228−2500

For local dealers and general dealers call the nearest law school library or consult *Books in Print* and *Law Books in Print* (Oceana).

Restatement (see paragraph 54; see also subject listings in this Alphabetical Appendix).

See also *Cohen*, p. 195; *How to*, pp. 290—295; *Pollack*, p. 364.

Rules of Court (see Civil Procedure).

Sales (see Commercial Law).

Securities.

BNA. *Securities Regulation and Law Report.* 2 v.

loose-leaf.

Business Lawyer. (ABA).

v. 31 published in 1976.

CCH. *Securities Law Reporter.* 5 v.

loose-leaf. Transfer binders for decisions affecting securities law.

Loss. *Securities Regulation.* 2d ed. and supp. (Little, Brown 1961, 1969).

Ratner. *Securities Regulation—Materials for a Basic Course.* (West 1975).

The introduction provides a basic understanding of legal materials in the field of securities.

Securities Law Review. (Clark Boardman).

v. 7 published in 1975.

Securities Regulation Law Journal. (Warran, Gorham and Lamont).

v. 2 published in 1975.

Standard and Poor. *Review of Securities Regulation.*

1 v. loose-leaf. monthly.

Secondary Materials (see paragraphs 37 *et seq.*).

Basically, all that is not a primary source, such as laws and opinions.

See also *Cohen*, p. 4; *How to*, p. 286.

Shepard's Citations (see paragraphs 59—69, 96).

See also *Cohen*, p. 61, 108; *How to*, pp. 160—183; *Pollack*, p. 281; *Research Group*, p. 64.

Slip Decisions.

This is the first official record of a court decision. As a practical matter, reprints of these decisions are more readily available from private publishers. West, loose-leaf services, U.S.L.W. are examples of publishers that provide opinions in lieu of the general unavailability and awkwardness of maintaining slip opinions.

See also *Cohen*, p. 73; *Pollack*, p. 20.

State Reports (see paragraphs 20—24).

See also *Cohen*, p. 26; *How to*, pp. 21—35; *Pollack*, p. 13.

State Statutory Material (see paragraphs 83, 84. see also Legislation).

See also *Cohen*, p. 93; *How to*, pp. 140—153; *Pollack*, p. 207; *Research Group*, pp. 49, 55.

Statutes at Large (see paragraphs 83, 84).

A session of Congress lasts two years. Laws passed during these sessions are first published as slip laws and then cumulated into a bound volume called the *Statutes at Large*. The slip laws contain the same pagination that appears in the bound volume. Laws begin as bill numbers preceded by a designation of "S" or "H," depending upon which chamber introduced the bill. When passed into law, they are numbered as follows: 92–109, which means 92d Congress, one hundred and ninth law passed. These laws can also be found in the *United States Code Congressional and Administrative News*, loose-leaf services, and elsewhere. *United States Law Week* publishes selective legislation.

See also *Cohen*, p. 79, *How to*, pp. 120–124; *Pollack*, p. 151.

Tax and Estate Planning.

Bittker and Eustice, *Federal Income Taxation of Corporations and Shareholders.* 3d ed. (Warren, Gorham and Lamont 1971).
  1976 supplement.
BNA. *Tax Management Portfolios.*
  monographs on all phases of tax law.
Casner. *Estate Planning.* 3d ed. (Little, Brown 1961).
  supplemented.
Chommie. *Federal Income Taxation.* 2d ed. (West 1973).
CCH. *Standard Federal Tax Reports.*
  loose-leaf. weekly. 9 v. plus citator and index volumes.
  Subscription includes bound volumes of cases, *United States Tax Cases.*
  CCH also publishes *Federal Estate and Gift Tax Reporter.*
Freeland and Stephens. *Cases and Materials on Fundamentals of Federal Income Taxation.* (Foundation 1972).
  Chapter I on orientation and Chapter II on tax practitioner's tools provide excellent basis for research in tax field.
Freeland, Ferguson, Stephens. *Federal Income Taxation of Estates and Beneficiaries.* (Little, Brown 1970).
  1971 supplement.
Law Reprints. *Tax Series.*
  Briefs and records of current tax cases. v. 8 was published in 1975/76.
Lowndes and Kramer. *Federal Estate and Gift Taxes.* 3d ed. (West 1974).
Mertens. *The Law of Federal Gift and Estate Taxation.* (Lofit).
  2 loose-leaf volumes, 1975 update; 15 bound volumes.
Michie's Federal Tax Handbook. 1974. 2 v.
Mertens. *The Law of Federal Income Taxation.* (Callaghan).
  loose-leaf. 40 plus volumes of commentary, code, rules.
  1975 supplement.
New York University. *Institute on Federal Taxation.* (M. Bender).
  v. 33 published in 1975.

Page on *Wills.* 8 v. (Anderson).
  1974–75 pocket parts.
Prentice-Hall. *Federal Taxes.*
  loose-leaf. weekly. Complete unit includes income tax, estate and gift tax,
  state and local tax (by state), citator volumes and bound volumes of court
  cases.
Rabkin and Johnson. *Federal Income, Gift and Estate Taxation.* 11 v.
  (M. Bender).
  loose-leaf. 1975 supplement.
Stephens, Maxfield, Lind. *Federal Estate and Gift Taxation.* 3d ed.
  (Warren, Gorham and Lamont).
  loose-leaf. 1974 pamphlet.
Tax Law Review. (Warren, Gorham and Lamont).
  Edited at New York University School of Law. v. 30 published in 1975.
Tax Lawyer. (ABA).
  v. 29 was published in 1976.
Taxes. (CCH).
  1975 is the last published volume.
Willis. *Partnership Taxation.* 2d ed. 2 v. (Little, Brown 1976).

Torts.
  BNA. *Product Safety and Liability Reporter.* 3 v.
    loose-leaf.
  Frumer and Friedman. *Products Liability.* 4 v. (M. Bender).
    loose-leaf.
  Harper and James. *The Law of Torts.* 3 v. (Little, Brown 1956).
  Hursh and Bailey. *American Law of Products Liability.* 2d ed. 6 v. (LCP).
    1976 supplement.
  Negligence and Compensation Cases Annotated.
      A multi-volume set containing leading cases and digest of cases in point.
    v. 16, 4th Series, published in 1975.
  Noel and Phillips. *Products Liability in a Nutshell.* (West 1974).
  Prosser on *Torts.* 4th ed. (West 1971).
  Restatement of Torts. (1931; *2d* 1965).
    tentative drafts for *2d* still being published.
  Rheingold and Birnbaum. *Product Liability.* 2d ed. (PLI 1975).
    A valuable compilation of leading law review articles.
  Schwartz. *Comparative Negligence.* (Allen Smith 1974).

Trade Regulation.
  BNA. *Antitrust and Trade Regulation Report.*
    loose-leaf. 2 v.
  Callman. *The Law of Unfair Competition, Trade Marks and Monopolies.* 3d
    ed. 5 v. (Callaghan).
    loose-leaf. 1975 supplement.

CCH. *Trade Regulation Reporter.* 5 v.
>loose-leaf plus bound volumes of *Trade Cases.*

Gellhorn. *Antitrust Law and Economics in a Nutshell.* (West 1967).

Howell's Copyright Law. 4th ed. by Latman. (BNA 1962).

Sullivan. *Hornbook on the Law of Antitrust.* (West announced 1976).

Toulmin. *A Treatise on the Antitrust Laws of the United States.* 7 v. (Anderson 1949–).

United States Patent Quarterly. (BMA).
>v. 187 published in 1976. covers patents, trademarks, and copyright.

United States. *Report* of the Attorney General's National Committee to Study the Antitrust Laws. (1955).

Van Cise. *Understanding the Antitrust Laws.* rev. ed.
(PLI 1966).

Treaties.
See *How to*, pp. 136–140, 418–425.

Trial Practice (See also Evidence).
Am. Jur. *Trials.* 23 v. (LCP).
>1975 pocket parts.

Bender's *Forms of Discovery.* 20 v.
>1975 supplement.

Figg, McCullough II, Underwood. *Civil Trial Manual.* (ALI/ABA 1974).

Goldstein and Lane. *Trial Technique.* 3 v. (Callaghan).
>loose-leaf. 1975 supplement.

Hunter. *Federal Trial Handbook.* (LCP 1974).

Jeans. *Trial Advocacy.* (West 1975).

Keeton. *Trial Tactics and Methods.* 2d ed. (Little, Brown 1973).

Schweitzer. *Cyclopedia of Trial Practice.* 2d ed. 10 v. (LCP).
>1975 supplement. Also publishers of *Proof of Traumatic Injuries.* 4 v.

Trial Lawyers Guide. (Callaghan).
>1957 to date.

Trial Manual 3 for the Defense of Criminal Cases. (ALI/ABA 1975).

Uniform Laws Annotated.
Uniform laws are not laws until adopted by some state. The National Conference of Commissioners on the Uniform State Laws publishes these laws in areas where states impinge upon one another and reciprocal treatment is advisable, such as the Uniform Support Act. In 1968 West began publishing a new annotated set of these laws as adopted by the conference, beginning with the Uniform Commercial Code. The laws are annotated and the states adopting the laws are listed along with notes as to any changes that may have been made by the adopting state. The *Handbook* of the conference has a chart of all uniform laws and also includes a good deal of information as to the work

of the conference and prints verbatim uniform laws that are presently being considered.

See also *Cohen*, p. 97; *How to*, pp. 146–149; *Pollack*, p. 376.

United States Code (see paragraphs 75–77).
See also *Cohen*, p. 82; *How to*, pp. 126–135; *Pollack*, p. 153.

United States Constitution (see paragraph 72).
See also *Cohen*, p. 88; *How to*, p. 116–117; *Pollack*, p. 133.

United States Reports (see paragraphs 21–25).
See also *Cohen*, p. 13; *How to*, pp. 35–37; *Pollack*, p. 34.

Words and Phrases.

An alphabetical arrangement of judicially considered words and phrases. It is published by West and supplemented annually. Each definition is followed by a citation to the case from which the quotation comes. Thus it can be a case finder as well as a key number finder. Do not cite. West also includes a words and phrases section with its state and federal digests in a less inclusive format. See *Cohen*, p. 59, *Pollack*, p. 81; and this appendix under Dictionaries.

Workmen's Compensation (see Labor).

Zoning (see Property).

✳ *Appendix B*

Courts: A Comparative Perspective

John P. Richert

Conflict is present in all social settings. As a result, each culture has developed a variety of procedures and institutions to resolve disputes. Conflict settling mechanisms range all the way from relatively informal procedures such as negotiations, mediation, and arbitration, to formal institutions such as administrative agencies and courts. In most instances such structures complement each other. Their relative importance is a product of cultural, social, historical, legal, and political factors which are unique to each nation.

Courts differ in several ways from other institutions which resolve conflicts. The following criteria are indicative of some of the major characteristics of courts:

1. Courts apply known rules to facts presented by litigants.
2. They follow an established procedure in the process of resolving disputes.
3. The outcome sought is a "just" one.
4. Decisions are made by one or several judges who enjoy a special legal status; judges are frequently assisted by laymen.
5. Decisions by courts are binding upon the parties.
6. Courts usually seek independence from outside pressures.

These criteria constitute an "ideal" model of a court. In reality, practices vary a great deal since they are a function of the needs and peculiarities of each legal system. But beyond individual differences, there are common patterns relating to the scope of the jurisdiction of courts, their organization, and their structure.

THE ORGANIZATION OF COURTS

The Jurisdiction of Courts

Two broad categories of courts may be distinguished on the basis of the scope of their jurisdiction: courts of general (or ordinary) jurisdiction and specialized courts.

Courts of General Jurisdiction. Courts of general jurisdiction are best defined as those whose trial jurisdiction is not assigned to a specialized court. Such courts hear the bulk of civil and criminal disputes. In some countries, for example, in the Federal Republic of Germany and in the United States, one institution usually hears both kinds of cases. In England, on the other hand, there are two sets of courts handling criminal and civil disputes, but judges are usually interchangeable. Another possibility is typified by France, which has separate civil and criminal courts each with its own judges. In virtually all legal systems, however, ordinary courts are supplemented by specialized jurisdictions.

Specialized Courts. The scope of specialized tribunals is by definition narrower than that of courts of ordinary jurisdiction. But the importance of the cases which they are empowered to hear may be considerable. The German Constitutional Court, for example, hears disputes involving violations of civil liberties. Like American courts, it has the power of judicial review, that is to say, it may declare a legislative act unconstitutional and therefore inapplicable. French administrative courts, such as the *Conseil d'Etat*, are competent in matters involving the relationships between private individuals and agencies of the government. Decisions by this court have played a major role in circumscribing the power of the state.

The range of specialized courts is considerable, but two major categories of specialized courts may be differentiated on the basis of the law which they apply, and the status of the litigants who appear before such courts. The two characteristics overlap in a number of instances. The first category of specialized courts includes social security courts (Germany), patent courts (the United States and Germany), bankruptcy courts (Australia), and, most notably, administrative courts (Argentina, Germany, Indonesia, and France).

Most specialized courts were created to serve the needs of special groups of individuals. The most common are juvenile courts, which exist in many countries. The development of such courts stems from the rapid increase of criminality of young people throughout the world and the belief that special treatment should be given to young offenders. Other specialized courts which are fairly common are military courts, which exist in France, Indonesia, Brazil, and the Soviet Union.

Other specialized courts designed to serve the needs of particular groups include labor courts. Such courts exist in France (*Conseil des Prud'Hommes*), the

Federal Republic of Germany (on the state and federal levels), and Brazil (on the federal level). Labor courts hear disputes arising out of collective bargaining agreements, workmen's compensation, or breaches of employment contracts. German labor courts are also competent in controversies dealing with the "right of co-determination" (*Mitbestimmungsrecht*), a new legal development which gives labor a share in the management of private corporations. One might cite, in addition, commercial courts (France and Germany), disciplinary courts for civil servants (Mexico and Germany), and religious courts (Indonesia and Middle Eastern countries). These courts exist at various levels of the judicial system, but in many cases, appeals from such courts go to ordinary courts of appeals. The list of specialized courts is virtually endless since they are created in response to situations often unique to each country.

Organization of Ordinary Courts

Two basic features characterize courts in most legal systems: their structure resembles that of a pyramid, and they are organized along a hierarchical pattern. This applies to specialized as well as to courts of general jurisdiction. However, because of the usually more limited scope of specialized courts, only ordinary courts will be examined.

The pyramidal structure of judicial systems results from differences in the function of courts, and the need to make the lower courts accessible to litigants. The function of trial courts, as well as courts of limited jurisdiction, is to decide controversies in the first instance: they are the courts which hear the disputes first. Since, as a rule, relatively few of these decisions are appealed, there is a lesser need for courts of appeal whose major function it is to review decisions by lower courts. As a result, trial courts and courts of limited jurisdiction are frequently organized on a geographic basis corresponding to a small political unit (city, county courts, *arrondissement, Bezirk*, etc.) easily accessible to litigants. Intermediate courts of appeal are usually set up on a regional basis incorporating several of the basic units, and the supreme court has jurisdiction over the entire system.

Most court systems consist of a triple layer of courts of ordinary jurisdiction. The first layer includes trial courts which hear disputes first. Many legal systems supplement these courts with courts of limited jurisdiction which hear minor civil and criminal cases.

Courts of appeals make up the second layer above the trial courts and the tribunals of limited jurisdiction. Their major function is to review the decision of the lower courts. The principle of review—or appeal—is common to all contemporary legal systems though it did not exist in some legal cultures; for example, traditional Muslim law before the eighteenth century. The review of a decision of a lower court by a higher court is made possible by the hierarchical organization of judicial systems. While the principle of appeal to a higher court is universal, its implementation varies considerably among legal systems. Many variations exist, for example, in the type of disputes which can be reviewed (in some cases, minor disputes may not be appealed), the number of services possible, whether the appeal is automatic or left to the intiative of one of the parties. Finally, the legal techniques through which appeals are made may also differ.

The court structure is capped by one or several courts of final review, frequently designated as a supreme court. Three patterns may be distinguished. In some countries, for example the United States, Canada, and India, the supreme court consists of one panel of judges. The supreme court in these countries may review cases tried in courts of general jurisdiction as well as those tried by specialized courts. In other countries, for example, France, the supreme court (*Cour de Cassation*) is a relatively large body divided into specialized panels which review cases in their respective specialities (e.g., civil, criminal). But provisions usually exist under which such courts can sit *en banc* (in one panel). A third pattern is best exemplified by the Federal Republic of Germany, which has several supreme courts, including a constitutional court, a supreme court of general jurisdiction, as well as courts reviewing administrative matters, labor cases, and social security disputes.

It may be pointed out that the names of courts are frequently a poor indicator of their function or their location in the judicial hierarchy. The terminology can be very misleading. In the United States, for example, the most frequent appellations for courts are district, circuit, and superior courts. These terms may apply to trial courts in some states, to the courts of appeals in others, and even to courts of limited jurisdiction. To complicate matters further, some state supreme courts are called Court of Appeals (N.Y.) or Supreme Court of Errors (Conn.). The supreme court of New York is not a supreme court: it is a trial court, and a separate division of the court serves as an intermediate court of appeals. In some cases the names of courts are not even indicative of their function. The British House of Lords falls in this category, as well as the French *Conseil d'Etat* and *Conseil des Prud'Hommes*.

Structural Models

The court systems of most nations fall into two major categories. Some, such as that of the United States, have a dual court structure in which two sets of courts coexist side by side. Other nations, for example, France and Italy, have a unitary system in which all courts are integrated into one structure along a hierarchical pattern.

Dual Court Systems.   The development of dual court systems may be attributed to two major factors. The first is the political infrastructure of a country. Many political systems organized on a federal or confederal principle have two courts systems because the concept of federalism implies a sharing of power and rule-making between the federal government and the various entities which make up the federation. It is therefore possible for each system to develop its own institutions to interpret and apply the laws. Political systems based on the unitary principle, on the other hand, tend to concentrate political power and rule-making at the national level, thereby eliminating the need for more than one court system. The duality of court structures may also result from cultural and social factors. This is often the case in developing nations in which political scientists frequently contrast the "traditional" and "modern" sectors. The "traditional" sector represents that part of the social system which still recognizes traditional norms and institutions. These may stress alternate means of dispute processing such as mediation, popular in Asia, or, in the event adjudication is used, rely upon tribal or customary law to resolve disputes, as is the case in many African nations. The "modern" sector, on the other hand, is characterized by a court structure which is often patterned after that of the former colonizer. Dual court systems may be further broken down into developed and undeveloped court systems.

Developed Dual Systems. The United States, Argentina, and Mexico may be placed in this category since all three nations have a federal judicial system and state or provincial courts. The federal judicial system in these countries consists of district courts at the trial level. Courts of appeals were created in Mexico, the United States (1891), and Argentina (1902) above the trial courts. A supreme court completes the federal court system. A major difference between federal courts in the United States and those of Mexico and Argentina is the absence of a well-developed system of specialized courts in the two latter countries.

The federal judicial system is closely patterned after the state court system in the United States and Mexico and the provincial courts in Argentina. All three have a triple layer of local courts supplemented, especially in the United States, by courts of limited jurisdiction.

Undeveloped Dual Systems. Most federal states have a court system in which federal courts exist only at the top of the local system. In such cases the federal courts do not duplicate the state courts. Rather, they provide an ultimate review for decisions handed down by state courts. In some cases the "ultimate" review could even be carried beyond the national level. For example, in Canada it was possible until 1949 to carry an appeal to the British Privy Council.

The role of the federal courts may extend beyond a mere review of state court decisions, since some federal courts have original jurisdiction. An example is the German Federal Constitutional Court (*Bundesverfassungsgericht*) which has original jurisdiction in the case of constitutional complaints dealing with infringements of civil liberties (*Verfassungsbeschwerde*).

The courts systems of Australia, Brazil, Canada, the Federal Republic of Germany, India, the Soviet Union, and Switzerland are based on this model. Each of these countries is characterized by a developed state or local court system, and a limited federal system involving only one stratum of federal courts. In some cases the federal courts are relatively new additions to the judicial system. This is the case in Switzerland where the federal court was created in 1848, and Canada where it was set up in 1875 after considerable debate.

Unitary Court Systems. Most nations which are not set up as federations have a unitary court system in which all courts are integrated in one structure. This system is typical of France, England (as distinguished from Britain), the Netherlands, Belgium, Scandinavian countries, Italy, Spain, Japan, and most of the countries of the Third World formerly colonized by Britain and France, though only in the "modern" sector as was noted above.

A unitary court system does not necessarily imply a unified one. The latter implies a logical and systematic integration of all courts in one structure in an effort to promote judicial efficiency. Most unitary systems are not unified, particularly those of American states. Rather, they represent the fruits of haphazard historical development. But efforts at unifying the courts are underway in many states and some foreign countries.

RULES APPLIED BY COURTS

The fact that courts resort to known rules distinguish them from other institutions settling disputes. These rules are specific to each legal system, but there are similarities both in the substance of the law applied, and in the procedure followed by courts.

Major Legal Families

Four major legal families (or legal cultures) are usually distinguished including the common law, the civil law, the Socialist legal tradition, and religious legal systems. Some of these may coexist in one country, for example, the common law in Canada and the civil law in Quebec. In many Middle Eastern countries traditional Muslim law coexists with legal systems inspired by the common law or the civil law. In many developing nations "modern" legal norms exist alongside customary rules.

The Common Law Legal Tradition. The common law (or Anglo-Saxon) tradition forms the basis of the legal systems of Britain, the United States, Canada, Australia, and New Zealand. It has also had a major influence on the legal system of most nations previously under British rule in Africa, the Middle East, and Asia such as Nigeria, Ghana, Tanzania, the Sudan, Israel, Jordan, Iraq, and India.

The common law differs from other legal traditions in several ways. The first concerns the source of law. Anglo-Saxon law developed essentially as case law. Other sources of law such as statutes, customs, and the writings of legal scholars have also had an impact on its development, but judicial precedents form the basis of the common law. Decisions by judges remain important sources of law today in common law countries. But statutory law plays an increasingly important role in all common law legal systems.

The application of *stare decisis* ("let the precedent stand") varies within common law systems. It is applied more rigidly in some countries, for example, in Britain, than in the United States, where it is not unusual for a supreme court to overrule itself and establish a new precedent. *Stare decisis* also plays a role in civil law countries but is an auxiliary in such systems rather than a major source of law. Indeed the French Civil Code specifically forbids French judges to elaborate "general principles" on the basis of the cases they hear, a procedure which is the essence of case law.

Secondly, the development of the common law is characterized by a great emphasis upon rules of procedure. A major result of this development is the solicitude of the common law toward individual rights which were frequently safeguarded because of procedural developments. The late Justice Frankfurter of the U.S. Supreme Court once noted that the history of liberty and the growth of due process can be viewed largely as the product of the development of procedural rules. The emphasis upon procedure and the possibilities which it offers is dramatized by Jefferson, who called judges "sappers and miners." His description was pejorative, but the terms highlight the role that judges and courts have played in the development of the common law. To put it in another way, one can say that the common law is essentially empirical in its growth since common law judges formulate general principles utilizing specific cases.

The Civil Law. The civil law, also known as continental law or Romano-Germanic law, is the second major legal family. It forms the basis of the legal systems of France, the Federal Republic of Germany, Austria, Switzerland, Italy, Spain, Portugal, the Netherlands, and Belgium. It has also been the major source for the Scandinavian legal systems, though the common law as well had some influence on their development. The civil law is also the dominant legal system of South America as well as most African nations previously under French rule such as Senegal, the Ivory Coast, and Dahomey. In addition, the civil law was literally exported to Turkey (which adopted the Swiss Civil Code), Taiwan, and Japan, though Anglo-Saxon law had some influence in the latter after World War II. The French civil code has also been the major source for the Civil Code of Quebec (1865) and the codes of Louisiana (1808, 1822). The civil law is derived from Roman law, especially Justinian's compilations (the Code, Digest, Institutes) which are a major restatement of Roman law published between 529 and 534 A.D. It also incorporates major portions of Germanic codes and was further restated by scholars in European universities during the renaissance of Roman law at the beginning of the twelfth century. The civil law is embodied in codes such as the Code Napoleon (1804) and the German *Burgerlischesgesetzbuch* (referred to as BGB, 1901).

A code is a systematic and logical restatement of the law in a particular field.

Codes are not mere collections of laws: they embody the basic legal principles and tenets of a legal tradition. Whereas the common law is essentially empirical, based on specific judicial decisions made in the past, codes are abstract documents stating general principles which judges apply to specific cases. The civil law and the common law therefore approach the law from opposite directions. The civil law differs therefore from the common law on the basis of its pattern of development. The latter grew under the aegis of English monarchs, but in a multitude of courts throughout the realm. It was and remains today a decentralized process which occurs at many levels in courts throughout the legal system. Codes, on the other hand, are enacted by national legislatures. The development of the law is therefore primarily a centralized process. This duality in the development of the two legal systems further highlights the deductive and abstract quality of the civil law, as opposed to the inductive features of the common law.

The Socialist Legal Tradition.   The Socialist legal tradition is based on the writings of Marxist theorists. It is the dominant legal system of Communist countries including the Soviet Union, the People's Republic of China, and Eastern European countries such as Poland, Rumania, Hungary, Bulgaria, and the Democratic Republic of Germany. Socialist law is of Western tradition, but it differs in important ways from the law of capitalist systems based on the common law and the civil law.

In the first place, the role of law in Communist countries is to serve as a means for the achievement of the Communist revolution. The law is not an end in itself, nor is it an embodiment of "justice" as law is often conceived in "bourgeois" states. Law in Socialist countries is used to organize the nation's economic system and to change the behavior and attitudes of citizens in order to facilitate the creation of a new Socialist "man." The perception of law merely as a tool is not compatible with the concept of natural law upon which both the civil law and the common law are anchored. Natural law implies a certain immutability whereas Socialist law, on the other hand, may be altered at any time, both in substance and procedure, to foster the revolution.

At the same time the concept of Socialist legality is now accepted, at least in the Soviet Union and European Communist states, despite its contradiction with the essence of Socialist law, which stresses the fluidity of the law. Indeed, disobeying the law in a Communist country does not constitute a mere infringement on the rights of private individuals, in the case of civil law, or an infraction against the state, in the case of criminal law, as it is perceived in "bourgeois" nations. Rather, it is viewed in its systemic implications since such behavior ultimately impedes the progress toward the Communist goal.

There are a number of significant differences between Socialist law and the legal systems of capitalist states. The first is that offenses against the state are far more numerous in Communist countries because of the expanded scope of the role of the state. Second, offenses against the state are regarded as more serious and are consequently more severely punished because they obstruct the progress toward communism. It is for this reason that such offenses as "profiteering" or "parasitism" are severely repressed. Third, because Socialist law is a superstructure, it need not be immutable or even stable. It can be changed to suit the needs of the proletariat. Furthermore, it need not be objective or unequivocal. These characteristics are diametrically opposed to the fundamental conception of the civil law as well as the common law.

These features of Socialist law have been an important impact upon the functioning of the courts. To begin with, courts are usually not independent from the political process in Communist countries. The lack of independence has prompted some scholars to argue that the concept of courts is actually incompatible with Socialist law. There is a divergence in the perception of the desirability for independence for tribunals among Communist nations. For example, the constitution of the Soviet Union (article 112) states that "judges are independent and subject only to the law." Chinese judges, on the other hand, are expected to clear their decisions with superiors. In reality, no courts in any judicial system are fully free from political pressures simply because courts do not operate in a vacuum. But compared to Anglo-Saxon or civil law courts, Socialist courts are considerably less independent. The lack of autonomy of judges is further reinforced by the role of such institutions as the *Prokurator* in the USSR, or its functional equivalent in other Communist countries. The *Prokurator* is a kind of super-prosecutor who enjoys wide latitude and authority to intervene in the judicial process at all levels. The *Prokurator* can—and does—intervene on behalf of a defendant as well as on behalf of the state in reversing decisions of courts, including those of the highest levels of the Soviet system.

Another difference is that Socialist courts play a major role in educating citizens and resocializing their attitudes in order to foster the development of a new Socialist personality. It is probable that courts anywhere play a role in educating citizens, but this role is specific and overt in Communist countries. It is perhaps best evidenced by some of the sanctions which Socialist courts may impose, such as "admonitions." The educational role of courts is particularly stressed in the courts of limited jurisdiction such as the Comrades' Courts of the Soviet Union. Such courts exist in virtually all Communist states though under a variety of names.

Religious Legal Systems. Religious legal systems encompass the Jewish tradition, canon law (Roman Catholic), the Hindu legal culture, various customary legal systems, and Muslim law. Most of these legal systems play a secondary role today either because they are restricted in their application to limited transactions of particular groups, or because they regulate the relations in the "traditional" sector of developing nations. The major exception is Muslim law which retains a considerable influence in many countries. But even in this case a notable evolution has taken place. It is only in Saudi Arabia, Yemen, Libya, and some small emirates of the Persian gulf that traditional Muslim law is followed exclusively. The common law has had a major impact in the Sudan, Jordan and Iraq, and Kuwait. The civil law has strongly influenced the legal systems of Egypt, Syria, Lebanon, Tunisia, Morocco, and Algeria. Many countries have abolished the traditional Muslim tribunals altogether including Turkey (1924), Egypt (1955), Tunisia (1956), and, more recently, Indonesia and Pakistan.

Basic Models of Procedure

Courts do not only apply known substantive rules, but they also rely on distinct procedures in the resolution of disputes. The procedures vary in their details, but two patterns emerge based on the differences in the criminal procedures used: the accusatory and inquisitorial models.

Accusatory Procedure. The adversary (or accusatory) procedure forms the basis of the criminal procedure of common law systems. It is the oldest of the two models since it was already in use in Ancient Greece and Rome. It differs from the inquisitorial approach by the manner in which the criminal proceedings are initiated, and by its greater reliance upon popular, as opposed to specialized, structures in the resolution of criminal cases.

Criminal proceedings under an accusatory system are initiated by a complaint filed by a victim of a crime. Initially, the right to complain belonged exclusively to the victim or a relative, but, because complaints were not always lodged, the state gradually designated a public official to intervene, especially in important cases, when no complaint was recorded by the victim. Thus the system of the prosecutor supplements the private complainant, it does not replace him. Structurally speaking, the accusatory criminal procedure is very much like the civil procedure.

A second feature of the accusatory model of criminal procedure is its emphasis upon such features as the publicity of the proceedings, the adversary nature of the debate between the accuser and the defendant, and the role of laymen in the process. Many of these features were embodied in the Bill of Rights of the American Constitution, as well as the constitutions of many states of the United States. The right to a public trial and to indictment by grand jury is guaranteed in the fifth amendment, while the sixth amendment guarantees the right to cross-examine one's accusers as well as providing for a trial by jury. In the United States members of both the grand jury and of the trial jury are laymen randomly selected from various rolls such as voter registration lists. It is in part for this reason that some authors argue that the adversary model of criminal procedure is more compatible with democratic systems of government, while inquisitorial forms of procedure are typical of more authoritarian nations.

Inquisitorial Procedures. The term "inquisitorial" is derived from the *inquisito*, or inquest, which marks the beginning of the criminal process under this procedural model. The criminal process begins with an inquiry into the alleged facts by a specialized judge, for example, the French *juge d'instruction.* The examining magistrate may begin such an inquiry following a complaint, as well as on his own. In any case he supplants the private complainant in the criminal process from this point on. The inquisitorial procedure was developed by the Church of Rome as early as the thirteenth century though its roots are to be found in Imperial Rome. Most civil law countries follow a criminal procedure which is based on this model which also constitutes the basic procedural model of Socialist states.

Specialists play a major role in inquisitorial systems. The examining judge dominates the first part of the criminal process during which the case is prepared and the evidence gathered. Civil law judges frequently actively participate in the trial. They may freely interrogate defendants, formulate opinions about their guilt, and thus participate, in fact, as adversaries in the proceedings, much more than a referee, which is what the trial judge is supposed to be in common law countries. While common law judges seek to supervise the criminal trial in order to ensure that the proper rules are applied, the civil law judge actively participates in the search for the "truth." The role of laymen is generally limited in inquisitorial systems. On the one hand laymen, unlike grand jurors, do not participate in the preliminary phases of the criminal proceedings. Furthermore, lay participation at the trial is usually in the form of lay assessors, who assist judges in the judicial decision-making process whereas jurors in accusatory systems actually determine the question of guilt and innocence. The position of lay assessors is one of subordination to the professional judges, while jurors are essentially independent.

Another significant difference between the inquisitorial and the accusatory procedures lies in the secrecy of the former, especially during the important phase of the *instruction* when the case is prepared. The trial is usually public, but the function of the trial differs in the two systems. In the adversary model of procedure, the trial is the stage at which the actual guilt or innocence will be determined (unless the accused pleads guilty, in which case there is no need for a trial). The trial plays a more symbolic role in inquisitorial systems since its basic function is to legitimize the findings of the investigating magistrate. That is not to say that a defendant will invariably be convicted when brought to trial in civil law countries. A court of assize may sometimes decide not to convict, but generally, if the investigating magistrate is unable to develop a substantial case, charges are usually dismissed before the case comes to trial.

A major practical difference between adversary and inquisitorial procedures is that the trial may be eliminated under the accusatory system, if the accused pleads guilty. This is possible for two reasons. First, there is a formal step in the criminal process at which the accused is given the opportunity to record his plea. This is not the case in inquisitorial systems. Second, the purpose of the trial in Anglo-Saxon legal systems is to prove the guilt, or establish the innocence of the accused. If the defendant *admits* his guilt there is simply no reason to demonstrate it in a court of law. Since the purpose of the trial in continental criminal procedure is to confirm the truth, the trial will be held anyway. The trial is simply the culmination of the entire criminal process rather than its central phase.

The possibility of eliminating the trial in common law countries leads to considerable pressures upon the defendant to plead guilty. This fosters the practice of plea-bargaining, also known as negotiated pleas, pleading for consideration, or "copping a plea." This technique is particularly common in the United States where it is estimated that 90 percent of all criminal cases are resolved by guilty pleas, and that many of these are negotiated. It would be incorrect, however, to consider plea-bargaining unique to common law systems. Plea negotiation is a manifestation of the universal problem of legal discretion which involves the application of general principles to specific facts. This process always necessitates some adjustment because there is usually no absolute congruence between norms and facts of a specific case. It is a reality in all legal systems, though it manifests itself at different stages of the process, in a variety of techniques, and is carried out by various persons. Plea-bargaining is simply one version of discretion in Anglo-Saxon legal systems. It may be argued that a functional equivalent in civil law countries is the decision by the examining magistrates to drop all charges and thereby eliminate the trial.

STAFFING THE COURTS

The primary function of courts is to settle disputes in a "just" manner according to known rules. In order to accomplish this task as efficiently and promptly as possible, those who do the actual "judging" need administrative support, for example, in scheduling cases, collecting and disseminating information, record keeping, or in providing security in the court room. While the problem of judicial administration is central to the achievement of justice, it extends beyond the scope of this essay, which will concentrate on those who are directly involved in "judging": judges and laymen who may assist them in this task.

Judges

Judges are the central figures in the judicial process in most legal cultures even though their actual role may vary between that of a referee to an active participant in the trial as was noted earlier.

The discussion here will be limited to an examination of the role of professional judges defined as individuals trained in the law who sit full time in courts. It should be noted, however, that lay judges play an important role in the lower courts of many legal systems such as Britain (magistrates), the United States (justices of the peace), and several Communist countries (for example, the Soviet Comrades Courts or the Cuban Popular Courts). In some instances, for example, the Federal Republic of Germany, laymen may sit in higher courts including the Federal Social Court and the Federal Labour Court.

Models of Judicial Careers. There are two distinct models of judicial careers. The first is characteristic of common law countries where judges are usually drawn from the bar after several years experience as practicing attorneys. The law often specifies the number of years an attorney must have practiced before he is eligible for a judicial appointment. In general, the prestige of the court and the number of years of experience required are directly related. In New Jersey, for example, judges of municipal courts may be appointed after five years' experience, while ten years are required for upper level judges. Ten years seems to be a common requirement since it is found in Canada and India, and in some cases, in Japan. Curiously enough, there are no such requirements for federal judges in the United States. But in practice, only experienced attorneys are selected in the majority of instances. In England, where the legal profession is divided into barristers and solicitors, professional judges were primarily selected from the ranks of barristers until the 1971 Court Act which made solicitors eligible for Recorder or Circuit Judgeships. Barristers usually become eligible for a judgeship only after having been selected as a Queen's Counsel by the Lord Chancellor, or, in colloquial terms, after becoming a "silk." Such a selection rarely occurs before ten years of advocacy. In any case, judges in common law legal systems are usually selected from the ranks of established attorneys who have achieved some form of professional distinction. This is particularly true of British judges, as well as judges in Canada, Australia, and India. It is also true of American federal judges and those of higher state courts, though it is less characteristic of lower state court judges.

The second major career pattern is that of civil law countries and, with notable exceptions, of Socialist legal systems. In these countries judges are, in effect, civil servants, though they frequently enjoy a special legal status, in order to insure their independence from political pressure. Typically, in civil law countries, a judge decides upon a judicial career upon graduation from law school and after passing a competitive examination. In this case a judicial career is an alternative to private practice; it does not usually follow years of practice as is the norm in most Anglo-Saxon countries. Lateral entry into the judiciary is possible in many instances though most judges begin their career at the entry level. A third method is in Scandinavian countries which select most of their judges after they have served a long clerkship in the courts. The length of the internship ranges from a few years, as in Norway and Sweden, to well over ten years in Denmark.

Differences in the career patterns of judges in civil law countries and those in common law systems have several consequences, including the question of judicial training and judicial advancement. It is apparent that graduates of law schools without any experience as practicing attorneys need some form of training before sitting as judges. As a result, many civil law countries provide executive training programs for judges. This is the case in Japan where the Japanese Legal Training and Research Institute provides a twenty-four months extensive program of courses and internships. In France the *Ecole Nationale de la Magistrature* (National School of the Judiciary) sponsors a twenty-eight months program of courses and internships for prospective judges. The French program has had a considerable impact in other countries of civil law tradition, because the National School of the Judiciary has trained judges from many countries including Tunisia, Greece, several African countries, Thailand, and, until recently, Cambodia. In addition it has influenced judicial training in such countries as Poland, Spain, Yugoslavia, and Lebanon.

Until recently, judges in most common law countries received only scant training. It was assumed that the mode of recruitment which emphasized practical experience implied that further training was not necessary. However, recent developments, particularly in the United States, suggest a growing emphasis upon judicial training. Well-established programs such as those of the Institute of Judicial Administration are being supplemented by new programs both at the state and federal levels. The Federal Judicial Center, for example, now organizes seminars for newly appointed federal judges and refresher courses for sitting judges. However, all of these programs are frequently ad hoc and often voluntary. In addition, many of them are financed through private grants, although the Law Enforcement Assistance Administration of the United States Department of Justice is providing an increasing share of the funds.

Second, the concept of a judicial career implies the expectation of promotion. As a rule, judges in civil law legal systems begin their careers in the lower courts. They progress to positions of greater responsibility and prestige during the course of their career. Promotion to higher judgeships usually involves a combination of seniority and merit. As a result, civil law judges are frequently evaluated on an annual basis by their superiors. The promotion from lower to higher courts tends to broaden the experience of judges and is a good complement to their preservice formal training. This is especially true when judges may be promoted from the bench to the prosecution (or vice versa) over the course of their career, as is the case in France. Judges in common law countries are rarely promoted though it is of course entirely possible that a judge may be elevated to a higher bench; such an elevation is usually construed as an honor rather than a normal career expectation. Recent American data show an increase in the appointment of federal judges who have some previous judicial experience.

Inherent in the practice of promoting judges is the possibility that judicial behavior may be affected by extra-judicial considerations. Subtle or overt political pressures may temper judicial behavior. The desire and possibility of advancement may be a real temptation for judges in civil law countries. The judicial process has political ramifications in all legal systems despite frequent assertions to the contrary. But the range of political influences varies considerably. England is an example of a legal system in which politics play a minor role in judicial selection and decision-making. In the United States on the other hand, politics play a more significant role, though essentially in the selection of judges. Previous political experience, party membership, and financial contributions to political campaigns often have an impact on who becomes a judge in America. Indeed some scholars argue that previous political experience constitutes an asset on such high courts as state supreme courts, or the United States Supreme Court, because of the range of issues which such courts hear.

The selection of judges in most civil law countries is virtually unaffected by political considerations, but political pressures may have an impact on individual careers. The degree to which such pressures are felt varies considerably. While it is generally minimal in Scandinavian countries, it is more substantial in France where individual careers may be significantly affected as a result of judicial compromises. Political pressures are particularly felt by investigating magistrates who enjoy considerable discretion in pursuing a case, or dropping charges. The extreme manifestation of the intrusion of political considerations upon judicial decision-making and selection is in Socialist countries.

The Selection of Judges. Judges have been selected by a variety of methods throughout the ages. Some tribal societies relied upon supernatural considerations in the selection of judges. Selection by lot was another popular mode of designating magistrates; it is still used, (with some modifications) to select laymen who assist judges in some countries. Hereditary succession was used under the French *Ancien Regime* where some judicial offices were actually the personal property of individual judges.

Contemporary legal systems rely primarily upon two techniques in the selection of judges: elections and appointment. The choice of the method may depend upon such considerations as the status of judges (professional judges vs. laymen), the function of the court on which they sit (trial vs. appeals), even the jurisdiction of courts (ordinary vs. specialized). Election and appointment may be combined in some cases, for example, under the American Bar Association merit selection plan.

Appointment. Most judges in most countries are appointed, but the method of initial selection, as well as the appointing authority, vary greatly. The executive is the most frequent body empowered to appoint judges, though the locus of power may vary within the executive branch and the degree of discretion of the appointing authority may differ. The president of the United States nominates all federal judges, but the actual selection of lower federal judges is usually performed by the deputy attorney general. English judges are officially appointed by the Crown, but they are selected for the most part by the Lord Chancellor. French judges are appointed by the president of the republic but they are usually selected following a competitive examination. In the Federal Republic of Germany local and regional judges are selected by the Ministry of Justice of each *Land* which also supervises the judicial training in a special division known as *Landesjustizprüfungsamt.*

In some cases, the executive branch does not have unlimited discretion in the appointment process. The authority may be shared by other organs of government, for example, the legislature as in the case of the Senate for American federal judges, and some state judges such as Delaware and New Jersey. The participation of the legislature may be a formal one as in the previous examples, or it may be informal. This is the case in the United States as a result of a practice known as senatorial courtesy. This technique allows a senator from the district (or state) in which the judge would serve to block the nomination and therefore, in fact, prevent the appointment. A second appointing authority may be a higher court. Under this system the supreme court may appoint judges of some lower courts. This is the case in Bolivia, El Salvador, Nicaragua, Uruguay, and Finland. In the United States some lower level judges are appointment by appeals judges in the states of Hawaii, Illinois, South Dakota, and Virginia. It is also not unusual for judges of the higher courts to be consulted informally by the executive in the selection or promotion of judges. This has been the case for justices of the United States Supreme Court, as well as judges of the high courts of France and India. The appointment process is used over a wide geographical spectrum and in systems representing most legal traditions since they include, in addition to the nations already discussed, the following countries: Australia, Canada, New Zealand, Norway, Denmark, Sweden, Spain, the Philippines, and many Latin American nations. However, the actual appointing discretion of the executive is often a function of the political regime in place rather than of the constitutional provisions.

Election of Judges.   There are two basic models of electoral selection of judges. The first is by popular election which is used in thirty-three American states, though some states use a mixed process under which some judges are appointed and others are elected. Elections may be used in the selection of trial judges as well as that of appeals judges as is the case of New York and North Carolina. Popular elections of judges may be organized on a partisan basis; they may also be bipartisan or even nonpartisan as in Minnesota. For this reason many judicial elections in the United States are actually noncompetitive because candidates for judgeships are not opposed in many cases. For example, only in 40 percent of the judicial elections in the state of Wisconsin were judges opposed between 1940 and 1963 while in Louisiana the proportion was 41.1 percent between 1945 and 1960.

Judges of courts of limited jurisdiction of some Socialist countries are also popularly elected. This is the case of the Soviet Comrades' Courts and the Cuban Popular Courts. But the electoral process in these cases is no more competitive than in some American states, because judicial candidates are often nominated and screened by the Communist party and then stand election by secret ballot. In either case, such a mode of selection is closer to a ratification or a plebiscite than an election.

The second model of judicial recruitment by election consists in the election of judges by legislatures. This system is in use in some American states such as Vermont and South Carolina. It is the usual method of selecting judges in some Soviet courts, such as the courts of the Region, Autonomous Region, and Autonomous Republics, as well as of the supreme court of the Union of the Republic. Federal judges are elected in Switzerland by the National Assembly and Senate sitting jointly as the National Assembly (*Bundesversammlung*). Judges of the German Federal Constitutional Court are also elected by the national legislature with half of them elected by the National Assembly (*Bundestag*) and half elected by the Senate (*Bundesrat*).

Finally, judges sitting in courts of specialized jurisdiction are frequently elected by members of professional organizations which they serve. This is the case of French labor and commercial tribunals. The former are elected by members of professional organizations while the latter are elected on the basis of a complex formula involving an electoral college. An interesting feature is that the various French forms of corporate entities are entitled to vote for judges of commercial courts.

The justifications of elections as a method of recruiting judges vary. The considerable reliance of American states upon elections may be explained by the desire to make judges responsive, in a general way, to the people. Many states which have adopted this method of selection have achieved statehood during the middle of the nineteenth century when Jacksonian democratic ideals were popular. The justification of popular election of judges is explained in a similar fashion in Socialist nations. The legislative selection of judges also reflects a desire to democratize the process. But there are frequently additional specific reasons which warrant this mode of selection. A major concern in Switzerland is with the maintenance of a proper linguistic and religious balance. In Germany it is thought appropriate for the legislature to elect judges of the Federal Constitutional Court because of the political ramifications of the cases which this court hears.

Mixed Modes of Judicial Selection.   It is obvious that the combination of the various methods can lead to an infinite number of possibilities. Thus Israeli judges are appointed by the executive branch of government on the basis of a recommendation of an appointment committee which includes judges, representatives of the organized bar, and of the parliament (*Knesset*). In the United States the Merit Plan (or Missouri Plan) combines appointment and election. This method is strongly supported by the American Judicature Society and the American Bar Association as a means to improve the quality of American judges, and in order to limit the impact of political factors upon the selection of judges. Under this plan, the executive appoints a judge from a list of eligible-and-screened-candidates. Within a year or so after the appointment, the judge stands for election in an unopposed contest. The only question on the ballot might read as follows: should Judge Smith continue in office?

The Participation of Laymen in the Judicial Process

Judges are frequently assisted by laymen in the resolution of cases. There are several justifications for such a development. The participation of the public in the judicial process may be viewed as the survival of an ancient practice rather than a new development since lay participation can be traced to Ancient Greece and Rome and was popular among the Germanic tribes as well as several non-Western tribal societies. Lay participation ensures the maintenance of societal norms as well as providing for modifications in the norms which are not reflected in the law. For example, one of the traditional justifications of the common law jury, and from an entirely different perspective of lay assessors in Communist countries, has been the desire to maintain democratic ideals. According to this view, the participation of laymen in the judicial decision-making is seen as a guarantee against governmental arbitrariness. Curiously though, lay participation has never been important in some of the oldest democracies, notably Switzerland. Service as a juror is frequently viewed as an honor and a basic duty of citizenship. For this reason many countries exclude by statute certain categories of individuals, such as convicted felons. Because jury duty may cause a hardship, other categories may be excluded or may qualify for individual dispensation. Another justification for lay participation in the judicial decision-making process offered by some scholars is the belief that such a participation will enhance the legitimacy of court decisions. According to this view, decisions by professional judges are more likely to be accepted by the public if laymen are associated in the decision-making process.

There are two basic models of public participation in the process of judging: juries and lay assessors who sit in so called "mixed tribunals."

Jurors. The jury system developed in England and was exported through British colonization to most former colonial possessions. It is in the United States that the jury is most popular both in terms of the scope of the legal disputes in which juries are used, and in terms of the total number of jury trials recorded per year since it has been estimated that 80 percent of all jury trials take place in the United States. A major feature of juries, as opposed to mixed tribunals, is the independence which jurors have since they sit apart from professional judges and usually deliberate outside of their presence. They are therefore more immune from pressures by professional judges than lay judges who may be swayed in the presence of trained judges. It would be incorrect, however, to state that jurors are totally immune from judicial influence. One instance in which American judges, for example, may influence jurors is in charging the jury when judges explain to the jury the law to be applied to the facts. It is conceivable that the charge may convey more than an interpretation of the law, without constituting an overtly biased statement.

Lay Assessors. Lay assessors called (*Schöffen*, in German; *échevins*, in French; and *scabini*, in Italian) sit in mixed courts, since they serve with professional judges. They occupy a middle position between judges and juries because they combine attributes of both roles. Like judges, they fully participate in the entire judicial process including an evaluation of the facts and the law applicable. This is emphasized symbolically since they frequently sit with judges on the bench. They are nonetheless adjuncts to professional judges who remain the central figure in the courts. Furthermore, their independence vis-à-vis nonprofessional judge is often limited by the fact that they deliberate with them and may therefore be influenced by their professional status. How can one expect a common man to argue with a professional judge garbed in crimson robes trimmed with rows of white ermine and wearing a high hat bound with gold braids?

The distinction between lay assessors and jurors is not always clearly made, even in the legal literature. French statutes, for example, continue to refer to the jury which was replaced in 1941 by a system of lay assessors. It is perhaps most useful to view the participants in the judicial process in terms of a continuum which includes at both extremes professional judges and jurors while lay assessors occupy a middle position. Lay assessors are characteristic of civil law legal systems. This form of public participation in the judicial process exists in the Federal Republic of Germany, Austria, Norway, Brazil, Denmark, Sweden, Belgium, France, Greece, Italy, and several Swiss *cantons*, as well as the Soviet Union and most other Communist nations. The specific composition of mixed tribunals varies and so does the scope of their authority. But in all cases they enjoy less independence than jurors in Anglo-Saxon systems.

Glossary

ABSTRACT OF RECORD. A complete history in short, abbreviated form of the case as found in the record.

ACCESSORY. An active participant in a crime by reason of participation only in its preliminaries (accessory before the fact) or in furthering its success (accessory after the fact).

ACCUMULATIVE SENTENCE. A sentence, additional to others, imposed at the same time for several distinct offenses; one sentence to begin at the expiration of another.

ACTION IN PERSONAM. An action against the person; founded on a personal liability.

ACTION IN REM. An action FOR A THING; an action for the recovery of a thing possessed by another.

AD DAMNUM. The amount of damages claimed to have been inflicted upon the party bringing the action.

ADJUDICATION. Giving or pronouncing a judgment or decree; also the judgment given.

ADMINISTRATIVE OFFICE OF THE STATE COURTS. The business office of state courts, established in several states, which supplies information on judicial business and court personnel to the highest court, or chief justice. The powers and duties of these offices are not uniform.

ADMINISTRATIVE OFFICE OF THE UNITED STATES COURTS. An agency within the judicial department of the United States which manages the business affairs of the courts and collects information and statistical data with respect to the courts.

ADVISORY OPINION. An opinion rendered by a court to a lower court or, in some cases, to the legislative or executive branch of government which is not binding nor decisive of a controversy.

ADVERSARY SYSTEM. The system of trial practice in the United States and some other countries in which each of the opposing, or adversary parties has full opportunity to present and establish his (her) opposing contentions before the court.

ALLEGATION. The assertion, declaration, or statement of a party to an action, made in a pleading, setting out what he (she) expects to prove.

AMICUS CURIAE. A friend of the court; one who interposes and volunteers information upon some matter of law.

ANSWER. A pleading by which defendant endeavors to resist the plaintiff's allegation of facts.

APPEARANCE. The formal proceeding by which a defendant submits himself to the jurisdiction of the court.

APPELLANT. The party who takes an appeal from one court or jurisdiction to another.

APPELLEE. The party in a cause of action against whom an appeal is taken.

ARRAIGNMENT. In criminal practice, to bring a prisoner to the bar of the court to answer to a criminal charge.

AT ISSUE. Whenever the parties to a suit come to a point in the pleadings which is affirmed on one side and denied on the other, they are said to be "at issue."

ATTACHMENT. A remedy by which plaintiff is enabled to acquire a lien upon property or effects of defendant for satisfaction of judgment which plaintiff may obtain in the future.

BAIL. A guaranty that a person arrested on a criminal charge will appear for trial or examination when required if he is temporarily released. The guaranty may take the form of a bond, a deposit of money or a deed to property, which is forfeited if the accused does not appear when required.

BAILIFF. A court attendant whose duties are to keep order in the courtroom and to have custody of the jury.

BARRISTER. In England, an advocate engaged in conducting the trial or argument.

BENCH WARRANT. Process issued by the court itself, or "from the bench" for the attachment or arrest of a person.

BEST EVIDENCE. Primary evidence, as distinguished from secondary; the best and highest evidence of which the nature of the case is susceptible.

BIND OVER. To hold on bail for trial.

BINDING INSTRUCTION. One in which jury is told if they find certain conditions to be true they must find for plaintiff, or defendant, as case might be.

BURDEN OF PROOF. In the law of evidence, the necessity or duty of affirmatively proving a fact or facts in dispute.

CALENDAR. A list of cases which are to be heard by a court during the court term.

CAPTION. The caption of a pleading, or other papers connected with a case in court, is the heading or introductory clause which shows the names of the parties, name of the court, number of the case, etc.

CASE. A suit in law or equity. In appellate procedure, the trial record made in the lower court, including the papers and testimony.

CASES AND CONTROVERSIES. Words appearing in section 2, article III of the United States Constitution, limiting the exercise of judicial power by the federal courts to actual cases between parties with adverse interests, as compared to hypothetical or friendly disputes.

CERTIFICATION. The submission of questions of law arising in a particular case by a lower court to a higher court for binding instructions.

CERTIORARI. A writ issued by a higher court requiring the record of a case in the court below to be sent up to itself for redetermination.

CHALLENGE TO THE ARRAY. Questioning the qualifications of an entire jury panel, usually on the grounds of partiality or some fault in the process of summoning the panel.

CHANCELLOR. Chief advisor of the English king. By issuing writs the office eventually became the Court of Chancery in the fourteenth and fifteenth centuries. In some states, he is the chief judge of the equity courts.

CHANGE OF VENUE. The removal of a suit begun in one county or district, to another, for trial, or from one court to another in the same county or district.

CHIEF JUDGE OR CHIEF JUSTICE. The presiding judge of a court. In addition to his judicial functions, he may have administrative tasks.

CIRCUIT. A division or territory for judicial business.

CIRCUMSTANTIAL EVIDENCE. All evidence of indirect nature: the process of decision by which court or jury may reason from circumstances known or proved to establish by inference the principal fact.

CITATIONS. References to legal authorities or decided cases.

CIVIL ACTION. An action which seeks the establishment, recovery, or redress of private and/or civil rights. Civil suits relate to and affect only individual rights whereas criminal prosecutions involve public wrongs.

CODE. A collection, compendium, or revision of laws systematically arranged into chapters, table of contents, and index, and promulgated by legislative authority.

CODICIL. A supplement or an addition to a will.

COMMIT. To send a person to prison, to an asylum, workhouse, or reformatory by lawful authority.

COMMON LAW. Law which derives its authority solely from usages and customs of immemorial antiquity, or from the judgments and decrees of courts. Also called "case law."

COMMON LAW PLEADING. A system of pleading and procedure in force in England until 1852 and until 1848 in most of the United States. Opposition to its extreme rigidity and technicality led to the adoption of code pleading in most American jurisdictions, fashioned after the Field Code adopted in New York in 1848.

COMMUTATION. The change of a punishment from a greater degree to a lesser degree, as from death to life imprisonment.

COMPARATIVE NEGLIGENCE. The doctrine by which acts of the opposing parties are compared in the degrees of "slight," "ordinary," and "gross" negligence.

COMPETENCY. In the law of evidence, the presence of those characteristics which render a witness legally fit and qualified to give testimony.

COMPLAINANT. Synonymous with "plaintiff."

CONCURRENT JURISDICTION. When two courts have the power to determine the same issues.

CONCURRENT SENTENCE. Sentences for more than one crime in which the time of each is to be served concurrently, rather than successively.

CONCURRING OPINION. An opinion by a judge of an appellate court indicating alternate grounds for agreeing with the result reached by the majority.

CONDEMNATION. The legal process by which real estate of a private owner is taken for public use without his consent, but upon the award and payment of just compensation.

CONSTITUTIONAL COURT. In the federal system, a federal court established by Congress pursuant to article III of the United States Constitution. Judges of constitutional courts serve during good behavior and cannot have their compensation reduced while in office. The United States Supreme Court, the United States Courts of Appeal, the United States District Courts, and the Court of Claims are constitutional courts. In the states, a court provided for under the constitution.

CONTINGENT FEE. One where the lawyer's compensation depends upon his achieving a successful result for his client.

CORPORATION COURT. A court of limited civil jurisdiction usually exercising its authority in a city or borough. In some American colonies the corporation court also heard criminal cases. These courts still are in existence in some states.

CORPUS DELICTI. The body (material substance) upon which a crime has been committed, e.g., the corpse of a murdered man, the charred remains of a burned house.

CORROBORATING EVIDENCE. Evidence supplementary to that already given and tending to strengthen or confirm it.

COSTS. An allowance for expenses in prosecuting or definding a suit. Ordinarily does no include attorney's fees.

COUNTERCLAIM. A claim presented by a defendant in opposition to the claim of a plaintiff.

COURT-MARTIAL A court convened to hear an offense committed by a person in the military. Under the 1950 Uniform Code of Military Justice, court-martial courts have jurisdiction to try any military person or civilian serving with the armed forces for an offense against military law. There is no jury.

COURT OF APPEAL. A court in which appeals from a lower court are heard.

COURT OF FIRST INSTANCE. A court in which a case must originally be brought. Usually a trial court.

COURT OF GENERAL JURISDICTION. The largest jurisdiction a court of first instance can have in a given political unit (i.e., state, federal, district, circuit, county).

COURT OF GENERAL SESSIONS. Criminal courts of general jurisdiction existing in some American cities.

COURT OF INTERMEDIATE APPEAL. A court of appeal established in several states to lessen the workload of the highest reviewing tribunal. Ultimate review can still be had in the highest court by its permission, or, in limited cases, as a matter of right.

COURT OF JAIL DELIVERY. A colonial court trying all persons accused of crime and held in jail until the court's arrival, and having the power to deliver, i.e., discharge, those who are acquitted. The name is still retained for criminal courts in some states.

COURT OF KING'S BENCH. Formerly the highest English common law court, now a department of the High Court of Justice. It is also referred to as the "King's Bench," or "Queen's Bench" when the Queen is the highest royal authority.

COURT OF LAST RESORT. A court from which no appeal lies to a higher court in the same jurisdiction. This may sometimes not be the highest court in the jurisdiction.

COURT OF RECORD. A court whose proceedings are permanently recorded, and which has the power to fine or imprison for contempt. Courts not of record are those of lesser authority whose proceedings are not permanently recorded.

COURT OF SPECIAL SESSIONS. A court of limited jurisdiction in criminal cases in some states.

COURT REPORTER. A person who transcribes by shorthand or stenographically takes down testimony during court proceedings.

COURT SESSION. The time during which a court sits and may exercise its judicial power.

COURT TERM. A division of the year during which the court holds it sessions.

CRIMINAL INSANITY. Lack of mental capacity to do or abstain from doing a particular act; inability to distinguish right from wrong.

CROSS-EXAMINATION. The questioning of a witness in a trial, or in the taking of a deposition, by the party opposed to the one who produced the witness.

CUMULATIVE SENTENCE. Separate sentences (each additional to the others) imposed against a person convicted upon an indictment containing several courts, each charging a different offense. (Same as accumulative sentence.)

DAMAGES. Pecuniary compensation which may be recovered in the courts by any person who has suffered loss, detriment, or injury to his person, property, or rights, through the unlawful act or negligence of another.

DE NOVO. Anew, afresh. A "trial de novo" is the retrial of a case.

DECLARATORY JUDGMENT. One which declares the rights of the parties or expresses the opinion of the court on a question of law, without ordering anything to be done.

DECREE. A decision or order of the court. A final decree is one which fully and finally disposes of the litigation; an interlocutory decree is a provisional or preliminary decree which is not final.

DEFAULT. A "default" in an action of law occurs when a defendant omits to plead within the time allowed or fails to appear at the trial.

DEFAULT JUDGMENT. Judgment entered in a civil case where the defendant has failed to appear to contest the claim asserted against him. Thus, uncontested, the case is won by the plaintiff.

DEFENDANT. A person who is being sued in a civil action or is prosecuted in a criminal action.

DEMUR. To file a pleading, called a "demurrer," admitting the truth of the facts in the complaint, or answer, but contending they are legally insufficient.

DEPOSITION. The testimony of a witness not taken in open court, but in pursuance of authority given by statute or rule of court to take testimony elsewhere.

DIRECT APPEAL. An appeal as of right from a lower court to an appellate court.

DIRECT EVIDENCE. Proof of facts by witnesses who saw acts done or heard words spoken as distinguished from circumstantial evidence, which is called indirect.

DIRECT EXAMINATION. The first interrogation of a witness by the party on whose behalf he is called.

DIRECTED VERDICT. An instruction by the judge to the jury to return a specific verdict.

DISCOVERY. A proceeding whereby one party to an action may be informed as to facts known by other parties or witnesses.

DISMISSAL WITHOUT PREJUDICE. Permits the complainant to sue again on the same cause of action; while dismissal "with prejudice" bars the right to bring or maintain an action on the same claim or cause.

DISSENTING OPINION. An opinion by a judge of an appellate court indicating his reason for disagreeing with the result reached by the majority.

DISTRICT COURT. In the federal system, the only type of trial court that exists; in state systems, also a trial court, with jurisdiction varying from state to state.

DOCKET. The record of the list of cases waiting to be tried.

DOMICILE. That place where a person has his true and permanent home. A person may have several residences, but only one domocile.

DOUBLE JEOPARDY. Charging an accused with a crime for which he has already been tried.

DUE PROCESS. Law in its regular course of administration through the courts of justice. The guarantee of due process requires that every man have the protection of a fair trial.

EMBEZZLEMENT. The fraudulent appropriation by a person to his own use or benefit of property or money intrusted to him by another.

EMINENT DOMAIN. The power to take private property for public use by condemnation.

EN BANC OR IN BANC. A judicial bench. The term is usually applied to a court of appeal when all of its judges sit together and jointly issue a decision or opinion.

ENTRAPMENT. The act of officers or agents of a government in inducing a person to commit a crime not contemplated by him, for the purpose of instituting a criminal prosecution against him.

EQUITABLE ACTION. An action which may be brought for the purpose of restraining the threatened infliction of wrongs or injuries, and the prevention of threatened illegal action. (Remedies not available at common law.)

EQUITY, COURTS OF. Courts which administer remedial justice according to the system of equity, as distinguished from courts of common law. Equity courts are sometimes called courts of chancery.

ESCHEAT. In American law, the preferable right of the state to an estate to which no one is able to make a valid claim.

ESCROW. A writing, or deed, delivered by the grantor into the hands of a third person, to be held by the latter until the happening of a contingency or performance of a condition.

ESTOPPEL. A person's own act, or acceptance of facts, which preclude his later making claims to the contrary.

ET AL. An abbreviation of et alii, meaning "and others."

ET SEQ. An abbreviation for et sequentes, or et sequentia, "and the following."

EX CONTRACTU. In both civil and common law, rights and causes of action are divided into two classes: those arising ex contractu (from a contract) and ex delicto (from a wrong or tort).

EX DELICTO. Rights and causes of action arising from a wrong or "tort."

EX POST FACTO. After the fact; an act or fact occurring after some previous act or fact, and relating thereto.

EX REL. An abbreviation for ex relatione, legal proceedings instituted by an attorney general or other government officer in behalf of the state, and on information from a party with a private interest in the litigation.

EXCEPTION. A formal objection to an action of the court, during the trial of a cause, in refusing a request or overruling an objection; implying that the party excepting does not acquiesce in the decision of the court, but will seek to procure its reversal.

EXCLUSIVE JURISDICTION. The power given to one court, as against all others, to handle a given type of case.

EXHIBIT. A paper, document, or other article produced and exhibited to a court during a trial or hearing.

EXPERT EVIDENCE. Testimony given in relation to some scientific, technical, or professional matter by experts, i.e., persons qualified to speak authoritatively by reason of their special training, skill, or familiarity with the subject.

EXTENUATING CIRCUMSTANCES. Circumstances which render a crime less aggravated, heinous, or reprehensible than it would otherwise be.

EXTRADITION. The surrender by one state to another of an individual accused or convicted of an offense outside its own territory, and within the territorial jurisdiction of the other.

FAIR COMMENT. A term used in the law of libel, applying to statements made by a writer in an honest belief of their truth, relating to official act, even though the statements are not true in fact.

FAIR PREPONDERANCE. Evidence sufficient to create in the minds of the triers of fact the conviction that the party upon whom is the burden has established its case.

FALSE ARREST. Any unlawful physical restraint of another's liberty, whether in prison or elsewhere.

FALSE PRETENSES. Designed misrepresentation of existing fact or condition whereby a person obtains another's money or goods.

FELONY. A crime of a graver nature than a misdemeanor. Generally an offense punishable by death or imprisonment in a penitentiary.

FIDUCIARY. A term derived from the Roman law, meaning a person holding the character of a trustee, in respect to the trust and confidence involved in it and the scrupulous good faith and candor which it requires.

FORCIBLE ENTRY AND DETAINER. A summary proceeding for restoring possession of land to one who has been wrongfully deprived of possession.

FRAUD. An intentional perversion of truth; deceitful practice or device resorted to with intent to deprive another of property or other right, or in some manner to do him injury.

GARNISHEE. The process whereby a person holding money belonging to another, such as an employer or a bank, can be required to pay it over directly to that person's creditor.

GARNISHMENT. A proceeding whereby property, money, or credits of a debtor, in possession of another (the garnishee) are applied to the debts of the debtor.

GENERAL ASSIGNMENT. The voluntary transfer, by a debtor, of all his property to a trustee for the benefit of all of his creditors.

GENERAL COURT. A common term for a colonial legislature which acted as a court.

GENERAL DEMURRER. A demurrer which raises the question whether the pleading against which it is directed lacks the definite allegations essential to a cause of action, or defense.

GOOD BEHAVIOR. An office held during good behavior is one from which the incumbent may not be removed except on proved charges of misconduct.

GRAND JURY. A body of men, the number of whom varies in different jurisdictions, sworn to inquire into crimes within the jurisdiction of the county or district.

GRATUITOUS GUEST. In automobile law, a person riding at the invitation of the owner of a vehicle, or his authorized agent, without payment of a consideration or a fare.

GREAT SEAL. The seal used by the king of England to authenticate important acts and documents involving an important exercise of sovereign authority. It was in custody of the Lord Chancellor who used it to issue writs and thus acquire his important position in law and exclusive jurisdiction in equity.

GUARDIAN AD LITEM. A person appointed by a court to look after the interests of an infant whose property is involved in litigation.

HABEAS CORPUS. "You have the body." The name given a variety of writs whose object is to bring a person before a court or judge. In most common usage, it is directed to the official or person detaining another, commanding him to produce the body of the prisoner or person detained so the court may determine if such person has been denied his liberty without due process of law.

HARMLESS ERROR. In appellate practice, an error committed by a lower court during a trial, but not prejudicial to the rights of the party and for which the court will not reverse the judgment; error which in the judgment of the appellate court would not have changed the verdict of the jury.

HEARSAY. Evidence not proceeding from the personal knowledge of the witness.

HOLOGRAPHIC WILL. A testamentary instrument entirely written, dated, and signed by the testator in his own handwriting.

HOSTILE WITNESS. A witness who is subject to cross-examination by the party who called him to testify, because of his evident antagonism toward that party as exhibited in his direct examination.

HYPOTHETICAL QUESTION. A combination of facts and circumstances, assumed or proved, stated in such a form as to constitute a coherent state of facts upon which the opinion of an expert can be asked by way of evidence in a trial.

IMPEACHMENT OF WITNESS. An attack on the credibility of a witness by the testimony of other witnesses.

IMPEACHMENT TRIAL. The hearing of charges of misconduct against a public official conducted by a legislative body.

IN CAMERA. In chambers; in private.

IN FORMA PAUPERIS. A proceeding whereby a court may absolve a poor person of certain legal costs upon appropriate application. These proceedings constitute a large number of the cases filed in the United States Supreme Court.

INCOMPETENT EVIDENCE. Evidence which is not admissible under the established rules of evidence.

INDETERMINATE SENTENCE. An indefinite sentence of "not less than" and "not more than" so many years, the exact term to be served being afterwards determined by parole authorities within the minimum and maximum limits set by the court or by statute.

INDICTMENT. An accusation in writing found and presented by a grand jury, charging that a person therein named has done some act, or been guilty of some omission, which, by law, is a crime.

INFERIOR COURT. In the federal system, all courts created under article III, section 1 of the United States Constitution, except the Supreme Court. In the state systems, all courts of limited original jurisdiction.

INFORMATION. A formal accusation made by an official prosecutor without presentment to a grand jury, charging a person with committing a crime.

INJUNCTION. A mandatory or prohibitive writ issued by a court.

INNS OF COURT. Societies of barristers in England.

INSTRUCTION. A direction given by the judge to the jury concerning the law of the case.

INTER ALIA. Among other things or matters.

INTER ALIOS. Among other persons; between others.

INTERLOCUTORY DECISION. A decision intervening between the commencement and the end of a suit which decides some point or matter, but which is not a final adjudication of the whole controversy.

INTERROGATORIES. Written questions propounded by one party and served on adversary, who must provide written answers thereto under oath.

INTERVENTION. A proceeding in a suit or action by which a third person is permitted by the court to make himself a party.

INTESTATE. One who dies without leaving a will.

IRRELEVANT. Evidence not relating or applicable to the matter in issue; not supporting the issue.

JUDGMENT. Determination by a court of competent jurisdiction of a controversy between two or more persons, which is brought before the court by proper procedure.

JUDICIAL ADMINISTRATION. The organization, procedures and operation of the judicial branch of the government.

JUDICIAL COUNCIL AND JUDICIAL CONFERENCE. The judicial council is usually an official continuing body for research, the collection of statistical data, and sometimes for the drafting of court rules. There are many variations in their membership, organization, activities and effectiveness. The membership of judicial conferences consists usually of the judges of the courts in a particular jurisdiction.

Both judicial councils and judicial conferences utilize the cooperation of the bar and the public and are dedicated to improving the administration of justice and relieving congestion and delay on the courts.

JUDICIAL POWER. The power of a court to decide and pronounce a judgment and carry it into effect between parties who bring a case before it for decision. This power includes the issuing of necessary orders to protect the court's jurisdiction.

JUDICIAL STATISTICS. Data which reveal the actual work of a court for a given period. This information includes the number and types of cases filed in court and disposed of by the courts, time intervals for obtaining a trial, operating expenses of the courts, and workload of individual judges.

JUDICIARY. The branch of government which has judicial power. Also, the name for all the courts of a jurisdiction taken collectively.

JURISDICTION. The authority of a court to exercise its judicial power in a specific case.

JURISPRUDENCE. The philosophy of law, or the science which treats of the principles of positive law and legal relations.

JURY. A certain number of men and/or women, selected according to law, and sworn to inquire of certain matters of fact, and declare the truth upon evidence laid before them.

JUSTICE OF THE PEACE. A public official with minor civil and criminal jurisdiction. In more serious crimes he may be authorized to conduct preliminary hearings and hold the accused for trial by a higher court.

LEADING QUESTION. One which instructs a witness how to answer or puts into his mouth words to be echoed back; one which suggests to the witness the answer desired. Prohibited on direct examination.

LEGISLATIVE COURT. A court created by Congress pursuant to a constitutional power other than article III of the United States Constitution. Judges of legislative courts, as contrasted to constitutional courts, are not automatically subject to nonreduction during their appointment. The legislative courts are the United States Court of Customs and Patent Appeals, the United States

Emergency Court of Appeals, the United States Customs Court, the Tax Court, the territorial courts, and the local courts for the District of Columbia.

LETTERS ROGATORY. A request by one court of another court in an independent jurisdiction that a witness be examined upon interrogatories sent with the request.

LEVY. A seizure; the obtaining of money by legal process through seizure and sale of property. The raising of the money for which an execution has been issued.

LIBEL. A method defamation expressed by print, writing, pictures, or signs. In its most general sense any publication that is injurious to the reputation of another.

LIMITATION. A certain time allowed by statute in which litigation must be brought.

LIS PENDENS. A pending suit.

LITIGANT. One who is involved in a lawsuit as a party. Both the plaintiff and the defendant in a civil action are litigants.

LOCAL COURT. A court whose jurisdiction is limited as to a specific place.

LOCUS DELICTI. The place of the defense.

MAGISTRATE. Title of a judge of an inferior court with limited criminal and sometimes limited civil jurisdiction.

MAJORITY DECISION. A decision by an appellate court by more than one-half of those judges hearing a case.

MAJORITY OPINION. The statement written by one appellate judge on behalf of a majority of his colleagues setting forth the conclusion of the court and the reasons therefor.

MALFEASANCE. Evil doing; ill conduct; the commission of some act which is positively prohibited by law.

MALICIOUS PROSECUTION. An action instituted with intention of injuring defendant and without probable cause, and which terminates in favor of the person prosecuted.

MANDAMUS. The name of a writ which issues from a court of superior jurisdiction, directed to an inferior court, commanding the performance of a particular act.

MANDATE. A judicial command or precept proceeding from a court or judicial officer, directing the proper officer to enforce a judgment, sentence, or decree.

MANSLAUGHTER. The unlawful killing of another without malice; may be either voluntary, upon a sudden impulse, or involuntary, in the commission of some unlawful act.

MASTER IN CHANCERY. An officer of a court of chancery who acts as an assistant to the judge.

MATERIAL EVIDENCE. Such as is relevant and goes to the substantial issues in dispute.

MAYOR'S COURT. An inferior court whose jurisdiction is limited to a city or a town.

MESNE. Intermediate; intervening.

MISDEMEANOR. Offenses less than felonies; generally those punishable by fine or imprisonment otherwise than in penitentiaries.

MISFEASANCE. A misdeed or trespass. The improper performance of some act which a person may lawfully do.

MISTRIAL. An erroneous or invalid trial; a trial which cannot stand in law because of lack of jurisdiction, wrong drawing of jurors, or disregard of some other fundamental requisite.

MITIGATING CIRCUMSTANCES. One which does not constitute a justification or excuse of an offense, but which may be considered as reducing the degree of moral culpability.

MOOT. Unsettled; undecided. A moot point is one not settled by judicial decisions.

MORAL TURPITUDE. Conduct contrary to honesty, modesty, or good morals.

MORTGAGEE. The party who takes or receives a mortgage.

MORTGAGOR. A person who, having title to property, pledges the property as security for a debt by means of a written instrument, or mortgage.

MULTIPLICITY OF ACTIONS. Numerous and unnecessary attempts to litigate the same right.

MUNICIPAL COURT. In the judicial organization of some states, courts whose territorial authority is confined to the city or community.

MURDER. The unlawful killing of a human being by another with malice aforethought, either express or implied.

NE EXEAT. A writ which forbids the person to whom it is addressed to leave the country, the state, or the jurisdiction of the court.

NEGLIGENCE. The omission to do something which a reasonable man, guided by ordinary considerations, would do; or the doing of something which a reasonable and prudent man would not do.

NEXT FRIEND. One acting for the benefit of an infant, or other person without being regularly appointed as guardian.

NO BILL. This phrase, indorsed by a grand jury on an indictment, is equivalent to "not found" or "not a true bill." It means that, in the opinion of the jury, evidence was insufficient to warrant the return of a formal charge.

NOLLE PROSEQUI. A formal entry upon the record by the plaintiff in a civil suit, or the prosecuting officer in a criminal case, by which he declares that he "will no further prosecute" the case.

NOLO CONTENDERE. A pleading usually used by defendants in criminal cases, which literally means "I will not contest it."

NOMINAL PARTY. One who is joined as a party or defendant merely because the technical rules of pleading require his presence in the record.

NON COMPOS MENTIS. Not sound of mind; insane.

NON OBSTANTE VEREDICTO. Notwithstanding the verdict. A judgment entered by order of court for one party, although there has been a jury verdict against him.

NOTARY PUBLIC. A public officer whose function it is to administer oaths; to attest and certify by his hand and official seal, certain classes of documents in order to give them credit and authenticity in foreign jurisdictions; to take acknowledgments of deeds and other conveyances, and certify the same; and to perform certain official acts chiefly in commercial matters, such as the protesting of notes and bills, the noting of foreign drafts, and marine protests in cases of loss or damage.

NOTICE TO PRODUCE. In practice, a notice in writing requiring the opposite party to produce a certain described paper or document at the trial.

OBJECTION. The act of taking exception to some statement or procedure in trial. Used to call the court's attention to improper evidence or procedure.

OF COUNSEL. A phrase commonly applied to counsel employed to assist in the preparation or management of the case, or its presentation on appeal, but who is not the principal attorney of record.

OFFENSE. A minor crime carrying a light penalty.

OFFICIAL REPORT. A report of a decided case, generally, in courts of appellate jurisdiction, containing statements of the facts, judgments, and opinions published by a government body. Several states publish such reports officially for selected trial courts.

OMBUDSMAN. A Scandinavian innovation to oversee those in power. The Ombudsman receives complaints about maladministration of governmental officials, investigates the complaints, attempts to right any wrongs, and may prosecute wrong-doing officials. The practice has recently been adopted in Great Britain and is being considered in the United States.

OPINION EVIDENCE. Evidence of what the witness thinks, believes, or infers in regard to fact in dispute, as distinguished from his personal knowledge of the facts; not admissible except (under certain limitations) in the case of experts.

ORDINARY. A judicial officer, in several of the states, clothed by statute with powers in regard to wills, probate, administration, guardianship.

OUT OF COURT. One who has no legal status in court is said to be "out of court," i.e., he is not before the court. For example, when a plaintiff, by some act of omission or commission shows that he is unable to maintain his action.

PANEL. A list of jurors to serve in a particular court, or for the trial of a particular action; denotes either the whole body of persons summoned as jurors for a particular term of court or those selected by the clerk by lot.

PARTIES. The persons who are actively concerned in the prosecution or defense of legal proceeding.

PER CURIAM. An opinion rendered by the court as a whole, rather than by one judge with whom others concur. These opinions are often very short.

PEREMPTORY CHALLENGE. The challenge which the prosecution, or defense may use to reject a certain number of prospective jurors without assigning any cause.

PETIT JURY. A body usually of twelve men and women or less selected from a larger panel to hear and find the facts in a trial at law, so called to distinguish it from the grand jury.

PETITION. A written request to a court for action upon a stated matter.

PLAINTIFF. A person who brings a law suit in law or equity. Sometimes the party appealing from a lower court to a higher court, the appellant, whether he was the plaintiff or defendant in the court below, is called the "plaintiff in error."

PLAINTIFF IN ERROR. The party who obtains a writ of error to have a judgment or other proceeding at law reviewed by an appellate court.

PLEA. The original answer given by the defendant to the accusation against him—usually guilty or not guilty.

PLEA BARGAINING. The process by which the prosecutor and the defense attorney bargain for dismissal for some charge in exchange for a plea of guilty to another charge.

PLEADINGS. Successive statements by which litigants set forth the allegations upon which they base their own claims or challenge the claims of their opponents.

POLICE COURT. A court for the trial of minor criminal offenses, and which may hold for trial by a higher court persons accused of more serious crimes.

POLLING THE JURY. A practice whereby the jurors are asked individually whether they assented, and still assent, to the verdict.

POWER OF ATTORNEY. An instrument authorizing another to act as one's agent or attorney.

PRAECIPE. An original writ commanding the defendant to do the thing required; also, an order addressed to the clerk of a court, requesting him to issue a particular writ.

PRECEDENT. A prior decision or authority that guides the court in deciding a case currently before it.

PREJUDICIAL ERROR. Synonymous with "reversible error"; an error which warrants the appellate court in reversing the judgment before it.

PRELIMINARY HEARING. Synonymous with "preliminary examination"; the hearing given a person charged with crime by a magistrate or judge to determine whether he should be held for trial.

PREPONDERANCE OF EVIDENCE. Greater weight of evidence, or evidence which is more credible and convincing to the mind, not necessarily the greater number of witnesses.

PRESENTMENT. An informal statement in writing by a grand jury to the court that a public offense has been committed, from their own knowledge or observation, without any bill of indictment laid before them.

PRESUMPTION OF FACT. An inference as to the truth or falsity of any proposition or fact, drawn by a process of reasoning in the absence of actual certainty of its truth or falsity, or until such certainty can be ascertained.

PRESUMPTION OF LAW. A rule of law that courts and judges shall draw a particular inference from a particular fact, or from particular evidence.

PROBATE COURT. A court which administers the estates of decedents, and which controls the adoption and guardianship of minors. It is sometimes referred to as an orphan's court or a surrogate's court.

PROBATION. In modern criminal administration, allowing a person convicted of some minor offense (particularly juvenile offenders) to go at large, under a suspension of sentence, during good behavior, and generally under the supervision or guardianship of a probation officer.

PROCEDURAL LAW. That part of the law that controls the mechanics of bringing, conducting, and deciding a lawsuit.

PROSECUTION. The bringing of a criminal proceeding or the authority conducting such a proceeding.

PROSECUTOR. One who instigates the prosecution upon which an accused is arrested or who prefers an accusation against the party whom he suspects to be guilty; also, one who takes charge of a case and performs function of trial lawyer for the people.

PROTHONOTARY. The title given to an officer who officiates as the principal clerk of some courts.

QUAERE. A query; question; doubt.

QUASH. To overthrow; vacate; to annul or void a summons or indictment.

QUASI JUDICIAL. Authority or discretion vested in an officer wherein his acts partake of a judicial character.

QUID PRO QUO. What for what, a fair return or consideration.

QUO WARRANTO. A writ issuable by the state through which it demands an individual to show by what right he exercises an authority which can only be exercised through grant or franchise emanating from the state.

QUOTIENT VERDICT. A money verdict determined by the following process: Each juror writes down the sum he wishes to award by the verdict; these amounts are added together, and the total is divided by twelve (the number of jurors) and the quotient stands as the verdict of the jury by their agreement.

RATIO DECIDENDI. The point of law upon which a court bases its decision on an issue.

REASONABLE DOUBT. An accused person is entitled to acquittal if, in the minds of the jury, his guilt has not been proved beyond a "reasonable doubt"; that state of the minds of jurors in which they cannot say they feel an abiding conviction as to the truth of the charge.

REBUTTAL. The introduction of rebutting evidence; the showing that statements of witnesses as to what occurred is not true; the stage of a trial at which such evidence may be introduced.

RECOGNIZANCE. In criminal law, a promise by the defendant to appear in court given in lieu of bail to obtain release.

RECORDER. A county officer in charge of public records. In some small towns, the recorder is the name of a local court with limited civil jurisdiction.

REDIRECT EXAMINATION. Follows cross-examination, and is had by the party who first examined the witness.

REFEREE. A person to whom a cause pending in a court is referred by the court to take testimony, hear the parties, and report thereon to the court. He is an officer exercising judicial powers and is an arm of the court for a specific purpose.

REMOVAL, ORDER OF. An order by a court directing the transfer of a cause to another court.

REPLY. When a case is tried or argued in court, the argument of the plaintiff in answer to that of the defendant. A pleading in response to an answer.

RES JUDICATA. Rule of law that a final judgment by a court of competent jurisdiction is conclusive as to parties and points of law in all subsequent suits on matters raised in the former action by the same parties.

RESPONDENT. The party against whom an appeal is taken.

REST. A party is said to "rest" or "rest his case" when he has presented all the evidence he intends to offer.

RETAINER. Act of the client in employing his attorney or counsel, and also denotes the fee which the client pays when he retains the attorney to act for him.

RULE NISI, OR RULE TO SHOW CAUSE. A court order obtained on motion by either party to show cause why the particular relief sought should not be granted.

RULE OF COURT. An order made by a court having competent jurisdiction. Rules of court are either general or special; the former are the regulations by which the practice of the court is governed; the latter are special orders made in particular cases.

SEARCH AND SEIZURE, UNREASONABLE. In general, an examination without authority of law of one's premises or person with a view to discovering stolen contraband or illicit property or some evidence of guilt to be used in prosecuting a crime.

SEARCH WARRANT. An order in writing, issued by a justice or magistrate, in the name of the state, directing an officer to search a specified house or other premises for stolen property. Usually required as a condition precedent to a legal search and seizure.

SELF-DEFENSE. The protection of one's person or property against some injury attempted by another. The law of "self-defense" justifies an act done in the reasonable belief of immediate danger. When acting in justifiable self-defense, a person may not be punished criminally nor held responsible for civil damages.

SEPARATE MAINTENANCE. Allowance granted to a wife for support of herself and children while she is living apart from her husband but not divorced from him.

SEPARATION OF WITNESS. An order of the court requiring all witnesses to remain outside the courtroom until each is called to testify, except the plaintiff or defendant.

SHERIFF. An officer of a county, chosen by popular election, whose principal duties are aid of criminal and civil courts; chief preserver of the peace. He serves processes, summons juries, executes judgments, and holds judicial sales.

SINA QUA NON. An indispensable requisite.

SLANDER. Base and defamatory spoken words tending to prejudice another in his reputation, business, or means of livelihood. "Libel" and "slander" both are methods of defamation, the former being expressed by print, writings, pictures, or signs, the latter orally.

SOLICITOR. In England, an attorney generally performing office duties rather than arguing cases.

SPECIFIC PERFORMANCE. A mandatory order in equity. Where damages would be inadequate compensation for the breach of a contract, the contractor will be compelled to perform specifically what he has agreed to.

STARE DECISIS. The doctrine that, when a court has once laid down a principle of law as applicable to a certain set of facts, it will adhere to that principle and apply it to future cases where the facts are substantially the same.

STATE'S EVIDENCE. Testimony, given by an accomplice or participant in a crime, tending to convict others.

STATUTE. The written law in contradistinction to the unwritten law.

STAY. A stopping or arresting of a judicial proceeding by order of the court.

STIPULATION. An agreement by attorneys on opposite sides of a case as to any matter pertaining to the proceedings or trial. It is not binding unless assented to by the parties, and most stipulations must be in writing.

SUBPOENA. A process to cause a witness to appear and give testimony before a court or magistrate.

SUBPOENA DUCES TECUM. An order by the court to a witness requiring that he produce a document, record, or other object at the trial.

SUBSTANTIVE LAW. The law dealing with rights, duties, and liabilities, as distinguished from adjective law, which is the law regulating procedure.

SUMMARY JUDGMENT. The disposition of a civil case without trial on the basis that the facts are so clear that reasonable men could not differ about them.

SUMMONS. A writ directing the sheriff or other officer to notify the named person that an action has been commenced against him in court and that he is required to appear, on the day named, and answer the complaint in such action.

SUPERSEDEAS. A writ containing a command to stay proceedings at law, such as the enforcement of a judgment pending an appeal.

SURROGATE. The name given in some states to the judge or judicial officer who has administration of probate matters. In other states he is called judge of probate, register, etc. He is ordinarily a county officer, with a local jurisdiction limited to his county.

TALESMAN. A person summoned to act as a juror from among the bystanders in a court.

TERRITORIAL COURT. A court established in a territory held by the United States.

TESTIMONY. Evidence given by a competent witness, under oath; as distinguished from evidence derived from writings and other sources.

TORT. An injury or wrong committed, either with or without force, to the person or property of another.

TRANSCRIPT. The official record of proceedings in a trial or hearing.

TRANSITORY. Actions are "transitory" when they might have taken place anywhere, and are "local" when they could occur only in some particular place.

TRAVERSE. In pleading, traverse signifies a denial. When a defendant denies any material allegation of fact in the plaintiff's declaration, he is said to traverse it.

TRIAL DE NOVO. A new trial or retrial had in an appellate court in which the whole case is gone into as if no trial had been had in a lower court.

TRIBUNAL. A court or administrative agency that decides questions of law or fact or both.

TRUE BILL. In criminal practice, the endorsement made by a grand jury upon a bill of indictment when they find it sufficient evidence to warrant a criminal charge.

UNDUE INFLUENCE. Whatever destroys free will and causes a person to do something he would not do if left to himself.

UNLAWFUL DETAINER. A detention of real estate without the consent of the owner or other person entitled to its possession.

UNOFFICIAL REPORT. Similar for the most part to official report, but published by a private company.

USURY. The taking of more for the use of money than the law allows.

VENIRE. Technically, a writ summoning persons to court to act as jurors; popularly used as meaning the body of names thus summoned.

VENIRE FACIAS DE NOVO. A fresh or new venire, which the court grants when there has been some impropriety or irregularity in returning the jury, or where the verdict is so imperfect or ambiguous that no judgment can be given upon it.

VENIREMEN. Members of a panel of jurors.

VERDICT. In practice, the formal and unanimous decision or finding made by a jury, reported to the court and accepted by it.

VOIR DIRE. To speak the truth. The phrase denotes the preliminary examination which the court may make on one presented as a witness or juror, as to his qualifications.

WAIVER. The voluntary relinquishment of a right.

WAIVER OF IMMUNITY. A means authorized by statutes by which a witness, in advance of giving testimony or producing evidence, may renounce the fundamental right guaranteed by the constitutions that no person shall be compelled to be a witness against himself.

WARRANT OF ARREST. A writ issued by a magistrate, justice, or other competent authority, to a sheriff, or other officer, requiring him to arrest the body of a person therein named and bring him before the magistrate or court to answer to a specified charge.

WEIGHT OF EVIDENCE. The balance or preponderance of evidence; the inclination of the greater amount of credible evidence, offered in a trial, to support one side of the issue rather than the other.

WILLFUL. A "willful" act is one done intentionally, without justifiable cause, as distinguished from an act done carelessly or inadvertently.

WITH PREJUDICE. The term, as applied to judgment of dismissal, is as conclusive of rights of parties as if action had been prosecuted to final adjudication adverse to the plaintiff.

WITHOUT PREJUDICE. A dismissal "without prejudice" allows a new suit to be brought on the same cause of action.

WITNESS. One who testifies under oath to what he has seen, heard, or otherwise observed.

WRIT. An order issuing from a court of justice and requiring the performance of a specified act, or giving authority and commission to have it done.

WRIT OF ERROR CORAM NOBIS. A common law writ, the purpose of which is to correct a judgment in the same court in which it was rendered, on the ground of error of fact.

Index

accusatory procedure. *See* adversary procedure
address, 27
administration of courts, 46–47; colonial, 3–4; and judges, 105, 106; states, 79, 85, 86, 94, 102, 106, 113–114, 141–144, 161–162; U.S. courts, 192–194
Administration of Justice Act, 71
administrative courts, 256
Administrative Office of the United States Courts, 183
admiralty cases, 4, 168, 180, 182, 192
adversary procedure, 264, 265–266
Advisory Commission on Intergovernmental Relations, 64
Alabama, 14; administration of courts, 49, 53, 57; federal courts, 183; judges, 22, 29, 46
Alaska, 14, 75–80; administration of courts, 49, 53, 79–80; appeals court, 8, 78; district court, 78–79; Judicial Council, 79; judges, 22, 29, 46, 79; jury, 68, 69; superior court, 75; supreme court, 75–76
Algeria, 264
American Academy of Judicial Education, 46, 80
American Bar Association, 48; Canons of Judicial Ethics, 27; Commission on Standards of Judicial Administration, 70–71; and judicial appointments, 8, 269, 271; and jury selection, 69, 73; and juvenile crime, 13; traffic court program, 45–46
American Judicature Society, 48, 271

Anglo-Saxon law, 260–261, 265–266
antitrust laws, 172
Apodaca v. Oregon, 69
appeals courts, 257, 259; colonial, 2, 4–5, 7; federal, *see* U.S. Court of Appeals; intermediate, 9–10; state, 82–83, 88–90, 98, 105, 110, 122–125
arbitration, 47, 135
Argentina, 256, 259
Arizona, 14; administration of courts, 49, 53, 57 domestic courts, 10–11; federal courts, 183; judges, 8, 22, 30, 46; jury, 69
Arkansas, 14; administration of courts, 49, 53, 57; federal courts, 183; judge, 22, 30; jury, 69; salaries, 9
Articles of Confederation, 5
attainder, bills of, 3
Australia, 256, 259, 260, 270
Austria, 261, 267, 273
automation, 11, 47, 80, 98, 134

bail, 91, 132, 192
bankruptcy, 179, 180, 256
Bartlett, Richard J., 144
Belgium, 260, 261, 273
Bolivia, 270
Boston Juvenile Court, 112
Boston Municipal Court, 111–112
Braun, Richard L., 61–62
Brazil, 256, 257, 259, 273
Breitel, Charles D., 144
Brown, Pat, 186
Bulgaria, 262
Burger, Warren E., 48, 175, 185

Cambodia, 268
canon law. 263, 265
calendaring, 47, 48
California, 14, 80–87; administration
of courts, 48, 49, 53, 57, 85–86; Center
for Judicial Education and Research, 46,
80, 87, 88; court of appeals, 82–83;
electronic recording, 80; federal courts,
179, 183; judges, 8, 11, 22, 30; Judicial
Council, 85–86, 152; salaries, 77;
superior court, 80; supreme court, 9,
80–81, 83–84, 86, 87
Canada, 258, 259, 260; judges, 267, 270
Canal Zone, 173, 179, 180
Carey, Hugh, 145, 146, 153
caseloads, 9, 12, 73, 133, 157; federal
courts, 168–169, 175–179, 180
certification, writ of, 159, 171
certiorari, writ of, 78, 88, 159; and U.S.
Supreme Court, 171, 172, 177
chancery courts, 3, 10, 117
China, 262, 263
circuit courts, 3; federal, 167, 168,
172–173, 194; state, 10, 99–101,
105–106
civil cases: administration, 144; appeal, 10;
federal courts, 172; state courts, 47, 78,
84, 91, 98, 101, 112, 118, 131, 137–138,
157, 160; juries, 47, 69, 71, 79, 90, 129,
135, proceedings, 182
Civil Justice in a Dynamic City, 136–137
civil law, 261–262; judges, 267, 268;
procedure, 264, 265, 273
civil liberties, 259
Civil Rights Act of 1964, 187
Clark, Tom, 72
clerks, 113
Code Napoleon, 261
codes, 261–262
colonial courts, 2–4
Colorado, 14, 87–95; administration of
courts, 48, 49, 53, 57, 93–94; court
of appeals, 88–90; judges, 8, 22, 31, 46,
94, 95; jury, 68, 71; supreme court, 9, 88
commercial courts, 257, 271
Commission on Executive, Legislative and
Judicial salaries, 173
Commission on the Revision of the Federal
Court Appellate System, 176–178
common law, 260–261, 264, 268
common pleas courts, 3, 4, 10
conciliation court, 83–84
Conference of State Court Administrators,
48
congestion. *See* caseloads
Connecticut, 14; administration of courts,
49, 53; colonial courts, 2; federal courts,

183; grand jury, 64; judges, 22, 31;
supreme court of errors, 8, 258
constitutions (state): amendments, 143–144,
145, 146, 148–149, 153, 154; and courts,
82, 83, 90, 105, 115, 121–122, 125, 128,
139, 140; and jury, 68–69
Constitution of the U.S. *See* U.S.
Constitution
county courts, 12, 90–91, 92, 137–139;
colonial, 3
court martial, 191
Courts of Assistants, 2
courts of first instance, 2–3, 4, 156
criminal courts, 264–265; appeals, 9–10,
101, 139; colonial, 3; federal, 182;
jurisdiction, 78, 111, 112, 131–133, 139;
jury trials, 67–68, 69, 118; procedure,
182
Cuban Popular Courts, 266, 270
Curia Regis, 3

Dahomey, 261
damages, 47
Dangerous Drug Control Program, 129–130,
141
death penalty, 125, 191
Delaware, 15; administration of courts, 49,
53; colonial courts, 4; domestic court, 12;
federal courts, 183; judges, 22, 31, 270;
supreme court, 8; trial court, 10, 12
delay in courts, 47–48
Democracy in America (Tocqueville), 71
Democratic Republic of Germany, 262
Denmark, 267, 270, 273
Denver (Col.) courts, 92–93
Desmond, Charles S., 72
district courts: federal, *see* U.S. district
courts; state, 78, 90, 101–102, 111, 156,
160
District of Columbia, 21, 26, 43, 57,
95–98; administration of courts, 48, 51,
55, 97–98; court of appeals, 98; federal
courts, 179, 180, 183; judges, 95;
superior court, 98
diversity jurisdiction, 181
domestic courts, 10–11, 12; colonial, 4;
judges, 45, 130; states, 78, 98, 101,
118–119, 144
Dominick Commission, 144, 148, 152
Douglas, William O., 65, 175
dual court system, 258–261
Dukakis, Michael S., 114
Duncan v. Louisiana, 67–68

Economic Stabilization Act Amendment
of 1971, 190
Egypt, 264

El Salvador, 270
electronic court recording, 80, 134, 160
Elliot, Sheldon, 75
England, colonies, 260; common law, 261; courts, 2, 3, 256, 260; grand jury, 65; judges, 267, 269; jury, 68, 71, 72
equity, 2–3, 10
evidence, rules of, 185

family courts, 130, 141; *see* also domestic courts
Federal Judicial Center, 193–194, 268
Federal Jury Selection and Service Act, 70
federal question jurisdiction, 180–181
Federal Republic of Germany: civil law, 261, 273; Constitutional Court, 256, 257, 258; judges, 267, 271
Federal Rules of Appellate Procedure, 185
Federal Rules of Civil Procedure, 182
Federal Rules of Criminal Procedure, 182
Feinberg, Wilfred, 179
financing of courts, 145–146, 148–150, 162
Finland, 270
Florida, 15; administration of courts, 48, 49, 53, 57; federal courts, 183; judges, 8, 11, 22, 31; jury, 68, 69
Ford Foundation, 48
foreign nationals, 171
France: civil code, 261–262; colonial law, 260, 261; Conseil d'Etat, 256, 258; Cour de Cassation, 258; courts, 257, 260, 271; judges, 268, 269–270; procedure, 265, 273
Frankfurter, Felix, 261
Freund Report, 175–176

general jurisdiction courts, 256
general sessions, 3, 10
Georgia, 15; administration of courts, 49, 53; federal courts, 183; judges, 22, 32
Germany. *See* Democratic Republic of Germany; Federal Republic of Germany
Ghana, 260
governors: appointment of judges, 8, 11, 83, 93, 103, 115, 116, 117, 118, 122, 129–130, 159, 161; colonial, 2, 3; and judicial misconduct, 121
grand jury, 61–65, 264
Greece, 268, 273
Guam, 21, 26, 43, 173, 179

habeas corpus, 78, 88, 172, 192
Harris County, Texas, 71
Harvard Law Review, 172
Hawaii, 14, 99–103; administration of courts, 49, 53, 102; circuit courts, 99–101; district courts, 101–102; federal courts, 173, 183; judges, 22, 32, 46, 102–103, 270; Judicial Council, 102; jury, 68; land court, 102; supreme court, 8, 99; tax court, 102
Hernandez Colón, Rafael, 157
House of Lords, 2
housing courts, 113, 135–137
Hruska, Roman L., 176, 186
Hungary, 262

Idaho, 15; administration of courts, 49, 53; federal courts, 183; grand jury, 64; judges, 23, 32, 46; jury, 68; supreme court, 9
Illinois, 15, 103–108; administration of courts, 49, 53, 57, 106–107; appellate court, 9, 105; circuit courts, 105–106; federal courts, 183; judges, 23, 32, 46, 107–108, 270; Judicial Conference, 107; supreme court, 104–105, 106, 107
immunity, 62–63
impeachment, 4, 27, 173
In re Gault, 12–13
India, 258, 259, 267, 270
Indian Claims Commission, 188
Indiana, 15; administration of courts, 49, 53, 57; appellate court, 9; federal courts, 183; judges, 8, 23, 33
indictment, bills of, 61, 62
Indonesia, 256, 257, 264
information, 63–64
injunctions, 186
inquisitorial procedure, 264–266
Institute for Court Management, 47–48, 142
Institute of Judicial Administration, 13, 45, 75, 80, 142
Intermediate Appellate Judges Seminar, 45
Internal Revenue Service, 181, 189
Iowa, 15; administration of courts, 49, 53; federal courts, 183; judges, 8, 23, 33, 46; jury, 68
Iraq, 260, 264
Israel, 260, 271
Italy, 260, 261, 273
Ivory Coast, 261

Japan, 260, 261, 267, 268
Jefferson, Thomas, 261
Johnson, Lyndon, 186
Johnson v. Louisiana, 69
Jordan, 260, 264
judges (federal), 171, 173, 187, 189, 190
judges (state): and administration, 3–4, 105, 106, 143–144, 145, 146–148; appointment, 7–8, 83, 85, 86, 90,

95–97, 101, 103, 105, 110, 146,
266–270; colonial, 3–4; conduct,
27–28, 79, 120–121, 146, 150–156, 162;
education, 45–46, 80, 87, 95, 103, 107–
108, 120; election, 8, 11, 78, 83, 84, 90,
119, 128, 131, 137, 140, 141, 145, 270–
271; part-time, 93; removal, 27, 43, 79,
97, 103, 107, 114–115, 121, 126, 146,
150, 153–154; retirement, 77, 97, 117,
122, 133, 135, 161; salaries, 8–9, 77, 78,
82, 83, 91, 92, 93, 98, 110, 111, 118,
119, 122, 129, 130, 131, 133, 135, 137,
140, 159; selection, 8–9, 10, 22–26, 82,
84, 91, 94–95, 105, 106, 110, 111, 112,
133, 145, 269–270; *see also* justices
(state)
Judicial Conference of the United States,
182–183, 192–193
Judiciary Act of 1789, 5, 167
jury, 67–73, 118, 182, 272–273; civil law,
4, 69, 71, 78, 79, 90, 111, 129; criminal
law, 67–68, 69, 79, 90, 112, 132–133;
costs, 72; history, 67, 264, 272; juvenile
courts, 90; selection, 69–71; size, 47,
68–69, 78, 111, 135; verdicts, 68
justices (state), 7–8; administration, 144,
156; appointments, 114, 115, 157;
education, 45, 46, 108; number, 77,
80–81, 108; organization, 48, 75–76;
retirement, 77, 99, 108, 117, 128; salary,
8–9, 77, 82, 99, 104, 108, 117, 128, 157
justices of the peace, 25, 87–88, 141, 160–
161, 266; colonial, 3; education, 45;
selection, 12, 160
Justinian code, 261
juvenile courts, 11, 12–13, 256; appeals,
90, 93, 112, 119; judges, 45, 119; state,
78, 92–93, 98, 101, 112, 118–119, 130

Kansas, 15; administration of courts, 49,
53; federal courts, 183; judges, 8, 23, 33,
46
Kaufman, Irving R., 13
Kentucky, 16; administration of courts, 49,
53, 57; court of appeals, 7; federal courts,
183; judicial selection, 23, 33
"key man" system, 70
King in Council, 2, 4–5
King's Bench, 2, 71
Kleindienst, Richard, 186
Kuwait, 264

labor courts, 256, 258, 271
Labor Relations Board, 172
landlord-tenant disputes, 112, 118
Law Enforcement Assistance
Administration, 11, 268
laymen, 265, 266, 272–273

Lebanon, 264, 268
legislatures: and administration of courts,
143, 144, 152; and appointment of
judges, 8, 11, 103, 129, 271; and jury size,
68–69, 111
Levin, A. Leo, 176, 178
Libya, 263
limited jurisdiction courts, 257, 259;
colonial, 3–4; states, 12–13, 78–79,
84–85, 88, 90–92, 111–113, 118–119
Los Angeles County Superior Court, 83–84,
86
Louisiana, 12; administration of courts, 50,
53; code, 261; federal courts, 183;
judges, 23, 34; jury, 68

McClellan, George, 186
magistrates, 3, 12, 64, 266; appointment,
77; education, 80; federal, 191–192;
honorary, 161; jurisdiction, 78–79, 132;
salaries, 78
Magna Carta, 68
Maine, 16; administration of courts, 50, 53;
federal courts, 184; judges, 23, 34;
supreme judicial court, 7, 8
mandamus, writ of, 78
marriage counseling, 83–84
marshals, 179
Maryland, 16; administration of courts, 50,
53, 57; colonial, 3, 4; court of appeals, 7;
federal courts, 184; judges, 8, 10, 23, 34,
46; salaries, 9
Massachusetts, 16, 108–115; administration
of courts, 50, 54, 113–114; appeals court,
110; colonial courts, 2; district courts,
111, 115; federal courts, 184; housing
courts, 113; Judicial Council, 114; judges,
11, 23, 35, 114–115; juvenile courts,
112; land courts, 113; probate court, 112,
113, 115; superior court, 110; supreme
judicial court, 7, 8, 108–110
Massachusetts Bar Association Committee
of Complaint, 115
mayor's court, 78, 133
Mexico, 257, 259
Michigan, 10, 16; administration of courts,
48, 50, 54, 57; federal courts, 184; grand
jury, 64; judges, 23, 35, 46; jury, 68, 69
military courts, 191, 256
Minnesota, 17; administration of courts,
50, 54; judges, 23, 35, 270; jury, 68
misdemeanors: courts, 91, 101, 132–133,
192; jury, 69
Mississippi, 10, 17; domestic court, 12, 46;
judges, 23, 35; jury, 68
Missouri, 17; administration of courts, 48,
50, 53, 54, 57; appeals courts, 9–10;

federal courts, 184; judges, 24, 36; jury, 68; supreme court, 8
Missouri Plan, 8, 271
Mitchell, John P., 186
Montana, 17; administration of courts, 50, 54; federal courts, 184; grand jury, 64; judges, 24, 36; jury, 68, 69
Morocco, 264
municipal courts, 12, 91–92, 111–112; appeal of decisions, 83, 84; judge, 45, 112, 119, 157, 161, 267
Muslim law, 257, 260, 263–264

Nassau County District Courts, 139–140
National Association of Trial Court Administrators, 48
National Association of Trial Judges, 135
National Center for State Courts, 46
National College of Juvenile Justice, 142
National College of the State Judiciary, 45, 80, 142
National Commission on Reform of Criminal Laws, 186
National Conference of Chief Justices, 48
National Council for Juvenile Court Judges, 45
National Court of Appeals, 176–179
National Survey of Court Organization, 11
Nebraska, 17; administration of courts, 50, 54; federal courts, 184; judges, 8, 24, 36, 46; jury, 68, 69
Netherlands, 260, 261
Nevada, 17; administration of courts, 48, 50, 54, 57; federal courts, 184; judges, 24, 36; jury, 68
New Hampshire, 17; colonial courts, 2; federal courts, 184; grand jury, 64; high court, 7; judges, 24, 37
New Jersey, 17, 115–121; administration of courts, 50, 53, 119–120; county courts, 118; domestic courts, 10–11, 118–119; federal courts, 184; judges, 10–11, 24, 37, 46, 120–121, 267, 270; jury, 68, 69; juvenile court, 118–119; municipal courts, 119; superior court, 117–118; supreme court, 8, 9, 115–117; surrogate court, 119
New Mexico, 18; administration of courts, 50, 54; federal courts, 184; judges, 8, 24, 37, 46; jury, 68
New York, 18, 121–156; administration of courts, 48, 50, 54, 57, 141–148; city courts, 140; Commission on Judicial Conduct, 154–156; county courts, 137–138; court of appeal, 7, 122–127, 146, 154, 258; court of claims, 129–130; district courts, 139–140; domestic courts, 12; family court, 11, 130; federal courts, 179,

184; financing of[...] 150; judges, 8, 1[...] 270; jury, 68, 6[...] 130, 145; surro[...] courts, 140–1[...]
New York City, 131–1[...] courts, 147–148; civil court,[...] criminal court, 131–135, 144; family court, 147; financing of courts, 147; housing court, 135–137; jury, 72; surrogate court, 130–131; traffic violations, 133–134
New Zealand, 260, 270
Nicaragua, 270
Nigeria, 260
Nixon, Richard M., 186
no-fault insurance, 47
North Carolina, 18; administration of courts, 50, 54; federal courts, 184; judges, 24, 38, 270
North Dakota, 18; administration of courts, 50, 54; federal courts, 184; grand jury, 64; judges, 24, 38; jury, 68
Norway, 267, 270, 272

Ohio, 18; administration of courts, 48, 50, 54, 58; federal courts, 184; judges, 24, 39, jury, 68
Oklahoma, 19; administration of courts, 51, 54; federal courts, 184; judges, 8, 24, 39, 40; jury, 68, 69
Oregon, 19; administration of courts, 51, 54; federal courts, 184; judges, 24, 40; jury, 68, 69; supreme court, 9
oyer and terminer courts, 3

Pakistan, 264
patents, 180, 256
Pennsylvania, 19; administration of courts, 48, 50, 54, 58; appeals court, 40; colonial courts, 2, 4; federal courts, 184; judges, 25, 40; supreme court, 9, 10
petit jury. *See* jury
Philippines, 270
Pitney, Justice, 62
plea bargaining, 266
Poland, 262, 268
Portugal, 261
preliminary hearings, 91, 101, 160
president: appointment of judges, 97, 170, 173, 189, 191, 269
pretrial conferences, 47
Privy Council, 2, 7, 259
probate courts, 4, 93; state, 10, 78, 83, 93, 112, 113, 118
prohibition, writ of, 78
psychiatry, 142
Puerto Rico, 21, 156–162; administration

courts, 51, 55, 58, 156, 161–162; district court, 16–17; federal courts, 173 179, 180, 184; Judiciary Act, 156, 162; justices of the peace, 160; superior court, 159–160; supreme court, 157–158

quarter sessions, 3
Quebec, 260, 261

recall, 27
recorder's court, 78
religious law, 257, 263–264
review, writ of, 78, 159
Rhode Island, 19, 182; administration of courts, 51, 54; colonial courts, 2; federal courts, 184; judges, 9, 11, 25, 40; supreme court, 8
Roman law, 261
Ross, David, 145
Rumania, 262

Saudi Arabia, 263
Securities and Exchange Commission, 172
self-incrimination, 62–63
senatorial courtesy, 270
Senegal, 261
sentencing, 45, 141
small claims court, 12, 78, 91, 98, 118, 135
social security courts, 256, 258
Socialist law, 262–263; judges, 266, 267, 270–271
South Carolina, 19; administration of courts, 51, 54; domestic courts, 12; federal courts, 184; judges, 25, 41, 46, 271; jury, 68; supreme court, 8
South Dakota, 19; administration of courts, 51, 54, 58; federal courts, 184; judges, 25, 41, 46, 270; jury, 69
Soviet Union, 259, 262–263, 266, 270–271
Spain, 260, 261, 268, 270
Spaniol, Joseph F., 187–188, 190
specialized courts, 256–257
split trial, 47
stare decisis, 261
State Judicial Training Profile, 46
State-Local Relations in Criminal Justice System, 64
Stevens, John Paul, 175
Sudan, 260, 264
Suffolk Co., Mass., 111, 113
Suffolk Co., N.Y. District Court, 139–140
superior courts: appeals, 84, 91, 117, 159; colonial, 2; powers, 78, 82, 83, 117; state, 77–78, 92, 98, 117–118, 159
Supreme Court. *See* U.S. Supreme Court
supreme courts (states), 4, 258; appeal

jurisdiction, 88, 99, 108, 126–127, 157–158; election, 88; original jurisdiction, 99, 104, 157; structure, 7–9, 75–76, 80–81, 99, 104–105, 108–115, 156, 157–158; *see also* justices
surrogate courts, 10, 130–131
Sweden, 267, 270, 273
Switzerland, 259, 260, 261, 271
Syria, 264

Taiwan, 261
Tanzania, 260
tax courts, 98, 102; appeals, 172, 188; federal, 189–190
Temporary Emergency Court of Appeals of the United States, 190–191
Tennessee, 19; administration of courts, 51, 54; federal courts, 184; judges, 25, 41; supreme court, 9
territorial courts, 180
Texas, 20; administration of courts, 51, 55; appeals court, 10; federal courts, 179, 185; judges, 25, 41, 46; jury, 68, 69, 71
Thailand, 268
Thompson, Edward J., 136, 137
Tocqueville, Alexis De, 71
traffic courts, 12, 98, 133–134; judges, 44–45
Traynor, Roger J., 27
trial courts, 10–12, 257
trial de novo, 11, 12, 78, 84, 85, 91, 110
Tunisia, 264, 268
Turkey, 261

ultimate review courts, 7–9; *see also* supreme courts
Uniform Jury Selection and Service Act, 70–71
unitary court system, 260
U.S. Commissioner, 191–192
U.S. Congress: and appointments, 270; and courts, 5, 167, 176–177, 182, 185, 187
U.S. Constitution, 5; fifth amendment, 63, 188, 264; fourteenth amendment, 13, 68; impeachment, 27; jury trial, 68, 182; sixth amendment, 67–68; 264; seventh amendment, 67, 68
U.S. Court of Appeals, 45, 168, 171, 172–175, 178–179, 189; judges, 173
U.S. Court of Claims, 173, 177, 187–188
U.S. Court of Custom and Patent Appeals, 177, 189
United States Courts: Their Jurisdiction and Work (Spaniol), 190
U.S. Criminal Code, 185–186
U.S. Customs Court, 188–189
U.S. district courts, 167, 179–186;

caseload, 168; judges, 173–174, 180; jurisdiction, 180–182; procedural rules, 182–186; three-judge, 186–187
United States Law Week, 170
U.S. Supreme Court, 168–172; administration, 194; appeals, 168, 171, 177, 178; caseload, 175–176; creation, 5, 167; decisions, 12–13, 67–68, 69, 170, 172, 186; jurisdiction, 150, 167, 171–172; justices, 167–168, 170–171, 174–175, 182, 192–193, 270; term, 168
Uruguay, 270
Utah, 20; administration of courts, 51, 55; federal court, 185; judicial selection, 8, 25, 41; jury, 68, 69; prosecution, 64

Vanderbilt, Arthur T., 47, 64–65, 115, 122
venire, 69–71
Vermont, 20; administration of courts, 48, 51, 55, 58; federal court, 185; judges, 25, 42; supreme court, 8
Virgin Islands, 173, 179, 180, 185
Virginia, 20; administration of courts, 51; colonial courts, 2; federal court, 185; judges, 25, 42, 46, 270, 271; supreme court, 8

Voting Rights Act of 1965, 187

Wagner, Robert, 133
Warren, Earl, 64, 185
Washington, 20; administration of courts, 51, 55; federal courts, 185; grand jury, 64; judges, 25, 42, 46; jury, 68, 69
Webster, Daniel, 72
West Virginia, 20; administration of courts, 51, 55; domestic courts, 12; federal court, 185; judges, 25, 42; jury, 68; supreme court of appeals, 7
Williams v. Florida, 69, 182
Wisconsin, 21; administration of courts, 51, 55; federal courts, 185; grand jury, 64; judges, 26, 43, 46; jury, 68, 69
writs, 78, 88, 108, 172
Wyoming, 21; administration of courts, 51, 55; federal court, 185; judges, 26, 43; jury, 68

Yemen, 263
Yugoslavia, 268

About the Author

Fannie J. Klein is an Associate Professor of Law, Emerita, New York University School of Law, a former Associate Director of the Institute of Judicial Administration and now Senior Consultant to the Institute. She received an LL.B. and an LL.M. from New York University School of Law and was admitted to the bar to practice law in New York City, in the United States District Courts, Southern and Eastern Districts of New York, and in the United States Supreme Court. She is the author of *Judicial Administration and the Legal Profession: Annotated Bibliography* (Oceana, 1963); *The Administration of Justice in the Courts*, 2 Vols. (Oceana, 1976); *Federal and State Court Systems—A Guide* (Ballinger, 1977); Co-Editor (with Professor Joel Lee) of *Arthur T. Vanderbilt, Selected Writings*, 2 Vols. (Oceana, 1967); as well as numerous pamphlets and articles. She is the recipient of numerous honors and awards and in 1968 was appointed by the New York Supreme Court, Appellate Division, First Department, to the Committee on Character and Fitness for the Bar, the first woman to serve on the 100 year-old committee. She has also served as consultant to the United States Department of Transportation in its *Automobile Insurance and Compensation Study* and to the National Criminal Justice Service (Law Enforcement Assistance Administration). She was president of the New York Women's Bar Association and is a member of the Board of Directors of the Committee on Modern Courts, Inc.

About the Contributors

Edward J. Bander is an Associate Professor and Associate Law Librarian at New York University School of Law. He is the author of *Mr. Dooley on the Choice of Law* (Michie, 1963); *Law Dictionary of Practical Definitions* (Oceana, 1966); *Justice Holmes Ex Cathedra* (Michie, 1967); *The Corporation in a Democratic Society* (H.W. Wilson, 1975); and numerous articles in law reviews and general periodicals. Mr. Bander has for many years taught legal research to law students and paralegals.

John P. Richert is an Associate Professor of Law & Political Science at Stockton State College and a Research Associate with the Institute of Judicial Administration (appointed 1975). He received his M.A. and Ph.D. in Political Science from Brown University; a B. ès L. and a J.D. from the University of Strasbourg Law School; and a C.E.S. from the University of Aix en Provence, France. The author of numerous journal articles and reviews, Professor Richert has also served as a consultant or member of several committees on the administration and enforcement of the law.

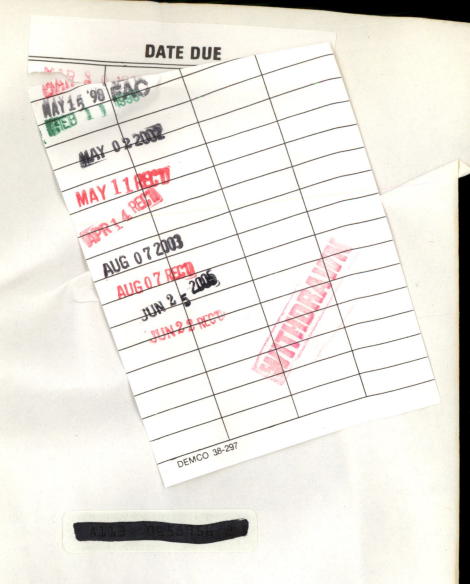